Complete French

For UK order enquiries: please contact Bookpoint Ltd, 130 Milton Park, Abingdon, Oxon OX14 4SB. *Telephone*: +44 (0) 1235 827720. Fax: +44 (0) 1235 400454. Lines are open 09.00–17.00, Monday to Saturday, with a 24-hour message answering service. Details about our titles and how to order are available at www.teachyourself.com

For USA order enquiries: please contact McGraw-Hill Customer Services, PO Box 545, Blacklick, OH 43004-0545, USA. *Telephone*: 1-800-722-4726. Fax: 1-614-755-5645.

For Canada order enquiries: please contact McGraw-Hill Ryerson Ltd, 300 Water St, Whitby, Ontario L1N 9B6, Canada. *Telephone*: 905 430 5000. Fax: 905 430 5020.

Long renowned as the authoritative source for self-guided learning – with more than 50 million copies sold worldwide – the Teach Yourself series includes over 500 titles in the fields of languages, crafts, hobbies, business, computing and education.

British Library Cataloguing in Publication Data: a catalogue record for this title is available from the British Library.

Library of Congress Catalog Card Number: on file.

First published in UK 1998 by Hodder Education, part of Hachette UK, 338 Euston Road, London NW1 3BH.

First published in US 1998 by The McGraw-Hill Companies, Inc.

This edition published 2010; previously published as *Teach Yourself French*.

The Teach Yourself name is a registered trade mark of Hodder Headline.

Typeset by Stephen Rowling, Springworks.

Illustrated by Barking Dog Art, Sally Elford and Stephanie Strickland.

Printed and bound in Dubai for Hodder Education, an Hachette UK Company, 338 Euston Road, London NW1 3BH.

The publisher has used its best endeavours to ensure that the URLs for external websites referred to in this book are correct and active at the time of going to press. However, the publisher and the author have no responsibility for the websites and can make no guarantee that a site will remain live or that the content will remain relevant, decent or appropriate.

Hachette UK's policy is to use papers that are natural, renewable and recyclable products and made from wood grown in sustainable forests. The logging and manufacturing processes are expected to conform to the environmental regulations of the country of origin.

Impression number 10 9 8 7 6 5 4

Year 2014 2013 2012 2011

Complete French

Gaëlle Graham

Advisory editor
Paul Coggle

Contents

Meet the author

Gaëlle Graham was born in Brittany, France, and went to University at La Sorbonne in Paris where she studied English. On moving to England Gaëlle taught French in London comprehensive schools for 25 years. She now works for the National Union of Teachers. She has a Master's degree in Applied Linguistics from the University of Kent at Canterbury. She is a regular contributor to *France Inter*, the French national radio, about English educational news.

Gaëlle enjoys travelling back and forth from London to Paris and to her beloved Brittany. She never travels without her camera and tries to capture the changes she observes in the course of her frequent visits to France. She believes the Vélib', a system of bike rental using a swipe card at bike stations dotted all over Paris, is the best way to appreciate the capital.

Gaëlle's other great loves are cinema and reading. She sticks to a very strict self-imposed reading pattern of alternating French and English books.

Gaëlle has been contributing to the Teach Yourself French course since 1984 and is always searching for new ways of making the course accessible and informative to learners. She endeavours to share with the readers the latest cultural, political or social developments and hopes therefore that you will enjoy having her as your guide as you embark on your study of French.

Only got a minute?

If you want to learn French to visit France or any French-speaking country, you will need to jump in at the deep end, even if you feel very nervous about it. When you have done it you'll feel great.

It is most likely that your first interactions in French will be in the street, in a café or in a shop. So they may well be:

Pardon, Madame, vous parlez anglais? (1)

S'il vous plaît, Monsieur…? (2)

Excusez-moi … l'Hôtel Ibis, s'il vous plaît? (3)

Bonjour, Madame, une baguette, s'il vous plaît? (4)

Merci beaucoup, Monsieur, au revoir! (5)

Encore du café, s'il vous plaît. (6)

So now you can ask a woman if she speaks English (1), say 'please' politely to a gentleman (2), ask where the Ibis Hotel is (3), say 'hello' to a woman and ask for bread in a shop (4), thank a man for giving you something and say 'goodbye' to him (5), and ask for more coffee in a café (6).

5 Only got five minutes?

If someone asks you **Parlez-vous français?** *Do you speak French?* **you might be able to answer Un petit peu!,** even if the only French you can speak at the moment is just that little bit of it (**un petit peu**). But there are many French expressions or words commonly used in English. So yes, you do already know some French words and expressions. Some of them are pretty complex too, and those listed opposite are just a few!

À la carte, when choosing from the menu (the card)

À la mode, fashionable

Apéritif, a drink before dinner

Après-ski, what you do after skiing

Art Déco (short for **Art décoratif**)

Art Nouveau, 'New Art'

Au contraire, 'on the contrary'

Avant-garde, advanced, before its time / ahead of time

Bon voyage! Have a good journey!

Café au lait, coffee with milk

Carte blanche, blank (white) card

C'est la vie! That's life! (**vie**, *life*)

Cuisine, cooking / cookery / kitchen plus of course many expressions used in cookery in English e.g. *blanched* (from **blanc** *white*), *sauté* (from **sauter**, *to jump*) and many more

Déjà vu, 'already seen' (when referring to something which is familiar)

Encore, 'again' (what the audience shouts when they want to hear more from the performers)

Fait accompli, 'done (accomplished) deed'

Femme fatale, 'deadly woman'

Force majeure, a major reason for an act or event

Idée fixe, set idea

Je ne sais quoi, 'I don't know what' (**je sais,** *I know*)

Joie de vivre, 'joy of living' (**vivre,** *to live*)

Moi! Me!

Nom de plume, 'pen name' (**nom,** *name*)

Raison d'être, 'reason for being'

Rendez-vous, meeting or meeting place (literally: you get there)

Risqué, risked / daring / provocative

Savoir faire, know-how (**savoir,** *to know,* **faire,** *to do*)

Tête à tête, 'head to head' as in a private or intimate meeting

Touché!, 'touched', meaning you've got it!

Voilà! There it is!

So how can these 50 or so words above that you already know give you a head start in this course? They can be pointers in something you read or hear.

Taking **déjà vu** as an example: if you hear someone say **J'ai déjà vu le film** you may be able to grasp that they are saying *I have already seen the film*. And so by extension if you hear **J'ai déjà lu l'article** and if you now learn that **lu** means *read* you may guess that the speaker is saying that he/she has already read the article.

So if you hear **J'ai déjà réservé ma place pour l'Eurostar** you may be able to guess what that person has already done!

In future if you come across what you think is a French word or expression used in English conversation or writing, just make a note of it and check it out later.

Introduction

Welcome to *Complete French*!

THE AIM OF THIS BOOK

If you are an adult learner with no previous knowledge of French and studying on your own, then this is the course for you. Perhaps you are taking up French again after a break from it, or you are intending to learn with the support of a class? Again, you will find this course very well suited to your purposes.

The language you will learn is introduced through everyday situations. The emphasis is first and foremost on using French, but we also aim to give you an idea of how the language works, so that you can create sentences of your own.

The course covers all four of the basic skills – listening and speaking, reading and writing. If you are working on your own, the recording will be all the more important, as it will provide you with the essential opportunity to listen to French and to speak it within a controlled framework. You should therefore try to get a copy of the recording if you haven't already got one.

THE STRUCTURE OF THE COURSE

The course book contains 25 course units plus a reference section at the back. There is also an accompanying recording which you must have if you are going to get maximum benefit from the course.

Each course unit contains most or all of the following:

Statement of aims
At the beginning of each unit there is a list of what you can expect to learn by the end of that unit.

Presentation of new language
This is usually in the form of dialogues, on the recording and in the book or in reading passages. Some assistance with vocabulary is also given in the vocabulary boxes. The language is presented in manageable chunks, building carefully on what you have learned in earlier units.

Exercises
Exercises are graded so that activities which require mainly recognition come first. As you grow confident in manipulating the language forms you will be encouraged to write and speak the language yourself.

Grammar
In these sections you will learn how to construct your own sentences correctly.

Pronunciation
The best way to acquire good pronunciation and intonation is to listen to the native speakers on the recording and to try to imitate them. However, as certain sounds in French are very unfamiliar we include specific advice on pronunciation within the course units. There is also a quick guide to pronunciation at the end of the book.

Information on French-speaking countries
Here you will find information on various aspects of everyday life such as the level of formality that is appropriate when you talk to strangers, and how the health service works if you should fall ill.

You will find a **Self-assessment test (unité de révision)** at the end of the book. This provides an opportunity for you to test yourself and judge whether you have successfully mastered the language in the book.

The reference section contains: a glossary of grammar terms, a key to the activities, transcripts of the recordings, a French–English glossary and an English–French glossary.

STUDY TIPS

Language learning is a bit like jogging – you need to do it regularly for it to do any good! Ideally, you should find a 'Study Buddy' to work through the course with you. This way you will have someone to try out your French on. And when the going gets tough, you will have someone to chivvy you along until you reach your target.

At the beginning of each course unit make sure that you are clear about what you can expect to learn. Read any background information that is provided, then listen to the first dialogue on the recording. Try to get the gist of what is being said before you look at the printed text in the book. Refer to the printed text and the vocabulary box in order to study the dialogues in more detail.

Don't fall into the trap of thinking that you have 'done that' when you have listened to the recording a couple of times and worked through the dialogues in the book. You may recognize what you have heard or read, but you almost certainly still have some way to go before you can produce the language of the dialogues correctly and fluently. This is why we recommend that you keep listening to the recording at every opportunity – sitting on the tube or bus, waiting at the dentist's or stuck in a traffic jam in the car – using what would otherwise be 'dead' time. Of course, you must also be internalizing what you hear and making sense of it – just playing it in the background without really paying attention is not enough!

Some of the recordings are listening-only exercises. The temptation may be to go straight to the transcriptions at the back of the book, but try not to do this. The whole point of listening exercises is to improve your listening skills. You will not do this by reading first. The transcriptions are there to help you if you get stuck.

As you work your way through the exercises, check your answers carefully in the back of the book. It is easy to overlook your own mistakes. If you have a study buddy it's a good idea to check each other's answers. Most of the exercises have fixed answers, but some are a bit more open-ended, especially when we are asking you to talk about yourself. Then, in most cases, we give you model answers which you can adapt for your own purposes.

We have tried to make the grammar explanations as user-friendly as possible, since we recognize that many people find grammar daunting. But in the end, it is up to you just how much time you spend on studying and sorting out the grammar points. Some people find that they can do better by getting an ear for what sounds right, others need to know in detail how the language is put together.

Before you move on to a new unit always check that you know all the new words and phrases in the current unit. Trying to recall the context in which words and phrases were used may help you learn them better.

We hope that you enjoy working your way through *Complete French*. Don't get discouraged. Mastering a new language does take time and perseverance and sometimes things can seem just too difficult. But then you'll come back another day and things will begin to make more sense again.

BEYOND THE COURSE BOOK

Where can I find real language?

Don't expect to be able to understand everything you hear or read straight away. If you watch French-speaking programmes on TV or buy a French magazine you should not get discouraged when you realize how quickly native-speakers speak and how much vocabulary there is still to learn. Just concentrate on a small extract – either a podcast, a video/audio clip or a short article – and work through it till you have mastered it. In this way, you will find that your command of French increases steadily.

Sources of real French

- ▶ *Newspapers (Le Monde, Libération, Le Figaro – the weekend issue is particularly interesting)*
- ▶ *Magazines (Le Nouvel Observateur, Cosmopolitan, Elle, Marie-Claire, Les Cahiers du Cinéma, Première)*
- ▶ *Satellite TV channels (For films: Ciné Cinéma, Paris Première. For news: CNN and Euronews)*
- ▶ *Radio stations on long wave (France Inter 162, RTL, Europe Un). You may wish to use the internet to download a radio programme, where possible, and listen to it again at leisure. For instance Radio France (which covers France Inter, France Info, France Culture and France Musique) keeps all the programmes archived for a week.*
- ▶ *World Wide Web: you can 'google' almost anything in French and you will get directly to a French website. Each unit has a list of websites relating to the topics, which may be used, and also some short web extension exercises, which, in most cases, can be done without internet access.*
- ▶ *Google* **TV5** *to access a whole range of francophone news programmes from all over the world. It includes the following topics: Programmes, Langue française, Musique, Sciences, Cultures du monde, Afrique, Cinéma, Jeux et divertissements, Football, Météo, WebTV, Blogosphère. TiVi5 also includes a French learning programme: Apprendre le français, and an information section for travellers: Voyageurs, Lettres d'information.*
- ▶ *You may wish to use an online-only daily free magazine, France Gazette, http://www.francegazette.com, which is specifically designed for those studying French. It gives readers access to up-to-date information on a wide range of topics, from political news to new films and to town twinning. It has a direct link to Métro, a free daily newspaper distributed in Paris and other main towns (Marseille, Lyon, Bordeaux, Nice, Cannes) as well as Planetantilles, a site with information on French overseas connections. Also Francophonie is a standard feature which covers cultural information, sports, political events etc. For those interested in a more in-depth use of France Gazette there is an archive section available on subscription.*

► *In London you can get information and activities at l'Institut Français, 17 Queensberry Place, London SW7 2DT (telephone 020 7073 1350 or visit www.institut.ambafrance.org.uk)*

French in the modern world

In all there are 180,000,000 people speaking French throughout the world, in French-speaking communities. Outside France, French is the first language for large communities in Belgium, Luxembourg and Switzerland. France also has four overseas **départements** which come under French administration and are part of the French Republic: Guadeloupe, Martinique, Réunion and Guyane. There are two territorial collectivities: Mayotte (one of the Comoro Islands, situated in the Indian Ocean, north of Madagascar, voted to become the 101st French department in 2009) and St-Pierre-et-Miquelon and other overseas territories which include Polynésie française, Nouvelle-Calédonie, Wallis-et-Futuna, terres Australes et Antarctiques (terre Adélie, Kerguelen, Crozet, St-Paul).

French is also spoken in countries which have been under French rule in the past. In North Africa, French is the second language after Arabic in Tunisia, Algeria and Morocco. The same applies to many central African countries such as Senegal. There is still an ageing population which speaks and understands French in Vietnam. In North America, Louisiana still has some vestiges of the French language. In Canada, in the province of Quebec, French is spoken by many people as their first language. French in Quebec has developed differently from the French spoken in France. The accent and the intonations are very different and it has more or less become a language in its own right although its speakers can understand and communicate with French people without difficulty.

If you are able to access the website http://www.tlfq.ulaval.ca/AXL/francophonie/dom-tom.htm you can get an interactive map of the world and a detailed list showing the four French overseas **départements** and other French regions, formerly called DOM/TOM and now known as **DROM** «**Départements et Régions d'Outre-Mer**».

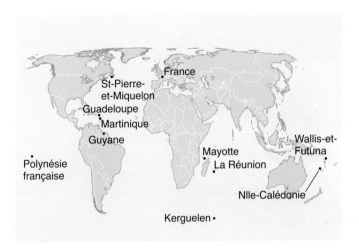

1

Salutations
Greetings

In this unit you will learn
* *how to say hello*
* *greetings for different times of the day*
* *greetings for special occasions*
* *a few places in the town*
* *food and drinks*
* *about gender and number*

1 Simple greetings

◀⁾ **CD1, TR 2**

You may be starting to learn French because you would like to be able to communicate with people you meet for business or leisure when you travel to France or other parts of the world where French is spoken. It might be because you have French acquaintances visiting you or because your children are learning French at school. Communicating starts with very few words or, indeed, without words at all, for example shaking hands with someone, which French people do whether they are meeting friends or meeting people for the first time. It is usual to give close acquaintances two, three or even four kisses on the cheeks. If you watch young people at the terrace of a café, for example, you will see how spontaneous and communicative it all is!

Insight

Your first few words are very important but also very simple:

Bonjour! *Hello! (literally Good day!)*
Salut! *(Hi!)*
Au revoir! *(Goodbye!)*

You will feel a great sense of satisfaction and achievement when you greet someone as if you have been speaking French all your life.

If you have the recording, listen to the following people saying hello and goodbye. It is daytime:

Bonjour Monsieur.

Bonjour Madame Martin.

Au revoir.

Bonjour! *Hello!*
Bonjour monsieur! *Hello! (to a man)*
Bonjour Madame Martin! *Hello! (to a woman – Mrs Martin)*
Salut Dominique! *Hi!/Hello! (to a friend or acquaintance – Dominique)*
Au revoir mademoiselle! *Goodbye (to a young, unmarried woman)*

Insight

If you know someone's name, for example a neighbour's, you greet them with their full name. Otherwise you greet them as **Madame, Monsieur** or **Mademoiselle**. You usually use first names for family and close friends only.

In addition, you need to know the correct greeting for each time of day:

À bientôt! À tout à l'heure! *See you soon!*
Bonjour! *Hello (any time in daytime)!*
Bon après-midi! *Good afternoon!*
Bonsoir! *Good evening!*
Bonne nuit! *Good night!*

Exercise 1 **Bonjour!**

◀) **CD1, TR 3**

Say the appropriate greeting to the following people:

- **a** *Hello* to Madame Corre
- **b** *Goodbye* to Marie-Claire
- **c** *Good night* to Paul
- **d** *Good afternoon* to a young woman at the cash desk in the supermarket
- **e** *See you soon* to Monsieur Jarre

Insight

When greeting someone raise your voice slightly at the end of each word or expression and make the last syllable linger a little.

Now listen to the recording to check whether you have got it right. If you do not have the recording just look up the answer at the back of the book.

2 Comment ça va?
How are you?

Listen to the conversation between two neighbours and see whether you can tell who is feeling fine and who is feeling 'so so!'.

CD1, TR 4

Madame Lebrun	Bonjour Monsieur Blanchard, comment ça va?
Monsieur Blanchard	Ça va bien merci et vous Madame Lebrun?
Madame Lebrun	Oh, comme ci, comme ça! Allez! Au revoir Monsieur Blanchard.

When asking somebody **Comment ça va?** it is not intended that the other person should give a full health bulletin in reply. Most of the time people reply **Ça va, ça va!** or **Ça va bien merci!** If someone replies **Comme ci, comme ça!** it indicates that all is not well, things could be better, but the person is unlikely to disclose more unless they are asked further questions.

When you listen to French people talking you are very likely to hear **Allez!** which comes from **Aller** *to go*.

Insight
Allez! This is an expression of encouragement at the end of a conversation, at the point when the speaker is leaving. The sense is *'Oh well, I'll leave you to it!'*

Allez, à bientôt! *Oh well, see you soon!*
Allez, bon appétit! *Oh well, have a good meal!*
Allez, bonne pêche! *Oh well, have a good catch! (to someone fishing)*

Exercise 2 **Cherchez la bonne phrase** *Find the right expression*

◀) **CD1, TR 5**

Listen to some more greetings on the recording. Try to match them to the correct English expressions.

1 Allez, bon voyage!
2 Bon week-end!
3 Allez, bonne route!
4 Bonnes vacances!
5 Bonne Année!
6 Bon anniversaire!

a Have a good weekend!
b Happy birthday!
c Have a good journey!
d Happy New Year!
e Have a safe journey!
f Have a good holiday!

Check your answers at the back of the book.

---

3 A votre santé!
To your good health!

French people always find a good reason to drink a toast. You will hear:

A votre santé!	*To your (good) health!*	These are said to all those assembled, or individually to someone you would address formally.
A la vôtre!	*To yours!*	
A ta santé!	*To your (good) health!*	These are said to one person you know well.
À la tienne!	*To yours!*	
Santé!	*Good health! Cheers!*	

Exercise 3 **Quelle est la fête?**
What's the celebration?
Listen to the recording. You will hear three
very short scenes. You have to decide what is
being celebrated in each of them:

Dialogue 1

CD1, TR 6

> – Bonne Année!
> – À votre santé!
> – Santé!
> – À la vôtre!

Are they celebrating:

a a good holiday?   **b** a wedding?   **c** New Year?

Dialogue 2

CD1, TR 7

> – Bon Anniversaire Françoise!
> – À la santé de Françoise!
> – À la tienne Françoise!
> – À la vôtre!

Are they celebrating:

a a good journey?   **b** a birthday?   **c** a good holiday?

Dialogue 3

CD1, TR 8

> – À la santé des mariés!
> – À la santé d'Estelle et Paul!
> – À la vôtre!

Are they celebrating:

a a wedding?   **b** an anniversary?   **c** New Year?

6

Vivent les mariés! *Long live the bride and groom!*
Vive le marié! *Long live the groom!*
Vive la mariée! *Long live the bride!*

Vivent les mariés!

Le PACS (PActe Civil de Solidarité): *a new law voted on 15 November 1999 gives the same rights to married and unmarried couples.*

Insight
Le PACS was introduced mainly for the purpose of providing same-sex couples with a contractual framework. In the first ten years of its existence **le PACS** has proved to be very successful and records show that more and more French couples prefer to adopt this formula.

4 Acheter et payer
Buying and paying

All you need to know is the name of what you would like to buy and how to ask for the price. Saying please and thank you will help you feel confident that you can express yourself, even if you are only using a few words.

S'il vous plaît (S.V.P.) *please*
Merci *thank you*
Merci bien *thanks a lot*
C'est combien? *How much is it?*
L'addition s'il vous plaît! *The bill please!*

Exercise 4 **Où sont-ils?** *Where are they?*
Look at the illustrations and listen to the three short dialogues.

Dialogue 1

◀) **CD1, TR 9**

Are the people **a** at home? **b** at a grocery shop? **c** in the street?

Dialogue 2

◀) **CD1, TR 10**

Are the people **a** in church? **b** in a café? **c** at a grocery shop?

Dialogue 3

◀) **CD1, TR 11**

Are the people **a** at the station? **b** in the street? **c** at a grocery shop?

Now check your answers by reading the dialogues you have just heard.

Dialogue 1

– Taxi! Taxi! La gare du Nord s'il vous plaît!
– Oui madame!

Dialogue 2

– Un café, une bière et un sandwich au fromage s'il vous plaît.
– Oui monsieur.
– L'addition s'il vous plaît.

Dialogue 3

– Une baguette, un camembert et un kilo de pommes s'il vous plaît.
– Oui mademoiselle!
– Merci bien. C'est combien?
– Cinq euros mademoiselle.

Exercise 5

Look again at the three dialogues above and find the French expressions for the following:

a *a kilo of apples*
b *five euros*
c *a cheese sandwich*
d *a beer*
e *the station*

Now check your answers at the back of the book.

5 Dans la rue
In the street

You want to find out where some places are in the village. The important thing is to know what to ask for, then people will point you in the right direction.

VOCAB

Pardon madame, la boulangerie s'il vous plaît? *Excuse me, where is the baker's please?*

Try to guess which places are mentioned in the following examples.

   a *Pardon monsieur, la poste s'il vous plaît?*
   b *Pardon mademoiselle, l'office du tourisme s'il vous plaît?*
   c *Pardon madame, le supermarché s'il vous plaît?*
   d *Pardon madame, le garage Citroën s'il vous plaît?*

Un peu de grammaire
A bit of grammar

So far you may have noticed three different ways of spelling the word for good:

Bon voyage!
Bonne année!
Bonnes vacances!

This is because in French, nouns (words which represent objects, people or ideas) have a gender; they can be either feminine or masculine. **Un voyage** *a journey* is masculine, **une année** *a year* is feminine, **des vacances** *holidays* is feminine but also plural.

The gender of nouns does not follow any logical pattern so you will need to be aware of the gender of every noun you learn.

Bon, bonne and **bons, bonnes** are four forms of the same adjective (a word which describes a noun) and they have the same gender as the nouns they describe, so we have masculine and feminine adjectives which can both be singular or plural.

French adjectives are spelt differently according to their genders. Generally (but not always) an -e at the end of an adjective is for feminine, an -s is for plural.

More examples:

If we take two other nouns **un raisin** *grape* (masc.) and **une pomme** *apple* (fem.) we have four spellings for **bon:**

un bon raisin *a good grape*   **une bonne pomme** *a good apple*
des bons raisins *good grapes*   **des bonnes pommes** *good apples*

des = *some/more than one*

Insight

In the plural form (more than one item) the use of **des** in front of a noun preceded by an adjective e.g. **des bons fruits** is what most French speakers use in everyday conversation; however you might also hear more formal French being spoken where the **s** of **des** is dropped.

Il y a de jolis villages en France	*There are some pretty villages in France*
Grand-mère fait de délicieuses confitures avec de bons fruits	*Grandma makes delicious jams with good fruit*

Pronunciation

▶ **Ça va** – C *with a cedilla (ç) sounds like an* s. *It is only used in front of* a, o *and* u: ça *[sa],* ço *[so] and* çu *[su].*
Note that there is no cedilla in **merci** *and that in* **comme ci, comme ça** *only* ça *needs a cedilla.*

▶ **Comment** – *the* t *at the end is silent and* en *is pronounced in a nasal fashion.*

▶ **Année, santé, enchanté, présente, appétit** *all have an* e *with an acute accent. It changes the neutral* e *sound into one close to the sound in the first syllable of 'ready'.*

Exercise 6 **La liste de provisions** *The shopping list*
Make your own shopping list using all the words for food and drinks in the unit.

1 kilo de pommes

Insight

Every time you use a noun, try to learn its article: **le** or **la**, **un** or **une**. The gender does not pertain to the object itself but to the noun describing it. It is either feminine or masculine: **le vélo** (*the bike*) but **la bicyclette** (*the bike*): one object or concept, two different nouns for it and two different genders!

6 Dites-le!
Say it!

Explication: dites comes from the verb **dire** (*to say*)

e.g. Dites-le avec des fleurs (*say it with flowers*)
          des chocolats
          un livre
          une carte

Grandmother (**Grand-mère**) is telling the children (**les enfants**) what to say. Please respond as if you were the children.

Grand-mère	Dites bonjour à Elise.
Les enfants	Bonjour Elise!
Grand-mère	Dites au revoir à Papa.
Les enfants	Au revoir Papa!
Grand-mère	Dites bon anniversaire à Maman.
Les enfants	Bon anniversaire Maman!
Grand-mère	Dites bonnes vacances à Mademoiselle Lapierre.
Les enfants	Bonnes vacances Mademoiselle Lapierre!
Grand-mère	Dites bonne fête à Catherine.
Les enfants	Bonne fête Catherine!

📶 CD1, TR 13

Surfez sur le web

- To send your best wishes in French you can find cards with greetings on the internet: http://carte.dromadaire.com/fr/
- Entraînez-vous sur le web
  Find the card category: **A fêter** (*to celebrate*) and click on the type of card you may use to celebrate 1. a wedding 2. a friend's name day 3. Bastille Day.

A) Without looking back at the previous pages put the following five expressions in chronological order (30 seconds):

1 *Bonsoir*

2 *Bonjour*

3 *Bon après-midi*

4 *Bonne nuit*

5 *Salut*

B) Say what expressions or greetings you would use for each of the following situations. Some apply to more than one situation (one minute):

1 *To people having a picnic*

2 *To a shopkeeper*

3 *At someone's birthday party*

4 *In a restaurant*

5 *At a wedding*

[Bon anniversaire!; C'est combien?; Vive la mariée!; A la vôtre! L'addition SVP!; Bon appétit!]

2

Premiers contacts
Meeting people

In this unit you will learn
- *how to give and understand information about marital status, family links, age and profession*
- *numbers up to sixty-nine*
- *four verbs:* **être** *to be,* **parler** *to speak,* **s'appeler** *to be called,* **avoir** *to have*

---

1 Enchanté de faire votre connaissance
Pleased to meet you

◄)) **CD1, TR 14**

There is a wedding in the family. People have travelled from all over the place. At the dinner table two people who have never met before find out each other's names and where they come from.

Listen to the recording.

a *What is the man's name?*

Now read the dialogue:

Homme	Bonjour, je m'appelle Alain. Et vous, comment vous appelez-vous?
Femme	Je m'appelle Claire.
Homme	Enchanté de faire votre connaissance, Claire! Vous êtes d'où?
Femme	Je suis de Paris. Et vous?
Homme	Moi, je suis de Marseille.

  b *What is the woman's name?*
  c *Where is Claire from?*
  d *Where is Alain from?*

un homme *a man*
une femme *a woman*
Comment vous appelez-vous? *What is your name?*
Je m'appelle … *My name is …*
Vous êtes d'où? *Where are you from?*
moi *me*

Find the French for:

  e *I am from Paris.*
  f *Pleased to meet you.*

To say where you are from you can name a town or a country:

Je suis de Bordeaux
Je suis de Londres
Je suis de New York
Je suis du Canada
Je suis du Pays de Galles   *I am from Wales*
Je suis des États-Unis   *I am from the United States*

Exercise 1 **D'où êtes-vous?** *Where are you from?*
You are François or Françoise, a guest at the wedding. You are
from Boulogne. Fill in your part of the dialogue.

CD1, TR 15

Lucien	Bonjour, je m'appelle Lucien. Et vous, comment vous appelez-vous?
Vous	a Give your name.
Lucien	Enchanté de faire votre connaissance. D'où êtes-vous?
Vous	b Say where you are from. Say 'And you?' to ask where Lucien is from.
Lucien	Je suis de Bruxelles.

Insight

In French even the names of countries are either feminine, masculine or plural:

Le Japon, le Portugal, le Mexique; la France, la Chine, la Russie; les Etats-Unis

Now do the exercise again, using your own identity.

Un peu de grammaire
A bit of grammar

◀) CD1, TR 17

DES NOMBRES ET DES CHIFFRES
Numbers and figures

The following table should allow you to work out numbers from 0 to 69.

0 zéro	10 dix	21 vingt et un
1 un	11 onze	22 vingt-deux
2 deux	12 douze	23 vingt-trois
3 trois	13 treize	30 trente
4 quatre	14 quatorze	31 trente et un
5 cinq	15 quinze	32 trente-deux
6 six	16 seize	40 quarante
7 sept	17 dix-sept	50 cinquante
8 huit	18 dix-huit	60 soixante
9 neuf	19 dix-neuf	61 soixante et un
	20 vingt	69 soixante-neuf

Look at the numbers above, listen to how they sound, and repeat after the speaker.

Exercise 2 **Le Loto**
Look at the KENO® lottery ticket and answer the questions which follow:

a *For each grid how many numbers can you tick?*
b *How many winning numbers are drawn every day?*
c *How much does it cost if you have two draws? If you have one draw?*
d *Listen to the recording. Write down all the numbers you hear and find out if you have any of the winning numbers.*

© Tous droits réservés à la Française des Jeux.

Did you know that the French National Lottery started in 1918 to fund the war widows' pensions, soldiers' disability pensions and the upkeep and education of the First World War orphans?

In 1933 it officially became **la Loterie Nationale** and it existed as such until 1990. The lottery is now run by a body called **La Française des Jeux**.

2 Je suis la mère d'Isabelle
I am Isabelle's mother

Isabelle Lejeune and David Miller are getting married in Rouen in Normandy. David is English but works in France. Isabelle is French. At the wedding there are lots of people from both families. Listen to one of the conversations where people introduce themselves.

Listen for the first time to the recording.

   a *Who is Hélène Lejeune?*
   b *Whose aunt is Anne Thompson?*

Listen once more.

   c *Is Anne Thompson English?*
   d *What is her husband's name?*

Listen a final time.

   e *Where does she live?*

◈ CD1, TR 18

Madame Lejeune	Bonjour Madame, je m'appelle Hélène Lejeune. Je suis la mère d'Isabelle. Et vous comment vous appelez-vous?
Anne Thompson	Enchantée de faire votre connaissance. Je m'appelle Anne Thompson, je suis la tante de David.
Madame Lejeune	Ah, vous êtes anglaise?
Anne Thompson	Non, non, je suis française. Je suis mariée à Mark Thompson, l'oncle de David. J'habite en Angleterre.
Madame Lejeune	Ah très bien! Enchantée!
Anne Thompson	Voici mon fils Raphaël et voilà ma fille Sophie. Raphaël, Sophie, je vous présente Madame Lejeune, la maman d'Isabelle.
Raphaël	Bonjour Madame.
Sophie	Bonjour.

20

Now read the written dialogue and try to find out how to say the following in French:

f *I live in England*
g *David's aunt*
h *Let me introduce you to Madame ...*
i *My son*
j *My daughter*

Check your answers at the back of the book.

Insight

The word for 'my' (known as the possessive adjective) changes according to the gender of the thing or person referred to. As a result there are three ways of saying 'my': **mon**, **ma** and **mes** (plural):

Le père + la mère = les parents   mon père + ma mère = mes parents

Un peu de grammaire
A bit of grammar

VOICI/VOILÀ *THIS IS/THAT IS*

Voici is used when introducing a first person, standing next to you.

Voilà is for introducing a second person, possibly standing further away from you.

More generally:

Voici is for pointing out someone or something close by.

Voilà is for pointing out someone or something slightly further away from you.

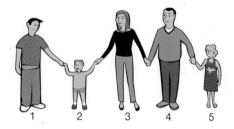

1 *Voici Jacques, le frère de Monsieur Norbert.*
2 *Voici Gaétan, le fils des Norbert.*
3 *Voici Madame Norbert.*
4 *Voici Monsieur Norbert.*
5 *Et voilà Joëlle, la fille des Norbert.*

Insight

In French, family names do not have an 's' in the plural form:
les Norbert = the Norberts; les Thompson = the Thompsons;
les Blanchard = the Blanchards etc.

Voici les Charcot   et   voilà les Bastide

3 Tu as quel âge?
How old are you?

The children at the wedding are getting to know one another.

Read what they say.

CD1, TR 19

Camille	Bonjour, je m'appelle Camille ... et toi comment tu t'appelles?
Sophie	Moi, je m'appelle Sophie. Et mon frère s'appelle Raphaël.
Camille	Moi je suis la sœur d'Isabelle. Je n'ai pas de frère.
Sophie	Tu as quel âge?
Camille	J'ai douze ans.
Sophie	Ah moi aussi j'ai douze ans! Mon frère, il a quatorze ans.

la sœur *the sister*
le frère *the brother*
moi *me*
ma sœur *my sister*
mon frère *my brother*
toi *you*

QUICK VOCAB

Remember that to say *my* in French you must use **ma** in front of a feminine word and **mon** in front of a masculine word.

Find the French for the following:

a *I am twelve years old.*
b *My brother, he is fourteen.*
c *I don't have a brother.*
d *Me too!*
e *How old are you?*

Pronunciation

◄》 **CD1, TR 20**

In French, words tend to be linked together, particularly when the second of two words starts with a vowel. When saying her age Camille says **J'ai douze ans**. These four short words are heard as two groups of sounds: [*jai douzan*].

Sophie says of her brother **Il a quatorze ans** which, again, is heard as two sets of sounds: [*ila quatorzan*].

It is important to know how the numbers are spelt because the last letter of the number is always linked with **an(s)** *year(s)*. Here are some more examples:

> *Isabelle? Elle a vingt-cinq ans. [ella vintcincan]*
> *Danielle? Elle a trente ans. [ella trentan]*

Note that the e at the end of **trente, quarante,** etc. is not heard.

> *Arnaud? Il a neuf ans. [ila neuvan]*

(an **f** sounds like a **v** when linking two words)

Exercise 3 **Quel âge avez-vous?** *How old are you?*

◄》 **CD1, TR 21**

Try saying the following in French:

a *I am twenty-one years old.*
b *He is thirty-eight.*
c *She is sixty-nine.*
d *He is forty.*

Now listen to the recording to hear the answers.

---

4 Vous parlez français?
Do you speak French?

Still at the wedding, Hélène and Anne discuss which language is spoken in the Thompson household.

Listen to the recording a few times and see whether you can answer the following questions.

a *Which two languages are mentioned?*
b *Does Anne speak English or French with Mark, her husband?*
c *What does Mark teach?*

Hélène	Vous parlez français avec les enfants?
Anne	Oui, je parle français à la maison. Les enfants parlent couramment les deux langues.
Hélène	Et avec Mark?
Anne	Avec mon mari je parle français ou anglais, cela dépend. Il parle bien le français, il est professeur de français.

♪ CD1, TR 22

avec *with*
à la maison *at home*
les enfants *the children*
couramment *fluently*
mon mari *my husband*
professeur *teacher*

Find the French for the following in the dialogue.

  d *He is a French teacher.*
  e *It depends.*
  f *I speak French or English.*
  g *I speak French at home.*
  h *The children speak both languages fluently.*
  i *He speaks French well.*

Un peu de grammaire
A bit of grammar

VERBS

In this unit you have already come across four important verbs. (A verb is the part of the language used to indicate an action or state of things.) Here is what you have learnt so far:

Être *to be*

Je suis française.	*I am French.*
Je suis mariée.	*I am married.*
Il est anglais.	*He is English.*
Il est professeur.	*He is a teacher.*
Vous êtes anglaise?	*Are you English?*

Être indicates a state of things.

Avoir *to have*

J'ai trente ans.	*I am (have) thirty (years).*
Il a dix ans.	*He is ten.*
Elle a vingt-cinq ans.	*She is twenty-five.*
Je n'ai pas de frère.	*I don't have a brother.*

S'appeler *to be called*

This a reflexive verb, that is, the subject and the object of the verb are one and the same. Word for word **s'appeler** means *to call oneself.*

Comment vous appelez-vous?	*What's your name? (lit. How do you call yourself?)*
Je m'appelle Anne.	*I am called Anne.*
Comment tu t'appelles?	*What's your name? (when speaking to a child or someone you know well)*

Parler *to speak*

Je parle français.	*I speak French.*
Je parle anglais.	*I speak English.*
Vous parlez français?	*Do you speak French?*
Ils parlent français.	*They speak French. (the **nt** in **ils parlent** is not pronounced)*

Exercise 4 **Cherchez la bonne phrase**

◀) **CD1, TR 23**

Listen to these French expressions. Link them to their English equivalents.

1 I am not married.
2 What's his name?
3 He has a brother and a sister.
4 I don't have a sister.
5 I don't speak English.

a Je n'ai pas de sœur.
b Je ne parle pas anglais.
c Je ne suis pas mariée.
d Il a un frère et une sœur.
e Comment il s'appelle?

Exercise 5 Qui est-ce?

Who is it? Read the explanations below and say what the family link is likely to be:

Your father? Your cousin? Your aunt? Your brother? Your grandmother?

a *C'est la mère de mon père.*
b *C'est le mari de ma mère.*
c *C'est la sœur de mon père.*
d *C'est la fille du frère de ma mère.*
e *C'est le fils de mes parents.*

Exercise 6 Trouvez l'intrus *(literally find the intruder)*

◄) **CD1, TR 24**

Listen and say which of the following people from my family is the odd one out.

1 *Annie, mon amie*
2 *ma mère*
3 *ma sœur*
4 *ma tante*
5 *mon oncle*
6 *ma cousine*

Insight

In French first names are often hyphenated compound names.

Boys' names: Jean-Paul; Jean-Pierre; Jean-Marie; Jean-Claude; Pierre-Henri

Girls' names: Marie-Christine; Marie-Pierre; Marie-Chantal; Marie-France*; Marie-Claire*; Anne-Marie; Anne-Elise

and many other combinations.

* You may recognize the two asterisked names as the titles of well-known French women's magazines. Fashions change and these names are not quite so commonly used nowadays.

Surfez sur le web

- Google 'origine des noms et prénoms' or go to http://www.lexilogos.com/noms_prenoms.htm
- Research the origin and popularity, in France, of four of the first names used in this unit: Anne, Hélène, David and Raphaël.
- You may find other sites and try your luck with your own first name and surname.

BONNE CHANCE!

TEST YOURSELF

Qui suis-je? *Who am I?*

1 *J'ai douze ans, j'ai un frère.*

2 *Je suis française, j'habite en Angleterre et mon mari est anglais.*

3 *Mon frère s'appelle Jacques.*

4 *Je suis de Bruxelles.*

5 *J'ai douze ans et je n'ai pas de frère.*

6 *Isabelle est ma fille.*

7 *Je suis professeur de français.*

8 *J'ai trente ans.*

9 *Mes cousins, Sophie et Raphaël, sont bilingues.*

10 *J'existe depuis 1918.*

3

On fait connaissance
Getting to know someone

In this unit you will learn
- *how to introduce yourself fully*
- *how to understand what other people say about themselves*
- *how to talk and ask about professions, employment and unemployment, leisure activities, likes and dislikes*
- *how to talk further about marital status and families*

1 En stage
On a training course

A group of people of all ages and backgrounds are on a weekend course (**un stage**) in Paris preparing for an amateur photography expedition to Vietnam. The first thing they do is a self-introduction exercise to get to know one another.

The course participants (**les stagiaires**) have been asked to say the following things about themselves:

- ▶ *Name*
- ▶ *Age*
- ▶ *Town/area where they live*
- ▶ *Marital status + family details*
- ▶ *Profession*
- ▶ *Languages spoken*

▶ *Likes (leisure, hobbies)*
▶ *Dislikes*

They all give the information in different ways, so listen for the expressions they use to say their name, their profession and what they like or dislike.

Listen to what the first person says and then stop the recording. You may need to listen more than once to understand what is being said.

_____

2 Natalie Le Hénaff

J'aime faire de la photographie.

Je n'aime pas faire le ménage.

◀ **CD1, TR 25**

Without looking at the text below can you answer the following questions about Natalie?

a *How old is she?*
b *Is she married?*
c *How many children does she have?*
d *Does she speak English?*
e *Can you tell at least one thing she likes doing?*

Listen to the recording again but this time you may look at the text.

> 'Bonjour! Je m'appelle Natalie Le Hénaff. J'ai trente-six ans.
> J'habite à Vannes en Bretagne.
> Je suis mariée. J'ai deux enfants, un garçon et une fille.
> Je suis professeur d'histoire dans un collège.
> Je parle français, anglais et espagnol.
> J'aime aller au cinéma, voyager, lire et faire de la photographie.
> Je n'aime pas faire le ménage.'

From the text above can you tell which French expressions Natalie uses to say the following things?

f *I am a history teacher.*
g *I love travelling.*
h *I live in Vannes in Brittany.*
i *I love going to the cinema.*
j *I don't like doing the housework.*

Insight

To say where we live or where we're from, we use **être de** (*to be from*) + name of town / country; **habiter à / vivre à** + name of town (*to live in*) or **habiter en / au** + name of the region:

Je suis de Bordeaux

J'habite à Bordeaux

Je vis à Bayonne au Pays Basque (le Pays Basque)

Je vis à Quimper en Bretagne (la Bretagne)

Un peu de grammaire
A bit of grammar

SAYING WHAT YOUR JOB IS

In French there is no indefinite article ('a' or 'an' in English) in front of the name of a profession.

Natalie says she is a history teacher in a secondary school:

Je suis professeur d'histoire dans un collège.

The next person, Antoine Durand (see Section 3), says he is a sound engineer for a French TV channel, France 3:

Je suis ingénieur du son à France 3.

The omission of the indefinite article also applies when Antoine says he is a bachelor:

Je suis célibataire.

(**Célibataire** is used for both unmarried men and women.)

HOW TO EXPRESS LIKES

- ▶ **J'aime** *(I like/love)*
- ▶ **J'aime bien** *(I like / I quite like)*
- ▶ **J'aime beaucoup...** *(I like ... a lot)*
- ▶ **J'adore** *(I adore/love)*

Je becomes **j'** in front of **aime** because **aime** starts with a vowel. The same rule applies with **adore** and with all other verbs starting with a vowel. **e** is the only letter which can be replaced by an apostrophe in front of a vowel.

J'aime les voyages.

J'aime bien lire.

J'aime beaucoup le sport.

J'adore la photographie.

AND HOW TO EXPRESS DISLIKES

▶ Je n'aime pas

To make a verb negative (the equivalent of adding 'not' in English), use **ne ... pas** (ne + verb + pas). Here **ne** becomes **n'** before a vowel (**aime**):

Je n'aime pas faire le ménage.   *I don't like doing the housework.*

You can also use expressions such as:

Je déteste / J'ai horreur de...   *I really don't like / I hate...*

Pronunciation

Look back at what Natalie says and find all the apostrophes. In each case, an apostrophe replaces an -e because the word that follows begins with a vowel or an **h**:

There is also one example of **de** losing its **e** in front of a vowel sound: **professeur d'histoire**. Here and in **j'habite**, the **h** is silent.

All these expressions are pronounced as if they were one word, specifically to avoid a harshness that the repetition of two vowel sounds would create:

je mappelle / jai / jabite / jaime / je naime pas / professeur distoire.

> ## Insight
> **Les liaisons**: linking words together gives fluidity to the sound. Try these three examples:
>
> **Je suis amoureux / amoureuse** (*I am in love*). This should be pronounced: *je suizamoorer / je suizamoorerze*
>
> **Bonjour mes amis** (*hello my friends*), pronounced *bonjour mezami* (the **s** at the end of **amis** is silent)
>
> **Bon appétit**, pronounced *bonappeti* (the **t** at the end of **appétit** is silent)

3 Antoine Durand

Try to answer the following questions about Antoine after listening to the next part of the recording a few times:

  a *How old is he?*
  b *Where does he live?*
  c *What foreign language does he speak?*
  d *What does he like doing best?*

Now look at the text:

> 'Alors moi, mon nom c'est Antoine Durand. J'ai vingt-neuf ans.
> Je demeure à Paris.
> Je suis célibataire.
> Je suis ingénieur du son à France 3.
> Je parle français et allemand.
> J'aime bien regarder des films et le sport à la télé. J'adore la
>   photographie et les voyages.
> J'ai horreur des voitures, alors je vais au travail à vélo.'

Using the text above find out the
following expressions:

e *I live in Paris.*
f *I like watching films on TV.*
g *I hate cars.*
h *I go to work by bike.*

Vélib': La Ville est plus belle à vélo
Since July 2007 **le Vélib'**, a new system of bike hiring, has
been introduced in Paris, together with cycling lanes. Paris is
fast becoming a city where people cycle to work or use bikes
for moving around the capital. (See Unit 20 Section 2 for
more details.)

Un peu de grammaire
A bit of grammar

ALORS

As soon as you hear French people talking amongst themselves you
will hear **alors** or **bon, alors** or **oui, alors**. It loosely means *then* or
so, similar to someone saying *well / so then…* in English. It is used
to fill a gap in the conversation. It also means *therefore*.

Task: Find two different uses of **alors** in what Antoine Durand says.

4 Monique Duval

Listen to the next part of the recording and answer the following questions about Monique:

a *How old is she?*
b *Who is Pierre?*
c *Where does she work?*
d *Does she speak English?*
e *How does she feel about football on TV?*

Now read the text below:

> 'Bonjour, je m'appelle Monique Duval. J'ai quarante-cinq ans. Je suis de Dijon.
> Je suis mariée à Pierre mais je n'ai pas d'enfants. Pierre a un fils d'un premier mariage. Il s'appelle Guillaume, il a vingt-cinq ans mais il ne travaille pas, il est au chômage.
> Je travaille à la poste.
> Je parle un peu l'anglais et j'apprends le vietnamien.
> J'aime beaucoup le sport, les voyages et la photographie.
> Je déteste le football à la télévision.'

Using the text above find out the following expressions:

f *I work at the post office.*
g *I speak a little bit of English.*
h *I don't have any children.*
i *I am learning Vietnamese.*
j *He is unemployed.*

5 Pierre Duval

Listen to Pierre speaking on the recording and answer the following questions:

a *How old is Pierre?*
b *What is his wife's name?*
c *Where does he work?*
d *Where does he live?*

Now read the text of what Pierre said:

> 'Alors je me présente: je m'appelle Duval Pierre.
> J'ai cinquante-deux ans. J'habite à Dijon.
> Je suis marié à Monique.
> Ma mère est veuve et elle habite chez nous.
> Je travaille chez Renault.
> Je comprends un peu l'anglais.
> J'adore les voyages et la lecture.
> Je n'aime pas la télé sauf les documentaires sur les voyages.'

The following words help you to understand what Pierre is saying.

avec *with*
chez *at*
sauf *except*
veuve *widow/widowed (woman)*

QUICK VOCAB

Using the text above find out the following expressions:

e *My mother is a widow.*
f *I work at Renault.*
g *She lives with us.*
h *I love travel and reading.*
i *I don't like TV except travel documentaries.*
j *I understand English a little.*

Insight

A formal way to introduce someone is by giving names in the order **Nom, prénom.** Pierre Duval says: **Je m'appelle Duval Pierre.** This is nearly always used for administrative or commercial purposes:

Monsieur Duval Pierre
16 Avenue de la Gare
DIJON

This not the usual practice for informal social occasions or in a professional or political context.

Un peu de grammaire
A bit of grammar

QUELLES QUESTIONS?

There is always more than one way to ask a question. Here are standard questions and answers about personal details.

Topics	Questions	Answers
Name	Comment vous appelez-vous?	Je m'appelle Nathalie.
	Quel est votre nom?	Mon nom c'est Josianne.
Age	Quel âge avez-vous?	J'ai trente-deux ans.
	Vous avez quel âge?	J'ai cinquante ans.

Where living	Où habitez-vous?	J'habite à Nantes.
	Où est-ce que vous habitez?	
	Où est-ce que vous demeurez?	Je demeure à Bordeaux.
Marital status	Vous êtes marié(e)?	Oui, je suis marié(e).
		Non, je suis célibataire.
Profession	Quelle est votre profession?	Je suis dentiste.
	Quel est votre métier?	Je suis dans le commerce.
	Quel travail faites-vous?	
	Où est-ce que vous travaillez?	Je travaille chez Renault.
Languages	Quelles langues parlez-vous?	Je parle français et anglais.
	Vous parlez anglais?	Oui, un petit peu.
Likes	Vous aimez le cinéma?	Oui, j'adore le cinéma.
	Vous aimez le football?	Non, j'ai horreur du football.

Exercise 1 **Je m'appelle...**

You are a participant on the Paris photography course. Try to make a statement giving the following information:

- ▶ *Your name is Anne-Marie Pélerin*
- ▶ *You are 45*
- ▶ *You live in Boulogne*
- ▶ *You are a dentist*
- ▶ *You speak French, English and German*
- ▶ *You love football and photography*

Exercise 2 Questions et réponses

You will need to look back at the statements made by the people on the photography course. In the boxes below enter the missing questions or the missing answers.

Names	Questions	Answers
Natalie	Comment vous appelez-vous?	
Antoine	Quel âge avez-vous?	
Natalie		Je suis professeur d'histoire
Monique	Où travaillez-vous?	
Pierre		J'habite à Dijon
Antoine		Je parle français et allemand
Monique		Oui, j'aime beaucoup le sport
Pierre	Vous êtes marié?	

Insight

The following six interrogative pronouns are likely to be key to your understanding what is being asked:

Qui êtes-vous? *Who are you?*
Comment voyagez-vous? *How do you travel?*
Quand partez-vous? *When are you leaving?*
Où allez-vous? *Where are you going?*
Pourquoi? *Why?*
Qu'est-ce que vous cherchez? *What are you looking for?*

Exercise 3 Vrai ou faux?

The following statements are not all accurate. Looking back at our four course participants say which statements are true (**vrai**) and which ones are false (**faux**):

a *Monique apprend le chinois.*
b *Pierre et Monique ont deux enfants.*
c *Natalie aime aller au cinéma.*
d *Antoine est célibataire.*
e *Antoine habite à Paris.*
f *Pierre travaille chez Citroën.*

Exercise 4 **Qui est l'aîné?**

◀ᴼ **CD1, TR 26**

Listen to the recording and say who is the oldest. First you need to learn the following two words:

plus *more*
moins *less*

a *Bernard a cinquante-trois ans.*
b *Sylvie a trente-neuf ans.*
c *Mona a cinq ans de moins que Sylvie.*
d *Marc a dix ans de plus que Mona.*
e *Etienne a trois ans de moins que Bernard.*
f *Martin a dix ans de plus qu'Etienne.*

Le chômage en France - *Unemployment in France*
  In March 2009 unemployment figures were 7.8% overall but 23% for the under 25s. The strikes and unrest were mainly due to the high level of unemployment amongst young people and a clumsy Government attempt to impose new rules for the **CNE**, **C**ontrat **N**ouvelles **E**mbauches (contracts for first time/new employees).

Surfez sur le web

  • Google: chômage en France. Choisissez le site www.educnet. education.fr/insee/chomage/default.htm
  • **Recherchez** les statistiques sur le chômage en France
  • **Cliquez** sur **Qui? Et suivez le lien** (*follow the link*)
  • **Répondez aux questions par Vrai ou Faux** (*answer with True or False*)
  (**L'Insee** is the French national institute for statistics and economic studies).

A) Using the information about the four course participants work out the answers to **Qui suis-je?** *Who am I?*

1 *Je travaille pour une chaîne de télévision française.*

2 *J'ai trente-six ans.*

3 *J'utilise le Vélib' pour aller au travail.*

4 *Le fils de mon mari est au chômage.*

5 *Ma mère habite avec ma femme et moi.*

B) Quelle est ma profession? *What is my job?*

1 *Je ne suis pas marié.*

2 *J'habite à Vannes.*

3 *J'apprends le vietnamien.*

4 *Je n'aime pas faire le ménage.*

5 *Je suis très sportive.*

4

Un voyage en bateau
A boat trip

In this unit you will learn
- *how to ask where something is situated*
- *how to understand some directions*
- *how to ask if something you need is available*
- *how to ask most forms of questions*
- *how to say what you would like to do*
- *how to count to 101*

Insight

Travelling to France on a cross-channel ferry to Caen or St Malo you may find that most of the staff are French. Although they are likely to speak English, use the opportunity to try out your French and to try French cuisine too if you travel on Brittany Ferries. On the other hand if you prefer crossing the Channel (**la Manche**) via the Channel Tunnel (**Le Tunnel sous la Manche**) it is a lot quicker.

1 Au pont cinq
On deck five

CD1, TR 27

Sarah Burgess is travelling to France with a French friend,
Dominique Périer. They have left their car on the car deck (**le pont**)
and now they are looking for their cabin.

Listen to the recording once through, then answer these questions:

   a *On which deck is their car?*
   b *On which deck is their cabin?*

Listen again.

   c *Where do they go to find out? On which deck is it?*
   d *Is it morning or evening?*
   e *Did you get the number of the cabin?*

Now read the dialogue.

Dominique	Bon, la voiture est au pont cinq. Maintenant allons à la cabine.
Sarah	Où se trouve notre cabine?
Dominique	Je ne sais pas. Allons au bureau d'information au pont sept.
Membre de l'équipage	Bonsoir madame.
Dominique	Bonsoir, j'ai réservé une cabine.
Membre de l'équipage	Oui, c'est à quel nom?
Dominique	Périer, Dominique Périer.
Membre de l'équipage	Oui, alors c'est la cabine 017 au pont huit. Prenez l'escalier à gauche.
Sarah	Allons-y.

la voiture *the car*
je ne sais pas *I don't know*
membre de l'équipage *a member of the crew*
c'est à quel nom? *which name?*
l'escalier *the staircase*
à gauche *on the left*
allons-y *let's go*

You may be able to work out some words and expressions for yourself. Link the English phrases below to the equivalent French expressions:

1 Where is our cabin?
2 Let's go to the information desk.
3 Take the staircase on the left.
4 I have reserved a cabin.
5 The car is on deck five.

a Prenez l'escalier à gauche.
b J'ai réservé une cabine.
c La voiture est au pont cinq.
d Où est notre cabine?
e Allons au bureau d'information.

Un peu de grammaire
A bit of grammar

OÙ SE TROUVE...?/OÙ EST...?

To ask where a place is use either **où se trouve...?** or **où est...?** These two expressions are totally interchangeable:

Où se trouve le bar?
Where is the bar? (lit. where does the bar find itself?)

Où est le bar?
Where is the bar?

Remember, if a noun is in the plural form, the verb will also be in the plural form:

Où se trouvent les toilettes? / Où sont les toilettes s'il vous plaît?

À, À LA, AU, AUX

These are prepositions. They are used to indicate a direction (to, at, in…) and are placed immediately before a noun.

Although all four words mean the same, you use the one that matches the gender (feminine or masculine) and number (one: singular, more than one: plural) of the noun it precedes.

▶ à *is generally used before the name of a place:*
Allons à Paris. *Let's go to Paris.*

▶ à la *is used in front of a feminine noun:*
Allons à la cabine. *Let's go to the cabin.*

▶ au *is used in front of a masculine noun.* au *is a contraction of* à + le:
La voiture est au garage. *The car is in the garage.*

▶ aux *is used in front of a plural noun, either feminine or masculine. It is a contraction of* à + les:
Allons aux jeux vidéo. *Let's go to the video games.*

Exercise 1 **Dans le bateau**

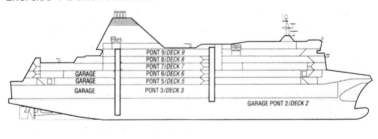

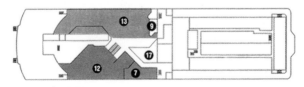

48

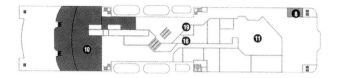

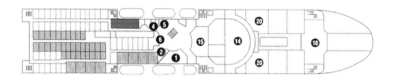

Now it is your turn to ask questions about various locations on the boat. Look at the four diagrams of the boat. The first one shows a plan of the boat; the others show various places on decks 7, 8 and 9.

Here are some of the places that you can identify on the three decks.

1 Bureau d'information	PONT 7	**a**	*Self-service restaurant*
2 Bureau de change	PONT 7	**b**	*Baggage room*
4 Sièges inclinables	PONT 7	**c**	*Children's playroom*
6 Local à bagages	PONT 7	**d**	*Information desk*
7 Salle de jeux enfants	PONT 9	**e**	*Shops*
11 Restaurant Self	PONT 8	**f**	*Bureau de change*
12 Salon de thé	PONT 9	**g**	*Reclining seats*
13 Le Bar «Le Derby»	PONT 9	**h**	*Tea shop*
15 Les boutiques	PONT 7	**i**	*Newsagent*
17 Le kiosque	PONT 9	**j**	*'Le Derby' bar*

Match the French names of places on the boat with their English equivalents. The numbers in the first column correspond to numbers of the decks on the diagrams.

Exercise 2 **Répondez aux passagers** *Answer the passengers' questions*

◀) **CD1, TR 28**

Look at the plan of the boat and imagine that you are a member of the crew answering passengers' questions.

Exemple:

Passager   Le restaurant self-service s'il vous plaît?
Membre de l'équipage C'est au pont huit, Monsieur.

Madame is used for a woman passenger (**passagère**), **monsieur** for a male passenger (**passager**).

How would you reply to these questions?

a **Passager**   Pardon, les boutiques s'il vous plaît?
  Membre de l'équipage   ...
b **Passagère**   Où est le salon de thé, s'il vous plaît?
  Membre de l'équipage   ...
c **Jeune garcon**   S'il vous plaît madame, où sont les jeux
                          pour les enfants?
  Membre de l'équipage   ...
d **Passager**   Le bar c'est à quel pont?
  Membre de l'équipage   ...
e **Passagère**   Il y a un bureau de change s'il vous plaît?
  Membre de l'équipage   ...

Un peu de grammaire
A bit of grammar

UN PASSAGER, UNE PASSAGÈRE

Nouns finishing with **-er** tend to change to **-ère** in the feminine form.

Other examples are:

masculine	feminine	
le boulanger	la boulangère	*the baker*
le fermier	la fermière	*the farmer*
le boucher	la bouchère	*the butcher*

Insight

Nouns for some professions have recently become feminine, as some adjustments have been made by law to reflect the place of women in society. For example in the case of nouns with no feminine equivalent, such as **le professeur** (*teacher*), **l'auteur** (*author*), **le ministre**, it is now recommended to use **la professeure, l'auteure, la ministre.**

---

2 Est-ce qu'il y a un cinéma?
Is there a cinema?

◀) **CD1, TR 29**

Sarah and Dominique are exploring the boat. What do they find?

Listen once to the recording and answer these questions:

  a *Is there a cinema on the boat?*
  b *Are they going to see* Pirates of the Caribbean?

Listen again.

  c *What film are they going to see?*
  d *Is the film they are going to see at 21.00 or at 22.30?*
  e *How much does it cost to get in?*

Now look at the script:

Sarah	Est-ce qu'il y a un cinéma sur le bateau?
Dominique	Oui, ici au pont 6, il y a deux cinémas. On y va?
Sarah	Oui d'accord!
Dominique	Il y a deux films. À quelle heure?
Sarah	Alors, il y a *Pirates des Caraïbes* avec Johnny Depp à vingt et une heures et à vingt-deux heures trente il y a *Le Come-back* avec Hugh Grant, le film s'appelle *Music and Lyrics* en anglais.
Dominique	Moi j'adore Hugh Grant, et toi?
Sarah	Moi aussi! Je voudrais voir *Le Come-back*. C'est combien?
Dominique	C'est dix euros.

QUICK VOCAB

On y va? *Let's go? (***On** *is frequently used in conversation to express a collective action)*
Oui d'accord *Yes O.K.*
Je voudrais + *verb I would like to...*
Je voudrais voir *I would like to see*
salon *lounge*
salle *room*
ici *here*

Link these English phrases to the equivalent French expressions from the script:

1 What about you? **a** Qu'est-ce que tu voudrais voir?
2 At 22.30 there is *Le Come-back*. **b** Moi aussi.
3 What would you like to see? **c** Et toi?
4 Me too. **d** À vingt-deux heures trente il y a *Le Come-back*.

Pronunciation

In French there is a tendency for groups of words to be pronounced as if all the letters were linked up. This applies to the following:

Il y a [ilia]   Y a t-il? [iatil]   Est-ce qu'il y a? [eskilia]

Insight: Liaisons Dangereuses

Liaising words is not always possible. Although **est** and **un/une** can be linked [*estun/une*], **et** and **un/une** cannot: they must be pronounced separately to avoid ambiguity. For example in **un homme et une femme** (*a man and a woman*), if **et** and **une** are liaised [*etune*] the meaning becomes 'a man is a woman'!

Un peu de grammaire
A bit of grammar

DES NOMBRES ET DES CHIFFRES DE 70 À 101

Look, listen and repeat.

70 soixante-dix [60 + 10]	90 quatre-vingt-dix
71 soixante et onze [60 + 11]	91 quatre-vingt-onze
72 soixante-douze	92 quatre-vingt-douze
79 soixante-dix-neuf	99 quatre-vingt-dix-neuf
80 quatre-vingts* [4 × 20]	100 cent
81 quatre-vingt-un	101 cent un
89 quatre-vingt-neuf	

*Only **quatre-vingts** is spelt with -s for plural (four twenties).

Exercise 3 **C'est combien?** *How much is it?*

🔊 **CD1, TR 31**

Sarah and Dominique are at the shop. They are checking the price of drinks and cigarettes.

Listen to the recording and answer these questions:

a *How much is the cognac?*
b *How much is the whisky?*
c *How much are the cigarettes?*
d *How much is the gin?*

Surfez sur le web

• Trouvez www.brittany-ferries.fr ou d'autres sites pour en savoir plus sur la traversée de la Manche (*the Channel*).

Insight: Un peu d'histoire *(A bit of history)*

Le saviez-vous? The Channel Tunnel (**le Tunnel sous la Manche**) is an idea that flourished throughout the 19th century. But it was on 12 February 1986 that a treaty was signed by the French President François Mitterrand and the British Prime Minister Margaret Thatcher. The project was finally adopted on 29 July 1987 and the inauguration of the tunnel took place on 6 May 1994.

Le saviez-vous? *(did you know it?)*
savoir *(to know)*

TEST YOURSELF

Fill the gaps with the appropriate word.

1 *Les __ jeunes femmes ont réservé une __ qui se __ au pont __.*
  La __ __ au __ __.
  [Use: pont; trouve; voiture; cinq; deux; cabine; est; huit.]

2 *Les deux passagères adorent les films avec __.*

3 *Au Québec et en Belgique 80 se dit __.*

4 *La femme du fermier est la __ et le mari de la boulangère est
  le __.*

5

On visite la vieille ville
Visiting the old town

In this unit you will learn
- *how to ask for various places in a town*
- *how to follow and give directions*
- *how to count from 102 to 10,500*
- *some adjectives*
- *the imperative*

---

1 Pour aller à...?
How do I get to...?

◆》 **CD1, TR 32**

Some tourists have just arrived in St Malo after their crossing on the ferry. They visit the old town, **la Vieille Ville**, which in St Malo is normally referred to as **L'intra muros** (the Latin phrase for 'inside the walls').

In this dialogue the tourist is asking for the station but the passer-by is not sure whether she means the bus station (**la gare routière**) or the railway station (**la gare SNCF**).

First read the key directions:

C'est tout droit/Allez tout droit	*It is straight ahead/Go straight on*
C'est à droite/Tournez à droite	*It is on the right/Turn right*
C'est la première rue à gauche/ Prenez la première rue à gauche	*It is the first road on the left/Take the first road on the left*
C'est la deuxième rue à droite/ Prenez la deuxième rue à droite	*It is the second road on the right/ Take the second road on the right*
C'est la troisième rue sur votre gauche/Prenez la troisième rue sur votre gauche	*It is the third road on your left/Take the third road on your left*

Now listen to the recording and choose the correct answer.

   a *Can you tell whether the tourist is looking for:*
      1 *the bus station?*
      2 *the railway station?*
   b *Is it:*
      1 *the first street on the left and the next one on the right?*
      2 *the first one on the left and then straight ahead?*
   c *How far away is it?*
      1 *one kilometre?*
      2 *one hundred metres?*
      3 *two hundred metres?*
      4 *more than two hundred metres?*

Now listen to the recording again and read the dialogue.

Touriste	Pour aller à la gare s'il vous plaît madame?
Passante	La gare routière ou la gare SNCF?
Touriste	Euh, la gare SNCF...
Passante	Oui alors vous prenez la première rue à gauche et c'est tout droit.
Touriste	C'est loin?
Passante	Non c'est tout près. C'est à deux cents mètres, au maximum.
Touriste	Merci beaucoup madame.

Link the English phrases to the equivalent French expressions:

1 at the most   a C'est à deux cents mètres.
2 Is it far?   b C'est tout près.
3 It's two hundred metres away.   c C'est loin?
4 It's straight ahead.   d Prenez la première rue à gauche.
5 Take the first street on the left.   e au maximum
6 It's very near.   f C'est tout droit.

Un peu de grammaire
A bit of grammar

FEMININE AND MASCULINE ADJECTIVES

You are already aware that there are feminine and masculine nouns
in French. Similarly, adjectives describe the nouns they are linked
up with and are feminine or masculine according to the gender of
the nouns they accompany.

In French adjectives can be placed before or after nouns, although
changing the position of an adjective can modify the meaning of
the phrase. In many cases -e is added for the feminine form of the
adjective and -s is added for the plural:

Masculine	
un village	*a village*
un joli village	*a pretty village*
des jolis petits villages	*pretty little villages*
un grand château	*a big castle*
des grands châteaux	*big castles*

Feminine	
une ville	*a town*
une jolie ville	*a pretty town*
des jolies petites villes	*pretty little towns*
une grande maison	*a big house*
des grandes maisons	*big houses*

But many adjectives change more radically from the masculine to the feminine:

le vieux port	*the old port*	**la vieille ville**	*the old town*
le premier jour du mois	*the first day of the month*	**la première rue à gauche**	*the first street on the left*

Masculine adjectives ending in **-e** remain the same in the feminine form:

le bonnet rouge	*the red hat*	**la fleur rouge**	*the red flower*
le deuxième magasin	*the second shop*	**la deuxième rue**	*the second street*

> ### Insight
> **Beau** (*beautiful / nice*), **vieux** (*old*), **nouveau** (*new*) are three adjectives which change according to the masculine noun they precede. In front of a vowel they become respectively **bel**, **vieil** and **nouvel**.

un **beau chêne** *a beautiful oak tree*
un **bel arbre** *a beautiful tree*
un **vieux copain**, un **vieil ami** *an old friend / mate*
un **nouveau copain**, un **nouvel ami** *a new friend / mate*

SOME ORDINAL NUMBERS

◀) **CD1, TR 33**

These are adjectives indicating a ranking position:

3rd **troisième**	20th **vingtième**
4th **quatrième**	36th **trente-sixième**
10th **dixième**	100th **centième**
15th **quinzième**	1,000th **millième**

---

2 Vous tournez à gauche
You turn left

◀) **CD1, TR 34**

As Sarah and Dominique leave the port they decide to visit Saint Malo before continuing with their journey. They ask for directions.

Listen to the recording once through, and answer the questions.

a *Who would like to visit the old town?*
b *Whom do they ask for directions?*

Listen again.

c *Is the old town far from the port?*
d *Are there problems with parking?*

Now read the text.

Dominique	Je ne connais pas St Malo. Je voudrais bien visiter la Vieille Ville. Et toi, tu connais?
Sarah	Non je ne connais pas. On y va! Demande la direction au monsieur, là.
Dominique	Pardon monsieur. Pour aller à la Vieille Ville s'il vous plaît?
Un passant	Oh c'est tout près d'ici! Alors vous allez au rond-point et là vous tournez à gauche. La Vieille Ville est à cinq cents mètres à gauche.
Sarah	Merci monsieur. Il y a un parking pas trop loin?
Passant	Pas de problèmes avec le stationnement à St Malo, il y a plusieurs grands parkings.
Dominique	C'est parfait! Merci monsieur!
Passant	De rien mesdemoiselles!

Link the English phrases to the equivalent French expressions.

1 there
2 at the roundabout
3 I don't know St Malo.
4 It's perfect!

5 Ask the way.
6 no problem with parking
7 several large car parks

a Je ne connais pas St Malo.
b C'est parfait!
c Demande la direction.
d pas de problème avec le stationnement
e plusieurs grands parkings
f là
g au rond-point

Un peu de grammaire
A bit of grammar

SAVOIR *AND* CONNAÎTRE

The verbs **savoir** and **connaître** both mean *to know*: **je sais** (*I know a fact*), **je connais** (*I know a place, something or someone*).

Je ne sais pas où c'est.	*I don't know where it is.*
Je ne connais pas la ville.	*I don't know the town.*

Insight

Savoir is frequently used in general conversation to indicate that you are on the same wavelength:

Il est malade, tu sais! *He is ill, you know!*

To which you can reply:

Oui, je sais, je sais!

DIRECTIONS: THE IMPERATIVE

Here are some verbs used for directions: **aller** *to go*, **prendre** *to take*, **tourner** *to turn*, **continuer** *to carry on*.

When someone is giving directions or orders they use a verb form called the imperative (*Go…!, Take…!, Turn…!*). If the directions are given to a stranger or someone the speaker is not acquainted with, the form of the verb used is different from the form used for family or friends or children.

To an adult:

Allez jusqu'au château, **tournez** à gauche puis **prenez** la deuxième rue à droite.

To a child or to an adult you know well:

Va jusqu'au château, **tourne** à gauche puis **prends** la deuxième rue à droite.

jusqu'à/jusqu'au *as far as*
puis *then*

VOCAB

VOUS *AND* TU

There are two ways of addressing people in French:

Vous to individuals who are not friends or relatives, and to more than one person (**vouvoyer** is the verb which describes the action of addressing someone as **vous**).

Tu to a friend, relative or young child (**tutoyer** is the verb which describes the action of addressing someone as **tu**).

Insight: Un peu d'histoire *(A bit of history)*

In old French people would used **tu** and **vous** when addressing someone according to moods or occasion. **Vous** would show more respect but **tu** would express more friendliness or affection. The king would be addressed as **vous** or **Votre Majesté**. Saying **tu** to someone became a sign of lack of respect and **vous** a sign of deference. Servants would be spoken to as **tu** but would have to address their masters as **vous**.

Today many people use **tu** to peers. There is almost a tacit agreement to **tutoiement** (calling each other **tu**) and the question to ask is **On se tutoie?** Unless you have misjudged the situation it is unlikely the other person will say **Non!**

DIRECTIONS: THE PRESENT TENSE

It is also possible to use the present tense to give directions:

Vous allez jusqu'au château, **vous tournez** à gauche puis **vous prenez** la deuxième rue à droite. (*You go as far as the château, you turn left then you take the second road on the right.*)

Exercise 1 Vous tournez à gauche encore
Look back at the dialogue in Section 2.
   a *Can you find examples of people saying* **tu** *to one another?*
   b *Can you find examples where someone gives directions using the present tense rather than the imperative?*

Exercise 2 La piscine, s'il vous plaît?

Look at the diagram below (this is not an accurate map of St Malo). The ten places numbered on the diagram are listed in the key words box.

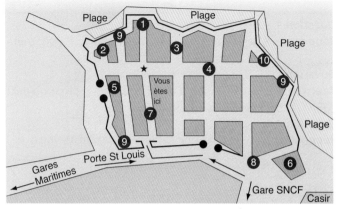

You are standing at the star, answering the questions of passers-by. Choose the correct reply.

1 **la piscine** *the swimming pool*
2 **le musée** *the museum*
3 **la cathédrale** *the cathedral*
4 **le marché aux poissons** *the fish market*
5 **le marché aux legumes** *the vegetable market*

6 **le château** *the castle*
7 **la Grand' Rue** *the High Street*
8 **l'Office du Tourisme** *the Tourist Office*
9 **les remparts** *the ramparts*
10 **le petit aquarium** *the small aquarium*

> **Question 1** La piscine s'il vous plaît?
> **Réponse** **a** C'est sur votre gauche. **b** C'est à droite.
> **c** Continuez tout droit.
> **Question 2** La Grand' Rue SVP*?
> **Réponse** **a** C'est ici la Grand'Rue. **b** C'est à gauche. **c** Prenez la deuxième rue à droite.
> **Question 3** Pour aller au marché aux poissons SVP?
> **Réponse** **a** Vous prenez la deuxième rue à gauche.
> **b** Allez tout droit. **c** Vous tournez à droite et c'est la deuxième rue sur votre droite.

*SVP stands for s'il vous plaît.

Exercise 3 **Quelle question?**

This time you are still standing at the same spot but you are asking the questions.

Question 1 ...
Réponse   Alors vous tournez à droite et vous continuez tout droit. C'est à deux cent cinquante mètres.
Question 2 ...
Réponse   Oui, alors tournez à droite et c'est la première rue à gauche.
Question 3 ...
Réponse   Tournez à gauche et prenez la deuxième rue à droite.

Un peu de grammaire
A bit of grammar

◀)) **CD1, TR 35**

DES NOMBRES ET DES CHIFFRES DE 102 À 10500

102 cent deux
170 cent soixante-dix
200 deux cents
900 neuf cents
926 neuf cent vingt-six

1000 mille
1900 mille neuf cents/dix-neuf cents
2000 deux mille
2020 deux mille vingt
10500 dix mille cinq cents

Note that when there is more than one hundred, **cent** is spelt with an **s** but if another number follows, the **s** is dropped:

deux cents *200* but **deux cent cinq** *205*

St Malo cité historique

St Malo was founded in the 6th century by the Welsh monk MacLow. It is the birth place of many sailors and discoverers. One of the most famous is Jacques Cartier who discovered Canada in the 16th century. There are still very strong links between St Malo and Canada, especially with Quebec. It is not unusual to see the Canadian flag flying in St Malo.

Insight

St Malo has remained a city of sailors and every four years La Transat Québec – St Malo, a high-calibre international transatlantic race, brings together the best professional sailors of mono- and multi-hulled vessels.

Exercise 4 **Répondez aux touristes**
It is your turn to answer questions asked by tourists.

Listen to the recording and answer the questions you will hear.

You need to know that:

a   *the swimming pool is on the right*
b   *the museum is 200 metres away*
c   *the cathedral is very near*
d   *the tourist office is straight ahead*
e   *the castle is on the left*

- Google St Malo and you will have access to many sites referring you to hotels and places to visit.
- For the best site go to www.saint-malo.com Le portail de Saint Malo et sa région for many fascinating sites on St Malo and its region.
- For a virtual visit of the region go to La vallée de la Rance maritime Découverte de l'histoire et des plus beaux sites du littoral du Nord de la Bretagne. Use the key words: **Cartes** (*maps*), **Diapos** (*for* **diapositives** = *slides*) and **Index**.
- TV5 Monde: **TV5** is a French language World TV channel. Try it out with a visit to the Quebec website http://www.tv5.ca

Insight

Here's **un bon tuyau** (*a good tip*) (colloquial), from **un tuyau** (*a pipe*), from which we get **un tuyau d'arrosage** (*watering pipe / hose*). If you own a satellite navigation system, set it to French when using it on familiar routes and you will hear a French voice ordering you about with verbs in the imperative form: **tournez à droite, tournez à gauche** etc.

TEST YOURSELF

Using the definite articles **le, la, l', les** test your memory of the gender of nouns you have learnt so far. Use the plural form where appropriate:

1 __ *château;*
2 __ *ville;*
3 __ *gare;*
4 __ *jolis petits villages de* __ *région;*
5 __ *port;*
6 __ *deuxième rue à gauche;*
7 __ *piscine;*
8 __ *aquarium;*
9 __ *rond-point;*
10 __ *village;*
11 __ *pont;*
12 __ *grandes maisons;*
13 __ *intra muros;*
14 __ *directions;*
15 __ *marché aux poissons;*
16 __ *vallée de la Rance;*
17 __ *direction;*
18 __ *stationnement;*
19 __ *parking;*
20 __ *oncle.*

70

6

Où stationner?
Where to park?

In this unit you will learn
* *how to understand instructions for car parking*
* *about using French money*
* *the time*
* *how to talk about daily routine*

---

1 Où stationner?
Where to park?

Dominique and Sarah are trying to find a car park space. They have a guide to all the parking zones in St Malo which they got from the Tourist Office: **l'Office de Tourisme.**

You are likely to hear a lot of French people refer to a car park as **un parking** but in an effort by various governments to remove the English and American influence on the French language you will notice that the official name for a car park is **une zone de stationnement.** On parking notices and tickets you will see:

Stationnement gratuit	*Free parking*
Stationnement payant	*Pay-parking*
Stationnement interdit	*Parking forbidden/No parking*
Stationnement autorisé	*Parking allowed*

Look at the information provided on the car parking leaflet and answer the following question:

What is the maximum amount of time you can stay in the short-stay car park?

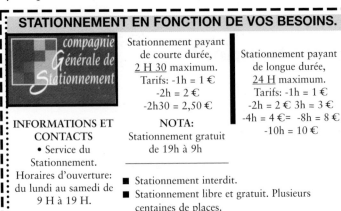

STATIONNEMENT EN FONCTION DE VOS BESOINS.

compagnie Générale de Stationnement

INFORMATIONS ET CONTACTS
• Service du Stationnement.
Horaires d'ouverture: du lundi au samedi de 9 H à 19 H.

Stationnement payant de courte durée, 2 H 30 maximum.
Tarifs: -1h = 1 €
-2h = 2 €
-2h30 = 2,50 €

NOTA:
Stationnement gratuit de 19h à 9h

Stationnement payant de longue durée, 24 H maximum.
Tarifs: -1h = 1 €
-2h = 2 € 3h = 3 €
-4h = 4 €= -8h = 8 €
-10h = 10 €

■ Stationnement interdit.
■ Stationnement libre et gratuit. Plusieurs centaines de places.

Nouveau: cartes de stationnement pour stationner dans la zone intra muros

You can buy a card which you can use as a pay-as-you-go system. This is a new system which most towns are now adopting. In St Malo the machine (**horodateur**) also allows for coins (**pièces de monnaie**) to be used – please note that parking tariffs increase regularly.

Insight: Un bon conseil *(a good piece of advice)*

You can leave your car outside the town and use the park-and-ride system (**navette** *bus*) to visit St Malo. You have to pay for the parking but **la navette** is free. **C'est gratuit!**

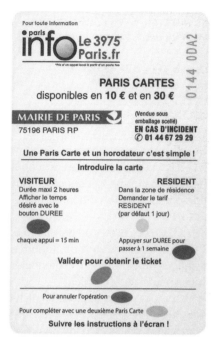

Pour toute information

info paris Le 3975
Paris.fr

Prix d'un appel local à partir d'un poste fixe

0144 0DA2

PARIS CARTES
disponibles en **10 €** et en **30 €**

MAIRIE DE PARIS
75196 PARIS RP

(Vendue sous emballage scellé)
EN CAS D'INCIDENT
☎ 01 44 67 29 29

Une Paris Carte et un horodateur c'est simple !

Introduire la carte

VISITEUR
Durée maxi 2 heures
Afficher le temps
désiré avec le
bouton DUREE

chaque appui = 15 min

RESIDENT
Dans la zone de résidence
Demander le tarif
RESIDENT
(par défaut 1 jour)

Appuyer sur DUREE pour
passer à 1 semaine

Valider pour obtenir le ticket

Pour annuler l'opération

Pour compléter avec une deuxième Paris Carte

Suivre les instructions à l'écran !

1 *With this Paris parking card what is the maximum time a visitor may park when using the card with **un horodateur**?*

2 *Do residents pay the same rate?*

3 *What do you get if you press the **Valider** button?*

---

2 Tu as de la monnaie?
Do you have any change?

◀) **CD1, TR 37**

Listen to the recording and then answer these questions.

1 *Which type of car park did Sarah and Dominique use?*
  a *long stay* **b** *short stay* **c** *free*

2 *How long did they plan to stay?*

3 *How much did they pay?*

4 *How did they pay?*
Tick the coins they used and say how many of each type they used:
a *50 centimes* **b** *1€* **c** *2€*
d *20 centimes* **e** *10 centimes*

Now read the text.

Dominique	Il y des horodateurs comme à Paris mais ici on peut aussi utiliser des pièces de monnaie. A Paris, il faut des cartes de stationnement sauf pour le mois d'août. Au mois d'août à Paris le parking, c'est gratuit!
Sarah	Tiens! Il y a des places au parking là-bas sur le quai.
Dominique	D'accord. C'est une zone de stationnement payant de longue durée. Tu as de la monnaie?
Sarah	Oui un peu. Il faut combien?
Dominique	Je ne sais pas. On reste combien de temps?
Sarah	Trois ou quatre heures.
Dominique	Alors quatre heures, cela fait quatre euros. J'ai une pièce d'un euro, une de deux euros et une de cinquante centimes, c'est tout.
Sarah	Pas de problème, moi j'ai une pièce de dix centimes et deux de vingt centimes.
Dominique	Quelle heure est-il?
Sarah	Il est dix heures et quart, donc on a jusqu'à deux heures et quart.
Dominique	Voilà notre ticket. Fin de stationnement autorisé: quatorze heures quinze.

Tiens! *Look!*
là-bas *over there*
C'est tout! *That's all!*
voilà *here is*
donc *therefore*

74

Link the following English phrases to the correct French expressions.

1 Are there spaces on the quay?   **a** Quelle heure est-il?
2 How long will we stay?   **b** Fin de stationnement autorisé
3 How much do we need?   **c** On a jusqu'à deux heures et quart.
4 What time is it?   **d** On reste combien de temps?
5 We've got until a quarter past   **e** Il y a des places sur le quai?
    two.
6 End of authorized parking   **f** Il faut combien?

Insight

What's free in France?

Le parking est gratuit à Paris au mois d'août. *Parking is free in Paris during the month of August.*

Les monuments historiques et les musées nationaux sont gratuits un fois par an. *Historical monuments and national museums are free once a year.*

Since 4 April 2009 everyone from the European Community under the age of 26 can visit all French national museums for free.

Un peu de grammaire
A bit of grammar

MORE NEW VERBS

▶ **Tiens!** *is the imperative form for the verb* **tenir** *to hold but it is frequently used as an expression of surprise* Look! *or* **Tiens! Tiens!** Well! Well!

▶ **Cela fait deux euros vingt-cinq.** That makes it 2,25 €. **Fait** *is the verb* **faire** *to do / to make in the present tense.*

▶ **Il faut combien?** *literally means* How much is necessary/required? *but it is best translated as* How much do we need? *The verb* **falloir** *means* to need / to have to. *It is only ever used with the pronoun* **il** it *in an impersonal form.*

Il faut *could also be translated as* one must:

Il faut manger pour vivre   *One must eat in order to live*
Il faut souffrir pour être beau / belle! *One must suffer to be beautiful*!

(**beau** is masculine, **belle** is feminine)

▶ **On** *is also an impersonal pronoun meaning* one, *but it is frequently used in conversation instead of* **nous** we.

FORMAL AND INFORMAL WAYS OF ASKING QUESTIONS

Most everyday conversations between people are informal. This is reflected in the way people ask questions.

In all cases the questioning is shown in the tone of voice which rises on the last syllables.

Formal	Informal
As-tu de la monnaie?	} **Tu as de la monnaie?**
Est-ce que tu as de la monnaie?	
Quelle heure est-il?	**Il est quelle heure?**
Combien faut-il?	**Il faut combien?**
Combien de temps reste-t-on?*	**On reste combien de temps?**

* see **On** above.

3 DES FAUX AMIS *FALSE FRIENDS*

There are a few French words which are deceptively similar to English words although their meanings are quite different. There are two examples in the dialogue above:

▶ **rester** *to stay*

On **reste** combien de temps? *How long are we staying?*

(*to rest* is **se reposer** e.g. **je me repose** *I am resting*)

▶ **de la monnaie** *change*

Tu as de la **monnaie?** *Have you got any change?*

Une **pièce de monnaie** is a coin (although **pièce** is usually used on its own).

Similarly **un billet** *a note* is short for **un billet de banque** *a bank note*.

(Money is **de l'argent**. Note that **argent** is also the word for silver.)

Exercise 1 **Remplissez les blancs**
Choose some of the words from **Des faux amis** above to complete the following sentences.

a *You are in a shop and you would like to get some change.*
J'ai un billet de 50 euros. Vous pouvez me faire la _____ SVP?
b *Je suis fatiguée. Je _____ _____ cinq minutes.*
c *On _____ quatre heures ici.*
d *Oh le joli bracelet en _____!*
e *Oh là là! C'est cent cinquante euros. Je n'ai pas d'_____.*

Insight: Proverbs
    L'heure c'est l'heure: avant l'heure ce n'est pas l'heure,
    après l'heure ce n'est plus l'heure!

    The time is the time: before the time is not the time and after
    the time it is no longer the time!

3 À l'heure française
On French time

🔊 **CD1, TR 38**

Two adults and two children have been asked three similar questions about their daily routine – **la routine quotidienne**:

1. *At what time do you get up in the morning?*
2. *At what time do you have lunch?*
3. *At what time do you go to bed?*

Questions aux adultes	Questions aux enfants
1 Vous vous levez à quelle heure le matin?	Tu te lèves à quelle heure?
2 Vous prenez votre déjeuner à quelle heure?	Tu prends ton déjeuner à quelle heure?
3 À quelle heure est-ce que vous vous couchez?	Tu te couches à quelle heure?

Before you listen to the recording, first check the French for the days of the week (later in this unit). Now look at the verbs in the three questions.

Se lever *to get up* and **se coucher** *to go to bed* are reflexive verbs. The first reflexive verb you came across in this book was **s'appeler** *to be called* (Unit 2). **Vous vous levez** literally means *you get yourself up*. The subject and the object of the action is the same person (**vous** *you*, in this case) in reflexive verbs.

Vous prenez / tu prends are the present tense of the verb **prendre** *to take*. To say you have a meal in French, you normally say **je prends...**

Look again at the three questions above.

a *What are the two expressions used for saying 'your lunch' (one to an adult and the other to a child)?*

b *Now listen to the recording and fill in this grid:*

	Question 1	Question 2	Question 3
Femme	7.30	?	?
Homme	?	1.00–1.30	?
Fille	?	12.00	?
Garçon	6.45	?	?

c *Who gets up between ten o'clock and half past ten on a Sunday morning?*

d *At what time does the boy claim he sometimes goes to bed at the weekend?*

Un peu de grammaire
A bit of grammar

L'HEURE *THE TIME*

There is a general tendency to use the 24-hour clock in France. It is used for transport timetables (**les horaires**), TV programmes (**les programmes de télévision**), computers (**les ordinateurs**), the Internet (**l'Internet**), working hours (**les horaires de travail**), school timetables (**les emplois du temps scolaires**), etc.

Most people use a mixture of the more traditional way of telling the time and of the 24-hour clock:

4h00 il est quatre heures / il est seize heures
4h15 il est quatre heures et quart / il est seize heures quinze
4h30 il est quatre heures et demie / il est seize heures trente
4h45 il est cinq heures moins le quart / il est seize heures quarante-cinq
12h00 il est midi (*midday*) / il est minuit (*midnight*)

Exercise 2 **Quelle heure est-il?**

◀) **CD1, TR 39**

Listen to the recording and write down the correct letter next to each of the following times:

1 1h20 ( )   **2** 23h45 ( )   **3** 17h05 ( )   **4** 12h30 ( )
5 8h56 ( )   **6** 11h15 ( )   **7** 3h00 ( )   **8** 6h45 ( )

Exercise 3 **Matin ou après-midi?**

◀) **CD1, TR 40**

Il est quatre heures du matin ou quatre heures de l'après-midi?

The distinction a.m. and p.m. has never been used in French. Listen to the recording to hear what people say when there is a need to make a distinction between morning and afternoon / evening.

  a *What time is it for Jean-Pierre in Paris?*
  b *What time is it for Martine in Sydney?*

Exercise 4 **À gagner!**
Anyone watching the nature programme on **la Cinquième** can win a prize. Read the competition details and then answer the questions below.

  a *Which TV channel do you have to watch?*
  b *Give the two dates and times when the programme is on.*
  c *What is the 'Question of the Week'?*

Exercise 5 **Le manoir de Jacques Cartier**

Un peu de lecture! Remember Jacques Cartier, the famous sailor from St Malo and discoverer of Canada?

You can visit le Manoir de Limœlou, his manor house, but when exactly? Look at the leaflet to find out. (Check with **Les jours de la semaine et les mois de l'année,** later in this unit.)

Visite commentée
du Manoir de Jacques Cartier

Musée ouvert toute l'année
Accès aux visites guidées
Tous les jours du 1ᵉʳ juillet au 31 août
sauf week-end du 1ᵉʳ septembre au 30 juin
Horaires des visites
du 1ᵉʳ juin au 30 septembre
de 10 heures à 11 h 30 et de 14 h 30 à 18 heures
du 1ᵉʳ octobre au 31 mai
à 10 heures et à 15 heures.

Prix réduit pour écoles
et groupes de 10 personnes minimum
(uniquement sur réservation)

Gratuit pour :
Enfants au-dessous de 5 ans.

a *Between which dates is it open every day of the week?*
b *Could you have a guided tour the first weekend in September?*
c *In July what are the opening times?*
d *In May what time of day is it open?*
e *Who can get a reduction? Under what condition?*
f *How much does it cost for a child under the age of five to visit Jacques Cartier's Manor House?*
g *Find the French expressions for the following:*
   museum open all year round
   every day from 1st July to 31st August
h *Can you spot a difference between French and English in the way that days and months are written?*

Un peu de grammaire
A bit of grammar

TOUT LE, TOUTE LA, TOUS LES, TOUTES LES

In front of nouns these words are adjectives (respectively masculine, feminine, masculine plural and feminine plural according to the noun they are used with). They mean *all* or *every*:

Il faut visiter toute la ville et toutes les vieilles rues.   *We must visit the whole town and all the old streets.*

J'adore tout le village et tous les monuments historiques.   *I love the whole village and all the historic monuments.*

Look at your answers to **g** above: **toute** agrees with **l'année** (fem.) and **tous** agrees with **les jours** (masc. pl.).

LES JOURS DE LA SEMAINE ET LES MOIS DE L'ANNÉE

◀) **CD1, TR 41, 0:44**

Les jours de la semaine

lundi	*Monday*	**vendredi**	*Friday*
mardi	*Tuesday*	**samedi**	*Saturday*
mercredi	*Wednesday*	**dimanche**	*Sunday*
jeudi	*Thursday*		

Les saisons

Le printemps	*Spring*	**L'automne**	*Autumn*
L'été	*Summer*	**L'hiver**	*Winter*

Insight: The calendar

•There is a saint for each day of the year in the French calendar and many people celebrate their name day as well as their birthday. Until relatively recently French children could only be given a name which appeared on this calendar. This is no longer the case as it would not be possible, considering the ethnic and religious diversity of the population.

JANVIER	FEVRIER	MARS	AVRIL	MAI	JUIN
1 J. DE L'AN	1 Ste Ella	1 Carème	1 St Hugues	1 F. DU TRAVAIL	1 St Justin
2 St Basile	2 Pres. Seign.	2 St Charles	2 Ste Sandrine	2 St Boris	2 Ste Blandine
3 Ste Geneviève	3 St Blaise	3 St Guénolé	3 St Richard	3 Sts Jacq./Philippe	3 St Kévin
4 Epiphanie	4 Ste Véronique	4 St Casimir	4 St Isidore	4 St Sylvian	4 Ste Clotilde
5 St Edouard	5 Ste Agathe	5 Ste Olive	5 Rameaux	5 Ste Judith	5 St Igor
6 St Mélanie	6 St Gaston	6 Ste Colette	6 St Marcellin	6 Ste Prudence	6 Norbert
7 St Raymond	7 Ste Eugenie	7 Ste Félicité	7 St J-B de la Salle	7 Ste Gisèle	7 Fête des Mères
8 St Lucien	8 Ste Jacqueline	8 St Jean de Dieu	8 Ste Julie	8 VICTOIRE	8 St Médard
9 Ste Alix	9 Ste Apolline	9 Ste Françoise	9 St Gautier	9 St Pacôme	9 Ste Diane
10 St Guillaume	10 St Arnaud	10 St Vivien	10 St Fubert	10 F. Jeanne d'Arc	10 St Landry
11 St Paulin	11 N-D Lourdes	11 Ste Rosine	11 St Stanislas	11 Ste Estelle	11 St Barnabé
12 Ste Tatiana	12 St Félix	12 Ste Justine	12 PAQUES	12 St Achille	12 St Guy
13 Ste Yvette	13 Ste Béatrice	13 St Rodrigue	13 Ste Ida	13 Ste Rolande	13 St Antoine
14 Ste Nina	14 St Valentin	14 Ste Matilde	14 St Maxime	14 St Matthias	14 Fête Dieu
15 St Rémi	15 St Claude	15 Ste Louise	15 St Paterne	15 Ste Denise	15 Ste Germaine
16 St Marcel	16 Ste Julienne	16 Ste Bénédicte	16 St Benoît Labre	16 St Honoré	16 St J.-F. Régis
17 St Roseane	17 St Alexis	17 St Patrice	17 St Anicet	17 St Pascal	17 St Hervé
18 Ste Prisca	18 Ste Bernadette	18 St Cyrille	18 St Parfait	18 St Eric	18 St Léonce
19 St Marius	19 St Gabin	19 St Joseph	19 Ste Emma	19 St Yves	19 St Romuald
20 St Sébastien	20 Ste Aimée	20 PRINTEMPS	20 Ste Odette	20 St Bernardin	20 St Silvère
21 Ste Agnes	21 St Pierre Damien	21 Ste Clémence	21 St Anselme	21 ASCENSION	21 Fêtes des Pères/ETÉ
22 St Vincent	22 Ste Isabelle	22 Ste Léa·	22 St Alexandre	22 St Émile	22 St Alban
23 St Barnard	23 St Lazare	23 St Victorien	23 JSt Georges	23 St Didier	23 Ste Audrey
24 St François Sales	24 Mardi-Gras	24 Ste Catherine	24 St Fidèle	24 St Donatien	24 St Jean-Baptiste
25 Conv. St Paul	25 Cendres	25 Annonciation	25 St Marc	25 Ste Sophie	25 St Prosper
26 Ste Paule	26 St Nestor	26 Ste Larissa	26 Jour du Souvenir	26 St Bérenger	26 St Anthelme
27 Ste Angèle	27 St Honnône	27 St Habib	27 Ste Zita	27 St Augustin de C.	27 St Fernand
28 St Thomas d'Aq.	28 St Romain	28 St Gontran	28 Ste Valérie	28 St Germain	28 St Irénée
29 St Gildas		29 Ste Gwladys	29 Ste Cather. de S.	29 St Aymar	29 Sts Pierre/Paul
30 Ste Martine		30 St Amédée	30 St Robert	30 St Ferdinand	30 St Martial
31 Ste Marcelle		31 St Benjamin		31 PENTECÔTE	

JUILLET	AOUT	SEPTEMBRE	OCTOBRE	NOVEMBRE	DECEMBRE
1 St Thierry	1 St Alphonse	1 St Gilles	1 Ste Thérèse E.-J.	1 TOUSSAINT	1 Ste Florence
2 St Martinien	2 St Julien	2 Ste Ingrid	2 St Léger	2 Défunts	2 Ste Vivance
3 St Thomas	3 Ste Lydie	3 St Grégoire	3 St Gérard	3 St Hubert	3 St François-Xavier
4 St Florent	4 St J-M Vianney	4 Ste Rosalie	4 St François d'Ass.	4 St Charles Boi	4 Ste Barbara
5 St Antoine-Marie	5 St Aber	5 Ste Raïssa	5 Ste Fleur	5 Ste Sylvie	5 St Gérald
6 Ste Marietta	6 Transfiguration	6 St Bertrand	6 St Bruno	6 Ste Bertille	6 St Nicolas
7 St Raoul	7 St Gaëton	7 Ste Reine	7 St Serge	7 Ste Carine	7 St Ambrose
8 St Thibaut	8 St Dominique	8 Nativité de N.-D.	8 Ste Pélagie	8 St Geoffroy	8 Imm. Concept.
9 Ste Amandine	9 St Amour	9 St Alan	9 St Denis	9 St Théodore	9 St Pierre Fourier
10 St Ulrich	10 St Laurent	10 Ste Ines	10 St Ghislain	10 St Léon	10 St Romaric
11 St Benoît	11 Ste Claire	11 St Adelphe	11 St Firmin	11 ARMISTICE	11 St Daniel
12 St Olivier	12 Ste Clarisse	12 St Apolinaire	12 St Wilfried	12 St Christian	12 Ste J.-F. De Chantal
13 Sts Henri/Joel	13 St Hippolyte	13 St Aimé	13 St Géraud	13 St Brice	13 Ste Lucie
14 FETE NATION	14 St Evrard	14 Sainte Croix	14 St Juste	14 St Sidoine	14 Ste Odile
15 St Donald	15 ASSOMPTION	15 St Roland	15 Ste Thérèse d'Av.	15 St Albert	15 Ste Ninon
16 N-D Mt Carmel	16 St Armel	16 Ste Edith	16 Ste Edwige	16 Ste Marguerite	16 Ste Alice
17 Ste Charlotte	17 St Hyacinthe	17 St Renaud	17 St Baudouin	17 Ste Elizabeth	17 St Judicael
18 St Frédéric	18 Ste Hélène	18 Ste Nadège	18 St Luc	18 Ste Aude	18 St Gatien
19 St Arsene·	19 St Jean Eudes	19 Ste Émilie	19 St René	19 St Tanguy	19 St Urbain
20 Ste Marina	20 St Bernard	20 St Davy	20 Ste Adeline	20 St Edmond	20 St Abraham
21 St Victor	21 St Christophe	21 St Matthieu	21 Ste Céline	21 Présentation	21 St Pierre Canis.
22 Ste Marie-Madel.	22 St Fabrice	22 St Maurice	22 Ste Salomé	22 Ste Cécile	22 HIVER
23 Ste Brigitte	23 Ste Rosa	23 AUTOMNE	23 St Jean de C.	23 St Clément	23 St Armand
24 Ste Christine	24 St Barthélemy	24 Ste Thècle	24 St Florentin	24 Ste Flora	24 Ste Adèle
25 St Jacques le M.	25 St Louis	25 St Hermann	25 St Crépin	25 Ste Catherine L.	25 NOEL
26 Sts Anne/Joachim	26 Ste Natacha	26 Sts Côme/Damien	26 St Dimitri	26 Ste Delphine	26 St Etienne
27 Ste Nathalie	27 Ste Monique	27 St Vincent de Paul	27 Ste Emeline	27 St Séverin	27 St Jean l'Apôtre
28 St Samson	28 St Augustin	28 St Venceslas	28 Sts Simon/Jude	28 St Jacques M.	28 Sts Innocents
29 Ste Marthe	29 Ste Sabine	29 Sts Michel/Gap	29 St Narcisse	29 Avent	29 St David
30 Ste Juliette	30 St Fiacre	30 St Jérôme	30 Ste Bienvenue	30 St André	30 St Roger
31 St Ignace	31 St Aristide		31 St Quentin		31 St Sylvestre

Surfez sur le web

- Tout sur St Malo: http://www.ville-saint-malo.fr/guide/

Web extension exercise
Choose from the following menu:

▶ **Se repérer** *to find one's way around*
▶ **Se loger** *where to stay*
▶ **Se restaurer** *where to eat*
▶ **Y circuler** *traffic information (including parking information)*
▶ **Y venir** *how to get there* *
▶ **Archives**
▶ **Multimédia**
▶ **Météo** – *weather forecast*
▶ **Adresses et numéros utiles**

Go to **Y circuler** for the latest updates on parking arrangements

Go to **se loger** to check the campsites. Have you discovered how many campsites there are in St Malo?

1 *How many altogether?*
2 *How many are municipal (run by the council)?*
3 *How many are private ones?*
4 *How many have four stars?*

there (y replaces the name of a place e.g **venir à Saint Malo** = y **venir** (*to get here / there*)

TEST YOURSELF

A) Tout est gratuit? Bien sûr que non! Of course everything is not free so read the items below and only tick what's free.

1 *Le parking à St Malo au mois d'août*

2 *La navette bus de St Malo*

3 *La visite des vieilles rues*

4 *Le stationnement à Paris en août*

5 *La visite des musées nationaux pour les jeunes européens de moins de 26 ans*

6 *La visite commentée du Manoir de Jacques Cartier pour les enfants au-dessous de 10 ans.*

B) Cela fait… / il faut de la monnaie

You are told how much something cost: **Cela fait 10,50€**

You work out what change you need: **Il faut un billet de 10€ et une pièce de 50 centimes** or the other way round!

1 *Cela fait 7,30€ →* __

2 __ *→ Il faut un billet de 20€, un billet de 5€ et deux pièces 20c.*

3 *Cela fait 3,10€ →* __

4 __ *→ Il faut un billet de 50€, une pièce de vingt centimes et une de cinq.*

7

L'hébergement
Accommodation

In this unit you will learn
- *how to find a hotel*
- *how to book a hotel room*
- *how to ask for various facilities*

À l'office de tourisme

Most French towns have **un Office de Tourisme**. The tourist office is an ideal place for you to get information and advice, **renseignements et conseils** whether you are on holiday or on a business trip, **en vacances ou en voyage d'affaires**. It can help you find somewhere to stay, somewhere to eat and also something interesting to do. Some offices will do the booking for you but if not they will give you all the information you need. As a general principle they deal with:

Hébergement
Where to stay

Restauration
Where to eat

Loisirs
What to do – leisure

1 Choisir un hotel
Choosing a hotel

You need to know which facilities you are looking for in order to choose somewhere to stay.

Match the following French and English expressions.

1 Une chambre simple

2 Une chambre double

3 Une chambre familiale (avec un grand lit + un lit pour enfant)

4 Une chambre pour personne handicapée

5 Pension (petit déjeuner + dîner)

6 Demi-pension (petit déjeuner)

a Full board (breakfast + dinner)

b A room for a disabled person

c A single room

d Half-board (breakfast)

e A double room

f A family room (with a double bed + a bed for a child)

Now match the symbols and the French explanations on the hotel facilities chart to their English equivalents.

1 Facilités pour handicapés/ pour voyageurs à mobilité réduite

a Main credit cards accepted

2 Ouvert toute l'année

b Bath and toilets

3 Catégorie (une/deux/trois/ quatre étoiles)

c Garage/private car park

4 Douches et wc

d Sea view

5 Salle de bains et wc

e Swimming pool

6 Garage/parking privé

f Children's games

7 Restaurant

g Lift

8 Principales cartes de crédit acceptées

h Facilities for disabled visitors

9 TV en chambres		i TV in rooms
10 Vue sur la mer		j Open all year round
11 Piscine		k Category (1/2/3/4 stars)
12 Ascenseur		l Pets welcomed
13 Jeux pour enfants		m Showers and toilets
14 Animaux acceptés		n Restaurant

2 Quelques renseignements
Some information

At the tourist office four tourists are requesting special facilities.

Listen to the recording, then answer these questions.

1 First tourist requires   **2** Second tourist requires
3 Third tourist requires   **4** Fourth tourist requires

Premier touriste	Je voudrais une chambre pour deux personnes pour une nuit dans un hôtel trois étoiles, avec vue sur la mer.	⊛ CD1, TR 42
Deuxième touriste	J'ai un petit chien alors je cherche un hôtel où l'on accepte les animaux.	
Troisième touriste	Je voudrais une chambre pour une personne dans un hôtel pas trop cher, avec restaurant et piscine.	
Quatrième touriste	Ma fille est handicapée et elle a un fauteuil roulant. Nous voudrions une grande chambre pour trois personnes dans un hôtel avec ascenseur.	

Un peu de grammaire
A bit of grammar

DES VERBES

There are three groups of verbs:

Group 1: verbs ending with **-er**. They very nearly all follow a regular pattern (**aller** is an exception).

Group 2: verbs ending with **-ir**. Some of them follow a regular pattern.

Group 3: mostly verbs ending with **-re/-oir**. They are mostly irregular verbs.

Vouloir *to want*
This is a very useful verb to express a wish / something you would like. As in English, it is more polite to use the conditional tense, rather than the present tense: *I would like* rather than *I want.*

Compare:

Je veux une glace!   *I want an ice cream!*

and...

Je voudrais une chambre à deux lits. *I would like a room with two beds.*

Nous voudrions louer des vélos. *We would like to hire bikes.*

Insight

Another meaning of the verb **vouloir**:

En vouloir à quelqu'un *To hold something against someone*

Ne m'en voulez pas trop! Literally *Don't hold it too much (against me)! / Don't be mad at me!*

Reply: **Mais je ne vous en veux pas du tout!** *But I don't hold it against you at all!*

Chercher or **rechercher** *to look for*

This is an easy verb to use. It is an **-er** verb because its infinitive (basic form) ends with **-er**. It is also a regular verb which means that it should provide you with a good example of how all regular **-er** verbs function.

Look carefully at the table below. It will provide you with some necessary information about French verbs in the present tense:

je cherche	Lit. *I look for* but best translated as *I am looking for*
tu cherches	*you are looking for* (see **tutoyer** Unit 5, Section 2)
elle/il cherche	*she/he/it is looking for*
on cherche	Lit. *one is looking for* but best translated as *we are looking for*
nous cherchons	*we are looking for*
vous cherchez	*you are looking for* (see **vouvoyer** Unit 5, Section 2)
ils/elles cherchent	*they are looking for* (pronounced the same way as **il/elle cherche**)

Exercise 1 Je voudrais une chambre double

Say what accommodation you require:

a *I am looking for a single room in a hotel with sea view.*
b *I would like a double room in a hotel.*
c *We are looking for a hotel with a swimming pool. (use* **nous***)*
d *We would like a hotel room for the weekend. (use* **on***)*

---

3 Quel mode d'hébergement choisir?
Which kind of accommodation should you choose?

Tourism and business tourism (**le tourisme d'affaires**) are booming in France and there are now lots of places to stay to choose from. Apart from the traditional range of hotels in towns there are also much cheaper and sometimes more convenient ranges of accommodation in out-of-town hotels, often in commercial estates (**zones commerciales**) or close to motorways (**les autoroutes**). **Hôtels Formule 1, Etap Hôtels, Hôtels Première Classe, Hôtels Campanile** are mushrooming all over France and Europe.

Camping is still very popular in the summer and for young people there are youth hostels (**auberges de jeunesse – centres de rencontres internationales**) but the fastest growing area for accommodation is the equivalent of the English bed and breakfast (**chambres d'hôtes**) with the cost of breakfast included (**nuit + petit déjeuner**). Many of them are located in genuine farmhouses and are registered with **Gîtes de France**.

Chambre d'Hôtes à la ferme

La chambre d'hôtes à la ferme, c'est le 'bed and breakfast' à la française chez des agriculteurs. Que ce soit pour une ou plusieurs nuits, vous serez reçus 'à la ferme'. Le matin, vos hôtes serviront un petit déjeuner campagnard. Dans certains cas, il vous sera même possible de prendre vos repas chez l'habitant (table d'hôtes). La chambre labellisée 'gîtes de France', c'est l'assurance de bénéficier d'un accueil de qualité dans un cadre chaleureux.

Read the text above and find the French words or phrases for:

a *at farmers' homes*
b *either for one or several nights*
c *a country breakfast*
d *your hosts will serve you*

Insight

Héberger is also a verb which means *to give shelter to*:
Nous pouvons vous héberger pour la nuit *We can put you up for the night*
Les sinistrés sont hébergés dans des tentes *The victims of the disaster are sheltered in tents*
Un centre d'hébergement pour des réfugiés *Refugee shelter*

Services 'plus' *Extras*

Now read the leaflet below from Campanile and make your own vocabulary list. Find the French words for the following objects:

a *toothpaste*
b *baby bottle warmer*
c *hair dryer*
d *toothbrush*
e *shaving cream*
f *a fax**

* This is a different French expression for 'fax', again created in an effort to move away from English and American influence on the French language. However **un fax** is still used most of the time.

Services "Plus" • Service "Extras"

• Dans la plupart de nos hôtels, possibilité de prendre une chambre 24h/24 grâce à notre système de paiement par carte bancaire

• In most of our hotels, possibility to take a room 24 hours a day thanks to our automatic payment system operating by credit card.

• Renseignements - réservation de votre prochaine étape chez Campanile

• Information - Booking your next stopover at Campanile

• Envoi d'une télécopie

• Sending a fax

• Vente de boissons (non alcoolisées)

• (Non alcoholic) beverages on sale

• La boutique Campanile : rasoir, crème à raser, dentifrice, nécessaire à couture, brosse à dents...

• The Campanile boutique : razor, shaving cream, toothpaste, sewing kits, toothbrush...

• Prêt d'un fer à repasser, sèche-cheveux, oreillers synthétiques, chauffe-biberon

• At your disposal : an iron, hair dryer, synthetic pillows, baby bottle warmer

4 Un petit hôtel
A small hotel

◀) CD1, TR 43

Having spent half a day in St Malo, Sarah and Dominique have decided that they want to see more of the town and the area around it (**la ville et ses environs/ses alentours**). They decide to stay for a few days (**quelques jours**) but are not sure about what to do and where to stay. At the tourist office they find that there is a lot of choice:

Listen to the recording and answer these questions.

   a *Are the two women likely to find something not too expensive for a few nights?*
   b *Would they like a hotel with a restaurant?*

Listen again.

   c *Do most hotels offer breakfast?*
   d *Can they arrange hotel bookings for customers at the Tourist Office?*

Now read the dialogue.

Dominique	Pardon monsieur, pouvez-vous nous renseigner? Nous passons quelques jours dans la région et nous cherchons un petit hôtel pas trop cher.
Employé	Oui, alors cela devrait être possible. Il y a beaucoup de petits hôtels deux étoiles qui sont très bien. Voici notre brochure… Vous voulez un hôtel avec ou sans restaurant?
Sarah	Sans restaurant. Il y a beaucoup de restaurants à St Malo.
Employé	Oh oui et la plupart des hôtels servent le petit déjeuner de toute façon.
Dominique	Vous vous chargez des réservations?
Employé	Non, je suis désolé madame! Nous ne nous chargeons pas des réservations, mais si vous voulez je peux téléphoner à l'hôtel de votre choix pour vérifier qu'il y a des chambres disponibles.

sans *without*
la plupart *most*
de toute façon *in any case*
disponible(s) *available*
vérifier *to check*

Find the French expressions for the following:

  e *It must be possible.*
  f *Could you give us some information?*
  g *Do you take care of reservations?*
  h *No, I am afraid not (madame)!*
  i *We are spending a few days in the area.*

Insight

For *'e-mail'*, we say **un courriel** (short for **courrier électronique**) or **un e-mail**.
Laissez-moi votre adresse e-mail et je vous enverrai un courriel *Leave me your e-mail address and I'll send you a mail*
To say *'at'* in an e-mail address (@), we use the word **arobaz**, and it's always said in full. So we would say this e-mail address (paul.dupont@gmail.com) as
Paul point Dupont arobaz gmail point com (**point** = *'dot'*)

Un peu de grammaire
A bit of grammar

ENCORE DES VERBES

There are several new verbs or new verb forms in the dialogue.

Vouloir *to want/to like to* (Section 2 above)
It is used with **vous** here:

Vous voulez un hôtel?	*Would you like a hotel?*
Voulez-vous une chambre?	*Would you like a room?*

Devoir *ought to/must*

▶ *In the present tense it mainly means* **must:**
Je dois partir.   *I must go.*

▶ *Just as* je **voudrais** *is a conditional form of* **vouloir,** *so* je
   devrais I ought to *is a conditional form of* **devoir:**
Je devrais téléphoner à ma   *I ought to phone my mother.*
   mère.

▶ *In the dialogue* **devoir** *is used with* **cela** *that / it (often
   shortened to* ça *as in* ça va? *See Unit 1 Section 5):*
Cela/ça devrait être bon.   *It ought to be good.*

Servir *to serve*
There are two examples of **servir** in this unit:

▶ *The first is in the dialogue:*
Les hôtels servent le petit   *Hotels serve breakfast.*
   déjeuner.

Note that **-ent** at the end is the plural form and you cannot hear it.
The singular form would be:

L'hôtel sert le petit déjeuner à   *The hotel serves breakfast from*
   partir de huit heures.   *8.00 a.m.*

▶ *The other is in* **Chambre d'hôtes à la ferme** *(Section 3 above):*
Vos hôtes vous serviront un   *Your hosts will serve you a*
   petit déjeuner campagnard.   *country breakfast.*

Ils serviront *they will serve* is the future tense of the verb **servir.**

Se charger de *to take responsibility for something*
This is a reflexive verb:

Je me charge de tout! *I'll take care of everything!*

L'Office de Tourisme de St Malo ne se charge pas des réservations.
This is best translated as *St Malo's Tourist Office does not deal with reservations.*

Exercise 2 **Chargez-vous de vos réservations avec l'Internet!**
Take care of your own bookings with the Internet. If you have access to the Internet 'google' **Tourisme et Hébergement en France** and choose the region of France you want to visit.

Insight

Using the website **La ville ou le village de votre choix** (www.France.com) you can easily find the town or village you're looking for - nothing could be easier! Click on a **département** on the map of France, choose a town or village from the list, and you'll have a map of the region with all the details you could want.

HOTEL**
DU
PALAIS

Hôtel situé dans la partie haute de la vieille ville: l'Intra Muros. Proche des remparts et de la plage, ainsi que des rues commerçantes très animées tout en restant dans un environnement dégagé et calme.
Accès aisé en voiture en toutes saisons.

CHAMBRES

18 Chambres – Toilettes, WC – Douche ou bain – Ascenseur
Télévision, Chaînes françaises et anglaises – Petit déjeuner
Prix de base: Chambre double (2 personnes) 45 € à 79 €

Here is the information provided by the Hôtel du Palais at St Malo:

a *Where is l'Hôtel du Palais situated?*
b *How many rooms have they got?*
c *Would you be able to watch* EastEnders?
d *What other facilities do they offer?*
e *What is their basic price for a double room?*

Surfez sur le web

- Où se loger? A l'hôtel? Au camping? Dans un gîte rural?
Pour chercher une chambre d'hôte sur le web visitez
http://www.chambre-d-hote.com.
Pour louer des vélos (*rent bicycles*) visitez
http://www.bretagnelocations.com/velos35s.php

louer   *to hire/to rent*
location *hiring/renting*

TEST YOURSELF

A l'hôtel, quels services recherchez-vous? *At the hotel, which services do you need?*

Do you know when to use the following verbs: vouloir, devoir, servir, se charger de? Fill in the gaps with the correct verb in its correct form:

1 *Nous __ une chambre à deux lits.*

2 *Je __ partir à six heures du matin.*

3 *Je recherche un hôtel où on __ le petit déjeuner au lit.*

4 *Est-ce que je __ réserver une place au chenil pour mon chien?*

5 *Nous __ louer des vélos.*

6 *Je __ un hôtel qui se __ de tout.*

7 *Vous vous __ du repassage* (ironing)?

8 *La plupart des hôtels __ le petit déjeuner dans la salle à manger.*

9 *Hum! Des croissants chauds* (hot, freshly baked), *ça __ être bon!*

10 *Je __ un hôtel avec une piscine.*

8

....

À l'hôtel
At the hotel

In this unit you will learn
- *how to express a preference and make some comparisons*
- *how to book a hotel, indicate requirements, understand instructions*
- *the alphabet, how to use accents and spell names*
- **du, de la, des**
- *the pronouns* **le, la, les**
- **vouloir, pouvoir, prendre**

---

1 Quel hôtel choisir?
Which hotel should you choose?

◄))) **CD1, TR 44**

Monsieur and Madame Olivier have some difficulties choosing a hotel. The choice is between:

L'HÔTEL DE LA GARE **   (*Station Hotel*)

L'HÔTEL DE L'ÉGLISE *   (*Church Hotel*)

L'HÔTEL DU CENTRE ****   (*Centre Hotel*)

L'HÔTEL DES VOYAGEURS *** (*Travellers' Hotel*)

Listen once to the recording, then answer these questions:

a *Which hotel does Monsieur Olivier suggest in the first place?*
b *He gives three reasons for his choice. Name one of them.*

Listen to the recording again.

c *Where is l'Hôtel des Voyageurs situated?*
d *Who makes the final choice?*
e *What reason is given for the choice?*

Now read the dialogue:

Madame Olivier	Alors quel hôtel choisis-tu?
Monsieur Olivier	Pas de problèmes, descendons à l'Hôtel de la Gare. C'est tout près de la gare. C'est plus pratique, c'est plus facile avec les bagages et c'est l'hôtel le moins cher!
Madame Olivier	Oui d'accord mais il y a aussi l'Hôtel des Voyageurs. C'est aussi tout près de la gare!
Monsieur Olivier	Oh je te laisse choisir, c'est plus simple!
Madame Olivier	Dans ce cas je choisis l'Hôtel du Centre. C'est plus loin de la gare mais c'est certainement plus confortable!

Link the following English phrases to the equivalent French expressions:

1 It's further from the station.
2 Yes OK but...
3 It's the cheapest.
4 It's certainly more comfortable.
5 It's more convenient.

6 It's easier.
7 I'll let you choose.

a Oui, d'accord mais...
b C'est plus pratique.
c C'est plus loin de la gare.
d Je te laisse choisir.

e C'est certainement plus confortable.
f C'est le moins cher.
h C'est plus facile.

Insight

The many uses of the verb **descendre**:

Nous descendons souvent à l'Hôtel de la Gare	*We often stay at the Station Hotel*
Je descends l'escalier en courant	*I run downstairs (lit. I come downstairs running)*
Ils habitent à Londres mais ils descendent à Paris plusieurs fois par an	*They live in London but they go (down) to Paris several times a year.*
Il s'est fait descendre par la mafia	*He got himself shot by the Mafia.*

Un peu de grammaire
A bit of grammar

DU, DE LA, DE L', DES

The names of the four hotels on the previous page have been used to show that there are four different ways to say *of the*.

Notice the word order in French: *Hotel of the Station* rather than *Station Hotel*.

You use **du, de la, de l'** or **des** according to the gender and number of the noun which follows. This can be illustrated with the following names of *streets* (**rues**) or *town squares* (**places**):

De + feminine noun = **de la**	**Rue de la Cité**
De + masculine noun = **du**	**Rue du Port**
De + singular noun beginning with a vowel or mute h = **de l'**	**Rue de l'Europe**
De + plural noun (fem. or masc.) = **des**	**Place des Québécois**

CHOISIR *TO CHOOSE*

In Unit 7 (Section 2) you met the verb **chercher**, an -er verb with a regular pattern. Similarly **choisir** which belongs to the second group of verbs (those regular verbs ending in -**ir**) is a useful model for other -**ir** verbs. (Unfortunately quite a few verbs ending in -**ir** are irregular and belong to the third group of verbs.) The letters underlined below show the pattern.

Choisir *in the present tense*

je chois<u>is</u>	*I choose/I am choosing*	**nous chois<u>issons</u>**	*we choose*
tu chois<u>is</u>	*you choose*	**vous chois<u>issez</u>**	*you choose*
il/elle chois<u>it</u>	*he/she/it chooses*	**ils/elles chois<u>issent</u>**	*they choose*

PLUS *MORE AND* MOINS *LESS*

In order to make a comparison you need at least two comparable things: **C'est plus pratique** effectively means that the Station Hotel is more convenient in terms of location than the other three hotels. **C'est plus pratique** is therefore a short cut for: L'Hôtel de la Gare est **plus** pratique **que** l'Hôtel du Centre, etc. (*more convenient than...*).

▶ *In more formal speech the sentence would start with* **Il est...**
  Il est plus pratique de descendre* à l'Hôtel de la Gare que de descendre à l'Hôtel du Centre.
    ***Descendre** *usually means* to go down, to alight *but here it means* to put up at a hotel. *In the dialogue* **Descendons à l'Hôtel de la Gare** *simply means* Let's go to ...
▶ **C'est moins cher** *is a short cut for:* **L'Hôtel de la Gare est moins cher que l'Hôtel du Centre** (less expensive than... / cheaper than ...)
▶ **C'est le moins cher** (it's the least expensive / it's the cheapest)

Exercise 1 **À qui sont les valises?**
Three suitcases have been left in the corridor. Whose are they?

Look at the people and at the three suitcases and say whether the following statements are true or false (**vrai ou faux**).

a *C'est la valise de la mère.*
b *C'est la valise du père.*
c *C'est la valise des enfants.*

Insight

Mais c'est sexiste cet Exercice 1! C'est peut-être la mère qui va à la pêche! Lecteur, c'est à vous de décider, ou bien si on se tutoie... Lecteur, c'est à toi de décider la bonne réponse.
(But this Exercise 1 is sexist! Maybe it's the mother who goes fishing! Reader, you can decide on the correct answer.)

Exercise 2 **Nommez les cafés!**
Choose the correct words to complete the name of each café.

EUROPE   VIEILLE VILLE   PORT   AMIS (*friends*)
a Café des ____   **c Café de la** ____
b Café du ____   **d Café de l'**____

Exercise 3 **Jeu du café mystère**

The name of a café, the name of a hotel and a name for the part of a town are hidden in the grid. Can you find them?

Mots cachés *hidden words*

```
C Q A D H B G T I C R V
H A P D E O U Y T N H I
S Q F X G L T W T T Y E
H O T E L D U P O R T I
R E G T D F M E D A W L
T G H W A E F P F M F L
A N G L A I S V I L L E
A M G L B I S Q C R U P
B C V N F T H W A Q S F
```

2 À l'hôtel de la Plage
At the Beach Hotel

◀) **CD1, TR 45**

Monsieur and Madame Landré are at the reception desk (**au bureau de réception**) of the Beach Hotel.

Listen once to the recording and answer these questions:
  a *Have Monsieur and Madame Landré reserved a room?*
  b *How long do they intend to stay?*

Listen to the recording again.
  c *On which floor is their room?*
  d *What is their room number?*

Listen one more time.
  e *At what time is breakfast?*
  f *At what time does the hotel door close?*

Now read the dialogue:

Réceptionniste	Bonsoir monsieur-dame. Vous désirez?
Madame Landré	Nous avons réservé une chambre pour deux personnes, pour deux nuits.
Réceptionniste	Bien, c'est à quel nom?
Madame Landré	Landré, Jacques et Martine Landré.
Réceptionniste	Cela s'épelle comment?
Monsieur Landré	L-a-n-d-r-e accent aigu.
Réceptionniste	Ah oui, voilà. Une chambre double pour deux nuits. Alors vous avez la chambre vingt-cinq au troisième étage. L'ascenseur est au bout du couloir. Voici votre clef. Vous prendrez le petit déjeuner?
Madame Landré	Euh oui! C'est à quelle heure?
Réceptionniste	Alors le petit déjeuner est servi dans la salle à manger de huit heures à dix heures mais vous pouvez le prendre dans votre chambre si vous voulez.
Monsieur Landré	Nous le prendrons dans la salle à manger, merci.
Réceptionniste	Très bien. Si vous avez besoin de quoi que ce soit, n'hésitez pas à m'appeler. Si vous sortez, gardez votre clef avec vous parce que la porte de l'hôtel ferme à vingt-trois heures. Bon séjour à l'Hôtel de la Plage, Monsieur et Madame Landré!
M. et Mme Landré	Merci bien Mademoiselle. A propos Mademoiselle, nous avons un petit problème. Nous avons un petit chien…
Réceptionniste	Pas de problèmes, ici les animaux sont acceptés.
M. et Mme Landré	Excellent! Merci Mademoiselle.

Vous désirez? *What can I do for you?* (**désirer** *to wish/desire*)
Cela s'épelle comment? *How do you spell it / how is it spelt?*
au bout du couloir *at the end of the corridor*
la salle à manger *the dining room*
avoir besoin de... *to need...*
quoi que ce soit *whatever it is*
parce que *because**

*Another word for *because* is **car** but it is more formal and it is used less frequently in speech and more often in formal written French.

Link the following English phrases to the equivalent French expressions:

1 on the third floor	**a** si vous sortez
2 Do not hesitate to call me.	**b** Nous avons réservé une chambre.
3 if you go out	**c** La porte de l'hôtel ferme à...
4 Keep your key.	**d** N'hésitez pas à m'appeler.
5 Have a good stay!	**e** au troisième étage
6 The hotel door closes at...	**f** Gardez votre clef.
7 We have reserved a room.	**g** Bon séjour!

Insight

In Dialogue 2 you have your first few examples of verbs used with the auxiliary verbs **être** (*to be*) and **avoir** (*to have*). In **Nous avons réservé une chambre**, **avons** (from **avoir**) plus a verb form of **réserver** indicates the past: *we have reserved*. The two examples with **être** are different: **Le petit déjeuner est servi** (*Breakfast is served*) and **Les animaux sont acceptés** (*Animals are accepted*), facts are established using **être** plus a verb form functioning as an adjective.

Pronunciation

◀) **CD1, TR 47**

Monsieur Landré was asked how to spell his name (**Cela s'épelle comment?**). If you need to spell your name, you will need to know the French alphabet – listen to it on the recording and repeat it:

A, B, C, D, E, F, G, H, I, J, K, L, M, N, O, P, Q, R, S, T, U, V, W (double V), X, Y (I grec), Z

In addition to spelling the letters you also need to spell accents and other signs. Listen to them and repeat them:

é = e accent aigu
è = e accent grave
ê = e accent circonflexe (also â, î, ô, û - often in place of s in earlier
     language e.g. *hostel* has become **hôtel**, *paste* – **pâte**, *hospital* –
     hôpital)
ë = e tréma (used to keep two vowel sounds separate e.g. **Noël**)
ç = cédille

Examples of double letters: deux c, deux f, deux m, deux s, etc.

Exercise 4 **Écoutez et écrivez**
Listen to the way people spell their names and write down what you hear:

1 Sylvie _____

2 _____ _____

3 _____ _____

4 Now can you spell your name in French?

Un peu de grammaire
A bit of grammar

PRONOUNS: LE, LA, LES

The receptionist says:

Vous pouvez le prendre dans   *You can take it in your room…*
votre chambre…

Le refers to **le petit déjeuner** *breakfast.* Le here is a pronoun, a word which stands in for a noun, although not necessarily in the same position. At a later stage you will learn how to use a whole range of pronouns but for the moment it is important to understand the difference between the articles **le, la,** and **les** which mean *the* and come in front of nouns, and the pronouns **le, la** and **les** which replace nouns altogether:

Vous prendrez le petit déjeuner?
Oui nous le prendrons.   *Yes we will have it.*
Vous gardez la clef?
Oui je la garde.   *Yes I am keeping it.*
Tu gardes les clefs?
Oui je les garde.   *Yes I am keeping them.*

VOULOIR, POUVOIR, PRENDRE, DIRE

These four verbs belong to the third group of verbs (mostly irregular which means that they do not all have the same spelling pattern). Here they are in the present tense.

Vouloir *to want*

je veux	*I want*	**nous voulons**	*we want*
tu veux	*you want*	**vous voulez**	*you want*
il/elle/on veut	*he/she/one wants*	**ils /elles veulent**	*they want*

Pouvoir *to be able to*

je peux	*I can*	**nous pouvons**	*we can*
tu peux	*you can*	**vous pouvez**	*you can*
il/elle/on peut	*he/she/one can*	**ils/elles peuvent**	*they can*

Prendre *to take*

je prends	*I take*	**nous prenons**	*we take*
tu prends	*you take*	**vous prenez**	*you take*
il/elle/on prend	*he/she/one takes*	**ils/elles prennent**	*they take*

Dire *to say*

je dis	*I say*	**nous disons**	*we say*
tu dis	*you say*	**nous dites**	*you say*
il/elle/on dit	*he/she/one says*	**ils/elles disent**	*they say*

Useful expression: **C'est à dire** *That is to say*

VERB + INFINITIVE

Vous pouvez prendre le petit déjeuner dans votre chambre. *You can have breakfast in your room.*

In this sentence **prendre** is in the infinitive (the basic form of the verb). That is simply because when one verb follows another, the second one remains in the infinitive, except after **avoir** *to have* and **être** *to be*.

Exercise 5 **Pouvoir et prendre**
a It is your turn to find the correct endings for the verb **pouvoir** *can* and for the verb **prendre** *to take*.

The first column is a list of the pronouns I, you, etc. (referred to as subject pronouns). Link each pronoun to the correct part of the verb listed in the second column (each pronoun can be linked to more than one verb form). Try to do this without referring back to the lists of these verbs, to see if you have learnt them.

Je	pouvez
Tu	prends
Il	prennent
Elle	prend
On	peuvent
Nous	peux
Vous	prenons
Ils	prenez
Elles	peut

b In Dialogue 2 there are two examples of **prendre** in the future tense (*I will take* etc.). Can you identify them?

c **Un proverbe!** *A proverb!* Here are two versions of the same French proverb:

> *Quand on veut on peut.*
> *Vouloir c'est pouvoir.*

Can you find an equivalent English proverb?

Insight

To check verb endings go to the verb tables at the end of the book. However, regular verb endings are mostly standard. For instance you know now that when you use **vous** in the present tense the ending of the verb is likely to be **-ez**, and with **nous** the ending is **-ons**.

UN ENTRETIEN AVEC SYLVIE LÉCAILLE, TOILETTEUSE

French people are very fond of animals, especially small dogs. This is something which has progressively developed in the last 20 years and with it a whole commerce related to animal care such as dog grooming salons. Author Gaëlle Graham (GG) interviews Sylvie Lécaille (SL), animal groomer.

GG	Sylvie, vous travaillez avec les animaux. Qu'est-ce que vous faites exactement?
SL	Je suis toiletteuse, c'est à dire que je prends soin de l'hygiène des animaux de compagnie.
GG	Tous les animaux?
SL	Non, je m'occupe en particulier du toilettage canin et également de l'hygiène des chats et des lapins.
GG	Vous aimez votre travail?
SL	Oui, c'est une passion d'enfance que j'ai réalisée récemment.
GG	Il faut des diplômes pour exercer ce métier?
SL	Non, ce n'est pas obligatoire mais dans mon cas j'ai obtenu le brevet de toiletteur canin et donc c'est un avantage au niveau technique.
GG	Du point de vue professionel, quel est le meilleur moment de la journée?
SL	C'est le moment où le client voit son toutou* transformé après le toilettage et sort de chez moi tout fier de son chien.
GG	Vous avez beaucoup de travail?
SL	Oui parce que les Français ont de plus en plus d'animaux de compagnie.
GG	Alors bonne chance Sylvie
SL	Merci beaucoup

1 *Sylvie grooms pets, which ones does she mention?*
2 *Is Sylvie qualified to do this particular job?*
3 *What makes her day?*

* un toutou = slang name for a pet dog.

RECHERCHEZ DES INFORMATIONS ET ENTRAÎNEZ-VOUS SUR LE WEB

Web extension
Go to http://www.tourisme.fr

Click on **préparer son voyage** at the top of the home page then on Informations pratiques → Animaux de compagnie → Voyager avec des animaux

Find out all you need to know about travelling in France with a pet.

Surfez sur le web

- Trouvez votre bonheur avec www.tourisme.fr, www.tourisme.gouv.fr
- Si vous connaissez Le Guide du Routard (French equivalent to the Rough Guides), allez voir www.routard.com

Insight: Encore un bon tuyau! *Another good tip!*
If you are using a French voice to direct you when using your satellite navigation system you already know the verb **prendre** in the imperative form:

Au rond-point prenez la deuxième sortie à droite. *At the roundabout take the second exit to the right.*

TEST YOURSELF

A) Vous devez choisir un hôtel plus / moins cher *You should choose a more / less expensive hotel*

L'Hôtel de la Plage**

L'Hôtel du Nord*

L'Hôtel des Voyageurs***

L'Hôtel l'Europe****

Assuming that a one-star hotel is less expensive than a two-star, etc., compare the cost of the four hotels:

   1 *L'Hôtel du Nord est __ __ que l'Hôtel de la Plage. C'est le __ cher.*

   2 *L'Hôtel l'Europe est __ __ __ l'Hôtel des Voyageurs. C'est le __ cher.*

B) What would you like for breakfast?

Place the following in the correct gap:

eau minérale
croissants
yaourts aux fruits
pain
café au lait
confiture

Pour le petit déjeuner je voudrais des __, du __, de la __, de l'__ __ bien fraîche, du __ __ __, et des __ __ __.

9

Une si jolie petite ville!
Such a pretty little town!

In this unit you will learn
- *places in a town and their location*
- *more about the time*
- *to plan for the near future*
- *parts of the day*

1 C'est à côté du commissariat
It's next to the police station

◀ **CD1, TR 48**

Dominique and Sarah visit the old town. They each go their own way.

Listen to the recording once, then answer these questions:

a *What is Sarah going to do?*
b *Can it be found on the map of the town?*

Listen to the recording again.

c *What is Dominique going to do?*
d *When will they meet again? In:*
  1 *two hours' time* **2** *an hour's time* **3** *half an hour's time*

Now read the dialogue:

Sarah	Je vais poster quelques cartes postales. Je vais essayer de trouver un bureau de poste.
Dominique	Regarde, la poste est indiquée sur le plan de la ville, là, PTT. C'est Place des Frères Lamennais. Tiens, regarde, c'est à côté du commissariat de police, en face de la cathédrale.
Sarah	Parfait, j'y vais! Et toi qu'est-ce que tu vas faire?
Dominique	Oh je ne sais pas, je vais peut-être faire un tour des remparts. On se retrouve dans une heure?
Sarah	OK! Où ça?
Dominique	Euh, au bout de la Grand'Rue, derrière la cathédrale, au coin de la rue Porcon de la Barbinais.
Sarah	Au revoir! Bonne promenade!
Dominique	Salut! A tout à l'heure!

QUICK VOCAB

à côté de *next to*
en face *opposite*
derrière *behind*
entre* *in between*
au coin de... *at the corner of/round the corner from*
chacun/chacune *each one*
de l'autre côté* *on the other side*
devant* *in front of...*
(**not in the text*)

Link the following English phrases (1–8) to the equivalent French expressions (a–h).

1 the police station

2 The post office is marked on the map.

3 look

4 I may go round the ramparts

5 What are you going to do?

a La poste est indiquée sur le plan.

b Où ça?

c Bonne promenade!

d On se retrouve dans une heure.

e le commissariat de police

6 Have a good walk!	**f** regarde
7 Let's meet again in an hour's time.	**g** Qu'est-ce que tu vas faire?
8 Whereabouts?	**h** Je vais peut-être faire un tour des remparts.

Vrai ou faux? Say whether the following statements are true or false.

   a *Le commissariat de police est derrière la cathédrale.*
   b *La poste est indiquée sur le plan.*
   c *Sarah cherche la cathédrale.*
   d *Dominique va à la poste.*
   e *Elles (les deux femmes) se retrouvent dans deux heures.*

Un peu de grammaire
A bit of grammar

ALLER

The verb **aller** *to go* appears several times in the dialogue. In Unit 7, you learnt that **aller** is the only verb ending in -**er** which does not follow the usual pattern. Here it is:

Aller *in the present tense*

je vais	*I go / I am going*	**nous allons**	*we go / are going*
tu vas	*you go / are going*	**vous allez**	*you go / are going*
il/elle/on va	*he/she/one goes/is going*	**ils /elles vont**	*they go / are going*

Aller + *a second verb in the infinitive*
This is used to indicate that an action will take place in the very near future:

Je vais poster quelques cartes postales.	*I am going to post a few postcards.*
Je vais essayer de trouver un bureau de poste.	*I am going to try and find a post office.*

In fact in this last example there are two verbs following **aller,** both of them in the infinitive.

Qu'est-ce que tu vas faire?	*What are you going to do?*
Je vais peut-être faire un tour	*Perhaps I'll take a walk around*
des remparts.	*the ramparts.*
Je vais faire une promenade.	*I am going to go for a walk.*

J'y vais *I am going (there)*
Y is a pronoun standing in place of a phrase beginning with **à.** When Sarah says **J'y vais** in the dialogue it is short for **Je vais à la poste.**

TROUVER – SE RETROUVER *TO FIND – TO MEET AGAIN*

re- at the beginning of a verb indicates that the action is being done again e.g. **faire** *to do* and **refaire** *to redo/do again*.

Se retrouver is like a reflexive verb but here it involves two people. The action is reciprocal (Sarah is going to find Dominique again and Dominique is going to find Sarah).

S'embrasser *to kiss one another* is another example of a reciprocal action:

Les amants s'embrassent. *The lovers kiss.*

Exercise 1 Faites des phrases

What are all the people whose names appear in column A going to do? For each sentence columns A and D remain the same. Columns B and C are jumbled. You have to find the right items from these two columns to complete each sentence. Can you find eight correct sentences? Can you say what they mean?

A	B	C	D
1 M & Mme Olivier	allons	visiter	des cartes postales
2 Tu	va	téléphoner	à ton frère
3 Sarah Burgess	vas	choisir	le petit déjeuner au lit
4 Vous	vont	chercher	la vieille ville
5 Je	vont	faire	à St Malo
6 On	allez	rester	du travail
7 Les enfants	va	voir (*to see*)	une promenade
8 Nous	vais	prendre	le dernier film de Spielberg

Les PTT ou La Poste

La Poste is no longer just a post office, it has changed its character to adapt to the needs of its customers. It has been privatized and is now also a bank and an organization which offers many of its services, including financial services, on the internet. For more information see the website for Le Groupe la Poste www.laposte.fr

---

2 Une si jolie petite ville!
Such a pretty little town!

Spend a few minutes studying the diagram overleaf. There is a multitude of small French towns where you can find all the buildings, shops and institutions pictured in it. You have already learnt some of the names and therefore you only need to concentrate on the new ones.

Look at the names of all the places in the town and say which of them are referred to in the second column.

Lieu *Place*
1 la Place de la République
2 le Bar-Tabac du Centre (bureau de tabac) *bar-tobacconist's*
3 l'église *the church*
4 la pharmacie *the chemist's*
5 le Commissariat de Police
6 la Mairie *the Town Hall* (l'Hôtel de Ville in larger towns)
7 la bibliothèque municipale *the public library*
8 la boucherie *the butcher's*
9 l'Office de Tourisme
10 la Maison de la Presse *the newsagent's + bookshop*
11 le Café de la Poste
12 l'Hôtel-Restaurant St Jacques
13 l'alimentation (l'épicerie) *general food store*
14 la poste
15 la boulangerie–pâtisserie *baker's/cake shop*
16 la banque *the bank*
17 la charcuterie *the delicatessen*
18 le camping municipal *the municipal campsite*

C'est où? *Where is it?*
a C'est entre la mairie et la boucherie.
b C'est derrière la poste, entre la banque et le bar-tabac.
c C'est entre le Café de la Poste et l'Office de Tourisme.
d C'est devant la bibliothèque et à côté de l'Office de Tourisme.
e C'est rue François Mitterrand, derrière l'alimentation.
f C'est à côté de l'église, près du Commissariat de Police.
g C'est derrière le bar-tabac et à côté du camping municipal.

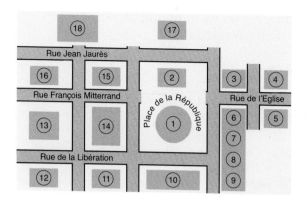

You are in **la Place de la République** when a passer-by stops you and asks you two questions. Complete the dialogue.

Passant	Excusez-moi Monsieur/Madame/Mademoiselle. Pour aller au _____ s'il vous plaît?
Vous	Le _____, c'est derrière la boulangerie et en face de la _____.
Passant	Merci bien! Et où est la _____ s'il vous plaît?
Vous	C'est à côté de la _____ municipale et en face du Commissariat de Police.

Insight: Les incontournables *(The unmissable)*
Toutes les petites villes et tous les villages de France qu'il faut absolument visiter. Il serait dommage de les contourner sans s'y arrêter. In other words there are so many lovely little towns and villages which deserve a visit.

Cherchez-les sur www.lesplusbeauxvillagesdefrance

3 Qu'est-ce qu'on va faire aujourd'hui?
What shall we do today?

🔊 **CD1, TR 49**

A family is staying in St Malo for the weekend. They are planning what they are going to do.

Listen once to the recording and answer these questions:

a *Who would like to go either to the beach or for a boat trip down the river?*
b *Who would like to go to Mont Saint Michel?*

Listen again.

c *What would the boy like to do?*
d *Who puts a stop to the discussion?*
e *At the end of the discussion what does the boy want to know?*

C'est samedi matin [discussion entre deux ados (adolescents) et leurs parents]	
Maman	Alors, soit on va à la plage et à marée basse on peut aller visiter la tombe de Chateaubriand sur le Grand Bé, ou bien on fait une excursion en bateau sur la Rance jusqu'à Dinan…
Jeune fille	Moi je voudrais aller au Mont Saint Michel!
Maman	Non, il y a beaucoup trop de monde au Mont Saint Michel le week-end!
Jeune garçon	Moi je veux prendre le petit train pour visiter St Malo. C'est moins fatigant et plus amusant!
Maman	Quel paresseux!
Papa	Bon, moi aussi j'ai une idée, on va visiter le barrage de la Rance. Plus de discussion!
Jeune garçon	Dis Papa et demain qu'est-ce qu'on va faire?

la marée basse *low tide*
soit... ou bien *either... or*
beaucoup trop de monde *far too many people*
aujourd'hui *today*
demain *tomorrow*
la marée haute* *high tide*
(**not in the text*)

QUICK VOCAB

Link the following English phrases to the equivalent French expressions:

1 We go to the beach.	**a** Quel paresseux!
2 I'd like to go on the little train.	**b** une excursion en bateau
3 What a lazy boy!	**c** C'est plus amusant!
4 a boat trip	**d** On va à la plage.
5 It's not so tiring.	**e** Je voudrais prendre le petit train.
6 It's more fun.	**f** C'est moins fatigant.

Insight

Où, quand et comment? *Where, when and how?*
Où allez-vous? Je vais à Paris
Quand y allez-vous? J'y vais demain / après demain / la semaine prochaine (*next week*) / bientôt
Comment y allez-vous? J'y vais en voiture / par le train / à vélo (*bike*)

Un peu de grammaire
A bit of grammar

THE IMMEDIATE FUTURE: **ALLER** *+ INFINITIVE*

You have already come across an easy way to talk about the future. You can use **aller** followed by another verb to refer to what will happen soon, for example in the next second, minute, hour or day, or even in the next few years in some cases:

Tu vas tomber!	You are going to fall over!
Il va pleuvoir.	It's going to rain.
Nous allons faire une promenade à vélo.	We are going to go for a bike ride.
Avec le nouveau gouvernement tout ça va changer!	With the new government all that is going to change!

In most cases the time scale is implicit but to be more precise use **aujourd'hui** *today*, **demain** *tomorrow*, **après-demain** *the day after tomorrow*, **bientôt** *soon*:

| Qu'est-ce qu'on va faire aujourd'hui? | What are we going to do today? |
| Qu'est-ce qu'on va faire demain? | What are we going to do tomorrow? |

Insight

Faire (*to make, to do*) is used in a multitude of expressions:
Il fait beau *The weather is nice*
Elle fait du 130 à l'heure *She is driving at 130 km/hour*
Faites attention! *Be careful!*
Arrête de faire le clown! *Stop mucking about!*
Ils font de la natation *They're swimming*

THE IMMEDIATE FUTURE: PRESENT TENSE

You can also use the present tense to express the immediate future:

Qu'est ce que tu fais cet après-midi?	What are you doing this afternoon?
Qu'est-ce que vous faites ce soir?	What are you doing this evening?
Ce midi nous allons au restaurant.	This lunch time we are going to the restaurant.
Cette année nous allons en vacances en Irlande.	This year we are going on holiday to Ireland.

AMUSANT *AMUSING/FUNNY*, **FATIGANT** *TIRING*

-ant in French is equivalent to *-ing* in English:

Marcher toute la journée, c'est très fatigant.	*Walking all day is very tiring.*
C'est un homme vraiment amusant.	*He's a really funny man.*

Amuser means *to amuse/to entertain* and the reflexive verb **s'amuser** means *to enjoy oneself*:

Les enfants s'amusent sur la plage.	*The children are enjoying themselves on the beach.*

DIS PAPA! / DIS MAMAN!

These are children's expressions generally used to attract the attention of adults. **Dis/dites** are the imperative forms of **dire** *to say*:

Dis-moi la vérité.	*Tell me the truth.*
Dites-le au maire.	*Tell it to the mayor.*

Chateaubriand is a French Romantic author born in St Malo in 1768. His grave is on a tiny island or rock, **Le Grand Bé**, which can be reached from the beach at low tide.

Le Barrage de la Rance or **Usine marémotrice de la Rance** is a tidal dam across the river Rance which uses the tide as a means to create electricity.

Exercise 2 **Le Petit Train de St Malo**
Read the advert for the little train and answer the questions below.

LE PETIT TRAIN
DE SAINT-MALO

**Visite touristique
et commentée**
*de l'intra-muros
et de ses alentours*

Départ et arrivée : porte St-Vincent
au pied du Château
NOCTURNE JUILLET/AOUT
Durée du trajet : 30 minutes

INFORMATIONS RESERVATIONS GROUPES
Tél. 02 99 40 49 49 - Fax 02 99 40 44 62
BP 173 35408 SAINT-MALO
ENGLISH GUIDED TOUR

a *What could you expect to see if you took the little train?*
b *What happens at Porte St Vincent?*
c *Could you take a night ride all year round?*

Exercise 3 **J'ai besoin de.../Je voudrais...**

◄) **CD1, TR 50**

Advise people where to go when you hear what they need (**avoir besoin de...**) or want. Listen to the recording and respond appropriately.

Exemple: J'ai besoin d'argent. **Vous:** Allez à la banque.

1 *Je voudrais du jambon et du pâté.*
2 *J'ai besoin de médicaments.*
3 *Je voudrais acheter des journaux.*
4 *Je voudrais des timbres poste.*
5 *Je voudrais du pain et des gâteaux.*
6 *J'ai besoin d'un plan de la ville.*

RECHERCHEZ DES INFORMATIONS ET ENTRAÎNEZ-VOUS SUR LE WEB

Web extension

1 *Log onto the Saint Malo official site*
   http://www.saint-malo.fr/guide/index.html
   find **Guide Pratique** *and click on* **se repérer** *(finding out where you are). You should see a map of St Malo and its area. You are invited to indicate your departure point. Please choose* **Dinard** *and then in the box below choose the type of itinary:* **Itineraire Bis,** *which is usually a tourist route, using secondary roads. Then click on* **Calculer l'itinéraire** *which will lead you to a box indicating the roads, the walking time (*itinéraire piéton*) and the distance. You can then click on* **Modifier les options** *and choose to go by car instead. Have fun calculating the distance, the time and how much you will spend on petrol, according to which type of car you drive and the petrol you use.*

2 *Log on* **le site du Petit Train de Saint Malo**
   www.lepetittrain-saintmalo.com
   L'accueil *(home page) describes the advantages of visiting St Malo with* **le Petit Train.** *Which are they? You are then invited to choose a category. Please choose* **Circuits.** *You will be presented with the train route and pictures of St Malo. You can also listen to a commentary (*écouter les commentaires*) while watching the panoramic views (*visualiser les vues panoramiques*). You can also read the commentary on each site. If you click on* **Accès** *you can read the following text and find information about distances between St Malo and other localities.*

Porte Saint-Vincent, … est à 50 mètres de l'office du tourisme, au pied des remparts et du château. Saint-Malo, c'est aussi à: 10 km de Dinard, 32 km de Dinan, 15 km de Cancale, 56 km du Mont St-Michel et à 1 heure environ des îles Anglo-normandes (Jersey, Guernesey).

Say where exactly Porte St-Vincent is.

TEST YOURSELF

Voici une ville typique

Look at the map of the French town earlier in this unit. Fill the gaps with the following words:

à côté, derrière, à gauche, à droite, en face, entre, centre, devant, renseignements, pain, timbres, lait, croissants, sucre

1 *La mairie est au __ du village, __ l'office de tourisme et le café, et __ __ de l'église.*

2 *Vous voulez acheter du __ et des __? Allez à la boulangerie, c'est __ le café.*

3 *Vous avez besoin de __ sur la région? Allez à l'office de tourisme, c'est __ __ de la Mairie et __ la médiathèque.*

4 *Nous avons besoin de __ et de __. Allons à l'épicerie, c'est __ le café et __ __ de l'église.*

5 *Je vais acheter des __. Je vais à la poste. C'est __ __ de l'office de tourisme.*

6 *L'église est __ la médiathèque et l'épicerie.*

10

....

Choisir un restaurant
Choosing a restaurant

In this unit you will learn
- *about eating out*
- *how to express an opinion*
- *about the French and their attitude towards food*

_____

1 Où est-ce qu'on mange?
Where shall we eat?

◀) **CD1, TR 51**

Sarah and Dominique are enjoying their stay in St Malo. As well as places to visit they discuss the restaurants and other places where they can have meals.

Listen to the recording and answer these questions:

a *What does Dominique suggest they do for lunch?*
b *Dominique sees a small restaurant. Where is it?*
c *How much would they have to pay for mussels, chips and a glass of wine?*

Now read the dialogue:

Dominique	Où est-ce qu'on mange ce midi? On fait un pique-nique?
Sarah	Non! Il ne fait pas assez beau. En fait on dirait qu'il va pleuvoir.
Dominique	Oui je pense que tu as raison. Alors qu'est-ce qu'on fait? On prend quelque chose de rapide dans une brasserie ou bien dans une crêperie? Qu'est-ce que tu en dis?
Sarah	Euh… J'ai envie de manger des moules avec des frites.
Dominique	Bonne idée! Tiens, regarde, il y a un petit restaurant de l'autre côté de la rue: repas express, moules-frites plus un verre de vin 10,50 € tout compris.
Sarah	C'est parfait. On y va!

QUICK VOCAB

avoir envie de… *to long for / to have a craving for/to feel like / to fancy…*
quelque chose *something*
un verre de vin *a glass of wine*
pleuvoir *to rain*

Link the following English phrases to the equivalent French expressions:

1 In fact it looks as if it is going to rain.

a Il ne fait pas assez beau.

2 What do you say to that?

b On prend un petit repas rapide?

3 The weather is not good enough

c J'ai envie de manger des moules avec des frites.

4 Where are we going to eat this lunch time?

d Je pense que tu as raison.

5 Shall we have a quick meal?

e Qu'est-ce que tu en dis?

6 Ten euros 50 centimes all included

f Où est-ce qu'on mange ce midi?

7 I think you are right..

g En fait on dirait qu'il va pleuvoir.

8 I fancy eating mussels with chips.

h 10,50 € tout compris.

Insight

Avoir envie de + verb in the infinitive ... *I feel like...* A handy key expression to use in everyday conversation.

J'ai envie de rire (*laugh*)
Il a toujours (*always*) **envie de sortir** (*go out*)
Elle a envie de dormir (*sleep*)
Ils ont envie d'aller au théâtre (*go to ...*)
J'ai envie de rester chez moi et de lire un bon livre (*stay at home + read*)

Un peu de grammaire
A bit of grammar

EXPRESSING AN OPINION AND SEEKING AN OPINION FROM SOMEONE

To express an opinion you can use **penser** *to think* or **croire** *to believe*:

Je pense que / Je crois que	*I think / I believe that...*
Je pense que oui.	*I think so.*
Je crois qu'il est malade.	*I believe he's ill.*

To seek an opinion you can use **penser** and **dire** *to say*:

Qu'est-ce que tu en penses?	*What do you think (of it)?*
Qu'est ce que tu en dis?	*What do you say (about it)?*

En is a pronoun which replaces whatever has just been said or suggested. Addressing someone more formally you will use **vous**:

Qu'est-ce que vous en dites?

Qu'est-ce que vous en pensez?

Exercise 1 La cuisine française

◀) **CD1, TR 52**

The following statement contains new vocabulary which is essential for slightly more complex conversations. Use the keywords, learn them and then read the text.

> *En général les Français sont très chauvins, c'est-à-dire qu'ils font souvent preuve de chauvinisme, surtout lorsqu'il s'agit de ce qu'il y a de plus important: la cuisine française. Pour beaucoup de Français, c'est la meilleure cuisine du monde.*

c'est-à-dire *that is to say*
souvent *often*
surtout *above all*
lorsque/quand *when*
partout *everywhere*
faire preuve de *to demonstrate / to show*
s'agir de *to be a matter of*
la meilleure cuisine *the best cooking*

Now answer the questions:

a *What national trait is mentioned here?*
b *When is this particular trait mostly evident?*

Listen to the recording. What do they say? Three people are arguing about the best cooking in the world.

c *How many think that French cooking is best?*
d *What is best about it?*
e *What other countries are mentioned as possible contenders?*
f *How many speakers think that the whole issue is a matter of taste?*

There are different types of eating-out places in France, apart from traditional restaurants:

• **Une brasserie** is often a large café which sells mainly beer and serves all sorts of quick meals. They are generally very good value for money.

• **Une crêperie** is a type of restaurant specialising in the cooking of pancakes with various types of fillings. **Crêpes** *pancakes* are a speciality from Brittany but there are now **crêperies** all over France. **Crêpes** can have a savoury or a sweet filling and therefore it  is possible to have a full meal eating a savoury pancake (or two) for the main course and a sweet one for dessert.

Brittany is also famous for its seafood and **plateaux de fruits de mer** (seafood platters with all sorts of shellfish which can be shared amongst several people).

Couscous, a North African dish, is often prepared and sold on certain days in campsites or supermarkets: **couscous à emporter** *couscous to take away*. There are also many North African restaurants, especially in Paris.

The latest trend is to eat at a farm house: **Une ferme auberge.** You can eat traditional French country cooking in traditional farm houses. Sometimes they are the same farms which offer **chambres d'hôtes.**

Insight

How to use **mieux / meilleur** (*best / better*)

mieux is the adverb, **meilleur** can be an adjective, an adverb or a noun!

J'aime mieux la bière. *I like beer best.*

Ces pommes sont meilleures. *These apples are better.*

La viande? C'est meilleur avec du vin rouge. *Meat? It's better with red wine.*

Beaucoup de gens pensent que les bières d'Alsace sont les meilleures du monde. *Lots of people think that Alsace beers are the best in the world.*

---

2 Les repas dans la vie des Français
Meals in the life of the French

Read this passage – you will understand it all!

> *Les Français aiment manger. Ils aiment la bonne nourriture* (good food) *et les bons repas* (good meals). *Toute occasion est bonne pour faire un repas de famille ou un repas entre amis: un baptême, une communion ou une confirmation, un mariage, un résultat d'examen, un anniversaire, et évidemment Noël et surtout le premier janvier.*

Did you understand it? Now answer these questions:

  a *What do French people like?*
  b *Name at least six occasions which are particularly good pretexts for a family meal or a meal with friends.*

Here is some more information:

Les heures des repas	Meal times
LES REPAS	*LES MOMENTS DE LA JOURNÉE*
Le petit déjeuner	*Le matin*
Le déjeuner	*À midi, entre midi et deux heures*

Le goûter	L'après-midi (surtout pour les enfants)
Le dîner	Le soir, vers sept, huit heures
Le souper	Plus tard le soir (repas assez léger)

Le midi les Français mangent à la cantine, à la cafétéria, au restaurant ou bien chez eux s'ils habitent près de leur lieu de travail.

le goûter *afternoon tea (nearest translation but not the same connotation)*
goûter *(as a verb) to taste/to appreciate*
assez léger *fairly light*
chez eux *at (their) home (lit. at theirs)*
leur lieu de travail *their place of work*

Obviously everybody does not have all these meals every day but generally French people are fairly punctilious about when they eat their meals. You might find that roads are almost empty at meal times because nearly everybody eats at the same time. Also far fewer French people have snacks or sandwiches at lunchtime.

Insight

Goûter is both a verb and a noun: **le goûter** (a noun, *taste*), **goûter** (a verb, *to taste*):
Goûtez mon gâteau, vous m'en donnerez des nouvelles! *Do taste my cake and let me know what you think!*
Alors, il a bon goût, mon gâteau? *So, does it taste good, my cake?*
Pouah! C'est dégoûtant! *Yuck! It's disgusting!*

Here are some more questions:

c *At what time are French people likely to have dinner in the evening?*
d *Who is* le goûter *mainly for?*
e *What is the difference between* le dîner *and* le souper?
f *Where do French people eat at midday?*

Exercise 2 Où est-ce qu'on mange ce soir?

Look at the following adverts and say which eating places best fit your requirements. (You can have more than one for each question.)

De quoi est-ce que vous avez envie?

a *You wish to eat seafood.*
b *You would like a meal to take away.*
c *You would like a Sunday lunch.*
d *You would like a pancake meal.*
e *You would like a restaurant with a sea view.*
f *You would like to take the children out for a meal.*
g *You are waiting for the boat to Ile de Sein.*
h *You would like a restaurant open every day until late in the summer.*
i *You would like a North African meal.*
j *You would like a seafood supper with mussels and chips.*

BAR - LOTO- PMU ①
4, place de la République - PONT-CROIX
Pizza à emporter
non stop, midi à 21 h 30
02 98 70 41 41

② ■ Pleuven :
Au Moulin-du-Pont, ***crêperie « Chez Mimi »***, sur la route des plages Bénodet-Fouesnant. Crêpes traditionnelles, spécialités glaces. Ouverte tous les jours sauf dimanche midi. Recommandée par le Guide du routard. **Tél. 02.98.54.62.02 - fax 02.98.54.69.91**

Crêperie de Pen al Lenn **OUVERTE** ③
dans un vieux moulin **TOUS LES JOURS**
avec terrasse couverte côté jardin *en juillet-août*
sur la route de la Forêt-Fouesnant *Service continu*
Fouesnant - ☎ 02.98.56.08.80 *de 11 h à 23 h*

Insight

Dégustation means *tasting*. The root of this noun is the same as in **goût** (and as in *gusto*). The **ût** in **goût** is a mutation of **ust** in **dégustation**. At Le Doris (in advertisement 4) you can enjoy seafood tasting: **Dégustation de crustacés.** Do you enjoy tasting wine in the regions you are visiting? You may be offered **dégustation gratuite!**

3 Le goûter à la ferme
Afternoon tea on the farm

This is an advert for a farm in the heart of Brittany – La Ferme des Monts – near an ancient site called La Roche aux fées (Fairies' Rock).

RESTAURATION
ILLE-ET-VILAINE

Contact	Descriptif
Jacques RUPIN Les Monts 35150 PIRE SUR SEICHE Tél. 02 97 37 55 92	Au pays de la Roche aux fées, près d l'axe Rennes-Angers, venez visiter les vergers de la ferme des Monts. Vous pourrez découvrir la fabrication traditionnelle du cidre, voir la cave et le matériel utilisé hier et aujourd'hui. Ensuite vous goûterez au jus de pomme, au cidre, aux crêpes et gâteaux maison accompagnés de confitures ou gelées. Vente directe sur place. Ouvert tous les après-midis sur réservation du 1/05 ou 15/09. Hors saison: ouvert sur RDV. Possibilité de recevoir des groupes.

You are not expected to understand every word in the advert but use the following keywords to answer the questions.

un verger *an orchard*
la cave *the cellar*
hier *yesterday/in the old days*
des confitures *jams*
des gelées *preserves*
RDV=rendez-vous *appointment*

  a *Name two things you could see or visit at the farm.*
  b *What could you drink?*
  c *What could you eat with the home-made cakes?*
  d *When is the farm open for* le goûter?
  e *What would you need to do before going there?*

Exercise 3 **Le souper marin**

🔊 **CD1, TR 53**

You and your friend Michel would like to go to the seafood supper at Plovan (see Unit 7 Exercise 2). Listen to the recording and answer Michel's questions.

Moules-frites is the type of snack meal you can eat in a brasserie anywhere in France nowaday but it is primarily a Belgian speciality. **Jacques Brel** (8 April 1929 – 9 October 1978), the famous Belgian singer, referred to **frites, moules et bières** in some of his songs. The chain of restaurants, Léon de Bruxelles, which specializes in **moules et frites**, has extended to Paris and most other parts of France.

Insight

Part of a song by the Belgian singer, Jacques Brel, from 'Jef', 1964:
On ira manger des moules et puis des frites, des frites et puis des moules et du vin de Moselle. *We'll go and eat mussels, and then chips, chips and then mussels and Moselle wine.*
On ira is from the verb **aller** in the future tense; **et puis** mean and then / and also.

Exercise 4
Cochez les cases – tick the boxes where required to make a meaningful sentence:

Les Belges ❏ les Suisses ❏ les Américains ❏ ne mangent pas ❏ n'aiment pas ❏ sont amateurs ❏ de beefburgers ❏ de moules-frites ❏ de couscous ❏ qu'ils mangent ❏ qu'ils boivent ❏ dans des restaurants ❏ dans des brasseries ❏ avec du vin rouge ❏ avec de la bière ❏ de la limonade ❏. Le chanteur et poète ❏ artiste peintre ❏ Jacques Brel ❏ a dénigré ❏ a célébré ❏ a refusé ❏ cette coutume nationale ❏ dans ses chansons ❏ dans son testament ❏.

Maintenant écrivez la phrase correcte.

- Vous aimez les moules-frites? Amusez-vous en visitant le site interactif de www.leon-de-bruxelles.fr.

Web extension exercise

Trouvez l'image du restaurant. Cliquez sur la première fenêtre à gauche de la porte d'entrée pour trouver des adresses. Cliquez sur la première fenêtre à droite de la porte pour des jeux (*games*) pour les enfants et pour les grands cliquez sur la porte.

VOCAB

la porte *the door*
la fenêtre *the window*
la porte-fenêtre *French windows*

TEST YOURSELF

Here are some new expressions:

avoir faim to be hungry

avoir soif to be thirsty

je meurs de faim / soif I'm dying of hunger / thirst (figurative)

Who is hungry? Who is thirsty?

Christophe a faim.

Jean-Michel n'a pas très faim.

Jacques a très soif.

Elise n'a pas soif.

Read the statements below and work out who is speaking:

1 *Je n'ai pas soif mais j'ai besoin d'un petit café.*

2 *Je meurs de faim! Je vais manger au restaurant, j'ai envie d'un bon bifteck-frites.*

3 *Je n'ai pas très faim, je vais manger un sandwich à la terrasse du café.*

4 *Je meurs de soif! Je vais commander une grande bière.*

11

La pluie et le beau temps!
Rain and shine!

In this unit you will learn
- *how to talk about the weather*
- *how to listen to a radio bulletin and read the weather forecast in the newspaper*
- *about the regions of France*
- *to express the present and future*

---

1 Il va faire de l'orage
It's going to be stormy

🔊 **CD1, TR 54**

Sarah et Dominique sont dans leur voiture. Elles vont visiter Dinan, une cité médiévale sur la Rance. Elles parlent de la pluie et du beau temps...

Listen to the recording and answer these questions:

a *When is it certainly going to rain?*
b *Why do they turn the radio on?*

Listen again.

c *The weather forecast mentions storms for at least three French regions. Can you name any of them?*

Now read the dialogue.

Dominique	Tu as raison, le temps change...il fait lourd, il va faire de l'orage!
Sarah	Oui, le ciel est couvert. En tout cas il va certainement pleuvoir cet après-midi.
Dominique	Ah oui, voilà les première gouttes de pluie.
Sarah	Écoutons les prévisions météorologiques.

Elles écoutent France Inter

...et pour les jours suivants le temps lourd va persister. Il fera encore chaud et ensoleillé. L'évolution orageuse sera plus marquée sur les Pyrénées, les Alpes et sur la Corse. Dans l'ensemble de la France les températures resteront cinq degrés au-dessus des températures de saison. C'était notre bulletin météorologique de la mi-journée. Vous pourrez écouter notre prochain bulletin sur France Inter à seize heures cinquante-cinq. Et voici maintenant notre bulletin d'informations de treize heures...

Dominique	Alors c'est partout pareil en France.
Sarah	Qu'est-ce qu'on fait demain? On va dans le Finistère comme prévu?
Dominique	Oui d'accord et après cela on commencera à descendre vers Bordeaux en passant par chez moi à St Nazaire et chez mon copain à Nantes.

Insight: Proverbs

Proverbs reflect French popular wisdom for forecasting the weather and the seasons:

En avril n'ôte pas un fil, mais en mai mets ce qu'il te plaît *In April do not remove a thread, but in May wear what you will.*

Noël au balcon, Pâques aux tisons *Christmas on the balcony, Easter by the fireplace.*

le temps *weather (in the text above) but also time*
le temps est lourd *the weather is close/muggy*
le ciel *the sky*
une goutte de pluie *a raindrop*
les prévisions météorologiques/la météo *weather forecast*
la mi-journée *midday/lunchtime*
au-dessus *above*
au-dessous *below*
pareil *the same*
prévoir *to forecast/plan*
comme prévu *as planned*
mon copain *my friend/boyfriend*
ma copine *my friend/girlfriend*

Reread the dialogue and answer these questions:

d *Will temperatures over France:*
   1 go up   2 go down   3 be higher than the seasonal norm
   4 be very low
e *The forecast is for:*
   1 today only   2 tomorrow only   3 the weekend
   4 the next few days
f *The weather bulletin was:*
   1 at 6 a.m.   2 just before the 1 o'clock news   3 at 4.55 p.m.
g *Tomorrow Dominique and Sarah:*
   1 plan to stay in St Malo   2 move on to Finistère
   3 get to Bordeaux
h *On their way to Bordeaux they will:*
   1 visit Paris   2 stop on the way in St Nazaire
   3 stop to see Dominique's boyfriend

Un peu de grammaire
A bit of grammar

French people tend to spend a lot of time talking about the
weather. To discuss today's weather they use the present tense and
the following structures:

QUEL TEMPS FAIT-IL AUJOURD'HUI?
What is the weather like today?

▶ **Il fait ...** *best translated as: It is...*
  Il fait *beau (nice)/ chaud (hot) / froid
  (cold) /lourd (muggy)/ du soleil (sunny)/
  du vent (windy)/ du brouillard (foggy) /
  de l'orage (stormy)*
▶ **Le temps est....** *The weather is...*
  Le temps est *ensoleillé (sunny) / nuageux
  (cloudy) / brumeux (misty) / pluvieux
  (rainy), orageux (stormy) / couvert
  (overcast)*
▶ **Il y a...** *There is ...*
  *Il y a du vent (wind)/des nuages
  (clouds)/de la pluie (rain)/de la neige
  (snow)*
▶ **Il pleut** *(it's raining) /* **il neige** *(it's
  snowing)*

You can see how to read and understand most of the weather
conditions on the map from the newspaper further on in the unit.

Insight: Proverbs
Many proverbs refer to swallows (**l'hirondelle**):
Par temps d'orage l'hirondelle monte aux nuages *In stormy
weather the swallow goes up into the clouds*
Une hirondelle ne fait pas le printemps *A swallow doesn't
make it spring*

QUEL TEMPS FERA-T-IL DEMAIN?

In conversational French you are likely to hear people using the immediate future: **il va** + infinitive:

▶ **Il va faire beau / il va pleuvoir** *(it's going to rain)* / **il va faire de l'orage** *etc....*

But in more formal situations (forecasts on the radio, TV or newspapers) the verbs are mainly in the future tense:

▶ *Il* **fera** *beau* (**faire** *in the future tense*)
▶ *Le temps* **sera** *orageux* (**être** *in the future tense*)
▶ *Il y* **aura**... (**avoir** *in the future tense*): *Il y aura des* **averses** *(showers), des* **éclaircies** *(bright periods), de la* **brume** *(mist)*
▶ *Le vent* **soufflera** *(the wind will blow)* (**souffler** *in the future tense*)
▶ *Il* **pleuvra** *(it will rain)/il* **neigera** *(it will snow)*

....
Insight: Proverbs

S'il pleut à la St Médard il pleuvra pendant quarante jours *If it rains on St Medard's Day (8 June) it will rain for the next 40 days.*
Hirondelle volant haut le temps sera beau, hirondelle volant bas pluie il y aura *If the swallow flies high the weather will be fine, if it flies low there will be rain.*
....

THE FUTURE TENSE

Look at the text accompanying the map of France later in this unit and you will be able to find many more examples of verbs in the future tense.

Using verbs in the future tense is simple for most verbs ending with **-er** or **-ir**:

▶ *When the subject is* **il/elle** *(it) use the verb (in the infinitive) + ending* **-a**:
Le soleil brillera The sun will shine. (**briller** + **-a**)

▶ When the subject is **ils /elles** *(they) use the verb (in the infinitive) + ending* **-ont:**
  Les températures **avoisineront** *les 30 degrés* Temperatures will be close to 30 degrees. (**avoisiner + ont**)
▶ *Whatever the verb, the endings for verbs in the future are always the same:*

je	-rai	nous	-rons
tu	-ras	vous	-rez
il	-ra	elles	-ront

Un peu de géographie

France is often referred to as 'L'Hexagone' because of its shape (six sides).

Look at the map of France overleaf and the article above it.

For weather forecast purposes France has been divided into seven broad areas, some representing a whole region and others several regions. The towns on the map can be used as markers for you to locate these regions.

Complete the following sentences either with the name of a town or with the name of a region of France:

1 *Rennes est en B_____, Nantes est dans les Pays de Loire, Rouen et _____ sont en Normandie.*

2 *_____et Amiens sont dans le Nord-Picardie, Paris est en Ile de France.*

3 *Metz et _____ sont dans le _____, Dijon est en Bourgogne et Besançon est en Franche-Comté.*

4 *Poitiers est dans le _____-_____, Orléans est dans le Centre et Limoge est dans le _____.*

5 *Toulouse est dans la région Midi-Pyrénées et _____ est dans l'Aquitaine.*

6 *Clermont-Ferrand est en A_____ et _____ est dans la région Rhône-Alpes.*

7 *Montpellier, _____ et _____ sont sur le Pourtour méditerranéen et Ajaccio est en _____.*

Note that Le Midi is used as a generic name for the South of France.

Les points cardinaux:

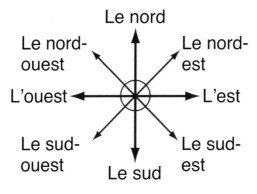

Le nord

Le nord-ouest

Le nord-est

L'ouest

L'est

Le sud-ouest

Le sud-est

Le sud

Pronunciation

🔊 **CD1, TR 55**

▶ le sud: *you can hear the* **d** *at the end of the word but in* le nord *the* **d** *is dropped*

▶ le sud-est / le sud-ouest: *are both pronounced linking the two words and the* -t *at the end of* est *and* ouest *is also pronounced:* [le sudest/le sudouest].

▶ le nord-est / le nord-ouest: *are both pronounced linking the two words but dropping the* -d *at the end of* nord: [le norest / le norouest]

Insight: Proverbs

The wisdom of the following proverb is that bad weather is never an excuse not to go to Paris:

Il ne fait jamais mauvais temps pour aller à Paris.

Un peu de grammaire
A bit of grammar

EN, DANS AND SUR

▶ **En** *is usually used in front of the name of a region or province:*
en Bretagne *in Brittany*
▶ **Dans** *is used in front of a geographical area:*
dans le nord-est *in the north-east*
▶ **Sur** *is used in association with the name of a region mainly with reference to the weather:*
sur la Bretagne et la Normandie *over Brittany and Normandy*

Exercise 1 **Le temps aujourd'hui**

◄◈ **CD1, TR 56**

Using the weather map and reading/listening to the text say where you can find the following weather conditions for the day (in some cases it applies to more than one area):

a *Thunderstorms from midday onwards*
b *Sunny all day*
c *Muggy in the afternoon*
d *Morning mist*
e *A light north-east wind*
f *Temperatures ranging from 30° on the coast to 35° inland*
g *Temperatures 5° above the seasonal norm*
h *Cloudy (veiled) sky in the afternoon*

Insight: Proverbs
A final weather-related proverb:
Après la pluie, le beau temps! *After the rain comes good weather*
Which may be translated in English as 'every cloud has a silver lining'!

LE TEMPS AUJOURD'HUI, RÉGION PAR RÉGION

Bretagne, Pays de la Loire, Normandie.
Sur la Bretagne et la Normandie, le
soleil brillera largement toute la journée.
Sur les Pays de la Loire, le soleil sera
bien présent, mais le ciel se voilera dans
l'après-midi. Il fera chaud, entre 24 et
30° du nord au sud.

Nord-Picardie, Ile-de-France. Après
quelques brumes matinales, le soleil
s'imposera largement. Un léger vent de
nord-est soufflera. Le thermomètre
indiquera entre 26 et 30° du nord au sud.

Nord-Est, Bourgogne, Franche-Comté.
Le temps sera chaud et bien ensoleillé.
Les températures avoisineront les 30°
soit 5 degrés au-dessus des températures
de saison.

Poitou-Charentes, Centre, Limousin. La
matinée sera bien ensoleillée mais le
temps deviendra lourd et des ondées
parfois orageuses se produiront sur
Poitou-Charentes et sur le Limousin. Le
thermomètre atteindra souvent les 30°.

Aquitaine, Midi-Pyrénées. Dans la
matinée, le temps deviendra lourd. Des
ondées orageuses se produiront l'après-
midi et des orages éclateront sur les
Pyrénées dès la mi-journée. Les
températures seront comprises entre 27
et 31°.

Auvergne, Rhône-Alpes. En Auvergne,
le temps deviendra lourd l'après-midi
avec des risques d'ondées orageuses.
Sur Rhône-Alpes, le temps sera
ensoleillé. Des nuages se développeront
sur les Alpes et quelques orages isolés
éclateront. Le thermomètre indiquera
entre 27 et 31°.

Pourtour méditerranéen, Corse. Sur le
Languedoc-Roussillon, la matinée
sera assez ensoleillée mais le temps
deviendra lourd l'après-midi avec des
ondées orageuses. Ailleurs, le soleil
brillera largement. Il fera chaud entre
30° sur les côtes et 35° dans
l'intérieur.

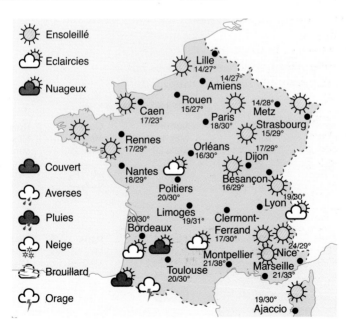

Exercise 2 **Où sont-ils en vacances?** *Where are they on holiday?*

◀) **CD1, TR 57**

a Listen to the recording and look at the list of cities below and their weather conditions. Then say where the following French people are spending their holidays.

Exemple: 'Bonjour, je m'appelle Étienne. La ville où je suis est ensoleillée et la température est entre 18 et 30 degrés.'

Réponse: Étienne est à Paris.

1 *Fabienne est _____ .*
2 *Jérôme est _____ .*
3 *Stéphanie est _____ .*
4 *Alexandre est _____ .*

b Say what the weather is like in the towns where you are holidaying.

1 *Vous êtes à Varsovie. Quel temps fait-il?*
2 *Vous êtes à Berlin. Quel temps fait-il?*

Le temps en villes

Alger
Mini 19
Maxi 33

Dublin
Mini 15
Maxi 21

Londres
Mini 14
Maxi 26

Oslo
Mini 12
Maxi 23

Rome
Mini 20
Maxi 31

Athènes
Mini 21
Maxi 29

Genève
Mini 16
Maxi 28

Madrid
Mini 20
Maxi 31

Paris
Mini 18
Maxi 30

Varsovie
Mini 17
Maxi 25

Berlin	**Istanbul**	**Moscou**	**Prague**
Mini 19	Mini 18	Mini 7	Mini 16
Maxi 27	Maxi 25	Maxi 12	Maxi 26

Surfez sur le web

- Vous pouvez voir une carte qui indique les prévisions météorologiques au jour le jour (*day by day*) sur le site de Météo France (www.meteofrance.com).
- Cliquez sur santé (*health*)/environnement pour accéder à des conseils sur la canicule (*heat wave*), les UVs et les pollens.

Web extension exercise
La canicule

La canicule tue chaque année à travers le monde, peut-être même plus encore que le froid…

Les ultraviolets

Qui n'a jamais souffert d'un coup de soleil?

Même si le soleil nous apporte bien-être et vitalité, il peut parfois se transformer en un terrible adversaire.

Les pollens

La pollinose, souvent appelée rhume des foins, est le nom donné à l'allergie au pollen des arbres, plantes, herbacées et graminées.

1 *Throughout the world what meteorological phenomenon kills more than the cold?*
2 *Find the expression for sunburn.*
3 *Find the expression for hay fever.*

TEST YOURSELF

Le temps aujourd'hui, demain et en fin de semaine

Draw lines between the columns. Six lines must be linked to each time expression.

Aujourd'hui (at present)   a **il fera beau**

                                             b **il va pleuvoir**

Demain (forecast)   c **il fait du brouillard**

                                             d **il fera de l'orage**

Ce matin (at present)   e **il neige**

                                           f **il fait du vent**

En ce moment (at present)   g **il va faire chaud**

                                           h **le ciel sera nuageux**

Après-demain (forecast)   i **il fait froid**

                                           j **le temps sera ensoleillé**

En fin de semaine (forecast) k **le soleil brille**

                                           l **le temps est pluvieux**

12

Au restaurant
At the restaurant

In this unit you will learn
- *how to order a drink in a café*
- *how to read a menu in a restaurant and how to order a meal*
- *some information on le Finistère*
- *how to recognize the past tense and how to express the recent past*

1 Un peu de lecture
A little bit of reading

Read the paragraph below.

> *C'est le mois de juillet. Nos deux amies, Dominique et Sarah, ont passé le week-end à Quimper pour les Fêtes de Cornouaille. Aujourd'hui elles viennent de visiter des chapelles dans le Pays Bigouden. Maintenant elles sont assises à la terrasse d'un café, Place de l'Église, à Plonéour-Lanvern. Il fait chaud et elles ont très soif.*

Now answer these questions:

1 *The month is:*
   a *June*   **b** *July*   **c** *January*

2 *Our two friends have spent the weekend:*
      a *in Cornwall* **b** *in St Malo* **c** *in Quimper*
   3 *They have just visited:*
      a *some chapels* **b** *some castles* **c** *some churches*
   4 *They are now:*
      a *in the church* **b** *in a restaurant* **c** *sitting at the terrace of a café*
   5 *The weather is:*
      a *muggy and they are tired* **b** *hot and they are very thirsty* **c** *cold*

Insight

The related words **venir** (*to come*), **venir de** (*to have just*), **revenir** (*to come back*), **l'avenir** (*the future*):

Viens ici mon Toutou! *Come here, my doggy!*

Je viens de déjeuner *I've just had lunch*

Je reviens dans cinq minutes *Ill be back in 5 minutes*

À l'avenir tu feras la cuisine! *In future you'll do the cooking!*

UN PEU DE GRAMMAIRE *A BIT OF GRAMMAR*

How to talk about events which have already happened
To say something has just happened use **venir** in the present tense + **de** + verb (in the infinitive):

Elles viennent de visiter des chapelles.	*They have just visited some chapels.*
Le bateau vient d'arriver au port.	*The boat has just arrived in the port.*
Tu viens de rencontrer le président.	*You've just met the president.*

Venir on its own means *to come* e.g. **Venez-vous souvent ici?** *Do you come here often?*

Venir de… indicates that something has just happened or has just been done.

Exercise 1 **Faites des phrases**
In the grid below, columns A and C remain the same. Columns B and D are jumbled.

Can you find the six correct sentences? Can you say what they mean?

A	B	C	D
1 Je	viennent	d'arriver	un bon film
2 Tu	venez	de finir	le gros lot au Loto
3 Jean-Paul	viens	de gagner	St Malo
4 Nous	vient	de visiter	à Paris
5 Vous	venons	de choisir	tes examens
6 Elles	viens	de voir	un menu

Insight

Talking about past events: the use of the perfect tense (perfect meaning perfected, in the sense of completed):

Elles ont passé le weekend au bord de la mer *They [have] spent the weekend at the seaside*

J'ai mangé des moules mais sans frites *I have eaten mussels but without chips*

Nous avons visité le phare *We have visited the lighthouse*

How to form the perfect tense
▶ *The perfect tense is formed with* **avoir** *or* être *in the present tense + another verb:* **j'ai choisi** I chose.

Avoir and être are called auxiliary verbs when they are used in this way. The verb which indicates the event or action which has been completed is in a form called a past participle. When Jean-Paul discovers that he has won the jackpot he says: J'ai **gagné** le gros lot. **Gagné** is the past participle of the verb **gagner** *to win*.

In this unit you will learn how to recognize and use the perfect tense with **avoir** which is the auxiliary verb used with the vast majority of verbs.

Verbs which end with **-er** and those which end with **-ir** are very easy to use:

All verbs ending with **-er** in their basic form (infinitive) have a past participle ending with **-é**.

All verbs ending with **-ir** have a past participle ending with **-i**.

visiter → visit**é**	finir → fin**i**
passer → pass**é**	choisir → chois**i**
gagner → gagn**é**	servir → serv**i**
aller → all**é** (though **aller** is used with **être**)	

Exercise 2 **Encore des phrases**

Once again columns B and D have moved. Can you find six correct sentences in the box below and say what they mean?

A	B	C	D
1 J'	avons	écouté	des moules-frites
2 Tu	ont	fini	les infos à la radio
3 On	avez	mangé	vos cartes postales
4 Nous	a	choisi	ton travail
5 Vous	ai	posté	une cabine
6 Sarah et Dominique	as	réservé	un hôtel pas trop cher

> **Insight: Un peu de couleur locale** *(A bit of local colour)*
>
> **Le Pays Bigouden est une partie du Finistère dans la région de Pont-L'Abbé. Il reste encore quelques vieilles Bigoudènes qui portent la coiffe qui fait partie du costume traditionnel. Ce costume est porté par des jeunes femmes à l'occasion des Fêtes de Cornouaille de Quimper (mi-juillet) ou du Festival Inter-Celtiques de Lorient, la première semaine d'août chaque année:** www.lepaysbigouden.com
>
> *In the Pays Bigouden (Finistère, Pont-L'Abbé region) there are still some old ladies who wear the lace head-dress which is part of the traditional costume. Young women wear it during summer festivals.*

2 Au Café de la Baie
At the Bay Café

◀ CD1, TR 58

Sarah et Dominique sont à la terrasse d'un café.

Listen to the recording once and answer these
questions:

  a *When the two women order their drinks
do they both order the same thing?*
  b *Does Sarah order anything else?*
  c *Does Dominique sound very
enthusiastic about it?*

Listen again.

  d *Who asks for the bill?*
  e *Who is going to pay? Why?*

Listen for a third time.

  f *How much is the bill? Do they leave a tip?*

Now read the dialogue.

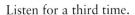

Serveur	Bonjour mesdames, qu'est ce que je vous sers?
Sarah	Alors pour moi une bière pression...et toi Dominique?
Dominique	Euh … je conduis alors je vais prendre un panaché.
Serveur	Alors une bière pression et un panaché.
Sarah	Et nous allons prendre des glaces aussi?
Serveur	Tout de suite madame, je vous apporte la carte.
Quelques minutes plus tard	
Sarah	Tu prends une glace Dominique?
Dominique	Non, je suis au régime!

Sarah	Eh bien prends un sorbet; il y a moins de calories.
Serveur	Vous avez choisi?
Sarah	Oui, alors une glace à la fraise et un sorbet au citron. Et l'addition s'il vous plaît.
Un peu plus tard	
Dominique	C'est moi qui paie cette fois-ci, toi tu as payé la dernière fois! C'est combien l'addition?
Sarah	Ça fait neuf euros cinquante.
Dominique	Dix avec le pourboire.

une bière *a beer*
un panaché *a shandy*
une glace *an icecream*
l'addition *the bill*
le pourboire *the tip*
conduire *to drive*
quelques minutes *a few minutes*
plus tard *later*
être au régime *to be on a diet*
cette fois-ci *this time*
tout de suite *right away*
apporter *to bring*

Now read the dialogue and find the French equivalent for the following sentences:

g *I'll bring you the menu.*
h *Have a sorbet; it's got fewer calories.*
i *A strawberry ice cream and a lemon sorbet.*
j *You paid last time.*
k *a few minutes later*
l *a short while later*

There are also two examples of the perfect tense in the dialogue. Can you find them and say what they mean? Now find the verbs in the present and the immediate future.

This tongue twister contains two verbs in the past historic, a written formal and literary equivalent of the perfect tense. It's about the goddess Dido who was said to have dined off the fat backs of ten fat turkeys!

Didon dîna dit-on du dos dodu de dix dodus dindons.

Un peu de grammaire
A bit of grammar

C'EST MOI QUI PAIE CETTE FOIS-CI. *IT'S ME WHO IS PAYING THIS TIME.*

In the dialogue, Dominique could have said **Je paie cette fois** *I am paying this time* but for emphasis she said **C'est moi qui paie.** In English we would probably use our voice for emphasis, stressing *I'm paying*.

Moi and other pronouns used in conversation to emphasize what is being said can be referred to as emphatic pronouns. In some cases (**elle, nous, vous, elles**) they are the same as subject pronouns, but the masculine singular pronoun is **lui** and the masculine plural pronoun is **eux**:

C'est *toi* qui as gagné?	*Is it **you** that won?*
C'est *lui* qui a choisi pas moi!	*He's the one that chose not **me**!*
C'est *elle* qui conduit!	***She's** driving!*
C'est *nous* qui avons visité la Corse.	***We're** the ones who've visited Corsica!*
Ce sont *elles* qui ont passé l'été en Bretagne.	***They're** the ones who spent the summer in Britanny! (fem. pl.)*
C'est *vous* qui habitez à Marseille?	*Is it **you** that lives in Marseille?*
Ce sont *eux* qui arriveront les premiers.	*It's **them** who arrived first. (masc. pl.)*

There are some regulations about the price of drinks in France. These are guidelines and there are discrepancies between various places. Prices of drinks in cafés and restaurants are not in any way comparable with the price of drinks you buy in a supermarket or any other shop.

When you ask for **une bière pression** you can expect a 25 cl glass of draft lager. Labelled beers in bottles are more expensive. For English people tempted to ask for a pint of beer, there is obviously not such a concept in France so the best thing is to ask for **une grande bière** which means that you will probably get half a litre of beer.

3 Au restaurant
At the restaurant

◆》 **CD1, TR 59**

Didier et Véronique Morin et leurs deux enfants, Armelle et Fabien, passent la nuit à l'Hôtel des Voyageurs. Ils ont décidé de dîner au restaurant de l'hôtel.

Listen once to the recording, then answer the questions.

   a *What seating arrangement does the waitress offer the family?*
   b *Do they wish to have an aperitif?*

Listen to the recording again.

   c *Apart from fixed price menus, what kind of menu do they ask for?*
   d *Would they like to see the wine list?*

Listen once more.

e *Véro asked for a 10 € menu. Why does the waitress say that she cannot serve it?*
f *What do they order?*

Now read the dialogue.

Serveuse	Bonsoir Monsieur-dame. J'ai une table pour quatre près de la fenêtre, est-ce que cela vous convient?
Didier	Oui, très bien.
Serveuse	Vous désirez prendre un apéritif?
Didier	Non non, apportez-nous le menu s'il vous plaît.
Serveuse	Vous voulez le menu à la carte?
Didier	Non, nous prendrons des menus à prix fixes. Vous avez un menu pour enfants?
Serveuse	Oui monsieur. Je vous apporte la carte des vins?
Véro	Oui merci.
Quelques minutes plus tard	
Serveuse	Monsieur-dame vous avez choisi?
Véro	Alors nous allons prendre un menu à 10 €, un menu à 20 €, deux menus pour enfants et une bouteille de Muscadet s'il vous plaît.
Serveuse	Je suis désolée madame mais le menu à 10 € est pour midi seulement.
Véro	Pas de problème, nous prendrons deux menus à 20 €.

la fenêtre *the window*
convener *to suit*
une bouteille *a bottle*
je suis désolée *I am sorry*
cela vous convient? *does it suit you?*

Exercise 3 **Bon appétit!**

🔊 **CD1, TR 60**

Look at the four menus which follow and listen to the recording. You have to enter in the table below what Luc and Florence have ordered. You may have to listen to the recording several times.

The last row is for you. There are gaps on the recording for you to respond to the waitress with your order from the 25 € menu.

	Menus (prix)	First course	Second	Cheese	Dessert
Luc					
Florence					
Vous	25 €	6 oysters served hot with seaweed	Grilled scallop kebab	Cheese	Strawberry ice cream

🔊 **CD1, TR 61**

MENU À 20€

ASSIETTE DE FRUITS DE MER
PLATE OF SEAFOOD
ou

COQUILLE SAINT JACQUES À LA BRETONNE
SCALLOPS 'À LA BRETONNE'

12 PALOURDES DES GLÉNANS FARCIES
12 STUFFED GLENAN CLAMS

BROCHETTE DE JOUE DE LOTTE À LA DIABLE
DEVIL MONKFISH KEBAB
ou

LE COQ AU VIN DU PATRON
COQ AU VIN SPECIAL
ou

CONTREFILET GRILLÉ MAÎTRE D'HÔTEL
GRILLED SIRLOIN STEAK MAÎTRE D'HÔTEL

SALADE DE SAISON

PLATEAU DE FROMAGES OU CHOIX DE DESSERTS
CHEESE PLATTER OR CHOICE OF DESSERTS

MENU À 25€

ASSIETTE DE FRUITS DE MER
PLATE OF SEAFOOD
ou

SALADE GOURMANDE AUX TROIS CANARDS
GOURMAND THREE DUCK SALAD
ou

6 HUITRES CHAUDES AU COCKTAIL D'ALGUES
6 OYSTERS SERVED HOT WITH SEAWEED COCKTAIL

BROCHETTE DE SAINT JACQUES AU BEURRE BLANC
GRILLED SCALLOP KEBAB IN BEURRE BLANC
ou

MAGRET DE CANARD AUX AIRELLES ET AU PORTO
MAGRET OF DUCK IN PORT AND BILBERRY
ou

CHÂTEAUBRIAND AUX CINQ POIVRES
STEAK CHÂTEAUBRIAND SEASONED WITH FIVE PEPPERS

PLATEAU DE FROMAGES
CHEESE PLATTER

CHOIX DE DESSERTS
CHOICE OF DESSERT

MENU À 35€

PLATEAU DE FRUITS DE MER
SEAFOOD PLATTER

BROCHETTE DE SAINT JACQUES GRILLÉE, BEURRE BLANC
GRILLED SCALLOP KEBAB IN WHITE BUTTER

ROGNONS DE VEAU BEAUGE AUX MORILLES
VEAL KIDNEYS IN CREAM AND MORREL SAUCE

PLATEAU DE FROMAGES
CHEESE PLATTER

FRAISES MELBA
STRAWBERRY MELBA

MENU À 45€

PLATEAU DE FRUITS DE MER
SEAFOOD PLATTER

HOMARD BRETON À NOTRE FAÇON
BRETON LOBSTER; CHEF'S SPECIAL

PLATEAU DE FROMAGES
CHEESE PLATTER

DESSERT
CHOICE OF DESSERT

Insight

Vous êtes végétarien / végétarienne? Le choix est encore limité mais on sert de plus en plus de très bonnes salades dans beaucoup de restaurants. *Are you vegetarian? Choice is still limited, but in many restaurants more and more very good salads are now served.*

When you get **l'addition** (*the bill*), check that service is included: **Vérifiez que le service est compris.** Restaurants have to indicate on their menus if the prices quoted include service (**prix nets**).

Vous aimez sortir au restaurant?
- Pour vos visites à Paris recherchez le restaurant de votre choix avec www.planresto.fr. Cliquez sur le chef et choisissez selon vos désirs: une envie (*a whim*), un budget, un lieu (*a place*), un nom.
- Pour choisir un bon vin www.cuisineetvinsdefrance.com est le site internet d'un magazine qui suggère le vin idéal pour toutes circonstances.

Web extension exercise
Le scénario

Vous êtes de passage à Paris. Vous avez invité un ami à manger au restaurant à midi, près de votre hôtel, dans le quatrième arrondissement, code postal 75004 (4th district of Paris). Votre budget est limité à 40 € maximum, pour vous deux. Vous visitez le site www.planresto.fr. Sélectionnez votre budget: **Indifférent? Prix le midi? Prix le soir?** C'est l'été, il fait chaud; à Paris, c'est la canicule. Vous sélectionnez un service supplémentaire pour pouvoir manger confortablement. Alors, vous choisissez un restaurant avec l'air conditionné ou bien avec terrasse?

C'est possible pour 40 €. Vrai ou Faux?

TEST YOURSELF

Une carte postale de la Martinique

As an introduction to the use of the perfect tense, all you need to do in this exercise is to identify the ten verbs in the perfect tense with **avoir**. You might also try to pick out a few verbs in the present and in the future. You need to know the following:

apprendre *to know*

prêter *to lend*

lire *to read*

écrire *to write*

Chère Sarah,

Je n'ai pas trouvé une seule minute pour t'écrire depuis mon arrivée ici il y a trois semaines. Mon amie Josiane a pris des vacances pour me faire visiter son île et nous avons fait des choses fantastiques. Elle m'a présentée à toute sa famille, j'ai goûté à la délicieuse cuisine locale, j'ai appris à surfer, j'ai nagé pendant des heures, nous avons fait des balades en mer et je n'ai pas lu une seule ligne du livre que tu m'as prêté. Je le lirai dans l'avion de retour.

Bon, je finis cette carte car mon avion part dans quelques heures. Je te verrai sans doute dimanche.

Bisous et à bientôt

Claire

13

Sur la route

On the road

In this unit you will learn
- *about French roads and driving in France*
- *useful expressions to use in a service station*
- *some vocabulary*
- *pronouns* y *and* en

1 Le coffre	6 Les phares
2 Le pneu	7 Le moteur
3 La portière	8 Le pare-brise
4 La roue avant	9 Le volant
5 Le parechoc	

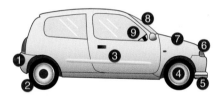

La voiture de Dominique

1 Il y a une déviation
There is a diversion

◆) **CD1, TR 62**

Sarah et Dominique sont en route pour St Nazaire où habite Dominique. Elles sont sur la RN (route nationale) 175. C'est Sarah qui conduit.

> ## TRAVAUX SUR RN 175
> ## ROUTE BARRÉE À 500M
> ## RALENTISSEZ!

Listen to the recording once, and answer these questions:

a *What's happening on the road?*
b *What is the speed limit?*

Listen again:

c *Where are they going to stop next?*
d *Is the place they are stopping at on the left or on the right?*

Now read the dialogue:

Dominique	Ah zut alors! Tu as vu le panneau? La route est barrée à cinq cents mètres.
Sarah	Oui il y a une déviation.
Dominique	Il faut passer par Auray. Ralentis un peu. Sarah, regarde le panneau: 'Travaux'. La vitesse limite est de cinquante kilomètres à l'heure. En plus il y a souvent des gendarmes sur cette route!
Sarah	De toute façon il faut qu'on s'arrête à la prochaine station service parce qu'il n'y a presque plus d'essence.

> **Dominique** Tiens, il y en a une sur la droite, ici, tout de suite. On devrait aussi vérifier le niveau d'huile et la pression des pneus tant que nous y sommes. Prends la première pompe, là, 'sans plomb'.
> **Sarah** On fait le plein?
> **Dominique** Oui il vaut mieux.

Zut! *Drat! (mild expletive)*
en plus *what's more*
de toute façon *in any case*
tout de suite *right here (immediately)*
il vaut mieux *we'd better*
il faut… *we must…*
il faut qu'on… *it's necessary that we …*
il n'y a presque plus de … *there is hardly any …*

QUICK VOCAB

Insight

La limitation de vitesse sur les routes françaises *(French speed limits)*
Cinquante kilomètres/heure dans les villes sauf si une autre limitation est indiquée. *50 kph in towns except if some other limit is shown.*
Soixante-dix ou quatre-vingt-dix km/h sur les autres routes (selon les indications). *70 or 90 kph on other roads (according to signage).*
Cent dix km/h sur les routes nationales à quatre voies. *110 kph on dual carriageways.*
Cent trente km/h sur les autoroutes sauf s'il pleut. *130 kph on motorways except in rain.*

Link the following English phrases to the equivalent French expressions:

1 There is a diversion.

2 Did you see the road sign?

3 The road is closed in 500 metres.

4 The speed limit is 50km/h.

5 We'll have to stop.

6 We ought to check the tyre pressure.

7 Shall we fill up?

8 Slow down a bit, Sarah!

a On devrait vérifier la pression des pneus.

b La vitesse limite est 50km à l'heure.

c On fait le plein?

d Ralentis un peu, Sarah!

e Il y a une déviation.

f Il va falloir s'arrêter.

g La route est barrée à 500 mètres.

h Tu as vu le panneau?

Un peu de grammaire
A bit of grammar

IL FAUT / IL FAUT QUE

The verb **falloir** *to be necessary* is only ever used in an impersonal form with subject pronoun **il: il faut.**

▶ Il faut + *verb in the infinitive:*
  Il faut conduire à droite.   *You must drive on the right.*
  Il faut se reposer souvent   *You must rest often when*
    quand on conduit sur de   *driving long distances.*
    grandes distances.

▶ Il faut que + *verb in a present form. As the second verb must be in the present subjunctive (see Unit 18) it is best to avoid this structure and use* **il faut** + *infinitive. However, for* -**er** *verbs the singular present subjunctive looks like the present tense you know:*

| **Il faut qu'on s'arrête à la prochaine station service.** | *We have to stop at the next petrol station.* |
| **Il faut que j'achète un litre d'huile.** | *I have to buy a litre of oil.* |

Insight

Using **il faut** + verb in the infinitive (*one needs to / must / should*):

Il faut manger pour vivre et non pas vivre pour manger. *One should eat to live, and not live to eat.*

In colloquial French, the **il** and the **il ne** are often dropped:

Faut pas jouer les riches quand on n'a pas le sou (Jacques Brel). *One mustn't play at being rich when one has no money.*

Faut pas faire ça! *Mustn't do that!*

Faut travailler! *Must work!*

NE ... PLUS / NE ... PAS / NE ... QUE

Il n'y a plus / il ne reste plus d'essence.	*There is no petrol left.*
Il n'y a presque plus d'essence.	*There is hardly any petrol left*
Il n'y a pas de station service sur cette route.	*There is no service station on this road.*
Il n'y a pas assez d'huile.	*There is not enough oil.*
Il n'y a que de l'essence super.	*There is only high-grade petrol.*
Il ne reste qu'un billet de vingt euros.	*There is only a 20 € note left.*

Reminder:

Use **ne** in front of a consonant and **n'** in front of a vowel.

PRONOUNS **Y** AND **EN**

▶ **Y** *(here / there) is used frequently in expressions like* **il y a** *(there is or there are):*

| **Tant que nous y sommes.** | *While we are about it. (Lit. here)* |

▶ **En** *is used with expressions of quantity and replaces a word already mentioned:*

Une station service? Il y en a *A service station? There is one*
  une sur la droite. *on the right.*
(en replaces **une station service**)

Il ne reste plus de bonbons, *There aren't any sweets left,*
  j'en achète? *shall I buy some?*
(en replaces **bonbons**)

▶ **Y** *and* **en** *are used in negative sentences:*
  – Il reste du pain? *Is there some bread left?*
  – Non, il n'y en a plus. *No, there isn't any (left).*
  – Tu as du lait? *Have you got some milk?*
  – Non, je n'en ai pas. *No, I haven't got any.*

Pronunciation

◀》 **CD1, TR 63**

▶ **Il n'y en a** *may seem difficult to pronounce but all the sounds roll into one [**ilniena**].*
  For **i** *your lips are straight but taut.*
▶ **Zut!** *Getting your* **u** *right is essential to sounding at all French. You may need to practise in front of a mirror in order to get the correct position for your lips, which should be tightly rounded, as though you are going to whistle. Now try to say* **ee** *– the result will be a French* **u***!*
  Try saying **i** *…* **u** *… i …u … i … u several times, alternately stretching your lips (***vos lèvres***) and then pursing them.*

> **Insight**
> When you've finished your 'lip exercises' try to repeat the following phrase several times:
> **Lulu lit la lettre lue à Lili.** *Lulu is reading the letter that was read to Lili.*

Exercise 1 **Il manque toujours quelque chose!** *There is always something missing!*
Link the first part of each sentence to the correct ending from the second column. You need to use all the information contained in the Grammar section, above.

1 Il n'y a plus d'essence, il faut
2 Il ne reste que cinquante euros, il faut
3 Je n'ai plus d'argent, il faut que
4 Il n'y a pas assez de café, il faut que
5 On n'a plus de fromage, il faut qu'
6 Il n'y a plus d'huile dans le moteur, il faut

a en remettre*.
b j'en achète.
c trouver une station service.
d je trouve du travail.
e trouver une banque.
f on en achète.

Note that there are two possible ways of ending sentences 1 and 6.

* **mettre** *to put* and **remettre** *to put more / again*

Exercise 2 **Qu'est ce qu'elles doivent faire?**
Look back at Dialogue 1. What is the third thing that Sarah and Dominique must do when they get to the petrol station?

1 *Faire le plein d'essence*
2 *Vérifier le niveau d'huile*
3 ...

Exercise 3 **À la station service**

◀》 **CD1, TR 64**

Choisissez la bonne pompe et le carburant qui convient à votre voiture.

Attention! Si vous avez un moteur diesel il faut mettre du gazole/diesel. La plupart des voitures modernes utilisent de l'essence sans plomb (*lead-free petrol*).

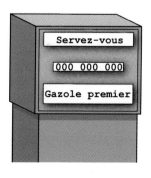

Listen to the recording and say which car each person is driving: **A**, **B** or **C**.

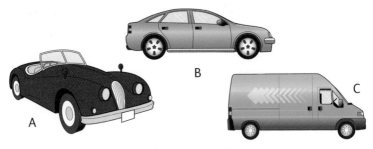

1 *La première personne conduit la voiture_____.*
2 *La deuxième personne conduit la voiture_____.*
3 *La troisième personne conduit la voiture_____.*

Filling up

essence *petrol*
essence super *leaded 4 star*
GPL (gaz de pétrole liquéfié) *liquid petroleum gas*
sans plomb *unleaded*
gazole *diesel*

Listen to the recording again.

4 *What do each of the three drivers ask for?*

Roulez à droite
The main thing not to forget if you are a British driver arriving in France is that you have to drive on the right-hand side. There are signs when coming out of the port or off the Shuttle.

ROULEZ À DROITE

CONDUISEZ À DROITE

> TOURISTES BRITANNIQUES
> N'OUBLIEZ PAS DE ROULER
> À DROITE!

> N'OUBLIEZ
> PAS!

La priorité à droite

There is one particular rule to remember on French roads. It is known as **priorité à droite** (*priority to the right*). It means that cars have to let vehicles coming from the right go first. This does not apply if you are on a **route prioritaire** (*a main road*). Smaller roads intersecting with the main ones have signs telling drivers to stop at the white line. It is important to check for signs indicating on which kind of road you are driving.

In small towns, street intersections often have **priorité à droite** and most drivers use their rights mercilessly. Many road accidents are due to this particular rule.

On some roads you are told if you do not have priority:

> ATTENTION!
> VOUS N'AVEZ PAS LA PRIORITÉ

Les routes

There are several kinds of roads in France:

A: Autoroute (a motorway; many motorways have a *toll*: **route à péage**)

E: Route Européenne (the same road as **A** but with a different number: the motorway from Dunkerque to Lille is the A 25 and also the E 42)

N: Route Nationale (e.g. the RN 175, equivalent to a British 'A' road)
D: Route départementale (maintained by the Département)
C: Route communale (municipal road maintained by the locality; not shown on 1/200 000 road maps.)

Opération Bison Futé is the code name for a police and national safety exercise which takes place any time there are major holidays (14 July and 15 August). Drivers are given advice via the radio and more police are out on the roads.

Exercise 4 **Quelle route?**

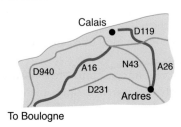

Look at the map of the North of France.

Find the numbers for the following roads:

a *The A road going from Boulogne towards Calais.*
b *The N road going from Calais towards Ardres.*
c *The D road from Boulogne to Calais via the coast.*

---

2 Les panneaux de la signalisation routière
Road signs

The following table from **La prévention routière** shows the four kinds of road signs which are used on French roads.

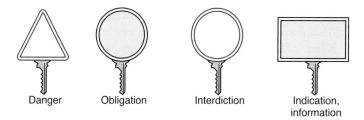

| Danger | Obligation | Interdiction | Indication, information |

La signalisation routière est une forme de langage très simple; elle peut être comprise par tous.

Il suffit d'en connaître **les clefs**

- La **FORME** permet de reconnaître facilement un panneau.
- La **COULEUR** précise la nature exacte du panneau: **ROUGE = interdiction, BLEU = obligation.**
- Un **SYMBOLE** facilement identifiable lui donne un sens précis.
- Enfin, une **BARRE OBLIQUE** sur un panneau signifiera toujours la fin d'une interdiction, d'une obligation ou d'une indication.

Ces quelques clefs suffisent à comprendre la signification de la plupart des panneaux routiers.

Les principales couleurs
blanc/blanche *white*
bleu/bleue *blue*
noir/noire *black*
vert/verte *green*
orange *orange*
rouge *red*
rose *pink*
Words for colours can be nouns or adjectives. As adjectives they change according to the gender (unless they end with an **-e**) and number of the noun they are linked to.
obligation *mandatory*
interdiction *strictly forbidden*

Maintenant vous comprenez les panneaux! Répondez aux questions.

a *What does it mean when there is a sign with an oblique line across?*

b *Which colour indicates that you have to do something?*

c *Which colour sign indicates that something is forbidden?*

d *Which colour and shape gives you some information?*

Un peu de lecture

In the checklist below tick only those sentences which reflect what is written in the two paragraphs accompanying these two road signs.

ZONES A VITESSE LIMITÉE

De nombreuses agglomérations ont vu la création de zones de circulation à vitesse limitée, dites 'Zones 30', à l'intérieur desquelles la vitesse des véhicules est réduite à 30 km/h. En l'absence de panneau, rappelez-vous qu'en agglomération, vous ne devez pas dépasser 50 km/h.

STATION DE GONFLAGE

Cette signalisation annonce une station de gonflage qui vous permettra de vérifier la pression de vos pneus (sans oublier la roue de secours!). Faites-le au moins une fois par mois et surtout avant un départ en vacances. Attention, la pression se vérifie sur un pneu froid ou ayant roulé moins de 15 km. En cas de mesure à chaud, il ne faut pas enlever de pression. N'oubliez pas que la profondeur des rainures ne doit pas être inférieure à 1,6 mm.

1 Don't forget to check the spare wheel. ❏

2 Most built-up areas do not have speed limit road signs. ❏

3 If there is no speed limit sign in a built-up area the maximum speed is 50 km per hour. ❏

4 Check your tyre pressure when your tyres are cold. ❏

5 Many built-up areas have ramps to slow down traffic. ❏

6 Check your tyre pressure before going on holidays. ❏

7 Check your tyres when you have driven less than 15 km. ❏

8 Ask someone to measure the grooves in your tyres. ❏

9 Check your tyres at least once a month. ❏

10 Many built-up areas have 30 km per hour speed limit signs. ❏

QUELS EMBOUTEILLAGES SUR LES ROUTES!

Un autocar

Des voitures

un camion

> When travelling in France during the summer it is important to remember two dates which can mean chaos on the roads – 14 July and 15 August. These are both bank holidays and people tend to take a few days off around them. For example if 14 July is on a Thursday most people are likely to take the Friday off. This practice is known as **faire le pont** *to do the bridge*. Special traffic measures are put in place to prevent accidents and excessive traffic jams at busy times (see **Opération Bison Futé**).

embouteillages *bottle necks*
bouchons *bottlenecks (Lit. corks)*

VOCAB

---

3 Les informations: un week-end meurtrier sur les routes *françaises*
The news: a murderous weekend on French roads

◄) **CD1, TR 64**

On the recording you will hear a news bulletin following a particularly bad weekend on French roads.

tué *killed*
meurtrier *murderous*
blessé *hurt*

VOCAB

You will need to listen to the recording several times in order to fill in the grid. Listen to all the news in the first place and then listen separately to each accident report.

Accidents	Type of vehicles involved in the accident	Place where accident occurred	Number of people killed	Number of people injured
1				
2				
3				

Once you have listened to the news you may read the article below, reporting one of the accidents mentioned on the radio. Use the information to help you fill in the grid.

FAITS DIVERS

Accident mortel sur la Route Nationale 10 Un camion sort d'un chemin privé devant un autocar bilan: 8 morts, 24 blessés

Comment l'accident s'est-il produit?
Un accident grave a fait huit morts et vingt-quatre blessés dans la nuit de mardi à mercredi, sur une section dangereuse de la Route Nationale 10 au sud de Bordeaux. Un autocar portugais a percuté un camion qui sortait d'un chemin privé devant l'autocar. Les deux chauffeurs portugais ont été tués. Le chauffeur du camion a été blessé.

Informations supplémentaires

If you are not used to driving in France, you need to be able to read these signs in order to drive safely.

Signs on other cars

Conduite accompagnée is the equivalent of a red learner's L, compulsory when people are learning to drive under supervision in a private car.

A red **A** at the back of a car indicates that the driver has passed the driving test less than two years ago. **A** stands for **apprentissage** *apprenticeship*.

And on the roads, especially on Routes Nationales and Autoroutes there is a constant dialogue between **La prévention routière** (*accident prevention department*) and drivers.

Insight: A new law for car registration plates

Les plaques d'immatriculation à vie depuis le 15 juin 2009: désormais tous les propriétaires de voitures auront une plaque avec un numéro pour la vie. On doit indiquer le numéro du département de son choix avec le logo de la région. La durée de vie d'une plaque est estimée à soixante-dix ans. Pour quelle raison? Pour un gain d'efficacité contre la fraude.

Number plates for life from 15 June 2009: from now on all car owners will have a car plate for life. You will have to show a department number of your own choosing with the logo of the region. The car plate is expected to last for 70 years. And why is this being done? As an anti-fraud measure.

Exercise 5 **Qu'est-ce que ça veut dire?**

Use the words in the vocabulary box to work out what the signs below mean.

un créneau de dépassement *overtaking lane*
le frein moteur *engine brake*
le pied *foot*
briser *to break (an object)*
la vie *life*

What do they mean?

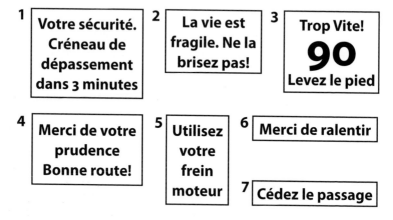

1 | Votre sécurité. Créneau de dépassement dans 3 minutes

2 | La vie est fragile. Ne la brisez pas!

3 | Trop Vite! **90** Levez le pied

4 | Merci de votre prudence Bonne route!

5 | Utilisez votre frein moteur

6 | Merci de ralentir

7 | Cédez le passage

Now match each of the signs above to its message below.

a You are going too fast! The speed limit is 90 kilometres per hour so be sensible, take your foot off the accelerator.
b You are not on a priority road so give way.
c Thank you for slowing down.
d Thank you for being careful. Have a good journey!
e You are going down a steep road. Use a low gear to slow down.
f Think about safety. Don't overtake now when in three minutes' time you can use the overtaking lane.
g Life is fragile. Don't break it!

Entraînez-vous sur le web

• http://www.code-route-facile.com leads to a driving test site where you can practise your knowledge of the French highway code: le Code de la Route. There are 20 topics and 7 slides for each topic.

• Consultez Bison Fûté www.bison-fute.equipementegouv.fr/ et vous voyagerez tranquille.

Web extension
Visitez le site des urgences
http://www.lesannuaires.com/numero-urgence-renseignements.html

Les numéros d'urgences en France

Pompiers – Incendies et urgences médicales	**18**
(fire brigade and medical emergencies)	
SAMU – Urgences médicales des grandes	**15**
agglomérations *(ambulance)*	
Police secours ou gendarmerie	**17**
Centre anti-poison	Paris: 01.40.37.04.04
SOS Médecin	0820.33.24.24 –
	Paris 01.47.07.77.77

En France, avec votre **téléphone mobile** faites le numéro **112 (cent douze)**. *112 will redirect you automatically to 15, 17 and 18.*

TEST YOURSELF

Practise responding in the negative in two steps. **Entraînez-vous!**
Examples:

Il y a du pain? Non, il n'y a pas de pain → **non, il n'y en a pas.**

Tu as du sucre? Non, je n'ai pas de sucre → **non, je n'en ai pas.**

Elle a acheté de l'essence? Non, elle n'a pas acheté d'essence →
elle n'en a pas acheté.

1 *Il y a une station service près d'ici?*
2 *Tu as acheté du lait?*
3 *Il a lu un livre?*
4 *Ils ont mangé des pommes?*
5 *Il y a du beurre dans le frigo?*
6 *Tu écris une lettre?*

Now you reply in the affirmative. Examples:

Il y a du chocolat? Oui, il y en a.

Tu veux des pommes? Oui, j'en veux.

7 *Il faut de l'huile?*
8 *Il y a du café?*

Now the question is in the negative and the answer in the
affirmative. Example:

Tu ne veux pas de chocolat? Si, j'en veux!

9 *Tu ne prends pas de lait dans ton café?*
10 *Il n'y a pas de vin?*

14

On cherche un appartement
Looking for a flat

In this unit you will learn
- *about housing in France*
- *about looking for a flat to rent*
- *how to enquire about a flat on the telephone*
- *more about pronouns*
- *adjectives ending with* -al

---

1 L'appartement de Dominique
Dominique's flat

◀) **CD2, TR 1**

Look at the plan of Dominique's flat on the next page and listen to the recording. Then answer these questions:

  a *On which floor is Dominique's flat?*
  b *Is there a lift?*
  c *Does she like her flat? Why or why not? (Give one reason)*

Listen again.

  d *Why is Dominique out of breath?*
  e *What does Sarah say is as good as aerobics?*

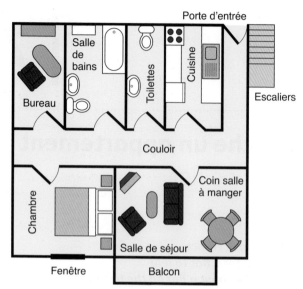

L'appartement de Dominique

Dominique Périer
5 Avenue de la Vieille Ville
St NAZAIRE 44600

Listen for a third time.

f *Who decorated Dominique's flat?*

g *What can they just about see when leaning out of the window?*

je te préviens *I am warning you* (**prévenir** *to warn*)
déménager *to move (house)*
louer *to rent*
les voisins *the neighbours*
à bout de souffle *breathless*
un copain *a friend/boyfriend*
une copine *a friend/girlfriend*
le tour du propriétaire *the tour of the property*
le propriétaire *the owner*
la propriété *the property*

Now read the dialogue.

Dominique	Je te préviens, mon appartement est au quatrième étage et il n'y a pas d'ascenseur dans l'immeuble.
Sarah	Tu devrais déménager alors!
Dominique	Non! Je l'adore, mon appartement! Je le loue pour presque rien, il y a une vue magnifique sur les anciens chantiers navals de St Nazaire, et puis mes voisins sont tranquilles. Ouf! Nous y sommes! Je suis à bout de souffle.
Sarah	Ne te plains pas, ma vieille! Monter et descendre les escaliers c'est aussi bien que de faire de l'aérobic, tu sais!
Dominique	Zut! Je ne trouve pas mes clefs. Ah si, les voilà!
Sarah	Oh là, là, quel bel appartement! C'est toi qui l'a décoré?
Dominique	Euh … oui, plus ou moins, avec l'aide de mon copain.
Sarah	Tu me fais visiter?
Dominique	Allons-y pour le tour du propriétaire: voici la salle de séjour avec le coin salle à manger, sans oublier le balcon. Ici c'est la cuisine et au bout du couloir il y a ma chambre, et mon bureau: tu vas dormir là, sur le canapé. Ici à gauche il y a la salle de bains et les toilettes.
Sarah	Il me plaît ton appartement. Bon, je m'installe!
Dominique	Tiens, ouvre la fenêtre. Viens voir, en se penchant on aperçoit la mer! Tu la vois?

Now link the following English phrases to the equivalent French expressions.

1 There is no lift in the building.   **a** Ouvre la fenêtre.
2 I rent it for next to nothing.   **b** la salle de séjour
3 going up and down stairs   **c** Ici c'est la cuisine.
4 with my friend's help   **d** Tu vas dormir sur le canapé.
5 the living room   **e** Je le loue pour presque rien.
6 Here is the kitchen.   **f** En se penchant on aperçoit la mer.

7 You are going to sleep on the sofa.   **g** monter et descendre les escaliers
8 When you lean out you can just about see the sea   **h** Il n'y a pas d'ascenseur dans l'immeuble.
9 Don't complain, old thing!   **i** Viens voir.
10 Open the window.   **j** Ne te plains pas, ma vieille.
11 Come and see.   **k** avec l'aide de mon copain

Insight

Using the verb **louer** *to rent / hire:*

Je loue une maison / un studio / une voiture. *I'm renting a house / studio / car.*

Depuis Noël j'habite chez mon copain et je loue mon appart à ma sœur. *Since Christmas I've been living with my friend and renting my flat to my sister.*

Location de voiture *Car rental*

Location saisonnière au mois ou à la semaine. *Seasonal accommodation by the month or week*

Appartement à louer *Flat to let*

Un peu de grammaire
A bit of grammar

LES PRONOMS: L'/LE/LA/LES

You already know these four pronouns, which are used to replace nouns.

In the dialogue above there are five examples of these pronouns. The first is:

Je l'adore mon appartement!   *I love (it) my flat!*

l' replaces **appartement**. This is an example where the pronoun is used first, in anticipation of the noun which comes next. It is used in spoken French to emphasize a point.

Remember that with pronouns and articles the **-e** is dropped in front of a vowel: **J'adore mon appart!** (**appart** is short for **appartement**). When the pronoun **le** is placed directly in front of the verb, the **-e** of **je** is reinstated and the **-e** of **le** is dropped instead: **je l'adore**. The same process applies with pronoun **la**.

À vous de les reconnaître *Your turn to recognize them*
  1 *Can you find the four other pronouns used in the dialogue above?*
  2 *Say which nouns they replace.*

LES PRONOMS: ME, TE, LUI, NOUS, VOUS, LEUR

At this point you need to be able to recognize these pronouns rather than use them yourself.

Tu me fais visiter?   *Can you show me round?*
Il me plaît ton appartement.   *I like it. Lit. It pleases me your flat.*

These pronouns are used in front of verbs. You have already met some of them in reflexive verbs but here their function is slightly different. They are used to target the recipient of an action, as for example **in faire visiter sa maison à quelqu'un** *to show one's home to somebody*:

Faire visiter à ...

tu *me* **fais visiter**	*you show **me** round*
je *te* **fais visiter**	*I show **you** (to one person, familiar)*
je *lui* **fais visiter**	*I show **him** or **her***
tu *nous* **fais visiter**	*you show **us***
je *vous* **fais visiter**	*I show **you** (to more than one person or one person you address formally)*
tu *leur* **fais visiter**	*you show **them***

A slightly different set of pronouns applies with a verb like **prévenir**. **Prévenir quelqu'un** means *to warn someone/to inform someone in advance of an event.*

If the verb is followed by **à** (**faire visiter à**) the above pronouns are used. However, if the verb is not followed by **à** (**prévenir**), **l', le, la, les** are used for *him, her, it, them.*

Compare the two examples:

Je préviens Sarah. *I warn Sarah.* **Je** *la* **préviens.**
Je fais visiter à Sarah. *I show Sarah round.* **Je** *lui* **fais visiter.**

Here are more examples of pronouns with **prévenir**:

Tu *me* **préviens s'il pleut, n'est-ce pas?**	*You'll let **me** know if it rains, won't you?*
Je *la* **préviens.**	*I am warning **her**.*
Je *le* **préviens.**	*I am warning **him**.*
Je préviens *mes parents* **de notre arrivée. Je** *les* **préviens.**	*I'm letting **my parents** know about our arrival. I'm letting **them** know.*

For more about these pronouns see the Grammar summary at the end of the book.

ADJECTIVES ENDING IN -AL

In the masculine form most adjectives ending in -**al** have a plural form ending in -**aux**:

un repas normal	*a normal meal*
des repas normaux	*normal meals*

In the feminine form all adjectives ending in -**al** take an -**e**, with a plural form ending in -**ales**:

une vie normale	*a normal life*
des vies normales	*normal lives*

But there are a few exceptions which you need to know about: in the dialogue above Dominique says that her flat has a fantastic view over the old shipyards:

Il y a une vue magnifique sur les anciens chantiers navals.

Naval is one of the extremely rare adjectives ending in -**al** which have a plural form with -**s**:

un chantier naval   **des chantiers navals**

> **Insight: Adjectives and nouns ending in** *-al*
> Usually adjectives ending in -**al** have the masculine plural ending -**aux**. But there are some exceptions:
> **un accident fatal - des accidents fatals** *fatal accident(s)*
> **un appartement glacial - des appartements glacials** *icy cold apartment(s)*
> **un incident banal - des incidents banals** *banal incident(s)*
> This happens with some nouns as well: **un bal - des bals** (*ball / dance*), **un carnaval - des carnavals**.

Pronunciation

WHEN **C** *BECOMES* **Ç**

The verb **apercevoir** (*to perceive/to catch a glimpse*) is one of the many verbs which changes **c** to **ç** in order to keep to an original [*s*] sound. This is necessary if the letter **c** is followed by **a/o/u** when it would normally have a [*k*] sound. To keep to the [*s*] sound the letter **c** becomes **ç**:

J'aperçois un ami là-bas.	*I can see a friend over there.*
Nous apercevons les montagnes.	*We can see the mountains.*
J'ai aperçu la Tour Eiffel.	*I spotted the Eiffel Tower.*

With other verbs this change does not always occur for the same part of the verb:

Nous commençons à apprendre l'anglais.	*We are beginning to learn English.*
Nous recevons des amis pour dîner.	*We are having friends for dinner.*
Il reçoit une récompense.	*He gets a reward.*

Exercise 1 **Comment déménager sans soucis**
Read the article opposite and the 20 questions on moving home:

Tick the correct answers only.

  a *Why are you moving?*
    1 *You are moving because you have got a new job.*
    2 *You are moving because your family needs more space.*
    3 *You have found the house of your dreams.*

  b *How are you going to manage it?*
    4 *It is simpler to do the lot yourself, with the help of your children.*

5 *Your friends can help.*
6 *You have to hire a van.*
7 *You have to make sandwiches for your friends.*
8 *You need lots of milk cartons.*
9 *You need to collect lots of cardboard boxes.*

COMMENT
déménager
SANS SOUCIS

Vous avez trouvé la maison de vos rêves! Votre petite famille aspire à un peu plus d'espace! Bref, vous devez déménager.

Pour déménager, la solution la plus simple reste de faire appel aux copains. On amasse les cartons, on loue une camionnette, on prépare des sandwichs et le tour est joué! Oui mais voilà, tout le monde n'a pas des amis disponibles. A fortiori quand on habite au dernier étage sans ascenseur ou quand le piano à queue pèse trois tonnes! Dans certaines situations, mieux vaut faire appel à des pros.

c *What problems are you likely to face?*
10 *You have no friends available for the task.*
11 *Your friends are a little bit careless.*
12 *Your friends are not strong enough.*
13 *Your front door is too narrow.*
14 *You live on the top floor.*
15 *Your washing machine weighs a ton.*
16 *You have a grand piano.*
17 *There is no lift.*

d *What should you do if in doubt?*
18 *Decide not to move.*
19 *Leave the piano in your old flat.*
20 *Call a professional removal firm.*

Insight

Using the verbs **déménager / emménager** (*moving out / moving in*) and **aménager** (*to organize*), and nouns related to them.

Nous emménageons demain *We're moving in tomorrow*
Il ne fait pas souvent le ménage. *He doesn't often do the housework.*
les travaux ménagers *domestic chores*
Je ménage la chèvre et le chou *I spare the goat and the cabbage*: old saying meaning trying to do one's best for both.
l'aménagement du temps scolaire *organization of the school day*

2 Où loger?
Where should I live?

◀) **CD2, TR 3**

Corinne is about to start her first year at university in Paris. She is looking for somewhere to live.

Listen to the recording once and answer these questions:

  a *Who is Corinne speaking to?*
  b *What did Corinne fail to get?*

Listen a second time.

  c *What does Corinne want to do?*
  d *She says that all she needs is a table, two chairs and a bed. How is she going to pay for it?*

Now read the dialogue.

Corinne	Allô Maman, c'est Corinne. Je téléphone pour te dire que je n'ai pas obtenu de chambre à la cité universitaire. Je crois que je vais chercher un studio à louer ou bien un appartement avec une ou deux copines.
Maman	Un studio! Mais c'est beaucoup trop cher! Et puis il faudrait le meubler!
Corinne	Bien sûr mais je vais travailler pendant les vacances pour acheter des meubles. J'ai besoin d'une table, deux chaises et un lit ou un sofa, c'est tout!
Maman	Non, il n'en est pas question! Alors tu m'écoutes: il serait beaucoup plus simple de prendre une chambre meublée chez des particuliers, dans une famille. Cherche dans les petites annonces dans le journal demain.
Corinne	OK! Je regarderai dans le journal, en cherchant bien j'arriverai à trouver un studio pas cher!

des meubles *furniture*
meubler *to furnish*
une chambre meublée *a furnished room*

VOCAB

Link the following English phrases to their French equivalent:

1 I am going to look for a studio to rent.

a Je vais travailler.

2 I need a table, two chairs and a bed.

b en cherchant bien

3 I am going to work.

c Je regarderai dans le journal.

4 It's out of the question.

d Je vais chercher un studio à louer.

5 I shall look in the newspaper.

e Il n'en est pas question.

6 by looking thoroughly

f J'ai besoin d'une table, deux chaises et un lit.

Un peu de grammaire
A bit of grammar

EN

You already know about the present participle of a verb: **-ant** in French is equivalent to *-ing* in English (see Unit 9).

When used with **en** *when/while* it is a verb form **le gérondif** referred to as a *gerund* in English:

En se penchant par la fenêtre on aperçoit la mer	*Leaning out of the window one can see the sea.*
en cherchant bien	*looking thoroughly*

But the gerund is not necessarily used in the English equivalent:

Ils sifflent en travaillant.	*They whistle while they work.*
Corinne fait ses devoirs en écoutant de la musique.	*Corinne does her homework whilst she listens to music.*

Insight

De la grammaire assommante en s'amusant! *Mind-numbing grammar while having fun!*
These little texts exemplify the use of the gerund (**forgeant** *working the forge*) and past participle (**chanté - dépourvue - venue** *sung - deprived - come*).
C'est en forgeant qu'on devient forgeron. *It is by working the forge that one becomes a blacksmith.* (Proverb)
La fourmi ayant chanté tout l'été se trouva bien dépourvue quand la bise fut venue. *The ant having sung all summer found itself deprived (of food) when the cold wind came.* (**La Fontaine**)

L'IMMOBILIER

If you are looking for a flat or a house to rent you can search for it in any newspaper under **annonces immobilières** or you can go to an estate agent, **une agence immobilière**. **L'immobilier** literally refers to what cannot be moved as opposed to **le mobilier**, another word for furniture.

There are three indicators to give you an idea of the size of places to rent or buy, whether it is a flat or a house (**une maison**): The letter **T** followed by a number indicates the number of people the place is designed to accommodate: **T1/T2/T3/T4/T5**. Some adverts indicate the number of rooms (**le nombre de pièces: 2P/3P** etc.). The number of rooms indicated includes all types of rooms except the kitchen and the bathroom. Finally there is always a figure ($25m^2$, $50m^2$, etc.) which relates to the measurements of the place in square metres and which will answer the question: **Il fait combien de mètres carrés?**

You also need to understand a vast number of abbreviations and vocabulary. The following list should help.

M°	métro *tube station* (this applies to Paris, Lyon and Marseille)
12è.	douzième arrondissement (Paris district number – 20 districts in all)
2è. étg/der. étg	deuxième étage/dernier étage
c.c./ch.comp	charges comprises *charges included*
sdb/wc	salle de bains/wc (*pronounced* les double v c *or* wouataires)
cuis.équip.	cuisine équipée
asc.	ascenseur
ch.perso.	chambre personnelle
10m² env.	10 m² environ *approximately*
ref.nf	refait neuf *newly decorated*
chauff.élec.	chauffage électrique
rép	répondeur automatique *answerphone*

3 Corinne cherche un studio à Paris
Corinne looks for a studio in Paris

Corinne a découpé des petites annonces dans des journaux. Elle n'a pas l'intention de prendre une chambre chez des particuliers. Elle cherche un petit appartement à partager avec une copine ou bien un petit studio pas cher. Elle a 450€ par mois pour payer son loyer.

Maisons & appartements

Particuliers
*46 € la parution
de 5 lignes
Tél.: 01.44.78.39.51*

Studios Location

a) 14è. M° PLAISANCE Studio
20m² Refait à neuf, 3è, étage
450 € ccJP2L01.43.35.15.40

---

b) ☐ 19è.CITE de la MUSIQUE
Studio meublé sympa
imm. très calme, pour 1 an
au moins, loyer 410 € cc.
Gilles 01.40.17.15.35

---

c) ☐ Paris 3è. Particulier loue
petit 2 P., 25m², wc, bains,
490 € cc. visite sur place lundi
1er septembre de 12h à 14h
4, RUE BLONDEL. 01.40.60.10.50

---

d) ☐ 18è.M° Marx-Dormoy
studio 18m², tbe. coin cuisine
s. de bains, 2è. et dern. étg.
clair, calme sur cour. Chauff.
élec. 350 € cc. 01.40.37.71.21

---

e) ☐ NATION - Studio 25m²
clair, calme, 1er. étg. sur cour,
salle de bains, wc, kitchenette,
480 € cc. Direct propriétaire
01.48.60.60.15

---

f) ☐ 20è. Pyrénées - Gd. studio
40m², 6è. étg. asc. beaucoup
de charme, poutres, ref. nf. cuis.
équip. vue dégagée, ds. imm.
PdT.620 € cc 01.43.61.49.37

---

g) ☐ 2è M° Strasbourg St-Denis
Studio 27m², séjour + vraie
cuis., sdb.libre le 1er octobre
460 € charges et chauffage
compris - 01.48.02.40.10

---

h) ☐ 3è. M° Fille du Calvaire
STUDIO MEUBLE
470 € ch. comprises
Tél.: 01.43.65.75.57

Partages

i) ☐ 20è. M° JOURDAIN
100m² Meublé sympa, sdb. +
chambre perso. 550 € cc.
Tél.: 01.43.65.80.15

---

j) ☐ 9e. Place Clichy Part. grd
appart. 120m2 Chbre. 400 € .
C.C. Tél.: 01.42.70.60.50

---

2 Pièces Location

k) ☐ M° LOUIS BLANC
2 Pièces 45m², cuisine équipée
nombreux rangements,
Libre tout de suite
Tél. 01.43.59.39.32

Look at the adverts Corinne has cut out from the newspaper and answer the following questions:

1 *How many studios, flat shares or small flats are within her price range?*

2 *Which ad is about a furnished studio flat for rent for at least a year?*

3 *Which ads should she call if she wants to move in immediately or no later than 1 October?*

4 *How much could she pay for a room in a flat share?*

5 *Which studio flat is on the 3rd floor and has recently been decorated?*

Insight: La cohabitation

En échange d'une chambre, l'objectif est de créer un lien entre des personnes seules ou âgées et de jeunes étudiants. Deux formules sont possibles: la formule « solidaire », une chambre gratuite en échange de la présence de l'étudiant; la formule « conviviale », une chambre pour environ 350€ par mois, sans engagement de présence.

The intention of this scheme is to create links between single or elderly people and young students. The student either agrees to provide companionship in exchange for a free room; or s/he pays around 350€/month without committing to provide companionship.

Exercise 2 **Un coup de telephone**
◀》 **CD2, TR 4**

You want to rent a studio flat in Paris. You have decided to phone about advert b opposite.

There are very few details about the studio so you need to ask a few questions.

The telephone conversation below is incomplete. The **propriétaire's** lines are in the correct place. Your lines have been jumbled up. You can find all your responses listed below the dialogue.

Propriétaire	Allô, j'écoute!
1 Vous	…
Propriétaire	Oui, c'est bien cela.
2 Vous	…
Propriétaire	C'est au sixième.
3 Vous	…
Propriétaire	Euh, non mais monter et descendre les escaliers est excellent pour la santé!
4 Vous	…
Propriétaire	Non, le chauffage est électrique.
5 Vous	…
Propriétaire	Oui il y a une cuisine moderne toute équipée.
6 Vous	…
Propriétaire	C'est bien cela. Vous pouvez visiter aujourd'hui?
7 Vous	…

a Il y a un ascenseur?
b Je viendrais cet après-midi si vous êtes disponible.
c C'est bien 400 € toutes charges comprises?
d Il y a une cuisine?
e J'ai vu une annonce pour un studio dans Libé. C'est bien ici?
f Il y a le chauffage central?
g C'est à quel étage?

Now listen to the whole dialogue and check your answers.

Surfez sur le web

Si vous voulez acheter ou louer une maison ou un appartement, vous pouvez visiter de nombreux sites sur le web.

- www.acheter-louer.fr
  Sur acheter-louer.fr, vous pouvez:
  Rechercher un **appartement** ou une **maison** neufs à la vente ou à la location (*renting*)
  Rechercher un **appartement** ou une **maison** rénovés à la vente ou à la location

> **Rechercher** tout type **d'appartements** ou de **maisons** à la
> **vente** ou à la **location**
> Pour rechercher un **appartement** ou une **maison**, venez
> visiter le portail immobilier acheter-louer.fr et **rechercher** en
> quelques secondes votre **appartement** ou votre **maison à**
> **vendre** ou à **louer**.
> Cliquez sur « les annonces », choisissez vos critères, regardez le
> diaporama.
> * www.maison.fr

Web extension exercise

Voici ce que vous offrent les agences immobilières (*estate agencies*). Vous
devez indiquer le type de bien (*type of property*) que vous cherchez,
le nombre de pièces (*number of rooms not including kitchen and
bathroom*) et le nombre de mètres carrés (*number of square metres*).
Imaginez que vous avez beaucoup d'argent. Amusez-vous bien!

Retrouvez nos annonces immobilières en location en France:

types de bien (types of property):

☐: Loft (penthouse) ☐: Garage ☐: Programme Neuf (new construction)

☐: Propriété ☐: Château Manoir ☐: Immeuble (block of flats)

☐: Parking ☐: Hôtel Particulier (town mansion) ☐: Haras (horse stables)

☐: Ferme ☐: Villa ☐: Habitation légère

☐: Autres ☐: Chalet

Infos prix et taille (price and size):

☐ Commerces (shop/commercial property)

Prix min (en €): [＿＿＿＿＿] Prix max (en €): [＿＿＿＿＿]

Pièces min: [＿＿＿＿＿] Surf. min (en m²): [＿＿＿＿＿]

Localisation (area):

Ville, cp: [＿＿＿＿＿] sur [＿＿＿＿▼] aux alentours (nearby)

Département: [＿＿＿＿＿] *(Essonne, 91)*

lancer la recherche

TEST YOURSELF

The object pronouns **le, la, l', les** look exactly like the definite articles but they have a different function:

Elle mange le gâteau d'anniversaire → Elle le mange.
J'emprunte ta voiture? → Non, tu ne l'empruntes pas! (emprunter = to borrow)
Je finis d'écrire mes cartes postales → Je finis de les écrire.
Je finis d'écrire ma lettre → Je finis de l'écrire.
Tu as compris le système? → Oui, je l'ai compris! / Non, je ne l'ai pas compris.

Over to you!

1 *Nous regardons la télé au lit* →

2 *Ils volent l'argent de la caisse (they steal the money from the cash desk)* →

3 *J'achète le journal au kiosque* →

4 *Il emmène sa fille en vacances de neige* →

5 *Je finis de lire mon livre* →

6 *Vous prendrez le petit déjeuner au lit? Oui, nous →; Non, nous* →

7 *J'ai fini le chocolat.* →

8 *Il n'a pas fini le ménage!* →

9 *Vous connaissez la route? Oui, nous →; Non, nous* →

15

Dans les grandes surfaces
At shopping centres

In this unit you will learn
- *about shopping in hypermarkets*
- *about buying clothes*
- *how to make comparisons, say something is better or worse*
- *how to find a bargain*
- *demonstrative pronouns:* **celui-ci, celui-là,** *etc.*

---

1 Rien dans le frigo
Nothing in the fridge

◀) **CD 2, TR 5**

Dominique has come home to an empty fridge. The two friends decide to go shopping. They go to one of the many out-of-town supermarkets.

Listen once to the recording, then answer these questions:

a *Name four items on Dominique's list.*
b *Who are the tins for?*
c *Who looks after him when Dominique is away?*

Listen again.

    d *Name three items on Sarah's list.*
    e *Who is the wine for?*

Listen for a third time.

    f *Dominique noticed that there were sales in the clothes and
       shoes department. What attracted their attention?*
    g *Do they buy anything?*
    h *Which colour suits Dominique best?*

Listen again for the last time.

    i *Which department do they go to?*

Dominique	Je n'ai plus rien dans le frigo. Il faut que j'achète de tout.
Sarah	N'oublie pas que tu as fait une liste ce matin.
Dominique	Ah oui, ma liste … je l'ai. Alors lait, fromage, yaourts, beurre, pain, poisson, fruits et légumes, liquide lave-vaisselle, sans oublier des boîtes pour Papaguéno!
Sarah	Pour qui?
Dominique	Papaguéno? C'est mon chat. Ma voisine s'en occupe quand je pars en voyage.
Sarah	Eh bien moi j'ai besoin de piles pour ma torche et puis d'une bonne bouteille de vin blanc pour boire avec le poisson et d'un gâteau de pâtisserie pour le dessert.
Dominique	Tu as vu, il y a des soldes de vêtements et de chaussures.
Sarah	J'aime beaucoup beaucoup ces chaussures - il n'y en a qu'une paire. C'est quelle pointure?
Dominique	C'est du trente-huit.
Sarah	Dommage, je chausse du trente-neuf!
Dominique	Regarde, il n'est pas mal ce pull! Et celui-ci est encore mieux!

> **Sarah** Oui mais j'ai vu meilleure qualité! Et puis le vert te va mieux que le bleu ... Ah non pas le rouge, c'est encore pire!
>
> **Dominique** Oh là là, tu es agaçante, tu as toujours raison! Allez viens, on va au rayon poissonnerie acheter du poisson. J'espère qu'ils ne vendent pas de poisson rouge sinon on ne mangera rien ce soir!

le frigo *short for* **réfrigérateur** *the fridge*
des boîtes *short for* **des boîtes de conserve** *tins*
une pellicule pour appareil photo *a film for a camera*
des vêtements et des chaussures *clothes and shoes*
le rayon poissonnerie *the fish counter*
un pull *short for* **un pullover**
la taille *size (for clothes)*
la pointure *size (for shoes)*
agaçante *annoying*
un poisson rouge *a goldfish*

Link the following English phrases to the equivalent French expressions.

1 I have nothing left in the fridge.	**a** Dommage, je chausse du trente-neuf.
2 washing-up liquid	**b** pour boire avec le poisson
3 My neighbour looks after him.	**c** Il y a des soldes.
4 to drink with the fish	**d** Le vert te va mieux que le bleu.
5 There are sales on.	**e** Je n'ai plus rien dans le frigo.
6 Pity, I take size 39.	**f** du liquide lave-vaisselle
7 Green suits you better than blue.	**g** sinon on ne mangera rien ce soir.
8 otherwise we won't eat anything tonight	**h** Ma voisine s'en occupe.

Dominique plaisante. At the end of the dialogue Dominique makes a joke which would be meaningless in translation. Why is it a joke in French and not in English?

On va à quel rayon pour nos provisions? Look at the map of the supermarket where Dominique and Sarah are now. Listen to the dialogue again and say which departments they go to (take their shopping lists into account). Tick the department numbers below.

1	2	3	4	5	6	7	8	9	10
11	12	13	14	15	16	17	18	19	20
21	22	23	24	25	26	27	28	29	30
31	32	33	34	35	36	37	38	39	40

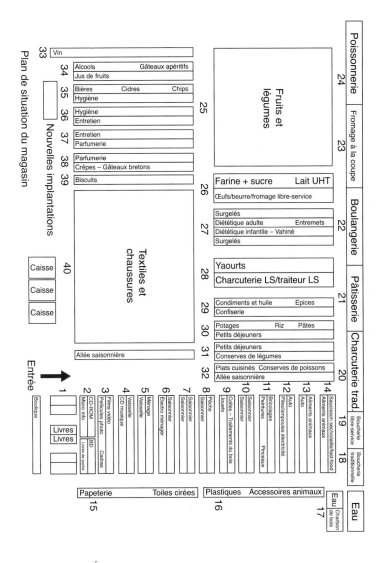

Plan de situation du magasin

Nouvelles implantations

33 Vin

34 Alcools · Gâteaux apéritifs
Jus de fruits

35 Bières · Cidres · Chips
Hygiène

36 Hygiène
Entretien

37 Entretien
Parfumerie

38 Parfumerie
Crêpes – Gâteaux bretons

39 Biscuits

40 Caisse · Caisse · Caisse

Textiles et chaussures

Allée saisonnière

Entrée →

Boutique

Livres
Livres

1
2 Micro info
CD-ROM
Livres de poche
3 Films vidéo
Pellicules photo
BD
Cadres
4 CD musique
5 Vaisselle
Ménage
Vaisselle
6 Electro ménager
7 Saisonnier
Saisonnier
8 Pêche
Saisonnier
9 Colles – Traitements du bois
Jouets
10 Saisonnier
Saisonnier
11 Bricolages
Peintures
Pinceaux
12 Auto
Piles/ampoules électricité
Auto
13 Aliments animaux
Aliments animaux
14 Saucisson sec/volaille/fast-food

Papeterie · Toiles cirées
15

Plastiques · Accessoires animaux
16

17 Eau de bois
Charbon
Eau

24 Poissonnerie

23 Fromage à la coupe

Fruits et légumes
25

24

Farine + sucre · Lait UHT
26 Œufs/beurre/fromage libre-service

27 Surgelés
Diététique adulte · Entremets
Diététique infantile – Vahiné
Surgelés

28 Yaourts
Charcuterie LS/traiteur LS

29 Condiments et huile · Epices
Confiserie

30 Potages · Riz · Pâtes
Petits déjeuners

31 Petits déjeuners
Conserves de légumes

32 Plats cuisinés · Conserves de poissons
Allée saisonnière

22 Boulangerie

21 Pâtisserie

20 Charcuterie trad.

19 Boucherie libre-service

18 Boucherie traditionnelle

Eau

Un peu de grammaire
A bit of grammar

EN

There is a further example of **en** in the dialogue:

C'est mon chat. Ma voisine s'en occupe.   *It's my cat. My neighbour looks after it.*

Here **en** replaces **de mon chat.** (**Ma voisine s'occupe de mon chat.**)

▶ **S'occuper de** *to mind/to look after/to take care of:*
Elle s'occupe de ma maison. Elle s'en occupe.

MAKING COMPARISONS

Plus/plus ... que
You have already met **plus ... que** *more ... than* and **moins ... que** *less ... than*: You can use **plus ... que** with almost all adjectives:

C'est plus cher qu'à Continent.   *It's more expensive than at Continent.*

Plus ... que can also be used with adverbs:

Tu marches plus vite que moi.   *You walk faster than me.*

Meilleur(e)(s)/mieux
Plus and **plus ... que** cannot be used with the adjectives **bon(s)/bonne(s)** *good;* **meilleur(e)(s)** *better* is used instead:

Les glaces à la fraise sont meilleures (que les glaces à la vanille).   *Strawberry ice creams are better (than vanilla ice creams).*

Le climat est meilleur dans le Midi de la France.   *The climate is better in the south of France.*

Meilleur can also be used as a superlative: the best!

Les vins français sont les meilleurs vins du monde.	*French wines are the best wines in the world.*
Les vins allemands, les vins italiens … sont bons aussi.	*German wines, Italian wines … are good too.*
Oui mais les français sont les meilleurs!	*Yes but French ones are the best!*
La championne olympique de natation c'est la meilleure nageuse du monde.	*The Olympic swimming champion is the best swimmer in the world.*

Plus and **plus … que** cannot be used with the adverb **bien** *good/ well*. **Mieux** *better* is used instead:

Le bleu te va bien.	*Blue suits you (Lit. Blue goes well with you.)*
Le vert te va mieux (que le rouge).	*Green suits you better (than red).*

Plus mauvais(e)(s) (pire) *and* **plus mal (pis)**
Although **plus** and **plus … que** can be used with the adjective **mauvais(e)(s)** *bad* and the adverb **mal** *badly*, you may come across their alternative forms: **pire** and **pis**. **Pis** is not commonly used in comparisons, but you will often hear the expression **Tant pis!** *Too bad!* (lit. So much the worse!)

Il est **mauvais** ce vin! Pouah!

Celui-ci est encore plus mauvais!	
Celui-ci est encore pire!	*This one is even worse!*
Marc conduit plus mal que son frère.	*Marc's driving is worse than his brother's.*

DEMONSTRATIVE PRONOUNS

You can use demonstrative pronouns when you need to refer to something which is present at the time of the conversation:

(masc.sing.)	**Celui-ci**	} this one	**Celui-là**	} that one
(fem.sing.)	**Celle-ci**		**Celle-là**	
(fem.pl.)	**Celles-ci**	} these ones	**Celles-là**	} those ones
(masc.pl.)	**Ceux-ci**		**Ceux-là**	

Exercise 1 **Trouvez les phrases correctes**
Choose the correct ending for each of the sentences below.

1	Ce poisson a l'air frais	**a**	mais celles-ci sont meilleures.
2	Cet artichaut est gros	**b**	mais celui-ci sent encore meilleur.
3	Ces pommes sont bonnes	**c**	mais celle-ci est meilleure.
4	Ce melon sent bon	**d**	mais ceux-ci sont meilleurs.
5	Ces gâteaux sont bons	**e**	mais celui-ci a l'air plus frais.
6	Cette bière est bonne	**f**	mais celui-ci est encore plus gros.

Les grandes surfaces

All French towns have out-of-town shopping centres with a vast range of supermarkets and hypermarkets (Auchan, Carrefour, Continent, Géant, Leclerc, etc.). They are generally referred to as **grandes surfaces** because of the large space they occupy. Some have up to thirty checkouts (**caisses**) and have a policy of employing young people on roller skates to help with customer service. Most of them are located in large shopping arcades, with a whole range of smaller shops, boutiques of all sorts and restaurants. In addition to the permanent shopping area, they frequently have seasonal products at competitive prices under a large marquee (**Sous Chapiteau**): wines in the autumn, chrysanthemums for All Saints Day on 1 November, oysters for Christmas and the New Year, bedding and furniture in the spring and camping equipment in the summer.

They all compete with one another by having promotional offers (**Promotions**), sales (**Soldes**), the bargains of the day (**Affaire du jour**), special offers (**Offres spéciales**). Once or twice in the year all the shops in an area all have sales on at the same time (**Grande braderie** or **Foire aux soldes**). They all advertise in the local press and have slogans like: **Guerre sur les prix** (*War on Prices*), **Prix fous** (*Crazy prices*) or **Prix défi** (*Price challenge*).

All **grandes surfaces** have **Un Point / Espace environnement** for recycling glass and plastic bottles.

Exercise 2 **Prix fous!**
Look at the adverts from local papers where local shops have
advertised their bargains.

A

PRIX FOUS ...

D

B

E

C

F

Answer these questions:

a *What is the bargain of the day at STOC?*
b *How long will it last?*
c *What day of the week is 3 August?*
d *Where and when in Auray is the Grande Braderie taking place?*
e *What is 'Monsieur Meuble' selling Sous Chapiteau? (Clue: first three letters of LITERIE)*
f *How much would one save at Brest Nautic?*
g *When does La Foire Aux Soldes end in Pont-L'Abbé?*
h *What is in the sales at 15 rue du Général de Gaulle?*

---

2 Au rayon charcuterie
At the delicatessen counter

◀) **CD2, TR 6**

Madame Rouzeau has a long list of delicatessen products she wants to buy: Bayonne ham, garlic sausage, farmhouse pâté, Greek mushrooms, scallops.

Listen to the dialogue as many times as necessary so you can identify everything on Madame Rouzeau's shopping list.

In the grid below fill in the quantity required for each item:

....

Bayonne ham
....

Garlic sausage
....

Farmhouse pâté
....

Greek mushrooms
....

Scallops
....

Now read the dialogue and check your answers.

Vendeuse	Soixante-quinze? C'est à qui le tour?
Madame R	C'est à moi. Mettez-moi six tranches de jambon de Bayonne s'il vous plaît.
Vendeuse	Ça vous va comme cela?
Mme R	Oui, c'est bien.
Vendeuse	Et avec ça?
Mme R	Alors il me faut douze tranches de saucisson à l'ail, ... deux cent cinquante grammes de pâté de campagne, ... deux cents grammes de champignons à la grecque, ... et quatre coquilles St Jacques.
Vendeuse	Et avec cela?
Mme R	Ça sera tout merci!
Vendeuse	Voilà Madame, bonne journée.

Dans les paniers de Madame Rouzeau il y a des fruits et des légumes frais. Look in Madame Rouzeau's baskets, and then try the wordsearch that follows.

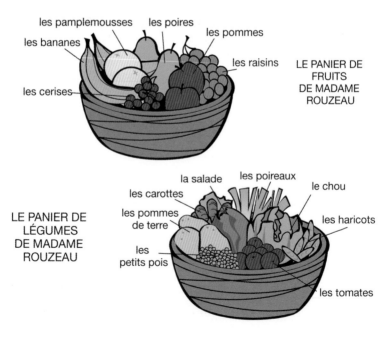

les pamplemousses les poires
les bananes   les pommes
                                     les raisins
les cerises   LE PANIER DE
                                         FRUITS
                                         DE MADAME
                                         ROUZEAU

LE PANIER DE   la salade   les poireaux   le chou
LÉGUMES   les carottes
DE MADAME   les pommes   les haricots
ROUZEAU   de terre
                      les
                      petits pois
                                                  les tomates

Find the names of fruit and vegetables hidden in the grid.

```
P  A  C  C  D  M  N  G  H  I  L  P  K
A  D  S  E  A  P  O  M  M  E  S  O  D
M  S  Q  R  D  S  A  T  E  E  G  M  H
P  E  T  I  T  S  P  O  I  S  K  M  K
L  R  G  S  F  T  Y  M  S  E  L  E  H
E  A  P  E  B  A  N  A  N  E  S  S  A
M  I  O  S  D  C  E  T  A  P  A  D  R
O  S  I  Z  A  H  R  E  T  O  L  E  I
U  I  R  C  V  O  B  S  M  I  A  T  C
S  N  E  R  H  U  S  G  D  R  D  E  O
S  C  A  R  O  T  T  E  S  E  E  R  T
E  T  U  Y  U  H  N  F  D  S  V  R  S
S  F  X  J  V  B  C  A  S  W  R  E  M
```

Insight

Colloquial expressions with fruit and vegetables:

Peach: **Il a la pêche en ce moment!** *He's in great form at the moment* (lit. 'He's got the peach…')

Cabbage: **Mon petit chou! Mon gros chou! Mon pauvre chou!** (terms of endearment); **le chouchou de la prof** *teacher's pet*

Pear: **Je suis bonne poire, moi!** *I am too good!* (lit. 'I'm a good pear!')

Apple: **Elle est tombée dans les pommes** *She fainted* (lit. 'She fell into the apples')

Mixed: **Quelle salade!** *What a mess!* (lit. 'What a salad!'); **Cinq fruits et légumes pour aujourd'hui!** *Five a day!*

Insight

In France chip and PIN cards (**les cartes à puces**) have been in use for many years. If you are paying with a debit or credit card you will be asked to insert your card in the machine. The following instructions will then appear on the screen.

Insérez votre carte → **Patientez** → **Composez votre code** → **Code bon** → **Retirez votre carte** *(remove your card)*

However in many places the directions will automatically appear in the language associated with your card.

Voulez-vous faire votre shopping sur le web? Alors visitez les sites suivants:

- Supermarchés Leclerc: http://fr.wikipedia.org/wiki/E.Leclerc
  Leclerc est une enseigne de supermarchés (*supermarket chain*) française. Elle regroupe des magasins indépendants respectant les exigences de l'organisation. Leclerc est le premier supermarché qui a eu l'idée de produire un sac pour la vie (*a bag for life*).
- Recherchez les faits et lisez un article de Wikipédia, l'encyclopédie libre, sur Leclerc et le sac plastique.
- www.supercasino.fr est un des plus grands hypermarchés français.

Web extension

Voici ce que vous pouvez lire dans l'article: le sac plastique ou sac de caisse est un sac offert, vendu ou prêté (*loaned*) par les **commerces** à leur **clients** pour faciliter le transport de leurs achats. Il est, à ce jour, composé essentiellement en **polyéthylène**.

▶ **1995**: *Leclerc arrête de distribuer des* **sacs plastiques** *jetables*

Maintenant visitez le site de supercasino et faites votre liste pour le petit déjeuner:

www.supercasino.fr → Vive la vie facile → Allons-y → liste de courses → choix de rayons → petit déjeuner

Petit déjeuner	
Café en grains	☐
Café soluble	☐
Pains suédois	☐
Thé	☐
Biscottes	☐
Café moulu (*ground coffee*)	☐
Céréales	☐
Chocolat en poudre	☐
Confitures (*jam*)	☐
Filtres à café	☐
Infusions	☐
Lait concentré	☐
Lait demi-écrémé (*semi-skimmed milk*)	☐
Lait écrémé	☐
Lait entier	☐
Miel (*honey*)	☐

Maintenant essayez la même chose avec les légumes frais, les boissons, les alcools etc...

Bonnes courses!

This one? That one? Which is the best? Is one better than the other?

Find the grammatically correct ending for each sentence:

1	Ce chocolat est plus sucré	a	plus gentille que son mari.
2	Ces pommes sont meilleures que celles-ci:	b	plus chères.
3	Madame Rouzeau est	c	mais je préfère la brune.
4	Ce vin n'est pas très bon…	d	ce sont les poires.
5	Cette femme est très belle…	e	que celle-là.
6	Pour moi, les meilleurs fruits	f	Oui, pas mal!
7	Celle-ci te plaît?	g	c'est le pire de tous.
8	Les baskets de ma sœur sont encore	h	mais celui-ci est encore pire.
9	Pouah! Alors celui-là	i	que celui-là.
10	Cette bière a meilleur goût	j	elles sont plus croquantes.

16

À la maison du peuple
At the community centre

In this unit you will learn
- *a little about multi-ethnic France*
- *about young people and out-of-school activities*
- *about tackling racism*
- *the perfect tense with* être

1 Je suis animateur
   I am a youth worker

🔊 **CD2, TR 7**

As planned Dominique and Sarah are on their way to Dominique's parents in Bordeaux but on the way they stop for one night at Dominique's boyfriend's house in Nantes.

Le copain de Dominique s'appelle Gildas Marrec. Il est Directeur de la Maison du Peuple dans un quartier populaire de Nantes.

Listen to the recording once, then answer the questions:

1 *Who is Djamel?*
   a *Gildas' brother* **b** *a colleague* **c** *a neighbour*
2 *Djamel works*
   a *with adults* **b** *in a college* **c** *with young people*
3 *What kind of activities does he supervise?*

Listen to the recording again.

4 *Where did Djamel and some young people travel to?*
5 *How long did they stay there?*
6 *How many young people and how many adults went on the journey?*

Listen for the last time to the recording.

7 *Where did some young people stay?*
8 *Who did they all meet?*

Now read the dialogue.

Gildas	Salut! Vous avez fait un bon voyage?
Dominique	Oui, très bien. Gildas je te présente Sarah.
Sarah	Enchantée!
Gildas	Enchanté! Dominique m'a beaucoup parlé de vous. Je vous présente Djamel, un collègue de travail. Djamel, Dominique, ma copine, et Sarah, une amie à elle.
Sarah	(*à Djamel*) Vous travaillez avec des jeunes aussi?
Djamel	Oui, je suis animateur, c'est-à-dire que j'encadre des jeunes dans de nombreuses activités en dehors du collège.
Sarah	Quel genre d'activités?
Djamel	Oh un peu de tout: du sport, de la photo, de la musique et même des voyages. Nous avons beaucoup de jeunes maghrébins dans le quartier. Ils n'ont pas grand'chose à faire, à part regarder la télé. Là on vient de rentrer d'un voyage au Maroc.
Gildas	Djamel est formidable avec les gamins.
Dominique	Combien sont allés au Maroc?
Djamel	Dix-huit et on était trois animateurs. On est resté trois semaines. Certains ont logé dans leurs familles.
Sarah	Ils ont rencontré des jeunes marocains?
Djamel	Oui, bien sûr. Ils ont tous fait énormément de découvertes.

un animateur (une animatrice) *someone organizing activities, youth worker (the full name for this profession is* **animateur socio-culturel**)
encadrer *to provide a framework for activities (* **un cadre***: a frame, support. In a work context it also means a manager)*
des jeunes maghrébins *young people with North African origins*
le quartier *the district / the area*

Insight: Possessive adjectives ('my', 'your', etc.)

Djamel est le frère d'Adidja: c'est son frère *(he is her brother)*
Sarah est la copine de Claire: c'est sa copine *(she is her friend)*
Sarah et Josiane sont les cousines de Sophie: ce sont ses cousines *(they are her cousins)*
Jean-Pierre et Jacques sont les cousins de Marie-Claire: Ce sont ses cousins *(they are her cousins)*

Link the following English phrases to the equivalent French expressions.

1 Dominique has told me lots of things about you

2 Do you work with young people too?

3 a bit of everything

4 There aren't many things for them to do.

5 Djamel is fantastic with kids.

6 We stayed three weeks.

7 Some stayed with their own family.

8 They met young Moroccans.

a Djamel est formidable avec les gamins.

b On est resté trois semaines.

c Ils ont rencontré des jeunes marocains.

d Certains sont restés avec leur famille.

e un peu de tout

f Vous travaillez avec des jeunes aussi?

g Ils n'ont pas grand'chose à faire.

h Dominique m'a beaucoup parlé de vous.

Un peu de grammaire
A bit of grammar

THE PERFECT TENSE WITH **ÊTRE**

Look back at Unit 12 where you met the perfect tense with **avoir**. Since then you have come across many examples of verbs which are formed with **avoir** in the perfect tense.

There are fewer verbs which form the perfect tense with être and they function slightly differently from those with **avoir**. They are closer to adjectives and in fact the past participle varies according to the gender and number of the subject in the same way that some adjectives do:

Elle est fatiguée (adjective)   *She is tired*

fatiguée ends with an -e for feminine because it is she who is tired.

Elle est allée (past participle) **en ville.**   *She went to town.*

allée also ends with -e because it is she who went.

The thirteen verbs with **être**

◀) **CD2, TR 8**

There are only thirteen frequently used verbs which form the perfect tense with être:

aller *to go*	**allé**	**naître** *to be born*	**né**
arriver *to arrive*	**arrivé**	**partir** *to leave*	**parti**
descendre *to go down*	**descendu**	**rester** *to stay*	**resté**
devenir *to become*	**devenu**	**sortir** *to go out*	**sorti**
entrer *to enter*	**entré**	**tomber** *to fall*	**tombé**
monter *to go up*	**monté**	**venir** *to come*	**venu**
mourir *to die*	**mort**		

Study carefully the examples below, paying particular attention to the spelling of the past participle:

- *Je suis **allée** à la banque. (a woman speaking)*
- *Tu es **arrivé** en retard ce matin, Pierre! (someone speaking to a young boy)*
- *Sophie est **devenue** très sage. (very well-behaved)*
- *Mathieu est **entré** à l'université.*
- *Nous sommes **descendus** de voiture (m.pl. – more than one man or a man and a woman)*
- *Nous sommes **entrées** à la Samaritaine (f.pl. – more than one woman speaking)*
- *Vous êtes **né** à Paris, Maurice? (addressing one male only)*
- *Vous êtes **partis** sans moi les garçons! (m.pl.)*
- *Ils sont **morts** dans un accident de voiture (Dodi and Princess Diana)*
- *Elles sont **venues** à pied (f.pl.) (They walked here.)*

*How to remember the verbs with **être***

The following story is a mnemonic device which you can use to remember easily most of these: It is the story of Henri, who was born in Marseille, went to Paris, went up the Eiffel Tower, went up to the second floor, stayed there half an hour, came down, came out, went to see la Seine, fell in it and died:

Henri est **né** à Marseille. À l'âge de trente ans il est **venu** à Paris. Il est **allé** à la Tour Eiffel. Il est **entré**. Il est **monté** jusqu'au deuxième étage. Il est **resté** là une demi-heure. Il est **descendu**. Il est **sorti**. Il est **allé** au bord de la Seine. Malheureusement il est **tombé** et il est **mort**.

You may write the story of Henri's twin sister, Henriette: **Henriette est née à Marseille...**

If you want to write a different version with Henri and Henriette both involved, its starts: **Henri et Henriette sont nés à Marseille** ... (One masculine + one feminine = masculine plural in French grammar rules.)

Reflexive verbs with **être**

In addition to these specific thirteen verbs, all reflexive verbs form the perfect tense with être. When they are not reflexive they form the perfect tense with **avoir**.

Exemples: couper *to cut,* past participle **coupé**

- ▶ *Caroline* **a coupé** *du pain avec un couteau. (perfect tense with* **avoir***) she cut the bread with a knife*
  BUT
- ▶ *Caroline* **s'est coupée** *avec un couteau. (perfect tense with* être*) She cut herself with a knife. (Reflexive verb has extra* -e *on past participle because Caroline is feminine.)*

Insight

Little words that sound the same but have very different meanings:

Caroline s'est coupée *Caroline cut herself* (verb **être** + past participle in the reflexive form)

Ces jeunes gens sont allés au Maroc *These young people went to Morocco*

Il ne sait pas où est son père *He doesn't know where his father is*

C'est difficile *It's difficult*

Exercise 1 **Faites six phrases correctes**
Find six correct sentences and say what they mean.

1 Djamel est l'animateur qui s'	**a** sont allés au Maroc.
2 Sarah et Dominique	**b** êtes parti avec un groupe de jeunes?
3 Je	**c** est occupé du voyage.
4 Les jeunes	**d** est resté trois semaines au Maroc.
5 Vous	**e** sont arrivées chez Gildas.
6 Le groupe	**f** suis monté(e) à la Tour Eiffel.

Exercise 2 **À votre tour de poser des questions**

◀) **CD2, TR 9**

It's your turn to ask questions – you are being told what to say.

You are speaking to Adidja, Djamel's friend, who is also an **animatrice socio-culturelle**.

a Vous	Ask her if she went to Morocco with the group.	
Adidja	Oui, j'y suis allée.	
b Vous	Ask her how many young people went to Morocco.	
Adidja	Dix-huit. Huit filles et dix garçons.	
c Vous	Ask her how long they stayed.	
Adidja	Nous sommes restés trois semaines.	
d Vous	Ask her if they met young Moroccans.	
Adidja	Oui beaucoup. C'était formidable.	

If you are satisfied with your questions you can now listen to the recording.

All French towns have places such as **centres socio-culturels, Maisons des Jeunes, Maisons du Peuple** or **Maisons de Quartier**. These centres are normally run by **la municipalité** (*the Council*) and do not only cater for young people. There are usually cultural and leisure activities for various groups of people at various times of the day. They can vary in terms of the facilities they offer but most of them have their own premises, sports halls, art rooms, games rooms, etc. They do not normally share buildings or facilities with schools. The role of the **animateur socio-culturel** is to provide a place for leisure and social purposes and also for education but clearly distinct from the school system. With French school children on a four-day week (see following 'Insight') now, the role of **animateurs socio-culturels** is vital although attendance at these centres is not compulsory. Part of the task includes tackling racism in a constructive way.

In the dialogue (at the beginning of this unit) Djamel refers **to jeunes maghrébins:** young people from the **Maghreb**, the area of North Africa which covers **la Tunisie, l'Algérie** and **le Maroc.** These countries were at one time French colonies. Most young people of Arabic origin were born in France but they live with a dual culture which is not always understood or accepted. Young Arabs are often pejoratively called **les beurs** or **les harkis** (born from North African parents – second generation people). In the 1980s young French people became aware of racial problems and under the leadership of a young black man called **Harlem Désir** started a movement called **SOS Racisme,** with a slogan 'Touche pas à mon pote!' (Don't touch my mate!) and an open hand as a symbol.

Insight

L'aménagement du temps scolaire *Organization of the school day* **Depuis la rentrée de septembre 2008 les élèves des écoles primaires doivent avoir 24 heures d'enseignement par semaines organisées à raison de 6 heures par jour les lundi, mardi, jeudi et vendredi.** *Since the beginning of the school year in September 2008 primary school children must have 24 hours of teaching a week: 6 hours daily on Mondays, Tuesdays, Thursdays and Fridays.*

---

2 Je suis né en France
I was born in France

◀) CD2, TR 10

Sarah continues the conversation with Djamel.

Listen to the recording and answer the questions.

  a *What question does Sarah ask Djamel?*
  b *Where was he born?*

c *Who did he go to Morocco with?*
d *How many times have they been there?*

Listen again.

e *Which language does Djamel speak at home?*
f *How many languages can he speak?*

Now read the dialogue.

Sarah	Et vous, c'est la première fois que vous êtes allé au Maroc?
Djamel	Non, non, je suis né en France mais avec mes parents et mes sœurs nous y sommes allés une dizaine de fois.
Sarah	Vous parlez l'arabe alors?
Djamel	Bien sûr, on parle l'arabe à la maison. Je pense que c'est enrichissant d'avoir une double culture. Je parle trois langues: le français, l'arabe et l'anglais. Je me sens ouvert et tolérant.

Insight: More on possessive adjectives ('my', 'your' etc.)
Djamel is speaking about his relatives:
Adidja, c'est ma sœur *(my sister)*
Gildas, c'est mon collègue *(my colleague)*
Je suis allé au Maroc plusieurs fois avec mes parents *(my parents)*

Exercise 3 **Un sondage d'opinion**
Lisez les résultats de l'enquête du *Nouvel Observateur*. Est-ce que la France mérite la réputation d'être le pays des droits de l'homme? *Does France deserve its reputation as the country of human rights?*

une enquête *an investigation*
étranger/étrangère *foreign*
des propos *remarks/utterances*
des comportements *attitudes*
accueil *welcome*

QUICK VOCAB

Now link the English phrases to the French expressions.

1 No opinion	**a** Tout à fait justifiée
2 Little justified	**b** Assez justifiée
3 Fully justified	**c** Ne se prononcent pas
4 Fairly justified	**d** Pas du tout justifiée
5 Not at all justified	**e** Peu justifiée

Exercise 4 **Combien de Français?**
Look at the results of the opinion poll (above) and answer the questions verbally only.

Reminder: **20% se dit 'vingt pour cent'**

Combien de Français d'origine étrangère:

    a *pensent que la réputation de la France est justifiée?*
    b *pensent que la réputation de la France n'est pas justifiée?*
    c *ont été victimes de racisme?*
    d *n'ont pas été victimes de racisme?*

Insight: Opinion polls

The French for 'opinion poll' is **sondages d'opinion,** from **une sonde** (*a probe*).

L'IFOP (l'Institut Français d'Opinion Publique) a été fondé en 1938, juste avant la deuxième guerre mondiale, pour sonder l'opinion des Français sur une question d'éducation.
The French Institute of Public Opinion was founded in 1938, just before the Second World War, to poll the French people's opinion about an educational matter.

Surfez sur le web

Trouvez des activités pour les jeunes.
- www.ufjt.org est le site de l'organisation Union des Foyers et des Services pour Jeunes Travailleurs
- http://fr.wikipedia.org/wiki/Lilian_Thuram

Web extension

Lisez le paragraphe ci-dessous sur le footballeur Lilian Thuram. Vous pourrez retrouver ce texte sur le site wikipédia http://fr.wikipedia.org/wiki/Lilian_Thuram.

Lilian Thuram (né le 1er janvier 1972 à Pointe-à-Pitre, Guadeloupe) est un **footballeur français,** qui évolue en défense. Au-delà de sa carrière sportive, il intervient dans la vie politique française, en particulier sur les questions d'intégration. Il est membre **du Haut conseil à l'intégration.**

Lilian Thuram, membre de l'équipe championne du monde de football en 1998, a surpris les médias le mardi 8 novembre 2005 par sa déclaration offensive*, 'Moi aussi j'ai grandi en banlieue'. Il a critiqué les propos de **Nicolas Sarkozy,** ministre de l'Intérieur à l'époque, en expliquant que ces jeunes ne sont pas des **racailles****: 'Avant de parler **d'insécurité,** il faut peut-être parler de **justice**

sociale.' Le ministre a plus tard répliqué, affirmant que 'Lilian Thuram ne vit plus en banlieue depuis longtemps'. Le 6 mai 2007 Nicolas Sarkozy a été élu Président de la République.

*confrontational **scum.

Répondez aux questions:

1 *Who is Lilian Thuram?*
2 *Where did he grow up?*
3 *Why was he critical of Nicolas Sarkozy's remarks?*
4 *What post did Sarkozy hold in November 2005?*
5 *What was his response to Thuram's statement?*

Postscript: **Lilian Thuram est maintenant à la retraite** (*has now retired*).

TEST YOURSELF

Une carte postale du Maroc

This time your task is to identify the seven examples of the perfect tense with **être** and any other verbs and tenses you recognize.

Salut Gildas,

Juste un petit mot pour te dire que tout va bien. Nous sommes arrivés à Marrakech samedi dernier. Les jeunes qui ont des contacts dans la région sont partis visiter leurs familles et sont restés quelques jours mais ils ont maintenant rejoint le groupe; tous sauf Yousef qui est parti chez sa sœur, et Nadima qui s'est installée chez sa tante. La tante est venue la chercher à l'aéroport et la ramènera quelques jours avant le départ.

Donc tout va bien. Pas d'incident à part Saïd qui s'est cassé la figure* en faisant l'idiot mais rien de grave heureusement. Je t'enverrai un mail la semaine prochaine.

A bientôt

Djamel

* **se casser la figure** (figurative) **to fall over** (lit. *to break one's face*)

17

On cherche du travail
Looking for work

In this unit you will learn
- *to talk about jobs and professions*
- *to look for jobs in the newspapers*
- *one more way to express the past: the imperfect tense to talk about unemployment*

1 Mon père était professeur
My father was a teacher

◀) **CD2, TR 11**

Dominique et Sarah sont arrivées chez les parents de Dominique, Monsieur et Madame Périer, à Pessac, une ville près de Bordeaux.

Listen once to the recording and answer these questions:

a *What does M. Périer think of Sarah's French?*
b *What does Dominique say about it?*
c *Who spoke French at home when Sarah was a child?*

Listen again.

d *What happened to Sarah's father?*
e *How long ago was that?*
f *How is Sarah's mother?*

Listen one more time.

g *Why does Mme Périer interrupt her husband?*
h *What is she going to show Sarah?*
i *How long ago did M. et Mme Périer retire?*

Now read the dialogue.

M. Périer	Mais vous parlez bien le français Sarah.
Dominique	Sarah est bilingue, Papa!
Sarah	C'est-à-dire que ma mère est française et elle m'a appris le français dès toute petite et le français était la première langue à la maison.
M. Périer	Ah bon! Et qu'est-ce qu'ils font vos parents?
Sarah	Mes parents étaient tous les deux professeurs de langues. Mon père était professeur d'allemand mais il est mort d'un cancer il y a cinq ans. Il parlait couramment le français et l'allemand.
Mme Périer	Je suis désolée. Votre maman va bien?
Sarah	Oui, oui, elle enseigne toujours le français dans une école à Londres.
M. Périer	Et vous, qu'est-ce que vous faites comme profession?
Sarah	Je suis éditrice dans une maison d'édition.
M.Périer	Ah, c'est un métier très intéressant! Dites-moi…
Mme Périer	Voyons François, tu vas fatiguer Sarah avec toutes tes questions. Je vais vous montrer votre chambre.
Un peu plus tard	
Sarah	Quelle belle maison! Qu'est-ce qu'ils font tes parents?
Dominique	Oh ils sont à la retraite depuis deux ans. Ma mère travaillait en tant que pharmacienne dans une grande pharmacie de Bordeaux et mon père était viticulteur.

Insight: More on possessive adjectives ('my', 'your' etc.)
'My': **mon père, ma mère, mes parents**
'Your': **votre / ton père, votre / ta mère, votre / tes parents**

apprendre *to learn but also to teach someone something*
dès *since*
dès que *as soon as*
enseigner *to teach (as a job)*
être à la retraite *to be retired*
couramment *fluently*
maison d'édition *publishing company*

QUICK VOCAB

In the grid below only the first row is completed correctly. Place the correct profession by each name and also its correct translation. Tick the names of those who are still working.

Noms	profession/métier	profession/job
Dominique	Prof de Philo	Philosophy teacher
Sarah	Professeur de français	Wine grower
Mme Périer	Viticulteur	French teacher
M. Périer	Editrice	Pharmacist
Mr. Burgess	Pharmacienne	German teacher
Mrs. Burgess	Professeur d'allemand	Editor

Un peu de grammaire
A bit of grammar

TALKING ABOUT PROFESSIONS

In Unit 3 you learnt that there is no indefinite article in front of the name of a profession. This applies with the following structure only: subject + **être** + name of profession:

Elle était pharmacienne.	*She used to be a pharmacist*
Elle est Ministre de l'Environnement.	*She is the Minister for the Environment.*
Il est ingénieur.	*He is an engineer.*
Je suis professeur d'allemand.	*I am a German teacher.*

But the definite article is required:

J'avais horreur de la prof de maths.	*I couldn't stand the maths teacher.*

APPRENDRE ET ENSEIGNER

- *Enseigner: to teach (e.g. in a school):*
  J'enseigne l'espagnol dans un lycée I teach Spanish in an upper secondary school.
- *Apprendre to learn:*
  J'apprends la musique. I am learning music.
- *Apprendre quelque chose à quelqu'un to teach someone something:*
  Mon professeur m'apprend à jouer du piano. My teacher teaches me to play the piano.
  Ma mère a appris à lire à tous ses enfants. My mother taught all her children to read.

ONE MORE WAY TO EXPRESS THE PAST: THE IMPERFECT TENSE

The various past tenses of verbs offer a range of nuances for what happened in the past. The perfect and the imperfect are often used in the same sentence to express when one event occurred in relation to another event.

How to form the imperfect
To form the imperfect tense you need to learn the following endings. They apply to all verbs without exception:

je	**-ais**	**nous**	**-ions**
tu	**-ais**	**vous**	**-iez**
il/elle	**-ait**	**ils/elles**	**-aient**

The four verbs below should provide you with a pattern for all other verbs in the imperfect.

Subject pronouns	être	parler	finir	prendre
je/j'	étais	parlais	finissais	prenais
tu	étais	parlais	finissais	prenais
il/elle/on	était	parlait	finissait	prenait
nous	étions	parlions	finissions	prenions
vous	étiez	parliez	finissiez	preniez
ils/elles	étaient	parlaient	finissaient	prenaient

When to use the imperfect tense:
1 When an action which was continuous or relatively lengthy is interrupted by a shorter one expressed by the perfect:

J'étais aux Etats-Unis quand **j'ai appris** la mort de mon père. *I was in the US when I learnt of my father's death.* (both events took place in the past but being in the US is longer than the few seconds it took to hear the news)

Nous sommes arrivées au moment où **il prenait** sa douche. *We arrived just as he was taking his shower.* (taking a shower is relatively longer than the action of arriving somewhere)

Les jeunes filles travaillaient au café quand **la bombe a explosé.** *The girls were working in the café when the bomb went off.*

2 When reminiscing, talking about and describing how things used to be and referring to events which occurred repeatedly in the past.

Quand **j'étais** petite **je passais** toutes mes vacances en France. *When I was little I used to spend all my holidays in France.*

Nous allions chez notre grand-mère en Provence. *We used to go to my grandmother in Provence.*

Nos grand-parents s'occupaient bien de nous. *Our grand-parents took good care of us.*

Nous travaillions dans les champs tous les étés. *We used to work in the fields every summer.*

Nous prenions le goûter tous les après-midi. **On mangeait** des confitures délicieuses. *We had tea every afternoon. We ate delicious jams.*

Exercise 1 **Qu'est-ce que vous faisiez quand vous étiez jeune?**
Answer with the verbs in the imperfect tense.

Start your answers with **Je/J'**:

a danser   **b** skier   **c** faire du basket

d aller à la pêche   **e** faire de la planche   **f** jouer du piano
                         à roulettes

Pronunciation

◀ **CD2, TR 12**

In Unit 14 you were given a few examples of verbs where **c** became **ç** in order to keep the same sound. A similar process takes place in the imperfect tense with verbs ending in **-cer** and verbs ending in **-ger**.

▶ **Commencer** *to begin:* **je commençais, elle commençait, ils commençaient**
   These are all pronounced the same way. With **nous commencions** *and* **vous commenciez** *the cedilla disappears again because it is not required:* **c** *followed by* **i** *sounds* [s].

▶ **Manger** *to eat,* **nager** *to swim*
   In order to keep the sound [je] *verbs ending with* **-ger** *keep the* **e** *after the* **g**:
   Je nageais, elle nageait, ils nageaient
   The **-e** *disappears with* **nous nagions** *and* **vous nagiez** *because* **g+i** *has a* [je] *sound.*

---

2 À l'A.N.P.E. (Agence Nationale Pour l'Emploi)

🔊 **CD2, TR 13**

Three unemployed young people are outside what is still referred to as l'A.N.P.E (pronounced by spelling out each of the letters of the acronym) but now officially renamed Pôle-emploi.

Listen to the recording once, then answer these questions:

   a *What kind of apprenticeship does Raphaël want to do?*
   b *What does Youssef say about his brother?*
   c *What does his brother do now?*

Listen again.

   d *According to Youssef what can't his brother do any longer?*
   e *At what time does he start work in the morning?*
   f *Where does Lætitia say she would like to work?*

Now read the dialogue.

Raphaël	Salut, vous venez avec moi?
Lætitia	Où ça? A l'A.N.P.E.? Qu'est-ce que tu vas faire?
Raphaël	Je voudrais des renseignements sur l'apprentissage.
Lætitia	Un apprentissage pour faire quoi?
Raphaël	Je ne sais pas moi, je vais demander ce qu'on peut faire.
Youssef	Mon frère Rashid, il était apprenti-boulanger.
Lætitia	Ah oui? Et maintenant qu'est-ce qu'il fait? Des croissants?
Raphaël	Arrête un moment Lætitia!
Youssef	Maintenant mon frère a un vrai boulot chez un boulanger. L'inconvénient, avant il aimait bien sortir en boîte et tout et maintenant il ne peut plus parce qu'il commence à travailler à cinq heures du matin.
Lætitia	Bon alors vous venez? On y va à l'A.N.P.E. mais pas pour devenir apprenti-boulanger! Moi j'aimerais bien travailler dans une pharmacie ou quelque chose comme ça. Alors tu viens Youssef, on va aider Raphaël à choisir son apprentissage.
Raphaël	Ah, non, elle me casse les pieds celle-là! Tu n'as qu'à en choisir un pour toi d'apprentissage!

Link the following English phrases to the equivalent French expressions:

1 Are you coming with me?

a Il commence à travailler à cinq heures du matin.

2 My brother used to be an apprentice.

b quelque chose comme ça

3 He starts work at five in the morning.

c Et maintenant qu'est-ce qu'il fait?

4 What does he do now?

d Vous venez avec moi?

5 something like that

e On va aider Raphaël à choisir.

6 We are going to help Raphaël choose.

f Mon frère était apprenti.

Pronunciation

◄》 **CD2, TR 14**

Because some words tend to be linked up together, you may frequently hear utterances which are not exactly grammatically correct but which are used in everyday conversation:

Tu n'as qu'à en choisir un pour toi!	*You'd better choose one. (Lit. You only have to choose one for yourself.)*

The structure is: **ne + avoir + que + à** but in everyday language the **ne** disappears, even in public talk by most eminent people (on TV, radio etc.).

This is high on the list of language used to give advice, for making suggestions in all sorts of circumstances but especially when people suggest what the government should be doing:

Ils n'ont qu'à... *all they need to do...* becomes **ils ont qu'à...** [*isonka*]
Tu n'as qu'à ... *all you need to do...* becomes **t'as qu'à...** [*taka*]
Il n'y a qu'à... *all that's needed...* becomes **y a qu'à...** [*yaka*]

You may even see YACKA used as the name of bars or cafés, places where people put the world right!

BAR - TABAC
LE YACKA

L'emploi

Le chômage, *unemployment*, is high in France. Between three to four million people are out of work (**au chômage**) and the trend is getting worse. **L'Agence Nationale pour l'Emploi**, the National Employment Agency which was created in 1967 has been replaced in 2008 by a multi-agency organization, Pôle Emploi, focusing on training and getting people back to work.

Le Contrat d'apprentissage (*apprenticeship*) has been revised, following the March 2006 demonstrations and the unrest created by government plans for new legislation on young people's work contracts (**Contrat Première Embauche** – *Contract for First Job*). The Government was forced to backtrack and came up with a more versatile plan for apprenticeship. This includes **L'Apprentissage Junior**, which can apply, under certain circumstances, to young people from the age of 14. The apprentice's salary is based on the Minimum Wage, **le SMIC** (**Salaire Minimum Interprofessionnel de Croissance** 8,71€ per hour) and various percentages apply according to age and number of years of contract. For example anyone under the age of 18 and in their first year of apprenticeship will get 25% of the minimum wage, 37% in their second year and 53% in their third and final year.

Insight: A brief introduction to the conditional

The endings are similar to the imperfect tense but the construction is similar to the future tense:

Mon grand-père travaillait à l'usine. (imperfect) *My grandfather worked at the factory.*

Après ses études ma sœur travaillera à Paris. (future) *After her studies my sister will work in Paris.*

Elle travaillerait si elle pouvait. (conditional) *She would work if she could.*

3 Le contrat d'apprentissage
The apprentice's contract

Read the excerpt from an
apprentice's contract and then
answer the questions. You are not
expected to understand every word
of the text.

1 *How old do you have to be to sign the contract?*
2 *How long is the apprenticeship for?*
3 *Can it be lengthened or shortened?*
4 *How long is the trial period?*
5 *What can happen during that time?*
6 *How many weeks' holiday does an apprentice have?*
7 *How much maternity leave does a young woman get?*
8 *How many days off do apprentices get:*
  a *to get married?*
  b *for the birth of a child?*
9 *What kind of course does the apprentice have to attend?*
10 *What proportion of the time has to be spent on a course?*

l'employeur *employer*
une période d'essai *trial period*
en fonction du métier *according to the job*
rompu *broken*
pendant laquelle *during which*
durée *duration*

LE CONTRAT D'APPRENTISSAGE

LE CONTENU DU CONTRAT

Le contrat d'apprentissage est un contrat de travail de type particulier qui permet au jeune d'acquérir une qualification professionnelle sanctionnée par un diplôme technologique ou professionnel, ou un titre homologué. Ce type de contrat associe une formation en entreprise et des enseignements dans un Centre de Formation d'Apprentis (CFA).

SIGNATAIRES Le contrat d'apprentissage est signé entre l'employeur, l'apprenti et le C.F.A. Il concerne tous les employeurs et tous les jeunes de 16 à moins de 26 ans.

DURÉE La durée d'un contrat d'apprentissage est en général de 2 ans. Elle peut être portée à 3 ans ou réduite à 1 an en fonction du métier, de la qualification préparée et du niveau initial de l'apprenti.

PÉRIODE D'ESSAI Les deux premiers mois constituent une période d'essai pendant laquelle le contrat peut être rompu.

CONGÉS ● L'apprenti bénéficie d'un congé annuel de 5 semaines.

● Au même titre que les autres salariées, l'apprentie peut bénéficier d'un congé maternité (6 semaines avant la date présumée de l'accouchement et 10 semaines après).

● Des congés pour événements familiaux sont également accordés, à savoir :
4 jours pour le mariage de l'apprenti,
3 jours pour sa présélection militaire,
3 jours pour la naissance de l'enfant de l'apprenti,
2 jours pour le décès du conjoint ou d'un enfant de l'apprenti,
1 jour pour le décès du père ou de la mère de l'apprenti.

TEMPS DE FORMATION Sur son temps de travail, le jeune suit une formation générale et technologique dans un centre de formation. La durée varie en fonction de la formation choisie (entre 1 à 2 semaines par mois).

Exercise 2 À l'A.N.P.E.

🔊 **CD2, TR 15**

(Since this exercise was recorded, l'A.N.P.E. has been replaced by the Pôle Emploi agency.)

You have decided to choose an apprenticeship. Tell the employee which category of work interests you.

Look at the list opposite, then listen to the recording to hear your questions.

Example:

Looking at the list, you think you are interested in the building trade:

Employé	Quel genre de métiers vous intéressent?
Vous	Je m'intéresse aux métiers du bâtiment.
a Employé	Quel genre de métiers vous intéresse?
Vous	*Say you are interested in the hotel industry.*
b Employé	Qu'est-ce qui vous intéresse?
Vous	*Say you are interested in photography.*
c Employé	Vous vous intéressez à quoi?
Vous	*Say you are interested in catering.*
d Employé	Quel genre de métiers vous intéresse?
Vous	*Say you are interested in jobs to do with health.*
e Employé	À quoi vous intéressez-vous?
Vous	*Say you are interested in the clothing industry.*

Métiers du bâtiment ....

Métiers de la chaudronnerie et de la métallerie ....

Métiers de bouche ....

Métiers de l'hôtellerie et de la restauration ....

Métiers de la santé et des soins personnels ....

Métiers de l'hygiène et de l'environnement ....

Métiers de l'habillement ....

Métiers de la photographie et des industries graphiques ....

Métiers du commerce et de la distribution ....

Métiers du secrétariat et de la comptabilité ....

Métiers du secteur agricole ....

Métiers de la pierre ....

Exercise 3 **Où chercher du travail?** *Where to look for work?*
Look at the adverts and answer questions a–h opposite.

http://www.liberation.com

PROFILS NET

Toutes les annonces
d'offres d'emploi
parues dans Libération depuis
quinze jours. Dès aujourd'hui
vous pouvez y répondre
instantanément en laissant votre CV.

OPPORTUNITES

Des *formations*,
des *voyages*, des *services*,
des *produits*

NOTRE OBJECTIF :

VOUS FORMER À L'INFORMATIQUE DE GESTION

Nous vous proposons une formation de 1200 heures à l'informatique, dans le cadre d'un contrat de qualification.

Dynamique, motivé, âgé de moins de 26 ans, vous êtes diplômé de mathématiques, physique, chimie, sciences économiques, gestion…, l'informatique vous intéresse et vous souhaitez en faire votre métier.

Alors n'hésitez plus, prenez contact avec nous, nous nous ferons un plaisir de vous présenter notre structure et nos projets de développement.

EMPLOIS OFFRES

COMMERCIAL VENTES

Sté LVG, vins de Bordeaux, recrute **2 VENDEURS** sur votre secteur, clientèle particuliers exclusivement, sur rendez-vous, profil, contact, convivialité, poste stable, débutants acceptés. Formation assurée. Tél. 02.99.55.74.74, pour rendez-vous, de 9 h à 17 h, sauf samedi.

EMPLOIS DU COMMERCE

Discothèque Finistère-Sud cherche **PORTIER.** Tél. 02.98.70.81.95.

METIERS DE BOUCHE

Recherche **PATISSIER** sérieux, sachant travailler seul, Pont-de-Buis. Tél. 02.98.73.00.77.

HOTELLERIE RESTAURATION

SERVEUSE, 2 ans expérience, recherche emploi **RESTAURATION** traditionnelle ou gastronomique, région Brest ou Quimper. Tél. 02.98.84.64.76.

APPRENTISSAGE

Recherche **APPRENTI(E) VENDEUR(SE)en charcuterie-traiteur.** Super U, Plestin-les-Grèves. Tél. 02.96.54.18.18.

GENS DE MAISON

LAVAL : recherche employée de maison, **temps plein,** logée, nourrie, pour s'occuper de deux enfants et entretien maison. Ecrire au Télégramme, 19, rue Jean-Macé, Brest, n° 12.787, qui transmettra.

Recherche DAME pour contrat temps plein, dans appartement **centre QUIMPER,** garde bébé, ménage, repassage. Tél. 02.98.95.28.58.

EMPLOIS DEMANDES

ADMINISTRATION COMPTABILITÉ

FEMME, 48 ans, avec expérience, cherche emploi temps partiel, **SECRÉTARIAT, COMPTABILITÉ ou COMMERCE,** secteur Quimperlé ou environs. Tél. 02.98.71.86.46.

TECHNIQUE PRODUCTION

ELECTRICIEN possédant CAP électroménager, bon bricoleur, expérience homme d'entretien, cherche **EMPLOI,** pour toutes propositions, tél. 02.98.96.45.18.

Sur internet

On the Internet, the national newspaper *Libération* has a site which you may wish to look up.

  a *What can you find on the Internet?*
  b *What if the advert is one week old, can you still find it?*
  c *How and when can you answer the job adverts?*

Dans les journaux locaux

  d *Can you name three jobs which are advertised in the local paper?*
  e *Can you give three types of jobs people are looking for?*
  f *If you wanted to be trained in information technology for management purposes how old would you have to be?*
  g *Which qualities would you have to demonstrate?*
  h *Which background would you need?*

Surfez sur le web

Surfez sur le web et trouvez un nouvel emploi.
- D'abord il vous faut un CV. Pour en savoir plus visitez: www.cvconseils.com

Si vous voulez trouver du travail, visitez les sites suivants:
- http://www.keljob.com
- http://www.cyber-emploi-centre.com
  Ouvrez le site, sur le troisième cadre, choisissez Echanges Européens → stages → Erasmus
- http://www.travail.gouv.fr et www.apprentissage.gouv.fr

Sur ce site vous pouvez aussi voir des vidéos.

TEST YOURSELF

Here are some words en vrac (*loose, in any order* – **when applied to food it is the opposite of packaged goods**):

> grand, chez, pâtissier, quand, les, pouvait, ma, toujours, incroyables, mais, était, mangeait, anniversaire, punir, fait, étais, jour, faim, racontait, énorme

You have to put them in the right places:

__ j'__ jeune __ grand'mère me __ des histoires __. Elle __ apprentie __ un __ pâtissier parisien et elle __ tous __ gâteaux qu'elle __ parce qu'elle avait __ très __. Un __ le __ l'a surprise __ au lieu de la __ il lui a __ un __ gâteau au chocolat pour son __.

18

On prend le TGV
Catching the high-speed train

In this unit you will learn
- *about travelling by rail, and how to buy a ticket*
- *all about la SNCF and le TGV*
- *more verbs in the imperfect tense*
- *the subjunctive*

---

1 Vous prenez le TGV?
Are you catching the TGV?

◆》 **CD2, TR 16, 1:36**

Sarah has spent a week visiting Bordeaux and Les Landes (vast pine forests south of Bordeaux). She is now planning to travel back to London via Paris.

Listen to the recording once through and answer these questions.

a *Why is Sarah leaving the Périers?*
b *Name two things which, according to Dominique, Sarah is starting to know well.*
c *What does Sarah think of the area?*

Listen again.

d *Where is Sarah going tomorrow?*
e *How is she getting there?*
f *How long will it take?*

Listen for a third time.

g *How long did it use to take to get to Paris when Monsieur Périer was a student?*
h *What could Sarah use the Minitel for?*

Listen one more time.

i *At what time is Sarah leaving tomorrow?*
j *Who is meeting Sarah on arrival?*

Now read the dialogue.

M. Périer	Alors Sarah, vous nous quittez déjà?
Dominique	C'est vrai, la semaine est passée très vite! Sarah commence à bien connaître Bordeaux et les Landes, les vins de la région...
Sarah	Oui, j'adore votre région mais il faut que je rentre à Londres, je reprends le travail lundi et j'ai promis à ma sœur de passer quelques jours chez elle à Paris.
M. Périer	Vous prenez le TGV?
Sarah	Oui, c'est très rapide.
Mme Périer	Ça prend combien de temps maintenant pour monter à Paris?
Sarah	Ça dépend des trains mais en choisissant bien c'est faisable en trois heures.
M. Périer	Incroyable! On n'arrête pas le progrès! Savez-vous que lorsque j'étais jeune j'étais étudiant à Paris alors je prenais souvent le train pour rentrer. Cela prenait douze heures, sinon plus!
Dominique	Eh oui le progrès! Au fait Sarah, tu as réservé ta place dans le TGV? Tu pourrais le faire par Minitel*.

Sarah	Non, je te remercie mais je préfère tout bonnement acheter mon billet à la gare. De toute façon on devait aller à Bordeaux cet après-midi, non?
Dominique	Oui bien sûr, c'est comme tu veux. À quelle heure tu pars demain?
Sarah	Je ne sais pas encore mais probablement entre quinze et seize heures: ma sœur viendra me chercher à Montparnasse après le travail, je pensais lui donner rendez-vous vers dix-neuf heures, dix-neuf heures quinze environ.

*Since this dialogue was recorded, Minitel has given way to the internet.

le TGV: Train à Grande Vitesse *high-speed train*
tout bonnement/tout simplement *very simply*
sinon plus *if not more*
la gare *the station*
lorsque *when*

QUICK VOCAB

Link the English phrases to the equivalent French expressions.

1 Well, then, Sarah, are you leaving us already?

2 Sarah is starting to know Bordeaux well.

3 I am going back to work on Monday.

4 Incredible! Progress never stops!

5 I used to be a student.

6 I often took the train to get home.

7 We were going to go to Bordeaux this afternoon, weren't we?

8 I thought I would arrange to meet her around 7 p.m.

a Je reprends le travail lundi.

b J'étais étudiant.

c Je prenais souvent le train pour rentrer.

d Alors Sarah, vous nous quittez déjà?

e Je pensais lui donner rendezvous vers 7h.

f Sarah commence à bien connaître Bordeaux.

g Incroyable! On n'arrête pas le progrès.

h On devait aller à Bordeaux cet après-midi, non?

Un peu de grammaire
A bit of grammar

PREPOSITIONS + INFINITIVE

You already know that when two verbs follow one another the second one is in the infinitive form:

On **devait aller** à Bordeaux.

Verbs following a preposition are also in the infinitive (prepositions are words which have a constant spelling, they are placed in front of nouns or pronouns or in front of verbs). The following prepositions are frequently used in front of verbs in the infinitive: **à** *at*, **de** *to, of*, **pour** *for / in order to*, **sans** *without*:

pour monter à Paris	*in order to get to Paris*
sans arrêter	*without stopping*
J'ai essayé de ranger.	*I tried to tidy up.*

THE SUBJUNCTIVE

The subjunctive is a verb form which is commonly used in French. In fact you have already come across it in Unit 13 in sentences starting with **il faut que**. The subjunctive is a verb form which has its own range of past tenses although the present tense of the subjunctive is the most used of all. This course will only provide you with examples of the present subjunctive and a few examples of the past form with **avoir** and **être**, as you are not likely to meet other forms when you hear spoken French.

The subjunctive is usually preceded by a verb + **que**. However, there are many verbs with **que** which are not followed by the subjunctive. So this alone is not a guide to whether or not you should use the subjunctive. Instead, look at the meaning of the sentence. The subjunctive is mainly used to express necessity, possibility, doubt, regrets, wishes, fear. The subjunctive is automatically used after the following expressions:

▶ *Necessity:* **Il faut que** *je rentre à Londres.*
   It is necessary that I should go back to London.
▶ *Possibility:* **Il est possible que** *je rentre à Londres la semaine prochaine.*
   There is a possibility that I shall return to London next week.
▶ *Doubt:* **Je doute que** *je rentre à Londres avant dimanche.*
   I doubt that I shall be going back to London before Sunday.
▶ *Regrets:* **Je regrette qu**'*elle rentre déjà à Londres.*
   I am sorry that she is already going back to London.
▶ *Wishes:* **Je veux qu**'*elle rentre à Londres immédiatement.*
   I want her to go back to London immediately.
▶ *Fear:* **J'ai peur qu**'*elle rentre à Londres sans moi.*
   I am afraid that she may return to London without me.

The ending pattern is similar for all verbs in the present subjunctive except for **avoir** and **être**.

Verb endings of the present subjunctive

je **-e**	nous **-ions** (**-yons** for **avoir** and **être**)
tu **-es**	vous **-iez** (**-yez** for **avoir** and **être**)
elle **-e**	ils **-ent**

Prendre *to take*

que je prenne	que nous prenions
que tu prennes	que vous preniez
qu'elle prenne	qu'ils prennent

Sometimes the subjunctive can be avoided by omitting **que** and using **de** + infinitive:

> Il est possible **que je rentre** à Paris la semaine prochaine. (subjunctive)
> Il est possible **de rentrer** à Paris la semaine prochaine. (infinitive after preposition **de**)

However the sense may be slightly changed.

When you feel ready to use the subjunctive you will find that your French has a slightly more authentic ring to it.

Pronunciation

🔊 **CD2, TR 17**

▶ **C'est faisable.** *It's feasible*
Here, -ai- has a neutral sound similar to the e of je [je].

▶ **On n'arrête pas le progrès. On arrête la voiture.**
*There is no difference in sound between the two phrases above. But the listener knows that the first example is a negative sentence because of **pas** after the verb.*

Exercise 1 **Quel temps?** *Which tense?*
See whether you can identify which tenses are being used in the following examples. Match the sentence with the correct tense.

Examples found in first dialogue	Tenses (jumbled)
1 tu as réservé ta place?	**a** present subjunctive
2 je te remercie	**b** perfect tense
3 je prenais souvent le train	**c** present indicative
4 il faut que je rentre à Londres	**d** imperfect
5 ma sœur viendra me chercher	**e** conditional
6 tu pourrais le faire par internet	**f** future

Exercise 2 **Ça prend combien de temps…?**

◀) **CD2, TR 18**

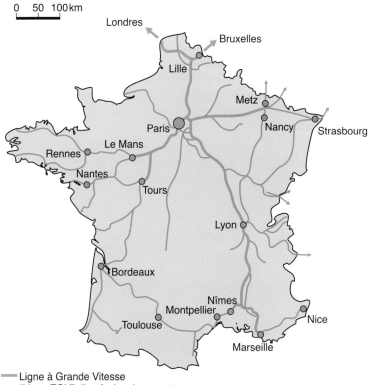

0 50 100 km

Londres

Bruxelles

Lille

Metz

Paris Nancy

Strasbourg

Le Mans

Rennes

Nantes

Tours

Lyon

Bordeaux

Nîmes

Montpellier

Toulouse

Nice

Marseille

— Ligne à Grande Vitesse
— "Ligne TGV" d'après les documents
   de la SNCF à destination du grand public
◦ "Ville de la Grande Vitesse"
● Métropoles régionales accessibles en TGV

©Bouron, 2005–2008 www.geotheque.org

If you want more detailed information, look at the map on the
TGV website: http://www.TGV.com (click on 'Découvrir le réseau
Grande Vitesse').

Look at the map, listen to the recording, and find out how long it takes
to get from Paris to (a) Nantes, (b) Toulouse, (c) Lyon and (d) Lille.

LES GARES DE PARIS

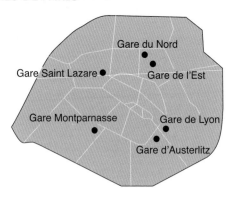

Starting or ending your journey in Paris? There are six main line stations which can take you to any corner of France. There are also links (**liaisons**) to airports and other major TGV stations around Paris. For instance if you are going to Disneyland your station is Marne la Vallée Chessy.

Look at the map of Paris above with the six main railway stations:

▶ *From the* **Gare Montparnasse** *you can go west (Altlantic coast, Brittany, south-west France and Spain).*

▶ *From the* **Gare St Lazare** *you can get to Normandy.*

▶ *From the* **Gare du Nord** *you can get to the north of France and Belgium.*

▶ *From the* **Gare de l'Est** *you can reach the east of France and Germany.*

▶ *From the* **Gare de Lyon** *you can go to the south-east of France, the Mediterranean and Italy.*

▶ *From the* **Gare d'Austerlitz** *you can reach places in central France.*

Insight: Le saviez-vous? *Did you know?*

Autrefois il y avait beaucoup plus de gares de chemin de fer à Paris. La Gare d'Orsay par exemple reliait Paris à Orléans. Cette gare est maintenant Le Musée D'Orsay, le plus grand musée de Peinture Impressionniste de Paris.

In the old days there were many more railway stations in Paris. The Gare d'Orsay, for example, connected Paris to Orléans. This station is now the Musée d'Orsay, the biggest French Impressionist museum in Paris.

---

2 Au guichet de la gare
At the station ticket office

◀» **CD2, TR 19**

Sarah and Dominique are at the ticket office at Bordeaux railway station. There are other customers in front of them.

Listen to / read the dialogue, and answer these questions.

a *How long does it take to go from Bordeaux to Poitiers?*
b *What kind of tickets do the old couple want? Single or return?*
c *Which day of the week do they wish to travel?*

Listen/read again and answer these questions.

d *One train leaves Bordeaux at 08.26. At what time does it arrive in Poitiers?*

e *Which train do they choose in the end?*

f *What is the advantage of taking this particular train?*

Listen/read once more.

g *Do they need to reserve their return tickets now?*

h *What does Sarah decide to do?*

Un vieux monsieur et une vieille dame sont juste devant Sarah au guichet.

Vieille dame	Nous allons à Poitiers, ça prend combien de temps avec le TGV?
Employée de la SNCF	Voyons, une heure trois quarts environ madame. Vous voulez réserver?
Vieux monsieur	Deux billets s'il vous plaît.
Employée	Deux billets simples ou deux aller-retours?
Vieille dame	Deux billets aller-retours, s'il vous plaît.
Employée	Quel jour désirez-vous voyager?
Vieille dame	Lucien, nous partons demain n'est-ce pas?
Vieux monsieur	Mais non Simone nous allons à Poitiers jeudi, c'est-à-dire après demain.
Employée	Jeudi? Vous prendrez le train de quelle heure?
Vieille dame	À quelle heure y-a-t-il un train dans la matinée?
Employée	Alors jeudi ... il y a un train qui part de Bordeaux à 08.26 et qui arrive à Poitiers à 10.09. Le suivant est à 10.37 et il arrive à 12.32, et finalement il y a un TGV à 11.59 qui arrive à Poitiers à 13.50.

Vieille dame	Dans ce cas nous prendrons celui de 10.37 et nous arriverons chez ma fille pour le déjeuner...
Employée	Et pour le retour?
Vieux monsieur	C'est-à-dire ... nous ne savons pas encore.
Employée	Ce n'est pas nécessaire de réserver votre retour maintenant, vous pourrez le faire plus tard. Vous avez votre carte Senior?
Vieux monsieur	Simone, c'est toi qui a les cartes Senior?
Vieille dame	Je ne sais pas où je les ai mises ... attendez, il faut que je réfléchisse.
Sarah à Dominique	Tu avais raison, je vais réserver mon billet à la billetterie automatique.

le suivant *the next one (verb* **suivre** *to follow)*
la carte Senior *SNCF concession card for old-age pensioners*
réfléchir *to reflect/to think back*
la billetterie automatique *the ticket machine*

QUICK VOCAB

Insight

Note the spellings used for the types of tickets mentioned.

Deux billets simples: adjective **simple + s** to reflect the plural of the noun - **billets**

Deux billets aller-retours: aller is a verb in the infinitive used here as part of a noun and therefore has no **s**; **retour** is a noun and as such is spelt with an **s** in the plural.

Les réservations

Link the following English phrases to the equivalent French expressions:

1 Would you like to make a reservation?	a Nous ne savons pas encore.
2 Which day would you like to travel?	b Nous partons demain, n'est-ce-pas?
3 We are leaving tomorrow, aren't we?	c Attendez, il faut que je réfléchisse.
4 We'll get to my daughter in time for lunch.	d Vous voulez réserver?
5 We don't know yet.	e Quel jour désirez-vous voyager?
6 Wait, I have to think.	f Je ne sais pas où je les ai mises.
7 I don't know where I put them.	g Tu avais raison.
8 You were right.	h Nous arriverons chez ma fille pour le déjeuner.

Exercise 3 À vous de réserver un billet

◀) CD2, TR 20

You are at the ticket office in Bordeaux station. You are travelling tomorrow. You want to reserve a single ticket on the TGV. You want to get to Paris by 11 a.m. Look at the train timetable and decide which train you need to catch.

Listen to the recording and respond to the employee's questions.

a **Vous**   *Say you would like to reserve a ticket to Paris, please.*
    Employée *Vous voyagez aujourd'hui?*
b **Vous**   *Say no, you are travelling tomorrow.*
    Employée *Vous prenez le train de quelle heure?*
c **Vous**   *Say the time of your train.*
    Employée *Vous prenez un billet aller-retour?*
d **Vous**   *Say no, you would like a single. Ask the price of the ticket.*

Arcachon → Bordeaux → Paris/Île de France

TGV vert: toutes les réductions (minimum 15%) sont calculées sur le prix normal de niveau 1

Pour connaître le prix de votre billet, consultez
- Si vous voyagez en 1re classe la page 46
- Si vous voyagez en 2e classe la page 47

TGV ne circulant pas ce jour-là

PRIX 1 3 1 / 1 2

HORAIRES

N° du TGV	Restauration	8402	8404	8410	8410	8412	7850	8414	7860(1)	8518	8420	8420 (4)	8526	8528
Arcachon	D					a	b	b	b	b			b	b
Facture	D					a	b	b	b	b			b	b
Bordeaux	D	4.59	6.01			6.08	6.46	7.05	7.59	8.22		8.26	10.37	10.44
Libourne	D	5.18			6.27			7.26						
Angoulême	D	6.03		7.10	7.10			8.11	8.58		9.25	9.25	11.44	
Ruffec	D				e				c			e	e	
Poitiers	D	6.47		7.55	7.55		8.28	8.56	9.43		10.09	10.09	12.32	
Châtellerault	D	7.04		8.12	8.12			9.37	10.23		10.25	10.25		
Saint-Pierre-des-Corps	D						9.08				10.54	10.54		
Massy TGV	D						9.58		11.13					
Marne la Vallée Chessy	D						10.34		11.53					
Aéroport Ch.de Gaulle TGV	D						10.49		12.06					
Paris-Montparnasse 1-2	D	8.20	9.00	9.30	9.30	9.40		10.35		11.25	11.50	11.50	14.05	13.50

Un peu de grammaire
A bit of grammar

◀) CD2, TR 21

There are two words for each of the following parts of the day and also for the year:

un jour	**une journée**	*a day*
un matin	**une matinée**	*a morning*
un soir	**une soirée**	*an evening*
un an	**une année**	*a year*

There is only a slight difference in meaning between the two forms and indeed that difference is not translatable in English. **Un jour, un matin, un soir, un an** are more likely to describe a portion of time defined by the calendar or the clock (objective connotation). **Une journée, une matinée, une soirée, une année** have a social connotation and are more likely to express the time experienced by individuals (more subjective):

Nous partirons dans trois jours.	*We'll leave in three days time.*
Nous avons passé une excellente journée au bord de la mer.	*We spent an excellent day at the seaside.*
Il passe un an à Paris.	*He is spending one year in Paris.*
Bonne année tout le monde!	*Have a good year everyone!*

Insight

Using **an** and **année** in the same phrase: **Le 31 décembre à minuit on fête le Nouvel An et on se souhaite une Bonne Année.** (*On 31 December at midnight we celebrate the New Year and wish everyone a Happy New Year.*) This example reinforces the point that the feminine form is used more to refer to the social aspect of time.

Exercise 4 **Choisissez le bon mot**
For each sentence choose one of the two words in brackets to fill the gaps.

a *Nous avons passé _____ magnifique chez nos amis. (un soir/ une soirée)*
b *Dans trois _____ il aura cinquante ans. (ans/années)*
c *Il y a sept _____ dans une semaine. (jours/journées)*
d *Mon frère a onze _____ de moins que moi. (ans/années)*

Insight

Remember that you can say **un nouveau livre** but you cannot use **nouveau** before a noun starting with a vowel. You have to say **le nouvel an, un nouvel ami, un nouvel appartement.**

3 Les points de vente et les billetteries automatiques
Sales points and automatic ticket machines

Read the information in the leaflet headed 'SNCF - Les points de vente' about buying tickets.

SNCF – Les points de vente

Accueil Grandes Lignes

Guide du voyager

Les**points de** V**ente**H**ABITUELS**

LES POINTS DE VENTE
Tous les billets sont vendus dans les gares, les boutiques SNCF et les agences de voyages.
Achetez-les à l'avance, ils sont valables 2 mois.
Que vous prépariez votre voyage ou soyez en instance de départ, tous les guichets délivrent, en principe, l'ensemble des prestations.
Certaines grandes gares disposent de guichets vous permettant de préparer votre voyage à l'écart des flux de départs immédiats.

LES BILLETTERIES AUTOMATIQUES
Ce sont des guichets en libre service qui vous permettent d'acheter un billet pour un trajet en France ou à destination de l'étranger (principales relations):
- de 61 jours à quelques minutes avant votre départ (sauf train autre que TGV avec réservation)
- avec ou sans réservation
- avec supplément éventuellement.

Vous pouvez également y réserver vos titres repas ou y retirer vos commandes passées par téléphone.
Comme moyen de paiement, la billetterie automatique accepte à partir de 2 € les cartes Bleues, Visa françaises ou étrangères, Eurocard/ Mastercard, American Express et Diner's Club International.
La billetterie automatique accepte les pièces jusqu'à un montant total de 15 € et rend la monnaie.

> La billetterie automatique vous permet d'éviter les files d'attentes aux guichets.

[www.sncf.com]

Vrai ou faux? Having read the information on where to buy tickets and how to use automatic ticket machines say whether the following statements are true or false (**vrai ou faux**):

   a *You cannot buy your tickets more than two months in advance at the ticket office.*
   b *All stations have a special ticket office for advance booking.*
   c *At the ticket machine you can only buy your ticket 61 days in advance of travelling.*
   d *If you use the ticket machine you can use up to 15 € in coins.*
   e *You won't get any change.*
   f *You can use your credit card for any journey.*
   g *You can get your meal reservation from the machine too.*

Surfez sur le web

- Trouvez la carte du TGV sur internet (www.res.ch/cartedu.htm) ainsi vous pourrez découvrir les nouvelles destinations du TGV en France et en Belgique.
- Si vous êtes passionné du train visitez le site de La Vie du Rail www.laviedurail.com. Pour entendre 'siffler le train' cliquez sur 'La vie du Rail' puis sur 'Trésor du Rail'. Sélectionnez 'Ambiances sonores.'

Web extension exercise

Voici ce que vous pouvez lire dans ce magazine hebdomadaire:

La Vie du Rail Magazine est n°1 dans le domaine du rail et des transports dans le monde. Hebdomadaire historique des cheminots, il comptabilise 600 000 lecteurs. Chaque semaine, découvrez toute l'actualité des transports, retrouvez les équipements, les technologies et les personnalités qui comptent, lisez les analyses et les partis pris des décideurs* du secteur, sans oublier les loisirs, des astuces** et des conseils pour être bien dans la vie.

* movers and shakers; ** tips

Cliquez ici pour

VOUS ABONNER

Ou téléphonez au 0 811 02 12 12

N° Azur, prox d'un appel local

Répondez aux questions

1 *What rank does* La Vie du Rail *occupy amongst rail buffs' magazines?*
2 *How often is it published?*
3 *What type of issues would you expect to read about?*
4 *Name two ways of subscribing to* La Vie du Rail.

Mots cachés

Find twenty words or expressions hidden in the grid. They all relate to train journeys and buying and booking tickets.

```
A R R I V E E S A R T Y U C V B M B T A
Z E F G H N M K L O S E R S T A Z C V L
D S I M P L E F S D F G H O R A I R E L
R E W A S V B G N M J D E P A R T S V E
G R A N D E S L I G N E S D I A S W B R
T V S A F T F E D D T Y U I N G S A N -
F A A W E G A H F E S V O Y A G E G D R
V T S S D G U J I U Y T R D G F A O F E
B I L L E T T E R I E S F F R D X N G T
C O F F G U O K L Y F D F G A S C R T O
V N D U W R M D G T R R M I N I T E L U
N E E J E G A R E S F F F U D B F S Y R
G U I C H E T F Z A G F G K E J G T U A
M F D H A B I L L E T D U Y V K H A E E
O G F N S S Q H G L N S I T I U J U A I
P B H F S A U K E R K G K F T T H R D O
V A L A B L E L K L H U U D E R T A F U
N P O I N T S D E V E N T E S D S N C F
F H W E T G G U I T H U T D S E F T G Y
G S D M O N T P A R N A S S E S R S E A
```

Hidden words in translation

arrivals, departures, name for French railway company, high-speed train, ticket machines, ticket office, Minitel*, main lines, timetable, single, return, ticket, stations, name of a Paris station, buffet car, valid, travel, booking, sales outlet, automatic.

*Minitel was used widely as an electronic telephone directory prior to the use of the Internet.

TEST YOURSELF

The present subjunctive is used to express ideas, thoughts, facts, fear, anxiety which are uncertain but not impossible or unrealisable. How is it used? In many cases in ready-made structures with **il faut que…, je doute que…, j'ai peur que…, quoiqu'il…**

Many expressions are idiomatic and even colloquial in the sense that they are used in pre-formed formulas common in everyday conversations:

Il faut que tu me dises tout! You must tell me everything!

Quoiqu'il en soit… Whatever the case may be…

These two structures are followed by a negative structure whem they express fear or anticipation:

Avant que… Before…

J'ai bien peur qu'il n'ait un accident. I'm very much afraid that there is an accident.

Complete the sentences below:

1 *J'ai bien peur qu'*	**a**	*cela ne changera rien.*
2 *Quoiqu'ils disent*	**b**	*que j'arrive.*
3 *Quoiqu'il en soit*	**c**	*puisse pas venir à Paris.*
4 *Je regrette qu'elle ne*	**d**	*avant qu'il ne pleuve.*
5 *Qu'ils n'attendent pas*	**e**	*il ne soit trop tard.*
6 *Fermez les fenêtres*	**f**	*ils ne font rien pour trouver du travail.*
7 *Quoique vous en pensiez*	**g**	*vrai.*
8 *Je doute que ce soit*	**h**	*je m'en fiche complètement!* (I could not care less!)

The sentences with **quoique** are more or less interchangeable in these examples.

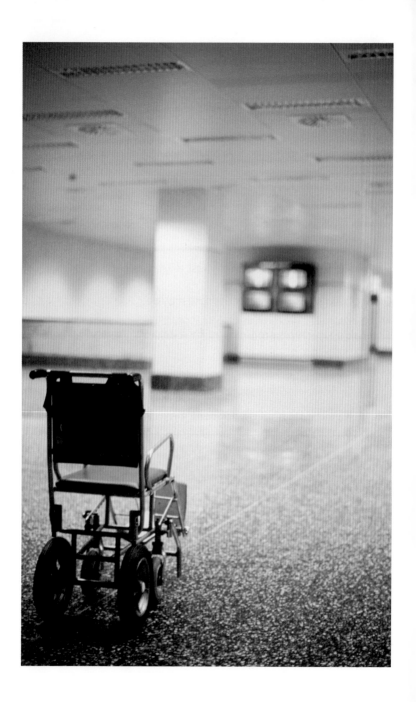

19

À l'hôpital
At the hospital

In this unit you will learn
- *more about public transport*
- *what to say at the hospital if you have to go in for a minor injury*
- *to recognize indirect object pronouns*
- *more about the subjunctive*

1 Sarah téléphone à sa sœur
Sarah telephones her sister

Read this short passage and the SNCF leaflet **L'horaire garanti** below.

Le train de Bordeaux arrive à Montparnasse à dix-neuf heures quinze, avec dix minutes de retard. Sarah descend, mais ne voit pas sa sœur sur le quai. Elle attend quelques moments puis elle décide de téléphoner chez sa sœur. Elle a son téléphone portable dans son sac.

Did you understand? Then answer these questions!

a *At what time does Sarah's train arrive in Paris?*
b *What was the scheduled arrival time? Will Sarah get any compensation? (see below:* **L'horaire garanti***)*
c *Can she see her sister on the platform?*
d *What does she decide to do after a few moments?*
e *What has she got in her bag?*

son téléphone portable *her mobile phone*
un portable/un mobile are both used
If you are using Pay as you Go, you can buy **une carte recharge** if you have run out of credit.

La SNCF s'engage...

ET TOUJOURS: L'HORAIRE GARANTI

Depuis le 1er septembre 1996, la SNCF s'engage à offrir une compensation **dès qu'un train Grandes Lignes est en retard d'au moins 30 minutes.**
Cette compensation représente:
– 25% du prix du billet du trajet concerné lorsque votre retard à destination est de 30 minutes à 1 heure,
– 50% du prix du trajet si le retard est supérieur à 1 heure.
Elle est réalisée sous forme de bons d'achat trains ('bons Voyage').
Pour en bénéficier, il est nécessaire d'avoir acquitté et effectué un parcours d'au moins 100 kilomètres en train Grandes Lignes.

Insight

Using words related to guarantee: **une garantie** (*guarantee* - a noun), **garanti(e)(s)** (*guaranteed* - an adjective), **garantir** (*to guarantee* - a verb):
J'ai un bon de garantie pour ma montre *I have a certificate of guarantee for my watch*
Ma montre est garantie deux ans *My watch is guaranteed for two years*
Je te garantis que c'est vrai! *I promise you it's true!*

2 Allô!
Hello!

🔊 **CD2, TR 22**

Sarah parle au téléphone à son beau-frère, Guillaume.

You may need to look at the words in the vocabulary list before you answer the questions.

Listen to / read the dialogue and answer the questions.

   a *What does Sarah think she has lost?*
   b *What is the telephone number that Sarah has just dialled?*

Listen/read again.

   c *Where is Marie-Claire?*
   d *How did she cut herself?*
   e *Does Guillaume think it is serious?*

Listen/read one more time.

   f *Who are Ariane and Pierre?*
   g *What does Guillaume suggest Sarah should do?*
   h *Is it because Sarah does not know her way round the métro?*

emmener *to take someone/something somewhere*
rejoindre *to rejoin/to meet someone somewhere*
un point de suture *a stitch (medical)*
une piqûre *an injection/insect bite*
J'ai perdu *I have lost*
Ouf! *Phew! (sigh of relief)*

QUICK VOCAB

Sarah	Zut! J'ai perdu mon portable! Ouf! le voilà! Alors … zéro un, quarante-huit, zéro cinq, trente-neuf, seize. Bon ça sonne! Allô!
Guillaume	Allô oui?
Sarah	Guillaume, ici Sarah. Tu sais où est…
Guillaume	Ah Sarah! Encore heureux que tu aies téléphoné! J'étais inquiet…
Sarah	Qu'est-ce qu'il se passe?
Guillaume	Marie-Claire a eu un petit accident, elle est aux urgences à l'hôpital.
Sarah	Quoi? Qu'est-ce qu'il lui est arrivé?
Guillaume	Rien de grave … elle s'est coupée en ouvrant une boîte pour le chat. La voisine l'a emmenée à l'hôpital.
Sarah	Tu veux que j'aille la rejoindre à l'hôpital?
Guillaume	Non, non elle ne devrait pas être longtemps … juste quelques points de suture et une piqûre anti-tétanique, c'est tout!
Sarah	Et les enfants? Où sont Ariane et Pierre?
Guillaume	Ici, avec moi. Ecoute … je suis désolé … prends un taxi.
Sarah	Non! Je connais bien le trajet en métro: je vais jusqu'à Châtelet, je change et je prends la direction Château de Vincennes et je descends à Nation.
Guillaume	Oui, c'est cela mais si tu as beaucoup de bagages un taxi sera plus pratique.
Sarah	Bon d'accord, j'arrive!

Link the following English phrases to the equivalent French expressions.

1 I was worried.
2 What is happening?
3 What happened to her?
4 nothing serious
5 She cut herself.
6 The neighbour has taken her to hospital.
7 She should not be long.
8 I get out at Nation.

a Elle ne devrait pas être longtemps.
b Elle s'est coupée.
c La voisine l'a emmenée à l'hôpital.
d J'étais inquiet.
e Qu'est-ce qu'il lui est arrivé?
f Je descends à Nation.
g Qu'est-ce qu'il se passe?
h rien de grave

Qu'est qu'il lui est arrivé? (asking about Marie – *What's happened to her?*)

For recognition only at this stage, you need to understand how this structure has been arrived at:

Il est arrivé xxx *xxx has happened*

xxx est arrivé à Marie → **à elle** (contraction of à + elle = lui)

Il lui est arrivé *It's happened to her*

Qu'est ce que + il → **lui est arrivé?** (contraction of que + il = qu'il)

Un peu de grammaire
A bit of grammar

INDIRECT OBJECT PRONOUNS

You have already come across the whole range of pronouns but there are still some complexities which need to be explained. In the dialogue Sarah says:

Qu'est-ce qu'il *lui* est arrivé?   *What has happened to **her/him**?*

The model for the structure in this particular example is:

Il est arrivé quelque chose à quelqu'un.   *Something has happened **to someone**.*

Qu'est-ce qu'il est arrivé à Marie-Claire?   *What has happened to Marie-Claire?*

When the object (here **Marie-Claire**) is linked to the verb by a preposition (here **à**), this object is called an indirect object. When a personal pronoun (here **lui**) is used to replace the indirect object it is referred to as an indirect object pronoun. The plural form of **lui** is **leur**. The other object pronouns (**me, te, nous, vous**) are the same whether the object is direct or indirect.

This can be more easily demonstrated in simpler examples, using the present tense:

Je donne les fleurs *à ma mère*.   *I give the flowers **to my mother**.*
Je donne les chocolats *à mes parents*.   *I give the chocolates **to my parents**.*

In both examples there are two objects after **donne** and it is possible to use two pronouns side by side to replace them but, taking one thing at a time, **à ma mère** is replaced by **lui** and **à mes parents** is replaced by **leur**:

Je *lui* donne les fleurs.   *I give **her** the flowers.*
Je *leur* donne les chocolats.   *I give **them** the chocolates.*

Other examples:

J'ai réservé une place *pour ma mère*.   *I've reserved a place **for my mother**.*
Je *lui* ai réservé une place.   *I've reserved **her** a place.*
Tu as écrit *à tes parents*?   *Have you written **to your parents**?*
Non, je ne *leur* ai pas écrit.   *No, I haven't written **to them**.*

> ## Insight
> Back to the more straightforward direct object pronouns:
> **Tu vois la Tour Eiffel? Ah oui, je la vois!** *Can you see the Eiffel Tower? Yes, I can see it!*
> **Tu as vu le quatre quatre!! Ouais! Je l'ai vu!** (both **le** and **la** become **l'** in front of a vowel) *Have you seen the 4x4!! Yes! I've seen it!*
> **Tu as fini ton travail? Non, je ne l'ai pas encore commencé!** *Have you finished your work? No, I haven't even started it!*

EMPHATIC PRONOUNS

These are generally used after a preposition: **à** *at*, **avec** *with*, **de** *from/of*, **dans** *in*, **chez** *at*, **pour** *for / in order to*, **sans** *without*, **sous** *under*, **sur** *on / on top of*:

Il est parti sans *moi*.   *He left without **me**.*

(sans **moi**, sans **toi**, sans **lui**, sans **elle**, sans **nous**, sans **vous**, sans **elles**, sans **eux**)

MORE EXAMPLES OF THE SUBJUNCTIVE

There are two examples in the dialogue. Did you find them?

Tu veux que j'aille la rejoindre à   *Would you like me to meet her at*
l'hôpital?   *the hospital?*

(The verb is **aller**.)

Encore heureux que tu aies   *Just as well you phoned!*
téléphoné!

In the second example the verb is in the past subjunctive, formed with **avoir** in the present subjunctive and the past participle of **téléphoner**.

Three essential verbs in the present subjunctive

	ALLER	AVOIR	ETRE
Il faut que	j'aille	j'aie	je sois
Il faut que	tu ailles	tu aies	tu sois
Il faut que	elle aille	elle ait	elle soit
Il faut que	nous allions	nous ayons	nous soyons
Il faut que	vous alliez	vous ayez	vous soyez
Il faut que	ils aillent	ils aient	ils soient

Exercise 1 Vous passez beaucoup trop de temps au téléphone!

🔊 **CD2, TR 23**

You have been telephoning all the people named in the box on the same day. Listen to the recording and fill in the grid. Say at what time you phoned them all. Remember to use the correct pronoun. A written example (a) is provided for you.

Names	Questions on the recording	Your answer
a Nadine (11.30)	A quelle heure avez-vous téléphoné à Nadine?	Je lui ai téléphoné à onze heures trente.
b Mathieu (12.00)		
c Chantal et Marc (17.15)		
d Votre sœur (18.45)		
e Vos parents (20.10)		
f Votre fiancé(e) (22.45)		

Pronunciation

la, là, l'a, l'as: all four sound the same *la, la, la, la* but they all mean something different.

▶ **la**   *Definite article:* la **voisine** the neighbour
▶ **là**   *An adverb:* **Marie-Claire n'est pas** là *(means there but frequently used to mean here)*
▶ **l'a**   *Pronoun* le *or* la *in front of verb* avoir: **La voisine** l'a **emmenée à l'hôpital**. *The neighbour took her to the hospital.*
▶ **l'as**   *Same as above but with* avoir *in the second person singular:* **Tu** l'as **vue?** *Have you seen her?*

What happens when the direct object is placed in front of the verb (for recognition only at the moment)?

Tu as entendu la chanson? Oui, je l'ai entendue. *Have you heard the song? Yes, I've heard it.*

In the answer there is an **e** at the end of **entendue** to reflect the fact that the direct pronoun is now placed before the verb.

---

3 À l'hôpital
At the hospital

C'est le mois d'août. A l'Hôpital d'Arcachon il y a beaucoup de personnes avec des maux et blessures en tous genres qui attendent de voir un docteur.

Look at the picture and the words in the vocabulary list below to find out more about parts of the body and what aches and injuries people have.

LES PARTIES DU CORPS

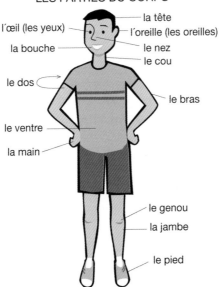

l'œil (les yeux)
la bouche
le dos
le ventre
la main
la tête
l'oreille (les oreilles)
le nez
le cou
le bras
le genou
la jambe
le pied

QUICK VOCAB

J'ai mal à la tête *I have a headache*
J'ai mal au ventre *I have a stomach ache*
Je me suis coupé *I cut myself*
Je me suis brûlé *I burnt myself*
Je suis blessé *I am injured*
J'ai une insolation *I have a sun stroke*
J'ai pris un coup de soleil *I have got sunburnt*
J'ai de la fièvre *I have got a high temperature*
J'ai du mal à respirer *I can't breathe properly*
Je me suis cassé la jambe *I've broken my leg*

Exercise 2 **Les maux et blessures** *Aches and injuries*
Listen on the recording to the eight young people at the hospital casualty department. They speak in the order listed in the grid, but what's wrong has got mixed up. Link their names to what they say is wrong with them. You may need to stop the recording after each person speaks and listen to it several times. Try to write just a word or two in French in the first column next to the name of each patient to say what's wrong with them.

Qu'est-ce qui ne va pas?	Noms	What's wrong?
	1 Marie-José	**a** infected mosquito bites
	2 Alain	**b** toothache
	3 Adrienne	**c** a hand burnt with an iron
	4 Benoît	**d** headache
	5 Elise	**e** hurt knees
	6 Julien	**f** probably a broken arm
	7 Cécile	**g** a backache
	8 Didier	**h** a foot cut walking on a broken bottle

4 J'ai mal au ventre
I have a tummy ache

Still at Arcachon hospital, a doctor is now seeing to a little girl called Magalie Dumas.

Listen to / read the dialogue and answer these questions:

  a *Is Magalie still crying?*
  b *Where does it hurt?*
  c *What is her temperature? Is it very high?*

Listen/read again.

  d *What is Magalie's mother worried about?*
  e *What did she have for lunch?*

Listen/read once more.

  f *What meal did she last eat?*
  g *When was she sick?*
  h *What does the doctor say should happen tonight?*

Dr Lebrun	C'est bien Magalie, tu ne pleures plus, tu es une grande fille. Alors montre-moi où ça fait mal.
Magalie	Là. Oh! Oh! J'ai mal au ventre.
Dr Lebrun	Ça fait mal quand je touche ici?
Magalie	Non. Aïe! Ici ça fait très mal!
Dr Lebrun	Elle a un peu de température, 38.2˚C.
Madame Dumas	Vous croyez que c'est une crise d'appendicite Docteur?
Dr Lebrun	Non, je ne pense pas. Est-ce qu'elle a mangé ce midi?
Madame Dumas	Non, elle n'a rien mangé depuis le petit déjeuner. Elle a vomi vers dix heures ce matin.
Dr Lebrun	Nous allons la garder en observation cette nuit. Si tout va bien elle pourra sortir demain matin.

pleurer *to cry*
vomir *to vomit*
montrer *to show*
garder *to keep*

Now link the following English phrases to the equivalent French expressions.

1 You are not crying any more.

a Montre-moi où ça fait mal?

2 Show me where it hurts.

b Elle a vomi vers dix heures.

3 She has a bit of a temperature.

c Tu ne pleures plus.

4 She has eaten nothing since breakfast.

d Elle a un peu de température.

5 We are going to keep her tonight for observation.

e Elle n'a rien mangé depuis le petit déjeuner.

6 She was sick at about 10 a.m.

f Nous allons la garder en observation cette nuit.

La pharmacie

For many French people **la pharmacie** is the first port of call in case of a minor injury or illness. **La Sécurité Sociale**, which is the equivalent of the National Health Service, is organized differently in France. When you go to your doctor you pay the full price of the visit, and at the chemist you pay the full price of the medicine, **les médicaments**, and then you fill in a form to claim re-imbursement. There are many people who cannot afford to pay up front for treatment and medicine and go to the pharmacist instead.

Before travelling in Europe, European citizens are advised to apply for their European Health Insurance Card, which is a certificate of entitlement to health benefits during a stay in a member state (for UK citizens go to www.dh.gov.uk/travellers).

Insight: Les pharmaciens (*Pharmacists*)

In France pharmacists are generally well disposed towards their clients.

Ils donnent des conseils. *They give advice.*

Ils donnent des renseignements. *They give information.*

Ils soignent les petits maux et blessures avec des médicaments ou des pansements. *They treat minor ailments and wounds with medicines and bandages.*

───

Exercise 3 **Tout savoir sur le mal de dos**

Look at the poster and answer the questions.

C.H.U. (Centre Hospitalo-Universitaire) means Hospital.

PLONEOUR-LANVERN
LE MAL DE DOS
RÉUNION - DÉBAT
Animée par le Docteur FRIAT, Médecin
Service de rééducation fonctionnelle du C.H.U. de BREST

Mercredi 21 MARS 2007, à 20H30
Salle Polyvalente, Plonéour-Lanvern
CAMPAGNE DE PRÉVENTION MENÉE PAR:

a *When is there a meeting at Plonéour-Lanvern?*
b *Who is leading the debate?*
c *What is the debate about?*
d *Where is the meeting taking place?*
e *Where does Dr Friat normally work?*

Exercise 4 **À vous de jouer à 'Jacques a dit'**

◄» **CD2, TR 27, 1:03**

This is a game similar to 'Simon Says' – you only do what Jacques says if Jacques' name appears before the command. You need to recognize the following commands, and others may be used:

▶ *Levez (raise)*
▶ *Baissez (lower)*
▶ *Grattez (scratch)*
▶ *Touchez (touch)*
▶ *Frappez (hit)*

Listen to the recording and write down how you responded to each of the commands.

Surfez sur le web

- Si vous avez mal au dos consultez le site www.undospourlavie.org (un dos pour la vie = Lit. *a back for life*). Vous trouverez des photos montrant des bonnes postures à adopter.
- Pour en savoir plus sur le jeu de "Jacques a dit" visitez le site http://www.tibooparc.com/anniversaire/jeu12.htm qui donne tous les détails sur ce jeu pour les enfants.

Web extension
Jeu de 'Jacques a dit'

▶ *Jeu calme (à partir de 5 ans)*
▶ *Intérieur*

Règle du jeu:

Un enfant est désigné comme étant 'Jacques'. Les autres sont en cercle autour de lui. 'Jacques' donne des consignes à ses petits camarades.

Quand la consigne est précédée des mots magiques: 'Jacques a dit', les enfants doivent exécuter l'ordre donné (ex: 'Jacques a dit levez les bras', tous les enfants doivent alors lever les bras).

Si la consigne n'est pas précédée des mots magiques, les enfants ne doivent pas bouger (ex: L'enfant dit juste 'Levez les bras', les autres ne doivent pas lever les bras).

Si un enfant se trompe il est éliminé. Le dernier restant devient 'Jacques' à son tour.

Un jeu parfait pour commencer la fête.

Web extension exercise
1 *How old should children be to play this game?*
2 *What are the magic words?*
3 *What happens if a child makes a mistake?*
4 *What happens to the winner?*

Insight

Jacques a dit: 'arrêtez-vous de travailler maintenant et ne vous inquiétez pas trop si vous n'avez pas tout compris aujourd'hui. Surtout ne vous donnez pas mal à la tête si vous n'avez pas encore compris cette histoire de pronoms!'
Simon says: 'Stop working now and don't worry if you haven't understood everything today. Above all don't give yourself a headache if you haven't yet understood all this pronouns business!'

TEST YOURSELF

Choisissez les bonnes réponses. Vous pouvez les vérifier dans les pages précédentes.

1 *Marie-Claire s'est blessée: a) en jouant au tennis; b) en traversant la rue; c) en ouvrant une boîte de conserve pour son chat.*

2 *Elle est allée se faire soigner: a) à l'hôpital; b) à la pharmacie; c) chez son médecin traitant.*

3 *On lui a fait: a) des points de suture; b) une piqûre anti-tétanique; c) un bandage.*

4 *C'est: a) sa sœur; b) son mari; c) sa voisine qui l'a emmenée à l'hôpital.*

5 *Comment le garçon s'est-il cassé la jambe: a) en tombant de vélo; b) en jouant au football; c) en tombant d'un arbre?*

6 *Julien s'est brûlé la main: a) au soleil; b) en faisant la cuisine; c) en faisant le repassage.*

7 *Cécile s'est coupé: a) le pied; b) le bras; c) le genou.*

8 *Magalie a mal: a) au ventre; b) aux dents; c) à la tête.*

9 *Elle restera en observation à l'hôpital: a) deux jours; b) une nuit; c) une semaine.*

10 *Vincent Van Gogh* s'est coupé: a) une oreille; b) les deux oreilles; c) le nez.*

* **On dit maintenant que c'est peut-être Paul Gauguin qui lui a coupé l'oreille. Saura-t-on jamais la vérité!?**

20

On prend le métro
Catching the métro

In this unit you will learn
* *what to say if you need to apologize*
* *everything you need to know about the Paris métro*
* *more on the perfect tense*

___

1 Je te prie de m'excuser
I must apologize

◄» **CD2, TR 28**

C'est mercredi matin. Marie-Claire est en congé de maladie. Elle bavarde avec sa sœur. Les enfants sont toujours en vacances. Sarah leur a promis de les emmener au zoo du Bois de Boulogne.

Listen to the recording several times, and then fill in the table below. You'll need to pause the recording several times when you hear the information required to fill in the table: what is Sarah doing or what will she be doing at each point in time? All this information is hidden in the chatting (**bavardage**) between the two sisters.

Calendar of events	What is Sarah doing / planning to do? Who with?
a Wednesday a.m.	
b Wednesday p.m.	
c Saturday p.m.	
d Sunday lunch time	
e Sunday 6.00 p.m.	
f Sunday 6.22 p.m.	
g Monday a.m.	

VOCAB

bouger *to move* **se débrouiller** *to manage*
s'inquiéter *to worry* **être bête** *to be silly*
prévenir *to inform/to warn*

Now read the dialogue.

Sarah	Bonjour grande sœur, ça va mieux?
Marie-Claire	Oh écoute, je te prie de m'excuser pour hier soir!
Sarah	Mais tu n'y pouvais rien! Ce n'est pas de ta faute!
Marie-Claire	Non mais tout de même, je suis désolée!
Sarah	Ce que tu es bête! Ne t'inquiète pas pour cela! De toute façon je me suis bien débrouillée! Tu ne m'as pas dit si tu allais mieux.
Marie-Claire	Oui, ça va un peu mieux. On m'a fait six points de suture mais ça me fait encore mal quand je bouge la main. Je vais prendre trois jours de congé maladie et je reprendrai le travail lundi matin. Au fait, tu restes jusqu'à quand?

Sarah	Jusqu'à dimanche soir. Il faudra que je sois à Paris-Nord à dix-huit heures pour enregistrer mon billet pour l'Eurostar de dix-huit heures vingt-deux. Moi aussi je reprends le travail lundi matin. Au fait Tante Eliane sait que je suis à Paris?
Marie-Claire	Oui, je l'ai prévenue. Elle nous invite tous à déjeuner dimanche midi. Je regrette mais je n'ai pas pu faire autrement.
Sarah	Non, cela ne fait rien, au contraire, je ne l'ai pas vue depuis Noël l'année dernière, ça me fera plaisir de la revoir.
Ariane	Maman, Tante Sarah a promis de nous emmener au zoo cet après-midi.
Pierre	Et puis aussi on va faire une grande balade dans le Bois de Boulogne et si on a le temps on s'arrêtera à Châtelet et on ira sur les quais voir les magasins d'animaux.
Marie-Claire	Eh bien dites-donc, vous en avez de la chance! Eh bien samedi soir on ira tous au cinéma.

Now link the following English phrases to the equivalent French expressions.

1 How silly you are!

2 In any case I managed!

3 I am feeling a bit better.

4 I am going to take three days of sick leave

5 to register my ticket for Eurostar

6 She is inviting us all for lunch.

7 I shall be pleased to see her again.

8 We are going to go for a long walk.

a Elle nous invite tous à déjeuner.

b pour enregistrer mon billet pour l'Eurostar

c Ce que tu es bête!

d Ça me fera plaisir de la revoir.

e De toute façon je me suis bien débrouillée!

f On va faire une grande balade.

g Ça va un peu mieux.

h Je vais prendre trois jours de congé de maladie.

Un peu de grammaire
A bit of grammar

HOW TO APOLOGIZE AND HOW TO RESPOND TO AN APOLOGY

Most of the expressions used here are from the dialogue above so that you can see how they fit in context.

Excuses: *Apologies*

Je vous prie de m'excuser. (a bit formal but not unusual in polite conversations) *I must apologize.*

Excuse-moi/Excusez-moi.
Excuse me. (more matter of fact)

Je suis désolé(e)/Désolé(e)!
I am sorry/Sorry!

Je regrette mais…
I am sorry but…

Je n'ai pas pu faire autrement.
I could not do anything different.

Je vous demande pardon.
Please forgive me. (e.g. asking forgiveness when walking in front of someone)

Vous pardonnez!/Pardonnez!
'scuse! (matter of fact, bordering on rude – much is in the tone)

Réponses/Réactions: *Responses*
Most of the responses apply to any of the apologies listed on the left.

Ne t'inquiète pas!
Don't worry about it!

Ne vous inquiétez pas!
Don't worry about it!

Ce n'est pas grave!
Nothing serious!

Cela/ça ne fait rien! ⎫ *It*
Ça n'a pas d'importance! ⎬ *doesn't*
Peu importe! ⎭ *matter*

N'y pense/pensez plus! *Forget it!*

Ce n'est pas de ta/votre faute.
It's not your fault.

Ne vous en faites pas.
Don't worry.

Il n'y a pas de mal!
There is no harm done!

Je vous en prie. *Go ahead / don't mind me.*

296

Exercise 1 **Répondre aux excuses**
Say how you would respond to the following. There is more than one answer in each situation.

a *Someone bumps into you in the tube and says:* **Oh excusez-moi!**
 Vous:

b *Someone breaks a vase in your house (not a collection item):* **Oh je suis désolé, j'ai cassé le vase!**
 Vous:

c *Someone phoning you on their mobile phone (un portable) to let you know they are late:* **Je regrette, je vais être en retard d'une heure. Je vous fais attendre...**
 Vous:

d *Someone saying why they were late (a problem at home):* **Je n'ai pas pu faire autrement, il y avait un problème à la maison, alors...**
 Vous:

Insight

Using the verb **penser** *(to think)*:
Je pense donc je suis. (Descartes, 1637) *I think therefore I am.*
That was a philosophical thought (**une pensée philosophique**)! And here are some idiomatic expressions:
Je pense bien! *I should think so!*
Penses-tu! *I doubt it! (lit. You think!)*
Tant que j'y pense... *While I think about it...*
And a historical afterthought, using the subjunctive mood:
Honni soit qui mal y pense

Un peu de grammaire
A bit of grammar

Note that if you are more interested in learning spoken French or background information about France you need not spend too much time on this section.

THE PERFECT TENSE AND AGREEMENT WITH THE DIRECT OBJECT

As usual there are several examples of the perfect tense in the dialogue:

dire to say: **Tu ne m'as pas dit.** *You did not tell me.*

promettre to promise: **Tante Sarah nous a promis.** *Aunt Sarah promised us.*

prévenir to inform: **Je l'ai prévenue.** *I have informed her (Tante Eliane).*

Have you noticed the difference between the two spellings of the past participle **prévenu**?

You might need to go back to Unit 16 to remind yourself about the difference between verbs with **être** with the perfect tense and those with **avoir**. With **être** (including reflexive verbs) the number and the gender of the subject affect the ending of the past participle:

Marie-Claire est **allée** à l'hôpital. (**allé** gains an **-e** because Marie-Claire is feminine.)

Les Dupont sont **partis** en Espagne. (**parti** gains an **-s** because there is more than one Dupont in the family.)

With verbs with **avoir** in the perfect tense there is no agreement between the subject and the past participle of the verb. If the subject is feminine or plural it does not affect the ending of the past participle: **Elle a vu sa tante à Noël.** *She saw her aunt at Christmas.*

But: **Elle l'a vue.** *She saw her.*

When a direct object (**sa tante/l'**) is placed before the verb, however, the past participle must 'agree' with the object i.e. it gains an **-e** if the object is feminine, an **-s** if it is plural and **-es** if it is feminine plural.

In the last example, a direct object pronoun (**l'**) is used instead of the direct object (**sa tante**). It precedes the past participle which consequently gains an **-e** in agreement (**vue**).

In this next example, as **Marie-Claire** (the direct object of the sentence) follows the verbs, there is no agreement between the object and the verb:

La voisine a emmené Marie-Claire à l'hôpital.   *The neighbour took Marie-Claire to the hospital.*

But in the following example, the object does agree with the verb because as a direct object pronoun it precedes the past participle. Thus **emmené** gains an **-e** to agree with **l'** (standing for **Marie-Claire**):

La voisine l'a emmenée.   *The neighbour took her.*

....
Insight: Conseil au lecteur *(Advice to the reader)*
If your goal is to communicate then with many verbs you can get by (**vous pouvez vous débrouiller**) without thinking too much about (**sans trop penser à**) the spelling of the endings of past participles: there is no audible difference between **emmené / emmenée / emmenés / emmenées** or between **vu / vue / vues / vus**, for example.

However, in some cases agreement of the past participle does make a difference to the sound of a verb:

J'ai mis la carte postale dans la boîte à lettres.   *I put the postcard in the post box.*

Je l'ai mise dans la boîte à lettres.   *I put it in the post box.*

Nous avons pris les clefs de la voiture.   *We took the car keys.*

Nous les avons prises.   *We took them.*

Mis sounds [**mi**] and **mise** sounds [**miz**]; **pris** sounds [**pri**] and **prises** sounds [**priz**].

Try to identify other examples in the next dialogue and the next units.

Les quais de la Seine

In the dialogue Sarah has promised Ariane and Pierre that if they have time they will stop **sur les quais** to go and have a look at pet shops. **Les quais de la Seine,** the river banks throughout the centre of Paris, are amongst the city's most interesting places, with hundreds of little wooden boxes which open as stalls where people sell old books, maps, stamps, postcards, etc. One of the most interesting **quais** is on the right bank of the **Seine** between **Châtelet** and **Pont-Neuf.** On one side there are **les bouquinistes** with their bookstalls and on the side of the buildings there is a multitude of pet shops with wonderful birds, cats, dogs and more exotic animals, next to flowers and seed shops selling a large variety of bulbs and seeds of all sorts. In recent years in the summer a section of the embankment has been transformed into a riverside resort.

Web Extension
Visitez le site http://marais.evous.fr/actualites/calendrier/paris-plage.html pour voir le programme de Paris-Plage pour chaque été.

Voyez aussi Wikipedia: http://fr.wikipedia.org/wiki/Paris-Plage

Voici ce que vous pouvez lire:

> **Paris-Plage** est aujourd'hui une opération **estivale** menée par
> la Mairie de Paris depuis **2002**. Chaque année, entre juillet
> et août, pendant environ 4 à 5 semaines, sur 3,5 km, la voie
> sur berge **rive droite** de la **Seine** et la **place de l'Hôtel-de-
> Ville** accueillent des activités ludiques et **sportives**, ainsi que
> des plages de sable et d'herbe, des **palmiers**,... La circulation
> automobile est interrompue sur cette portion de la voie
> rapide Georges-Pompidou pendant la durée de l'opération,
> de son installation à son démontage.

Web extension exercise

1 *When did the Mayor of Paris launch this new institution?*
2 *When exactly does it take place?*
3 *Where exactly is it situated?*
4 *What activity is temporarily suspended because of it?*

---

2 Acheter des tickets
Buying tickets

◀) **CD2, TR 29**

*Sarah, Ariane et Pierre sont en route pour leur
promenade. Ils sont à la station de métro Nation.
Ils se dirigent vers le guichet.*

Listen to / read the dialogue and answer these questions.

a *Does Sarah need to get tickets for the children?*
b *What kind of tickets have they got?*
c *Who says that Sarah is a child?*

Listen / read again.

d *Why does Sarah say to the children she wants to think for a minute?*

e *What does she get in the end?*

Listen / read once more.

f *Which direction will they take to go back?*

g *Why do the children choose les Sablons as the station where they want to get off?*

Sarah	Attendez les gamins! Il faut que j'achète des tickets.
Ariane	On en a, nous, des tickets.
Sarah	Ah oui? Bon très bien mais ce sont des tickets demi-tarifs pour les enfants et moi je ne suis plus une enfant!
Ariane	Si, tu es une enfant!
Sarah	Eh bien voilà! Je vous remercie les petits! Sérieusement, est-ce que je prends une carte ou un carnet? Laissez-moi réfléchir une minute.
…	
Sarah	Pardon madame, c'est combien la carte Mobilis, Zone 1 et 2?
Employée	Cela dépend où vous allez et combien de voyages differents vous allez faire…
Sarah	Ah oui, je vois. Je vais prendre un carnet de tickets s'il vous plaît.
Ariane	Moi, je sais quelle ligne il faut prendre, c'est la ligne 1, en direction de la Grande Arche de La Défense. C'est facile, il n'y a même pas de changements.
Pierre	Et pour rentrer c'est la direction Château de Vincennes. A quelle station on descend?
Sarah	On a le choix entre la Porte Maillot et les Sablons. C'est plus ou moins la même distance pour le zoo. Si on descend aux Sablons on peut prendre le petit train du Bois de Boulogne.
Ariane et Pierre	Les Sablons!

demi-tarif *half-fare*
un carnet de tickets *a book of tickets (10)*
une station de métro *a tube station*
une gare R.E.R./une gare S.N.C.F. *an RER or SNCF train station*
un changement *connection (on métro or railway line)*

Link the following English phrases to the French equivalent expressions.

1 Children, wait!	**a** A quelle station on descend?
2 I am no longer a child.	**b** Moi, je sais quelle ligne il faut prendre.
3 Do I get a travel card or a book of tickets?	**c** Attendez les gamins!
4 I know which line we have to take.	**d** C'est plus ou moins la même distance pour le zoo.
5 At which station do we get off?	**e** Je ne suis plus une enfant.
6 It's more or less the same distance to the zoo.	**f** Est-ce que j'achète une carte ou un carnet?

Les transports parisiens

La Grande Arche de la Défense is a métro station named after the monument it leads to. *La Grande Arche* is President Mitterand's legacy to Paris. It is a tall futuristic building built under Mitterand between 1983 and 1989. It is spectacular in itself for its view over Paris and l'Ile-de-France but also because of its location which symbolically lines it up with l'Avenue de la Grande Armée and les Champs-Elysées and therefore with L'Arc de Triomphe and l'Obélisque de Louxor, Place de la Concorde.

Travelling around Paris you can use the bus or the métro which are run by *la R.A.T.P. (Réseau Autonome des Transports Parisiens) and le R.E.R. (Réseau Express Régional)*, a train service which serves the Parisian suburbs of l'Ile-de-France.

Les titres de transports is the official name for tickets. In normal usage there are two separate words for ticket in French: **un billet (de train)** and **un ticket de bus / de métro.** Paris commuters have a range of season tickets which they can use but for visitors there are three options: the individual ticket (not economical unless you only have one journey to make), **un carnet de tickets** with ten tickets and finally **la carte Mobilis** which is a day travel card with options for all zones. Within Paris you can use just one ticket for any journey, whether you have two stops or twenty on your journey; the cost is the same. You can also use one of your tickets for the cablecar in Montmartre, **le Funiculaire de Montmartre.**

Insight: Se déplacer à vélo (*Getting around by bike*)

Le 15 juillet 2007 la Mairie de Paris a lancé 'l'Opération Vélib' (Vélos libres). Dans Paris même il y a maintenant des stations Vélib' partout. Il est possible de circuler à vélo presque gratuitement. La première demi-heure est gratuite et chaque demi-heure supplémentaire coûte un euro. Visitez le site Vélib' velib.paris.fr **pour en savoir plus.**

On 15 July 2007 the Paris Mayor's office launched 'Operation Vélib', an almost free bikes scheme. All over Paris itself there are now Vélib points. You can ride around by bike almost for free. The first half-hour is free and each following half-hour costs one euro. Visit velib.paris.fr *to find out more.*

Exercise 2 **Vous vous déplacez de temps en temps**
Look at the leaflet and answer the questions.

a *Which of the three cards advertised is only a travel card?*
b *What do these three cards entitle tourists to do?*
c *Where can you buy your Passport for Disneyland Paris?*
d *Where can't you buy one?*
e *Which card has a half-fare tariff for children aged between 4 and 12?*
f *Can you buy a Carte Musées et Monuments for one day? For six days?*

Et pour les touristes

A Paris Visite:

C'est la carte idéale pour voyager à volonté sur tous les réseaux de transports urbains d'Ile-de-France dans la limite des zones choisies pendant 1, 2, 3 ou 5 jours.

Une carte pour voyager malin: pas de perte de temps, les enfants de 4 à moins de 12 ans paient moitié prix, accès à la 1re classe en RER et sur les trains Ile-de-France.

Elle n'a que des avantages: 14 partenaires proposent réductions, offres exceptionnelles, en exclusivité.

En vente également

B Carte Musées et Monuments

Un laissez-passer de 1, 3 ou 5 jours pour visiter 70 musées et monuments de la région Ile-de-France.

C Passeport Disneyland® Paris

En même temps que votre titre de transport, vous pouvez acheter votre passeport Disneyland Paris dans toutes les gares RER de la RATP (sauf Marne-la-Vallée/Chessy), les principales stations de métro, les Agences Commerciales RATP, les terminus bus de la Gare de Lyon et de la Place d'Italie, le Carrousel du Louvre et les points RATP de l'aéroport Roissy Charles-de-Gaulle.

Insight

Using the verb **déplacer** (*to move, get about*): **se déplacer** is a reflexive verb meaning *to travel (lit. to move oneself from one place to another)*. Remember to place the appropriate pronoun (**me, te, se, nous, vous**) in front of the verb:

Je me déplace partout pour mon travail. *I travel all over the place for my work.*

Je suis souvent en déplacement. *I am often away.*

Comment vous déplacez-vous dans Paris? *How do you get about in Paris?*

Points de vente et mode de paiement

Now look at the second leaflet, below, and answer these questions.

g *Make a list of all the places where you can buy Mobilis, Tickets, Ticket jeunes.*

h *How much do you need to spend before you can pay your fare with a credit card?*

Les titres de transport

Mobilis: un seul ticket pour toute une journée.

Pendant une journée entière, Mobilis vous ouvre l'accès aux réseaux RATP, SNCF Ile-de-France, APTR et ADATRIF (à l'exception des dessertes aéroportuaires).

Muni de votre carte nominative et d'un coupon valable pour une journée, vous pouvez, à votre gré, combiner les trajets et vous déplacer dans les zones géographiques que vous avez choisies.

Economique, Mobilis propose un tarif forfaitaire en fonction des zones sélectionnées.

Zones de validité	Tarifs Mobilis
Zones 1–2	5,80 €
Zones 1–3	7,70 €
Zones 1–4	9,60 €
Zones 1–5	12,90 €
Zones 1–6	16,40 €

Ticket Jeunes: se déplacer partout le samedi, le dimanche ou un jour férié.

Pour tous les titulaires de la Carte Jeunes (française ou étrangère), le Ticket Jeunes permet de se déplacer partout pendant toute une journée, le samedi, le dimanche ou un jour férié. Le Ticket Jeunes est nominatif et permet de circuler en 2e classe sur les réseaux RATP (sauf Orlyval), SNCF Ile-de-France, APTR et ADATRIF dans la limite des zones choisies.

Zones de validité	Tarifs Mobilis
Zones 1–3	3,20 €
Zones 1–5	6,40 €
Zones 1–6	8,00 €
Zones 3–6	4,00 €

Points de vente Mobilis, Tickets, Ticket Jeunes:
- Toutes les stations de métro, gares RER.
- Terminus des lignes de bus.
- Commerces et bureaux de tabac signalés par le visuel RATP.
- Distributeurs automatiques pour les tickets.

Vous vous déplacez de temps en temps

Ticket ou Carnet: **pour un ou plusieurs déplacements dans Paris et Ile-de-France.**

Un ticket pour un seul voyage, c'est idéal pour un déplacement occasionnel. Il peut être vendu soit en carnet.

Dans le métro, et dans le RER à l'intérieur de Paris, un seul ticket suffit quelles que soient les correspondances effectuées et la longueur de votre parcours.

Dans le RER en banlieue, le tarif varie selon la longueur de votre parcours.

Dans le bus à l'intérieur de Paris, un ticket permet un seul trajet, sans correspondance, quelle que soit la longueur du parcours (sauf sur les lignes PC, Balabus et Noctambus).

Pour les Noctambus, une tarification spéciale est appliquée.

Dans le bus et le tram, en banlieue et pour tout trajet incluant un parcours hors des limites de Paris, un ou plusieurs tickets sont nécessaires selon le nombre de sections parcourues.

Dans le Funiculaire de Montmartre, un ticket permet d'effectuer un seul trajet (montée ou descente), sans correspondance possible avec le métro ou le bus.

Tickets	Plein tarif	Demi-tarif
A l'unité	1,60 €	3,20 €
Carnet de 10 tickets	11,60 €	5,80 €

Surfez sur le web

- Visitez le site de la RATP et découvrez des tas d'informations utiles: http://www.ratp.fr/. Vous y trouverez aussi un plan interactif des transports parisiens.

TEST YOURSELF

Connaissez-vous bien Paris? Testez vos connaissances.

1 *Le Métro*
2 *Le Musée d'Orsay*
3 *La Tour Eiffel*
4 *La Pyramide du Louvre*
5 *L'Obélisque de Louxor*
6 *L'Hôtel de Ville*
7 *Le Pont-neuf*
8 *Les bouquinistes des quais de la Seine*
9 *La Plage*
10 *l'Arc de Triomphe*

Now link each of the definitions below to one of the 10 sites above:

a *Une construction pyramidale en verre construite sous la présidence de François Mitterrand dans la grande cour du Louvre.*
b *La Mairie de Paris.*
c *Un Musée d'art impressionniste situé dans une ancienne gare qui reliait Paris à Orléans.*
d *Une arche construite sous le règne de Napoléon 1er pour y faire passer ses armées triomphantes.*
e *Un événement estival annuel qui transforme 3,5 kilomètres de la rive droite de la Seine en espace ludique.*
f *Un monument construit en 1889 par l'ingénieur de la statue de la Liberté.*
g *Le plus vieux pont de Paris.*
h *Des marchands de vieux livres sur les bords de la Seine.*
i *Un monument égyptien au milieu de la place de la Concorde.*
j *L'abréviation du nom du chemin de fer souterrain et aérien qui transporte des millions de voyageurs à travers Paris.*

21

....

Si on gagnait le gros lot...
If we won the jackpot...

In this unit you will learn
- *about some places to visit in Paris*
- *how to discuss where to go and what to visit*
- *how to express what you would like to do if you had more time and money (the conditional)*

---

1 On pourrait sortir
We could go out

C'est vendredi matin. Marie-Claire est toujours en congé de maladie mais elle se sent beaucoup mieux. Sarah et Marie-Claire font des projets pour la journée. Les deux sœurs s'entendent très bien.

Listen to / read the dialogue. Sarah and her sister are chatting about places they might be going to and about what they might do when they get there. Tick only what they have agreed to do.

a *to go to the Louvre*
b *to go to the Musée d'Orsay*
c *to go and see the Impressionist paintings*
d *to go to the Bazar de l'Hôtel de Ville*
e *to go to the Samaritaine*
f *to go for a cup of tea*

Listen/read again and answer these questions.

g *Considering that Marie-Claire is still on sick leave, why do the two young women decide to go out?*

h *What does Marie-Claire wish for?*

Sarah	Toi ça va mieux, cela se voit! Tu es de meilleure humeur ce matin! Si tu allais mieux on pourrait peut-être sortir.
Marie-Claire	Oui je me sens beaucoup mieux et puis les gosses sont chez la mère de Guillaume jusqu'à ce soir, le mari au travail ... À nous la liberté!
Sarah	Tu veux venir avec moi, je pensais faire une balade dans Paris?
Marie-Claire	Mais pourquoi pas? Ma main est encore douloureuse mais je ferai bien attention. Tu n'aurais pas envie d'aller au Louvre?
Sarah	Le Louvre ... non, ça ne me dit rien et puis nous n'aurions pas assez de temps, il y a toujours une telle queue!
Marie-Claire	Oui, je sais, si j'avais le temps ... et l'argent ... je sortirais beaucoup plus souvent.
Sarah	Écoute, si on allait au Musée d'Orsay on pourrait juste aller voir les Impressionnistes, non? Et après si on voulait, on aurait assez de temps pour faire les grands magasins: le Bazar de l'Hôtel de Ville ou je ne sais pas moi…ou bien alors on pourrait aller à L'Orangerie qui vient d'être rénovée.
Marie-Claire	Génial! J'adore Monet et je n'ai pas encore vu la nouvelle salle aux Nymphéas…mais au lieu du Bazar de L'Hôtel de Ville on pourrait aller à la Samaritaine …mais non! Que je suis bête! La Samaritaine est fermée pour rénovations.
Sarah	Ah oui c'est vrai! C'est dommage! Mais ça ne fait rien, on ira prendre une tasse de thé à la terrasse du BHV.

Insight

C'est dommage! *It's a pity!* This can be a free-standing expression of regret. **C'est dommage + que** requires the use of the subjunctive with the verb which follows:

C'est dommage que nous ne puissions plus aller à la Samaritaine. *It's a pity that we can't go to the Samaritaine any more.*

C'est dommage que tu n'aies pas le temps de visiter le Louvre. *It's a pity that you don't have time to visit the Louvre.*

être de bonne humeur *to be in a good mood*
de meilleure humeur *in a better mood*
se sentir mieux *to feel better*
douloureux/se *painful*
Cela ne me dit rien (colloquial). *I don't fancy it.*
au lieu de *instead of*
une telle queue *such a queue*
les gosses *kids* (similar to **les gamins** but slightly pejorative)
Que je suis bête! *How silly of me!*

QUICK VOCAB

Link the following English phrases to the French.

1 It shows!

a Nous n'aurions pas assez de temps.

2 The kids are at Guillaume's mother's.

b Cela se voit.

3 Do you fancy going to the Louvre?

c On ira prendre une tasse de thé tout en haut à la terrasse.

4 We would not have enough time.

d Les gosses sont chez la mère de Guillaume.

5 We would have time to go to the department stores.

e Tu as envie d'aller au Louvre?

6 We'll go for a cup of tea at the terrace at the top.

f On aurait assez de temps pour faire les grands magasins.

Un peu de grammaire
A bit of grammar

FAIRE

Faire can mean a lot more than *to make* or *to do*.

faire les grands magasins *to go window-shopping*, Lit. *to do the shops*

faire du lèche-vitrine *to go window-shopping*, Lit. *to do window licking*

Faire is also used to express that someone has done it all:

Il a fait la Chine, l'Afrique, l'Amérique du Sud... *He's done China, Africa, South America...*

Ça ne fait rien, *It does not matter*, Lit. *It does nothing*

THE CONDITIONAL AND THE IMPERFECT

You have already met and used the conditional (see Unit 7). It conveys the notion that if conditions were fulfilled something would happen. It is used frequently in conversational French, especially with a few verbs which you are now familiar with. Here are two verbs in the conditional and the conditional verb ending pattern:

Aller	Finir	Ending pattern for all verbs in the conditional		
j'irais	je finirais	je	_____	**rais**
tu irais	tu finirais	tu	_____	**rais**
elle irait	elle finirait	elle	_____	**rait**
nous irions	nous finirions	nous	_____	**rions**
vous iriez	vous finiriez	vous	_____	**riez**
ils iraient	ils finiraient	ils	_____	**raient**

Je voudrais faire une balade	*I would like to...* **(vouloir)**
Je devrais rentrer chez moi	*I ought to...* **(devoir)**
On pourrait aller au cinéma	*We could...* **(pouvoir)**
Il faudrait partir avant la nuit	*We should...* **(falloir)**

You have noticed before that within one short conversation people use many different tenses. The imperfect tense and the conditional are often used together in the same sentence to convey the notion that if the condition was (imperfect) right something would (conditional) happen.

Look at the examples in the dialogue at the beginning of this unit. First of all note that **si** *if* together with a verb in the imperfect is often used with the conditional:

Si ça allait mieux on pourrait peut-être sortir.	*If you were better we could go out.*
Si j'avais le temps et l'argent je sortirais beaucoup plus souvent.	*If I had more time and money I would go out more often.*
Si on allait au Musée d'Orsay on pourrait aller voir...	*If we went to the Musée d'Orsay we could go and see...*

The emerging pattern here is therefore:

▶ *si + verb in the imperfect + verb in the conditional*
   or
▶ *verb in the conditional + si + verb in the imperfect*

It is also possible to have the conditional on its own with the condition unspoken but present in the mind of the speaker and understood by the listener:

Nous n'aurions pas assez de temps.	*We would not have enough time.*

Note that when the doubt is lifted or when the condition is fulfilled the future tense is used instead of the conditional:

On ira prendre une tasse de thé...   *We'll go for a cup of tea...*

It has been agreed by the sisters that this is exactly what they will do rather than what they would like to do.

Reminder: The ending pattern for the future tense is as follows:

je	___rai	nous	___rons
tu	___ras	vous	___rez
elle	___ra	ils	___ront

(See also Unit 11.)

Insight: Proverbs

These two proverbs, which are roughly equivalent to the English 'If 'ifs' and 'ands' were pots and pans, there'd be no work for tinkers', demonstrate the use of the conditional:

Avec des si et des mais le monde serait bien différent! *With 'ifs' and 'buts' the world would be very different!*

Avec des si et des mais on mettrait le monde en bouteille! *With 'ifs' and 'buts' you could put the world in a bottle!*

Exercise 1 **Faites des phrases**
Find the ending for each of the sentences in the left-hand column.

1 Si je savais son numéro de téléphone je...	**a**	réussirait à ses examens.
2 Si j'étais riche je ...	**b**	iraient à l'hôpital.
3 Si Corinne travaillait mieux elle ...	**c**	n'aurait pas d'accidents.
4 Si vous aviez le temps qu'est-ce que vous ...	**d**	ferais un voyage autour du monde.
5 S'il conduisait moins vite il ...	**e**	saurais ce qui se passe. (**savoir**, *to know*)
6 Si tu lisais le journal tu ...	**f**	nous changerait les idées.
7 S'ils étaient malades ils ...	**g**	lui téléphonerais.
8 Si on allait au cinéma, ça ...	**h**	feriez?

Paris

The following Paris landmarks are mentioned in the dialogue:

• **Le Louvre** is a vast art gallery and museum on the right bank of the Seine which used to be the residence of French kings before they moved to Versailles. In 1989 a large glass pyramid was added to it which in fact operates as a large dome for the underground reception area.

• **Le Musée d'Orsay** is an old main line station which stopped being used for main-line purposes as long ago as 1939. Since 1986 it has been an art museum and a cultural centre which houses many works of the Impressionists.

• **Le Bazar de l'Hôtel de Ville** (www.bhv.fr) is the oldest department store in Paris. Its old rival, **La Samaritaine**, also on the right bank of the Seine, immediately opposite **Le Pont-Neuf** (despite its name, the oldest bridge in Paris), closed down in March 2006, for renovation. Its terrace was one of the best vantage points in Paris. Both places are within close walking distance from the Métro station **Châtelet**. From **Châtelet** you can also walk to **Le Centre Pompidou**, a contemporary art museum and one of the best venue to see street theatre and entertainment. It was built in the 1970s on the site of **Les Halles de Paris**, which used to be the central market for the capital. Nearby, **Le Forum des Halles**, is a vast underground shopping centre which includes shops, a swimming pool, a multiplex cinema, and a **FNAC** (Fédération Nationale d'AChats), a vast book, DVD and music shop and ticket office for shows.

• **L'Orangerie**, situated in **Le Jardin des Tuileries** (between **la Place de La Concorde** and **Le Louvre**) was chosen by Claude Monet as a permanent exhibition hall for his water lily paintings. It reopened in 2006 after major renovation works.

2 Qu'est-ce que tu ferais?
What would you do?

Sarah et Marie-Claire sont assises à la terrasse de la Samaritaine. Elles se relaxent un peu en jouant un jeu.

Listen to / read the dialogue, and answer the questions.

    a *What game are they playing?*
    b *What would she have if it happened and why?*

Listen / read again.

    c *Why would she live in Paris?*
    d *Would she carry on working?*

Listen / read once more.

    e *When would she swim?*
    f *What would she do in Paris? (try to list everything mentioned, but if you can't, find at least three)*
    g *Who would be with her in her paradise?*

sans tricher *no cheating*
c'est dingue *it's crazy* (colloquial expression)
also **dingo: il est dingo** *he is mad*

> ## Insight
> The conditional is also used with **sans** (*without*):
> **Sans l'aide de leurs parents ils ne pourraient pas continuer leurs études.** *Without their parents' help they wouldn't be able to continue their studies.*
> When the meaning implies a duty or a necessity:
> **Tu devrais chercher du travail.** *You ought to look for work.*
> With the verb **valoir** (*to be worth*), when it is always used in an impersonal form:
> **Il vaudrait mieux rentrer ce soir.** *It would be best to return tonight.*

Sarah	Dis-moi Marie-Claire, honnêtement et sans tricher, ce que tu ferais vraiment si tu gagnais le gros lot au Loto?
Marie-Claire	Alors d'accord … euh … Eh bien j'aurais un grand appartement à Paris, parce que j'adore vivre à Paris, et une maison sur la Côte d'Azur parce que j'aime bien le soleil.
Sarah	Tu continuerais à travailler?
Marie-Claire	Euh, non! Comme cela j'aurais plus de temps pour moi.
Sarah	Et qu'est-ce que tu ferais avec tout ce temps?
Marie-Claire	J'irais à la piscine tous les jours, je lirais tous les livres que je voudrais, j'irais au cinéma, au théâtre, à l'Opéra, dans de très bons restaurants. Et puis de temps en temps je ferais des petits voyages quelque part, aux sports d'hiver par exemple. C'est dingue tout ce qu'on pourrait faire!
Sarah	Tu serais toute seule dans ton paradis?
Marie-Claire	Non, je serais avec toute ma famille, toi y compris!
Sarah	Merci, ma chère, c'est très aimable à toi!

Exercise 2 **Qu'est-ce que vous feriez?**

CD2, TR 32

You are asked: 'Qu'est-ce que vous feriez si vous gagniez le gros lot au Loto?'

a *Work out how you would say that you would have a big house in Brittany, that you would have a boat, that you would go fishing and watch TV in the evening.*

b *How would you say that you would take a trip round the world?*

c *Listen to the recording and check your answers.*

Exercise 3 **Les jeux instantanés** *(scratch cards)*
Vous avez acheté une carte jeu. Vous l'avez grattée (**gratter** *to scratch*). Est-ce que vous avez gagné?

© Tous droits réservés à la Française des Jeux.

Look at the scratch card and answer these three questions.

a *What is the rule of the game?*
b *What is the cost of this scratch card?*
c *What happens if you find 3 ☆ on your card?*

> Gagner, cela n'arrive pas qu'aux autres®
>
> (Lit. *Winning does not happen only to others.*)

....

Insight

In the slogan from the French Loto company the verb **gagner** in the infinitive is the subject of the sentence. You might like to try out your own sentences following the pattern of these examples: **Faire du sport est bon pour la santé.** *Doing sport is good for one's health.*

....

Exercise 4 **Avez-vous gagné au Loto?**

Look at the grid on the Loto card. There are two days of the week when the Loto is drawn and on each of these days there are two draws within a few minutes of one another.

a *On which days is the lottery drawn each week?*
b *How much would you pay if you opted for eight numbers on only one of the two days?*
c *How much would you pay if you opted for eight numbers on both days?*
d *How many numbers would you be able to tick for 252 €?*
e *Up to how many weeks could you have a subscription for?*
f *How much would you pay for four weeks, having ticked eight numbers for both days?*

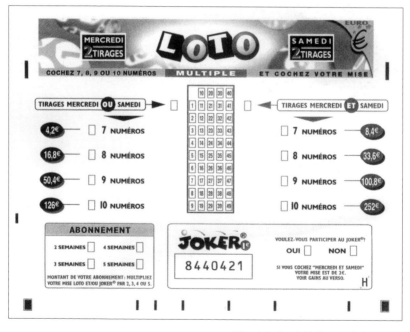

© Tous droits réservés à la Française des Jeux.

Exercise 5 **Vous avez coché?**

◄ **CD2, TR 33**

Tick eight numbers on the Loto card. In order to win anything you need to get between three and six numbers correct.

Écoutez et voyez si vous avez gagné! Ne trichez pas!

Pas de chance? Mais si vous aviez choisi les bon numéros, vous auriez gagné le gros lot...

Insight: Le Métro(politain)

Saviez-vous que c'est la loi du 30 mars 1898 qui a déclaré que l'établissement d'un chemin de fer métropolitain d'intérêt local, fonctionnant à la traction électrique sur soixante-cinq kilomètres, serait d'utilité publique? C'est l'approche de l'Exposition Universelle de 1900 qui a précipité la décision.

Did you know that it was the law of 30 March 1898 which declared that the establishment of a local electric 65-km metropolitan railway line would be of public benefit? This decision was precipitated by the imminence of the 1900 Universal Exposition.

---

3 Un peu de littérature
A little bit of literature

Here is an extract from *Dora Bruder*, a novel by the contemporary French writer Patrick Modiano.

Elle allait certainement le dimanche retrouver ses parents qui occupaient encore la chambre du 41 boulevard Ornano. Je regarde le plan du métro et j'essaye d'imaginer le trajet qu'elle suivait. Pour éviter de trop nombreux changements de lignes, le plus simple était de prendre le métro à Nation, qui était assez proche du pensionnat. Direction Pont de Sèvres. Changement à Strasbourg-St-Denis. Direction Porte de Clignancourt. Elle descendait à Simplon, juste en face du cinéma et de l'hôtel.

(Editions Gallimard 1997, page 46)

And here's what the Larousse dictionary says about Patrick Modiano:

MODIANO (Patrick), écrivain français né à Boulogne-Billancourt en 1945. Ses romans forment une quête de l'identité à travers un passé douloureux et énigmatique.

Did you understand it all? Now answer these questions.

a *What did Dora most certainly do on Sunday?*
b *Where did her parents live?*
c *What is the author imagining?*
d *At which station would she catch the métro? Where would she get out?*
e *How many changes did she have to make?*
f *What was there next to the hotel?*
g *What is Modiano's date of birth?*
h *What are his novels mainly about?*

trajet *route*
roman *novel (book)*
éviter *avoid*
quête *enquiry*
pensionnat *boarding school*
à travers *through*
écrivain *writer*
douloureux *painful*

Les promenades dans Paris: il y a beaucoup de choses à voir à Paris, par exemple les promenades à pied ne coûtent rien. Découvrez le Canal St Martin, la Promenade Plantée ou le parc des Buttes Chaumont. Pour en savoir plus visitez http://www.a-paris.net/A-paris-balade-paris.htm. C'est le site internet le plus utile sur la capitale, malgré les fautes d'orthographe!

Si vous aimez lire des romans historiques et que vous avez lu le roman de Tracy Chevalier *The Lady and the Unicorn* profitez d'une visite à Paris pour visiter le Musée du Moyen Age pour voir de près la du tapisserie de la Dame à la Licorne. En attendant visitez le site http://www.musee-moyenage.fr/. Cliquez sur 'information' pour trouver l'adresse du musée puis sur 'plan du site' → les collections → les tapisseries pour avoir un aperçu des collections.

Web extension exercise
Did you find the six tapestries? Five of them represent the senses. Find the French words for sight, hearing, touch, smell and taste.

TEST YOURSELF

Et vous, que feriez-vous si vous gagniez le gros lot à la Loterie?
Look at Marie-Claire's ideas and complete each sentence using the
verbs in bracket in the conditional:

1 *Elle dit qu'elle arrêterait de travailler mais moi je pense que je
(continuer) pour mieux apprécier mes loisirs.*

2 *Elle irait à la piscine tous les jours mais moi je (acheter) une
grande maison et je (faire) construire une piscine chauffée.*

3 *Elle irait au cinéma mais moi, dans ma grande maison, il y
(avoir) une salle de cinéma avec un écran géant et tous mes
amis (pouvoir) venir voir les derniers films chez moi.*

4 *Elle ferait des petits voyages de temps en temps, mais moi je
(acheter) un bateau de croisière et je (passer) un an ou deux à
voyager autour du monde.*

5 *Elle irait dans des bons restaurants mais moi je (employer) un
des meilleurs chefs du monde. Je (exiger) un menu différent
tous les jours. Mes copains (être) toujours les bienvenus
pour partager ma table. Nous (vieillir) ensemble sans aucun
problème d'argent.*

Quel égoïste! Et le reste de la planète alors?

22

....

Les grèves
Strikes

In this unit you will learn
- *about the French media*
- *about possessive adjectives and pronouns*
- *about strikes and French trade unions*

_____

1 C'est le mien!
It's mine!

C'est vendredi soir. Les enfants sont tous les deux dans la chambre d'Ariane. Soudain on entend des cris: ils se disputent. Leur père va voir ce qu'il se passe.

Listen to / read the dialogue, and answer the questions.

    a *Why are they fighting?*
    b *Where is Pierre's game?*
    c *Whose game has he got now?*

Listen/read again.

    d *Who shouted?*
    e *What does Pierre claim he can prove?*
    f *What does Guillaume tell them to do?*

Listen/read once more.

g *Why does Pierre call Ariane a liar?*
h *How does she retaliate?*
i *What does Guillaume tell them to do?*

Ariane	Donne-moi ça! C'est à moi!
Pierre	Non, c'est le mien!
Ariane	Mais non, tu as laissé le tien chez Bonne Maman et tu le sais bien!
Guillaume	Qu'est-ce que c'est que tout ce bruit? Qui a crié?
Ariane	C'est Pierre, il a pris mon jeu et il dit que c'est le sien!
Pierre	Mais elle est complèment dingue! C'est le mien, je peux te le prouver!
Ariane	Je te dis que ce n'est pas le tien!
Guillaume	Bon, ça suffit! Vous allez venir vous asseoir avec nous dans la salle de séjour et vous allez regarder la télé tranquillement. Il y a un programme très intéressant sur les animaux.
Ariane	J'aime pas les animaux!
Pierre	Menteuse! Aïe!! Elle m'a donné un coup de pied dans la jambe!
Guillaume	Bon, c'est terminé pour ce soir. Ni jeux, ni télé mais le lit! Immédiatement!

un cri* *a shout*
crier *to shout*
un coup de pied *a kick*
menteuse/menteur *liar*
ni … ni… *neither … nor…*
Ça suffit! *That's enough!*

*Cri is another **faux-ami**; *to cry* is **pleurer**.

Link the following English phrases to the equivalent French expressions.

1 Give me that!
2 You left yours at Grandma's.
3 What's all this noise?
4 It's mine and I can prove it to you!
5 That's enough!
6 She kicked me in the leg.
7 You are going to come and sit with us.
8 No games, no TV but bed!

a Ça suffit!
b Elle m'a donné un coup de pied dans la jambe.
c Vous allez venir vous asseoir avec nous.
d Donne-moi ça!
e Ni jeux, ni télé mais le lit!
f Tu as laissé le tien chez Bonne Maman.
g Qu'est-ce que c'est que tout ce bruit?
h C'est le mien, je peux te le prouver!

Insight:

Demonstrative adjectives are for pointing to places, people, objects. Here we show 'this' and 'these' for masculine and feminine singular, and masculine and feminine plural:

ce ballon, cette voiture, ces DVDs, ces cigarettes - *this ball, this car, these DVDs, these cigarettes*

Demonstrative pronouns are for referring to what has already been identified. Here we refer to the same objects as above in the same order:

celui-ci, celle-ci, ceux-ci, celles-ci - *this one, these (ones)*

Un peu de grammaire
A bit of grammar

POSSESSIVE ADJECTIVES AND PRONOUNS

Possessive adjectives and pronouns are used to say that something belongs to someone. The following examples show three different ways of saying something belongs to 'me':

C'est **à moi**
C'est **mon jeu** / C'est **le mien**
C'est **ma chambre** / C'est **la mienne**
Ce sont **mes chaussures** / Ce sont **les miennes**
Ce sont **mes crayons** / Ce sont **les miens**

To express possession you can choose between:

1 *an emphatic pronoun:* **c'est à moi**, *when you are talking about something you can point to;*
2 *a possessive adjective before a noun:* **mon jeu, mes chaussures.** *Remember, the adjective agrees with the gender and number of the noun it accompanies;*
3 *A possessive pronoun which replaces the noun altogether:* **le mien, les miennes.** *Here the form of the pronoun depends on the number and gender of the noun it replaces.*

Study the following table which shows the whole range of possessive adjectives and pronouns and also the use of the emphatic pronoun following a preposition (in this case **à**).

Emphatic pronouns	Possessive adjectives	Possessive pronouns
C'est **à moi**	C'est **mon/ma**…	C'est **le mien / la mienne**
	Ce sont **mes**…	Ce sont **les miens / les miennes**
C'est **à toi**	C'est **ton/ta**…	C'est **le tien / la tienne**
	Ce sont **tes**…	Ce sont **les tiens / les tiennes**
C'est **à lui/**	C'est **son/sa**…	C'est **le sien / la sienne**
à elle	Ce sont **ses**…	Ce sont **les siens / les siennes**

C'est **à nous**	C'est **notre**…	C'est **le nôtre / la nôtre**
	Ce sont **nos**…	Ce sont **les nôtres**
C'est **à vous**	C'est **votre**…	C'est **le vôtre / la vôtre**
	Ce sont **vos**…	Ce sont **les vôtres**
C'est **à elles/**	C'est **leur**…	C'est **le leur / la leur**
à eux	Ce sont **leurs**…	Ce sont **les leurs**

Insight

Interrogative pronouns: which one to use? **Lequel? Laquelle? Lesquel? Lesquelles?** The teacher here is asking individual pupils about their possessions. **Dans le bureau du prof il y a…** (*In the teacher's office there are… Which is / are yours?*)
des cagoules (fem.)(*hoods*): **Laquelle est la tienne?**
des mobiles (masc.): **Lequel est le tien?**
des lunettes de soleil (fem. pl.): **Lesquelles sont les tiennes?**
des chewing gums (masc + pl.): **Lesquels sont les tiens?**

Exercise 1 **Au bureau des objets trouvés**

Maintenant vous êtes au bureau des objets trouvés (*lost property office* but literally *found property*). You report that you have lost seven items in the following order: umbrella, roller skates, reading glasses, wallet, keys, bag and watch. Work through the grid below, item by item, and say if the object shown to you is yours or not. (The gender of the article is indicated.)

Exemple:

Vous	J'ai perdu mes lunettes de soleil (*sunglasses*).
Employée	Ce sont les vôtres?
Vous	Non, ce ne sont pas les miennes.

Employée du bureau des objects trouvés		*Vous*
a C'est votre parapluie?	(masc.)	Non, ce n'est pas…
b Ce sont vos patins à roulettes?	(masc.)	Oui, ce sont…
c Ce sont vos lunettes?	(fem.)	Oui…
d C'est votre portefeuille?	(masc.)	Non…
e Ce sont vos clefs?	(fem.)	Oui…
f C'est votre sac?	(masc.)	Oui…
g C'est votre montre?	(fem.)	Non…

Exercise 2 **Oui, c'est le mien**

◀) **CD2, TR 35**

This time the items are yours (four of the above but not in the same order). Listen to the recording and claim your property.

Exemple:

| **Employée** | Ce sont vos lunettes de soleil? |
| **Vous** | Oui, ce sont les miennes. |

Insight

À qui c'est cela? (*Whose is it?*)
La prof de Maths: **Ils sont à qui ces chewing gums? À toi, Xavier?** *Whose are these chewing gums? Yours, Xavier?*
Xavier: **Non, Madame, ils sont à lui.** *No, Miss, they're his.*
La prof: **Elles sont à qui, ces cigarettes? Elles sont à toi, Michel?** *Whose are they, these cigarettes? Are they yours, Michel?*
Michel: **Non, je (ne) fume pas moi, Madame! Elles (ne) sont à personne!** *No, I don't smoke, Miss! They're no one's!*

---

2 On regarde la télé
Watching television

◀) **CD2, TR 36**

Les enfants sont couchés. Marie-Claire regarde le programme de télévision.

Look at the TV listings for this evening, listen to the recording, and answer the questions below.

a *Guillaume has heard on the news that lorry drivers might go on strike. When is the strike likely to start?*
b *Why is he telling Sarah?*
c *What is Sarah's first reaction?*

Listen again.

d *What has already started on Canal+?*
e *Which programme would Guillaume like to watch after the film?*
f *Why should it interest Sarah?*

LUNDI 28 OCTOBRE

T E L E V I S I O N

TF1 F2 F3 C+ 5e ARTE M6 Câble et satellite

TF1 20.45	F2 20.55	F3 20.50	C+ 20.35	5e ARTE 20.45	M6 20.45	Câble 20.30
LA BELLE VIE Téléfilm humoristique français de Gérard Marx (2/2) (1997). 120 min. VF. Avec : Jean Yanne (Julius), Danièle Evenou (Linda), Paulette Dubost (Mamé), Vanessa Devraine (Fanny), Christian Rauth (Gaspard). Une famille d'origine modeste devient milliardaire et rachète un château pour y habiter.	**URGENCES** Série médicale américaine. Deux épisodes : Se voiler la face. – Boomerang. VF. 90 min.	**LES CONQUÉRANTS DE CARSON CITY** Film américain d'André De Toth (1952). Western. 84 min. VF. Avec : Randolph Scott (Jeff Kincaid), Lucille Norman (Susan Mitchell), Raymond Massey (Big Jack Davis). Un ingénieur se bat pour l'ouverture d'une ligne de chemin de fer.	**RIDICULE** Film français de Patrice Leconte (1996). Comédie. 102 min. VF. En 16/9. Redif le 30. Avec : Charles Berling Fanny Ardant. Un jeune noble naïf et passionné découvre les artifices et les dangers de la cour de Versailles. **22.15** Flash infos.	**LA LEÇON DE PIANO** Film de Jane Campion (1992). 125 min. VO. En 16/9. Avec : Holly Hunter (Ada), Harvey Keitel (Baines). Une jeune pianiste muette entre deux hommes, en Nouvelle-Zélande. **22.40** Kinorama.	**D.A.R.Y.L.** Film américain de Simon Wincer (1985). Science-fiction. 100 min. VF. Avec : Barret Oliver (Daryl), Mary Beth Hurt (Joyce Richardson), Kathryn Walker (Ellen Lamb). Un robot rêve de devenir un humain.	**M. HIRE** Film français de Patrice Leconte (1989). Drama. 90'. En 16/9. **21.50** La main gauche du seigneur. Film américain d'Edward Dmytryk (1955). Aventures. VO. 85'. **Le femme secrète.** Film français de Sébastien Grall (1986). Comédie dramatique. 90'. En 16/9. **0.55** Secret mortel. Film américain de Michael Scott (1995). Policier. 88'.
22.55 LE DROIT DE SAVOIR Magazine présenté par Charles Villeneuve. «Un enfant à tout prix». Un reportage réalisé par Cathelyne Hemery, David Gosset et Philippe Véron en 1997. L'adoption d'enfants à l'étranger, en particulier au Viêt-nam et en Russie.	**22.35 MOTS CROISÉS** Magazine présenté par Arlette Chabot et Alain Duhamel. «Quelle école pour nos enfants ?» Invités : Claude Allègre, Alain Madelin **23.50** En fin de compte. **23.55** Journal **MOTS CROISES** le magazine politique mensuel de la rédaction présenté par **Arlette CHABOT Alain DUHAMEL** ce soir 22h35	**23.15 TERREUR A L'OUEST** Film américain d'André De Toth (1954). Western. 80 min. VO. Avec : Randolph Scott (Jim Kipp), Marie Windsor (Alice Williams), Dolorès Dorn (Julie). Un justicier solitaire poursuit trois criminels dont il ignore encore le signalement. **0.35** La dernière séance. Tex Avery.	**22.20 PARTY** Film franco-portugais de Manoel de Oliveira (1996). 90 min. VF. 1ère diff. Redif le 28. Avec : Michel Piccoli, Irène Papas. Un séducteur impénitent s'efforce de charmer sa jeune hôtesse, lors d'une garden-party. **23.55** Caméléone. Film de Benoît Cohen (1996). Policier. 92 min. VF. En 16/9. Dern. diff.	**22.55 L'ARGENT** Film de Robert Bresson (1983). 85 min. VF. Avec : Christian Patey (Yvon), Sylvie van den Elsen. **0.15** Court circuit - Bon voyage. Court-métrage d'A. Hitchcock. **0.45** La rate. Téléfilm de Martin Buchhorn **2.15** Tracks.	**22.40 COUPS POUR COUPS** Film américain de Deran Sarafian (1990). Policier. 90 min. VF. Avec : Jean-Claude Van Damme (Louis Burke), Robert Guillaume (Naylor). Pour enquêter sur une série de meurtres inexpliqués dans un pénitencier, un inspecteur de police endosse l'identité d'un gangster.	**20.30** Arsène Lupin. Film américain de Jack Conway (1932). Policier. NB. VO. 86'. **22.00** Fanny Elssler. Film allemand de Paul Martin (1937). Romanesque. NB. VO. **23.25** Fabiola. Film italien d'Alessandro Blasetti (2/2) (1949). Aventures. 90'. **0.45** L'empereur de Californie. Film allemand de Luis Trenker (1936). Western. NB. VO. 90'.

Now read the dialogue.

Guillaume	Sarah, je viens d'écouter le journal de dix-neuf heures sur France Inter, les routiers menacent de se mettre en grève à partir de dimanche, ça pourrait affecter ton voyage de retour!
Sarah	Super! Comme cela je resterai à Paris! Sérieusement parlant, je ne pense pas que l'Eurostar soit affecté par le blocage des routes mais on ne sait jamais. On verra bien!
Marie-Claire	Au fait il y a *Ridicule* qui passe à Canal+. Ça fait presque une demi-heure que cela a commencé.
Sarah	Parce que vous avez Canal+ maintenant?
Marie-Claire	Oui, c'est surtout pour les nouveaux films puisque nous ne sortons presque pas.
Sarah	Eh bien c'est bien! Alors on regarde le film?
Guillaume	Oui mais je voulais voir *Mots Croisés* après.
Marie-Claire	Ah oui, c'est vrai. Toi qui aimes la politique, Sarah, ça t'intéressera sûrement.

le journal (d'information)/les informations/les infos *the news*
France Inter is part of **Radio France**, the French national radio organization. **Radio France** broadcasts many other radio stations such as **France Musique**, **France Culture**, **France Info**. You can use Podcasts to listen to their programmes.
les routiers (short for **chauffeurs routiers**) *lorry drivers*
mots-croisés *crosswords*
Here, on *France 2*, it is the name of a televised political debate between politicians (the title plays on the expression **mots croisés**)

Link the following English phrases to the equivalent French expressions.

1 I have just listened to the news.   **a** On ne sait jamais.
2 It could affect your return journey.   **b** Les routiers menacent de se mettre en grève.
3 We'll see.   **c** Puisque nous ne sortons presque jamais.

4 You can never tell.

5 The lorry drivers are threatening to go on strike.

6 Since we hardly ever go out.

d On verra.

e Ça pourrait affecter ton voyage de retour.

f Je viens d'écouter le journal.

Insight

The verb **mettre** (*to put*) is frequently used in idiomatic expressions in the reflexive form, **se mettre**:

Les pêcheurs se sont mis en grève pour protester contre les quotas. *The fishermen went on strike to protest against the quotas.*

Nous nous mettons à table à une heure. *We sit down to eat at one o'clock.*

On se met en route à quelle heure? *At what time are we setting off?*

Ils se sont mis en ménage. *They moved in together.*

À vous de choisir

Look at the TV listing again and answer the questions below (there may be more than one answer for some of the questions).

VF: Version Française *dubbed*
VO: Version Originale *with subtitles*

VOCAB

Which channel would you watch and at what time...

a ...if you wanted to watch a film in English?

b ...if you wanted to watch a medical comedy?

c ...if you wished to see the late night news?

d ...if you wanted to watch a political debate?

e ...if you wanted to watch a programme on the adoption of children from other countries?

f ...if you fancied watching a science-fiction film?

g ...if you wanted to see Monsieur Hire, a film you have been meaning to see for a long time?

h On which condition would you be able to watch it?

i Look at the small ad for Mots Croisés. Can you find the word which indicates that it is a monthly programme?

j What is the theme of this month's debate?

On regarde beaucoup les jeux à la télé en France

French people have always been keen on television games.
Now many are hooked by games such as **Le Maillon Faible**
(*The Weakest Link*) – an exact replica of the English and
American versions presented by Laurence Boccolini, who
acts and dresses like Ann Robinson. There is also the most
popular: **Qui Veut Gagner Des Millions?** With a maximum
prize of one million euros, which is not as much as in the
English version of the programme, **Loft Story**, one of the
Télé Réalité games which was very successful for a few
years is no longer on French TV but seems to have taken
by storm the province of Québec (see the Canadian website
www.loftstory.tqs.ca for updates on the latest show).

---

3 *Loft Story*
La version canadienne

◄) **CD2, TR 37**

*Si possible visitez le site de la version canadienne de Loft Story
dont l'adresse est indiquée au paragraphe précédent.*

Les six gars et les sept filles qui participent à LOFT STORY
circulent dans des locaux d'une superficie de 7000 pieds carrés
sur deux étages. En plus des pièces comme les chambres, la salle à
manger et le salon, les lofteurs et les lofteuses pourront se tenir en
forme dans une salle de conditionnement physique ultramoderne.

Le confessionnal, cette pièce où les participants peuvent s'isoler
pour s'adresser en privé aux téléspectateurs, sera situé au deuxième
étage du loft, au-dessus des chambres. Dans chacune des pièces,
on retrouvera des fenêtres-miroirs, permettant aux caméramans de
filmer les allées et venues des lofteurs et des lofteuses.

Vingt-deux caméras robotisées seront installées un peu partout afin de
ne rien manquer des échanges entre les gars et les filles... Cinquante-

cinq microphones seront dissimulés dans chaque pièce afin de bien comprendre ce qui se dira et se tramera entre les participants.

Dans ce loft d'une dizaine de pièces, les six gars et les sept filles disposeront de tout l'espace nécessaire pour nous faire partager leurs états d'âme et s'adonner à de nombreuses activités.

a *How many participants are there?*
b *Make a list of all the rooms in the house.*
c *What is the most private room in the house?*
d *Where is it situated? What is its use?*
e *List the different pieces of equipment used to record the participants' every utterance and action.*
f *What can the participants do to keep in good shape?*
g *What is the use of the two-way mirrors?*
h *In square feet, what is the size of the Loft?*

Les grèves et les syndicats

Only 10% of French workers belong to a trade union but when serious issues are raised there is usually a spontaneous response from the vast majority of people within a profession or an industry. Workers join in if a strike is called whether they are members of a trade union or not. All categories of workers go on strike at one time or other and take to the streets. Doctors, nurses, dentists, teachers and even lawyers (see headlines below) go on strike when they need to put pressure on the government.

In the spring of 2006, following social unrest in the Paris suburbs, the Government tried to introduce a new formula for young people's first work contracts. This was strongly objected to by thousands of workers and students who demonstrated and went on strikes for several weeks. In the end the government relented and changed its plans. This movement was the follow-up to a first period of unrest that took place in the autumn of 2005 in '**les cités**', the social housing estates, often deprived and run down, situated in '**les banlieues**' (the suburbs) of Paris and other French towns. See the website for Libération http://www.liberation.fr/dossiers/banlieues/actualite/210864.FR.php

Also for comments from the most looked-up archives from other papers see www.giga-presse.com.

Menace de grève des avocats

Les bâtonniers protestent contre le manque de moyens.

Les bâtonniers is a term sometimes used to refer to barristers. They are threatening to go on strike because of insufficient funding.

There are two main trade unions in France: both cover all trades and professions and have within them groupings for the various categories of workers. The difference between them is now a historical division which no longer applies but still marks each one's tendencies:

▶ **La CGT** (**C**onfédération **G**énérale du **T**ravail) *was traditionally affiliated to the French Communist Party. It has not significantly declined since the demise of communism.*
▶ **La CFDT** (**C**onfédération **F**rançaise **D**émocratique du **T**ravail) *is more aligned with the French Socialist Party.*

There are also two much smaller trade union organizations:

▶ **FO** (**F**orce **O**uvrière – *the name means workers' power) is of a moderate and reformist tendency.*
▶ **La CFTC** (**C**onfédération **F**rançaise des **T**ravailleurs **C**hrétiens) *is a Christian trade unionists' organization.*

Quote from a lorry driver interviewed on France Inter: **'Ce que nous n'obtiendrons* pas par la négociation, nous l'obtiendrons par la rue.'** For this reason strikes by some categories of workers such as **les routiers** *lorry drivers* have a wide impact!

* future of **obtenir,** *to obtain*

4 Que disent les journaux?
What do the newspapers say?

Read the following newspaper article and answer the questions.

La grève dans les écoles de la Seine–Saint-Denis va-t-elle faire boule de neige?

Les syndicats d'enseignants de quinze établissements scolaires de la région de Créteil ont appelé à la grève pour protester contre «les graves insuffisances pour faire face aux besoins et lutter contre l'échec scolaire». Le ministre de l'Education Nationale avait proposé des réformes scolaires «pour donner aux élèves le goût d'apprendre et de se cultiver tout au long de la vie avec des itinéraires de découvertes». Les enseignants disent que «ces itinéraires prétendent résoudre l'échec scolaire. Or pour leur faire place dans l'emploi du temps on a été obligé de diminuer les horaires de français, mathématiques et histoire-géographie de deux heures par semaines.» Les professeurs réclament aussi la création de 6000 postes supplémentaires dans le 93*.

*93 is the number for the area of La Seine–Saint-Denis. In France each 'département' has a number which is linked to its alphabetical order, except for those for Paris suburbs which all have numbers in the 90s.

les enseignants *teachers*
établissements scolaires *schools*
l'échec scolaire *school failure*

une boule de neige *snowball*
lutter *to fight*
résoudre *to resolve*

VOCAB

1 *What question is raised in the title of the above article?*
2 *How many schools are facing strike action?*
3 *Where are these schools?*
4 *What new initiatives does the Minister wish to introduce?*
5 *What are teachers protesting against? Why?*
6 *What else do teachers want for this particular area?*

Un entretien avec Jean-Marc Four

Author Gaëlle Graham (GG) interviews journaliste Jean-Marc Four (JMF).

GG	Jean-Marc, vous êtes journaliste, que faites-vous en Angleterre?
JMF	Je suis le correspondant de Radio France.
GG	Vous aimez votre travail?
JMF	Oui, il faut aimer ce travail pour l'exercer.
GG	Est-ce que c'est difficile?
JMF	Ni facile, ni difficile, c'est une question de formation et de curiosité.
GG	Du point de vue professionnel, quel est le meilleur moment de la journée?
JMF	Le moment où l'on parle en direct à la radio.
GG	Cela fait combien de temps que vous travaillez à Londres?
JMF	Quatre ans.
GG	Vous aimez Londres?
JMF	Beaucoup, Londres est une ville passionnante pour un journaliste.
GG	Vous pensez y rester encore quelques années?
JMF	Non, je m'apprête à partir car les contrats de correspondants étrangers durent quatre ans.
GG	Ah c'est dommage! Vous êtes content de rentrer à Paris ou est-ce que vous regretterez Londres?
JMF	Les deux. J'aime Londres mais c'est agréable aussi de rentrer dans son pays.
GG	Alors bon retour en France et bonne chance!
JMF	Merci et bonne chance à vous également!

De retour en France Jean-Marc Four travaille maintenant à la Maison de la Radio à Paris.

Insight

Encore un tuyau utile pour faire des progrès en français: écoutez France Inter, soit sur longues ondes (162LW), soit sur l'internet, où vous pouvez podcaster les programmes qui vous intéressent le plus. Avec l'internet vous pouvez aussi réécouter les progammes autant de fois que vous voulez. Le site: http://www.radiofrance.fr/franceinter/accueil

Here's another useful tip for making progress in French: listen to France Inter, either on long wave (162m) or on the Internet, where you can download the programmes that you find most interesting. With the Internet you can also listen again as many times as you want: http://www.radiofrance.fr/franceinter/accueil

TEST YOURSELF

Exemples:

Cet iPod, c'est le vôtre? → Non, ce n'est pas le mien, c'est celui de ma sœur.

Ces lunettes sont les vôtres? → Non, ce ne sont pas les miennes, ce sont celles de mon père.

1 *Ce portable c'est __ __? Non, ce n'est pas __ __, c'est __ de __ fils.*

2 *Ces patins en ligne* ce sont __ __? Non, → (fille).*

3 *Cette voiture c'est __ __? Non, → (mari).*

4 *Ces valises ce sont __ __? Non, → (enfants).*

5 *Cet ordinateur c'est __ __? Non, → (professeure).*

6 *Ces livres ce sont __ __? Non, → (mon collègue).*

7 *Ces cigarettes ce sont __ __? Non, → copain.*

* **des patins en ligne** = *roller blades* but **des rollers** is commonly used.

23

La vie de famille
Family life

In this unit you will learn
- *about the cinema*
- *about sport in France*
- *one more past tense: the pluperfect*

1 Moi, j'en ai ras-le-bol!
I'm fed up!

◀) **CD2, TR 38, 1:37**

C'est samedi matin et Marie-Claire est débordée!

Listen to / read the dialogue. You need to concentrate on what the various people in the family are planning to do. Complete the grid according to what each person is doing in the morning, afternoon and evening.

Saturday	Marie-Claire	Guillaume	Sarah	Ariane	Pierre
Morning	Housework Shopping				
Afternoon		Football match	Cinema		
Evening	Cinema			At home	

débordée *snowed under*
aider *to help*
le ménage *housework*
en avoir ras-le-bol *to be fed up* (lit. *up to the brim*)
la rentrée *start of the new school year*
ranger *to tidy up*

Ariane	Maman, c'est aujourd'hui que tu nous emmènes au cinéma? Tu avais dit qu'on irait voir *Azur et Asmar*…
Marie-Claire	Oui ma chérie, mais nous n'avons pas encore décidé ce que nous allons faire aujourd'hui.
Pierre	Tu nous avais promis!
Marie-Claire	Oui je sais mais c'est un peu compliqué…
Guillaume	Marie-Claire, je t'avais prévenue qu'aujourd'hui c'est le sport toute la journée … Je pars dans cinq minutes, là…
Marie-Claire	Quoi? Mais où vas-tu?
Guillaume	Mais je te l'ai dit avant-hier! Ce matin je vais à Bercy faire une partie de tennis avec les copains du bureau et cet après-midi je vais au foot avec Lionel. On va voir Paris-Saint Germain. C'est le premier match de la saison, on ne peut pas rater ça!
Marie-Claire	Il est possible que tu me l'aies dit mais j'avais complètement oublié. Moi j'en ai ras-le-bol! Je comptais sur toi pour m'aider à faire le ménage et les courses pour la semaine prochaine. Tu as sans doute oublié que c'est mardi, la rentrée!
Sarah	Bien, moi je vous propose une solution: Guillaume tu vas à Bercy et à ton match de foot, les enfants, ce matin on va tous aider Marie-Claire avec le ménage et les courses et si vous avez bien travaillé, je vous emmènerai voir *Azur et Asmar* cet après midi. Maman profitera du calme pour se reposer.
Ariane	Super! Je vais ranger ma chambre. Tu viens Pierre?
Guillaume	Et moi, ce soir je garderai les enfants et vous deux vous pourrez aller au cinéma si vous en avez envie.

Link the English phrases to the equivalent French expressions.

1 You had said we would go and see.	**a** On va tous aider.
2 I was counting on you to help with the shopping.	**b** On ne peut pas rater ça!
3 I told you the day before yesterday.	**c** Je garderai les enfants.
4 I shall look after the children.	**d** Tu avais dit qu'on irait voir.
5 We are all going to help.	**e** Je te l'ai dit avant-hier.
6 We can't miss that!	**f** Je comptais sur toi pour les courses.

Insight

More on the demonstrative adjectives **ce, cet, cette, ces** (*this, these*):

ce matin, cet après-midi, cette semaine, ces derniers jours, ces dernières semaines - *this morning, this afternoon, this week, these last few days, these last few weeks*

The odd one out is **cet après-midi**. Just as the adjectives **nouveau** and **beau** become respectively **nouvel** and **bel** in front of a masculine noun starting with a vowel, **ce** becomes **cet**.

Un peu de grammaire
A bit of grammar

THE PLUPERFECT

This is another past tense, used for an action which took place prior to something else happening:

Tu avais dit qu'on irait voir *Azur et Asmar*.   *You had said that we would go and see Azur et Asnar.*

Ariane is reminding her mother what had been said prior to today.

There is very little difference between the structures of the pluperfect and the perfect tense.

▶ *Perfect:* **avoir** *or* **être** *in the present tense + past participle*
▶ *Pluperfect:* **avoir** *or* **être** *in the imperfect tense + past participle*

J'ai dit	*I have said*	**Elle est partie**	*She has left*
J'avais dit	*I had said*	**Elle était partie**	*She had left*

Other examples in the dialogue:

Tu nous avais promis.	*You had promised.*
Je t'avais prévenue.	*I had warned you.*
J'avais oublié.	*I had forgotten.*

Note that in many cases the pluperfect and the perfect are used in the same sentence, for example when:

▶ *Something was planned, said or done but more recent events altered the situation:*
Michael Schumacher, deux fois champion du monde, **avait voulu** gagner mais à Jerez il **a** tout **perdu** dans un accrochage avec Jacques Villeneuve.
Michael Schumacher, twice world champion, had wanted to win but at Jerez he lost everything in a collision with Jacques Villeneuve.

This example is from a 1997 newspaper article. The old affinity between France and Canada meant that, at the peak of his career, francophone Jacques Villeneuve received support and full media attention in France.

Et Schumacher? En tout il a été sept fois champion du monde. Jacques Villeneuve ne l'a été qu'une seule fois, en 1997!

▶ *something is done as a consequence of a prior state of things:*
Le garçon **a volé** des pommes parce qu'il n'**avait** pas **mangé** depuis deux jours.

344

The boy stole some apples because he hadn't eaten for two days.

Check that you know your past participles:

prendre	pris
pouvoir	pu
devoir	dû
boire	bu
pleuvoir	plu
perdre	perdu
avoir	eu

Insight

Note the spelling of **dû**, the past participle of **devoir** (*to have to*):
Il avait dû boire toute la bouteille de vin. *He must have drunk the whole bottle of wine.*
The circumflex on the **û** is used to differentiate between **dû**, the past participle, and **du**, the indefinite article (as in **du pain, du vin et du fromage**).

Exercise 1 Terminez les phrases

Find a suitable end for each of the sentences.

1 Sylvie avait beaucoup travaillé

2 Les Durand avaient gagné le gros lot;

3 J'avais pris mon parapluie;

4 Loïc avait dit qu'il viendrait à Paris

5 Les jeunes avaient trop bu

6 Laurent était allé en Angleterre pour les vacances

7 Il a appelé la police

8 Le voleur est entré sans effort;

a mais malheureusement il n'a pas pu.

b pour déclarer qu'on lui avait volé sa voiture.

c on avait dû laisser la porte ouverte.

d et elle a réussi son examen.

e et il a décidé d'y rester.

f malheureusement ils ont tout perdu.

g alors il n'a pas plu.

h et ils ont eu un accident.

Les Français et le sport

Lots of people are keen to watch sports on TV but not so keen to participate. The attitude to sport has been changing slowly though. In the 80s and 90s most French towns started to build well-equipped sports centres. If you want one, look for a sign saying: **Salle omnisports**. The biggest sports centre in France is **Le Palais Omnisports de Paris-Bercy** – a vast centre built mainly for indoor games and also for international competitions, with a capacity for 17,000 spectators. French people are also getting away from lazy beach holidays and spending more time walking, cycling through the countryside on their **VTT** (**Vélos Tous Terrains,** *mountain bikes*), surfing and wind surfing, skiing, swimming and sailing.

And when you hear some French people say: **Je fais du footing**, what they mean is that they go jogging. **Jogging** is also used.

But spectator sports are as popular as ever with **Le Tour de France Cycliste** (watched by millions from the roadsides) at the top of the list and **le foot** close second, and third, horse racing, **la course de chevaux/hippique**. In the dialogue, Guillaume is going to **Le Parc des Princes** to see his team **Paris-Saint Germain. Paris-SG** or **le PSG** is the only first-division club in Paris.

Les clubs français
These are some of the major teams:
Lyon: **Olympique de Lyon**
Auxerre: **Association Jeunesse Auxerroise**
Bordeaux: **Les Girondins de Bordeaux**
Guingamp: **En avant Guingamp** (*Forward Guingamp* – from a tiny Breton town)
Marseille: **Olympique de Marseille**
Lens: **Racing Club de Lens**
Monaco: **Association Sportive de Monaco**
Nantes: **Football Club Nantes Atlantique**
Paris: **Paris-Saint Germain (PSG)**

Many sporting events take place or finish in Paris every year. Look at the table:

Calendrier annuel des événements sportifs à Paris

DATES ET ÉVÈNEMENTS SPORTIFS	LIEUX: OÙ DANS PARIS
Premier janvier Départ du Rallye de Paris-Dakar	Esplanade de Vincennes
Dernier dimanche de janvier Prix d'Amérique (course de chevaux)	Hippodrome de Vincennes
Février – mars Tournoi des Six Nations (rugby)	Parc des Princes
Avril Marathon de Paris; Festival d'Arts Martiaux	À travers Paris; Palais Omnisports de Bercy
Première quinzaine d'avril (un dimanche) Prix du Président de la République	Hippodrome d'Auteuil
Fin mai / début juin Internationaux de France de Tennis	Stade Roland-Garros
Juin Finale de la coupe de France de Football; Course des serveuses et garçons de café	Stade de France; Des Champs-Elysées à la Bastille
Troisième dimanche de juin Grand Steeple-Chase	Hippodrome d'Auteuil
Dernier dimanche de juin Grand Prix de Paris	Hippodrome de Longchamp
Mi-juillet Arrivée du Tour de France Cycliste	Champs-Elysées
Mi-septembre (un samedi) Prix d'été	Hippodrome de Vincennes
Premier dimanche d'octobre Prix de L'Arc de Triomphe	Hippodrome de Longchamp
Octobre Les Vingt Kilomètres de Paris (course à pied)	Tour Eiffel
Deuxième dimanche d'octobre Course de côte de voitures anciennes (*uphill race*)	Rue Lepic (Montmartre)
Fin octobre Tennis: Le Tournoi de Paris (*Paris Open*)	Paris-Bercy

Exercise 2 **Les événements sportifs**
Look again at the table of sporting events in
Paris, and answer these questions.

  a *How many types of sporting events are*
      listed?
  b *What are they?*
  c *When is the barmen and women's race?*
  d *Where does it take place?*
  e *When is the Prix du Président de la*
      République?
  f *What race starts and finishes at the Eiffel Tower?*

Exercise 3 **Est-ce que vous connaissez bien les deux meilleurs
footballeurs français?**

L'un, maintenant en retraite, est toujours la personnalité
préférée des français, malgré son expulsion pour avoir
donné un coup de tête volontaire dans la poitrine de Marco
Materazzi, au cours de la Coupe du Monde 2006, l'autre a
joué plusieurs années pour l'équipe anglaise d'Arsenal. Il joue
maintenant pour l'équipe de Barcelone et il est toujours le
chouchou des foules.

Using the information listed below fill in the gaps in the box below:

Marseille, française, Zidane, 1,88m, Arsenal FC, Paris, Real
Madrid, 23 juin 1972, milieu de terrain, Zinédine, 1,85m,
attaquant, française, 17 août 1977, Henry.

1. Prénom:	1. Prénom: Thierry
2. Nom:	2. Nom:
3. Nationalité:	3. Nationalité:
4. Date de naissance:	4. Date de naissance:
5. Lieu de naissance:	5. Lieu de naissance:
6. Taille:	6. Taille:
7. Poste:	7. Poste:
8. Club avant la coupe du Monde:	8. Club avant la coupe du Monde:

Insight

Sporting euphemisms:

Les Français sont fous* de sport. Dans les bars les discussions tournent inlassablement autour du ballon rond, du ballon oval de la petite reine, et de la grande boucle.

You've probably guessed that **le ballon rond** (*the round ball*) is football, **le ballon oval** (*the oval ball*) is rugby and that **la grande boucle** (*the big loop*) is the Tour de France, but do you know what **la petite reine** (*the little queen*) is? You'll find the answer later in this unit.

* **fous** = *mad*

Surfez sur le web

Si vous êtes sportif ou sportive visitez les sites suivantes:

- Pour le football visitez www.maxifoot.com
- Pour tout savoir sur les derniers transferts et sur les clubs français et étrangers visitez www.football365.fr
- Pour tous les résultats du monde du basket trouvez www.basketzone.com
- Pour les amateurs de rugby allez voir www.totalrugby.com et www.rugbyrama.com
- Google Olympique Lyonnais or go to www.olweb.fr (site officiel) or www.olympiquelyonnais.com

---

2 Aller au cinema
Going to the cinema

◀)) **CD2, TR 39**

Sarah et Marie-Claire ont finalement décidé d'aller au cinéma. Elles ont acheté L'Officiel des Spectacles (a weekly guide to what's on in Paris) et cherchent des films qu'elles aimeraient voir.

Listen to the recording and look at the list of films below selected by Sarah and Marie-Claire then answer the questions:

a *Why does Sarah say she will let Marie-Claire choose the film?*
b *What does Marie-Claire say about* Paris je t'aime?
c *Which film do they choose to see?*

La liste de Sarah et Marie-Claire (par ordre alphabétique)

Arthur et les Minimoys (2006 1h35) Aventure et animation de Luc Besson: comme tous les enfants de son âge Arthur est fasciné par les histoires que lui raconte sa grand-mère pour l'endormir. Mais..si ces histoires étaient vraies?

Azur et Asmar (2004 1h39) Animation de Michel Ocelot: il y a bien longtemps, deux enfants étaient bercés par la même femme. Elevés comme deux frères, les enfants sont séparés brutalement …

Hors de Prix (2006 1h43) Comédie de Pierre Salvadori avec Audrey Tautou et Gad Elmaleh. Jean, serveur timide d'un grand hôtel, passe pour un milliardaire aux yeux d'Irène, une aventurière intéressée. Quand elle découvre qui il est réellement elle le fuit aussitôt. Mais Jean, amoureux, se lance à sa poursuite et la retrouve sur la Côte d'Azur.

Les Infiltrés (VO) (2006 2h30) Film américain de Martin Scorsese avec Leonardo Di Caprio, Matt Damon et Jack Nicholson:
le 'parrain', Lou Costello règne en maître sur Boston. Pour le démasquer la police locale charge un jeune flic, Billy Costigan, d'infiltrer le gang du vieux malfaiteur.

Marie-Antoinette (2005 2h03) Film américain de Sofia Coppola. Drame historique où la jeune Marie-Antoinette découvre un monde hostile et codifié, un univers frivole où chacun observe et juge l'autre...

Paris je t'aime (2006 1h50) Film à sketches collectifs: voyages dans différents arrondissements de Paris à travers une série d'anecdotes amoureuses. Avec Fanny Ardant, Juliette Binoche, Steve Buscemi, Sergio Castellitto, Willem Dafoe, Gérard Depardieu, Marianne Faithfull, Ben Gazzara, Bob Hoskins, Nick Nolte, Natalie Portman, Gena Rowlands et Ludivine Sagnier.

Sarah	Je te laisse choisir parce que je sors beaucoup plus souvent que toi quand je suis à Londres. De toutes façons j'aimerais certainement ton choix.
Marie-Claire	J'ai coché *Azur et Asmar* mais en fait tu l'as vu samedi avec les enfants. Je les emmènerai sans doute voir *Arthur et les Minimoys* samedi prochain.
Sarah	*Les Infiltrés* c'est la version originale sous-titrée en français je crois. Le titre anglais est *The Departed*. J'aime bien les films de Scorsese mais je le verrai certainement à Londres.
Marie-Claire	*Paris Je t'aime* vient de sortir en DVD, je te l'offre pour ton anniversaire si tu veux. C'est formidable, c'est plein d'acteurs connus et ce sont des histoires qui se passent dans chaque arrondissement de Paris.
Sarah	Bon eh bien il nous reste le choix entre *Marie-Antoinette* et *Hors de Prix*. Qu'est ce que tu préfères?
Marie-Claire	Moi j'adore Audrey Tautou, tu as vu *Amélie*?
Sarah	Bien sûr, j'ai adoré, bon alors c'est décidé on va voir *Hors de Prix*! Je suis sûre que nous ne serons pas déçues.

je te laisse choisir *I let you choose*
la version sous-titrée *subtitled version*
de toutes façons *in any case*
déçues/déçu/e *disappointed*

QUICK VOCAB

Exercise 4
   a *Say you would like to see* Paris je t'aime *because you love Paris.*
   b *Say you would like to see* Arthur et les Minimoys *because you love films directed by Luc Besson.*
   c *Say you would like to see* Marie-Antoinette *because it is interesting to see an American film about French history.*
   d *Say you would like to see* Azur et Asmar *because the story, the animation and the music are beautiful.*

Insight

We use the pluperfect to talk about something that happened before the time we are speaking about. In a 'then and now' situation:

J'avais adoré Audrey Tautou dans 'Amélie' mais dans le rôle de Coco Chanel elle est sublime. *I'd loved Audrey Tautou in 'Amélie' but in the role of Coco Chanel she is sublime.*

In a 'before and then' situation:
Marion Cotillard était peu connue mais avec 'La Môme' cela a été une révélation. *Marion Cotillard had been little known but with 'La Môme' this was a revelation.*

With an implicit pre-existing condition:
Isabelle Adjani était préprogrammée pour son rôle de professeure dans 'La Journée de la jupe'. *Isabelle Adjani had been preprogrammed for her role of professor in 'La Journée de la jupe'.*

Exercise 5 Abonnez-vous
Et si vous aimez vraiment le cinéma abonnez-vous!

The form below is for a year's subscription to *Les Cahiers du Cinéma*, the oldest and most famous cinema magazine which, from its early days, has been influential on French cinema.

Fill in the form (as an exercise!) and answer these questions.

   a *What was the special offer?*
   b *How many issues would you receive for that price?*
   c *How can you pay?*

Pour les amateurs de cinéma surfez sur le web pour trouver des informations sur les derniers films et tous les grands classiques du cinéma.

- www.cahiersducinema.com.
  If you are a real film buff this is the site for you.
- www.MK2.com
  Depuis 1974, mk2 distribution a distribué plus de 300 films de plus de 30 nationalités différentes.
- www.cinemathequefrancaise.fr
  La Cinémathèque Française has moved its premises to Parc de Bercy. See website for special events.
- http://www.azuretasmar-lefilm.com/demo.html (this is a good example of a trailer available on the web)

Insight

So what is **la petite reine** (*the little queen*)?

C'est le nom donné affectueusement par les Français à la bicyclette. La troisième passion sportive de millions de Français est évidemment la course cycliste, et particulièrement le Tour de France qui a lieu au mois de juillet chaque année.

It's the affectionate French name for the bicycle. The third sporting passion of millions of French people is obviously cycling, and in particular the Tour de France, which takes place in July every year.

TEST YOURSELF

Link the sentences.

1 *Je n'avais pas vu ce film*

2 *Ils étaient montés à la Tour Eiffel*

3 *Il avait voulu faire des courses*

4 *Elle était tombée en panne;*

5 *J'étais sortie sans mon parapluie*

6 *J'avais dû m'endormir;*

7 *Nous avions décidé de partir en voyage;*

8 *Nous avions prévu un pique-nique*

9 *Nous étions partis de bonne heure*

10 *Ils m'avaient prêté de l'argent*

a *malheureusement mon mari est tombé malade.*

b *heureusement qu'il y avait un garage tout près.*

c *et j'ai pu prendre un taxi pour rentrer chez moi.*

d *mais il a plu et nous avons mangé dans la voiture.*

e *mais les magasins étaient fermés.*

f *mais il faisait du brouillard et ils n'ont rien vu.*

g *mais le DVD vient de sortir.*

h *mais ma sœur m'a prêté le sien.*

i *heureusement que le téléphone m'a réveillé.*

j *mais nous sommes arrivés en retard.*

24

Un repas familial
A family meal

In this unit you will learn
- *about French meals*
- *recipe vocabulary*
- *how to talk about the family*
- *how to talk about travelling*
- qui *and* que *(relative pronouns)*

1 Mettre le couvert
To lay the table

◀) **CD2, TR 40**

*La famille se retrouve chez tante Eliane, Rue du Docteur Blanche,
à Passy dans le seizième arrondissement de Paris. Bruno, un de ses
fils, est enseignant à Lyon mais en ce moment il est en vacances
chez sa mère. Son autre fils, Daniel, travaille à l'étranger.*

Listen to the recording and answer the questions.

   a *What does aunt Eliane ask the children to do?*
   b *What does she ask them to be careful with?*
   c *What does she give them to take to Bruno?*
   d *What will they drink with the meal?*

Listen again, several times if necessary.

e *And now write down Tante Eliane's menu in French and say what it means.*

Menu
de Tante Eliane
Dimanche 31 août

Tante Eliane	Vous venez avec moi dans la salle à manger les petits, vous allez m'aider à mettre le couvert.
Ariane	Moi, je sais mettre le couvert.
Pierre	Et moi aussi je sais.
Tante	Alors faites bien attention à ma vaisselle, surtout les verres. Alors vous faites comme cela. La petite assiette sur la grande assiette, la fourchette à gauche, le couteau à droite et la cuillère à dessert devant le verre. Voilà, c'est bien!
Pierre	On a fini!
Tante	Bon, tu veux demander à Bruno de m'ouvrir la bouteille de vin blanc qui est au frigo? Tiens, donne-lui le tire-bouchon.
Ariane	Qu'est-ce qu'on mange? J'ai faim!
Tante	Ah! J'aime bien que les enfants aient de l'appétit! Je vous ai préparé un très bon menu. Alors comme entrée on a du bon melon et après je vais vous servir une truite au champagne et raisins avec des pommes de terre sautées.
Pierre	Et pour le dessert?
Tante	Ah mais avant le dessert il y a de la salade et du bon fromage et pour le dessert ... une tarte aux pommes!
Pierre et Ariane	Miam-miam!

Le couvert

In the dialogue can you find the French for the following items of crockery, cutlery, etc.?

a a glass
b a plate
c a knife
d a fork

e a spoon
f crockery/dishes
g a corkscrew

Link the following English phrases to the equivalent French expressions.

1 You are going to help to lay the table.

2 Mind my dishes.

3 Do you mind asking Bruno to open the bottle of wine for me?

4 Give him the corkscrew.

5 I like it when children have an appetite.

6 And for dessert ... an apple tart.

a Donne-lui le tire-bouchon.

b Et pour le dessert ... une tarte aux pommes.

c J'aime que les enfants aient de l'appétit.

d Vous allez m'aider à mettre le couvert.

e Faites attention à ma vaisselle.

f Tu veux demander à Bruno de m'ouvrir la bouteille de vin?

......

Insight

Use of the relative pronouns **qui** (*who / which*) and **que** (*that / which*): in

La bouteille de vin qui est dans la cave et que ton grand-père garde depuis dix ans

qui stands for **la bouteille de vin** when it's the subject of the clause (*which is in the cellar*); **que** refers to **la bouteille de vin** when it's the object of the sentence (*which Grandpa has been keeping for ten years*).

......

La cuisine et la nourriture *Cooking and food*

French home cooking has been very traditional for a long time but now people are starting to experiment. There is also the influence of North-African cooking such as couscous-based dishes which are integrated into what people eat at home.

There is a slight attempt to eat things other than meat for the main course. However, the pattern of serving the lettuce after the main course, followed by the cheese followed by dessert is absolutely standard.

An important family meal on a special occasion such as a wedding, a communion or a christening (**un baptême**) would probably have either a seafood dish to start with or **un plateau de charcuterie** with various cooked meats. There would be a fish course followed by a meat dish. Traditionally only one vegetable is served, often a potato dish. Big family reunions often take place around the table and often last for hours. Lots of wine tends to be served.

Everyday cooking can be more sober but even when people are on their own they take pleasure in cooking something nice: **se mijoter un bon petit plat**. **Mijoter** means *to stew*, but in terms of French cooking, **mijoter** means cooking slowly, with care and attention, just the correct proportion of ingredients, making sure that the sauce is just right.

Insight

Cooking and table expressions are often used figuratively with a derogatory meaning.

Je ne sais pas ce qu'il mijote! (in the sense of plotting)

Elle met les petits plats dans les grands (*to make an effort to please or impress*, lit. *She puts the little dishes in the big ones*)

Il est soupe au lait (*he loses his temper easily* – just as a milky soup boils over)

2 Une bonne recette: La grande truite au champagne et aux raisins frais
A good recipe: trout in champagne with fresh grapes

Before you can read this recipe you need a few items of vocabulary which are new to you. Some can be guessed but others need to be learnt. The vocabulary can be divided into three categories: ingredients and other nouns, adjectives describing the condition of the ingredients, and instructions (here verbs in the infinitive). Once you can read this recipe you can tackle others.

In each of the three boxes match the equivalent French and English expressions. Some have already been done for you.

Qu'est-ce qu'il faut?

Les ingrédients		
1 échalotes	**a**	mushrooms
2 beurre	**b**	salt and pepper
3 champignons	**c**	shallots
4 jaunes d'œufs	**d**	fresh dill leaves
5 feuilles d'aneth fraîches	**e**	butter
6 sel et poivre	**f**	egg yolks
Les procédés (*processes*) **et les ustensiles de cuisine**		
7 le temps de cuisson	**g**	boiling point
8 ébullition	**h**	cooking time
9 la lèchefrite ⟶	**i**	cooking pan (in oven)
10 le four ⟶	**j**	the oven

Comment sont nos ingrédients?

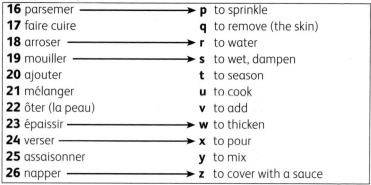

11 épluché(e)(s) ⟶	**k** peeled
12 lavé(e)(s)	**l** heated
13 vidé(e)(s) ⟶	**m** gutted (emptied)
14 haché(e)(s) ⟶	**n** chopped
15 chauffé(e)(s)	**o** washed

Maintenant que faut-il faire?

16 parsemer ⟶	**p** to sprinkle
17 faire cuire	**q** to remove (the skin)
18 arroser ⟶	**r** to water
19 mouiller ⟶	**s** to wet, dampen
20 ajouter	**t** to season
21 mélanger	**u** to cook
22 ôter (la peau)	**v** to add
23 épaissir ⟶	**w** to thicken
24 verser ⟶	**x** to pour
25 assaisonner	**y** to mix
26 napper ⟶	**z** to cover with a sauce

Et voilà! La cuisine de A à Z!

Vous pouvez maintenant suivre n'importe quelle recette française!

Lisez la recette! Now read carefully the recipe for trout in champagne, and answer the questions which follow.

- **a** *This recipe is for how many persons?*
- **b** *How long will it take to cook?*
- **c** *How much champagne is used?*
- **d** *What must be done to the champagne before pouring it on the trout?*
- **e** *When do you need to add the champagne?*
- **f** *What needs to be done to the trout's tail and head?*

UNE ENVIE DE VRAI

*à découvrir la truite de France
et ses recettes
mode et tradition*

AU FOUR,
EN FETE, LA GRANDE TRUITE
AU CHAMPAGNE ET RAISINS FRAIS

Ingrédients

- 1 grande truite d'env. 2,5 kg
- 3 échalotes
- 100 g de beurre
- 125 g de champignons de Paris
- 1/2 bout. de champagne
- 10 grains de raisin noir frais épluchés
- 10 grains de raisin blanc frais épluchés
- Asperges
- 125 g de crème fraîche
- 2 ou 3 jaunes d'œufs
- Baies de poivre rosé
- Feuilles d'aneth fraîches
- Sel et poivre

Temps de cuisson
Environ 45 minutes.

Préparation pour 6/8 personnes.

La truite étant vidée et lavée, saler et poivrer l'intérieur. Garnir le fond d'une léchefrite d'une feuille d'aluminium, la parsemer d'échalotes hachées et de champignons, y déposer la truite, après avoir enveloppé la tête et la queue de papier d'aluminium. Saler, poivrer, mouiller avec la moitié du champagne, couvrir le plat d'aluminium.

Faire cuire à 200°C (thermostat 6) pendant 45 minutes environ. Une ou deux fois en cours de cuisson, arroser la truite de champagne chauffé en soulevant la feuille d'aluminium.

Sortir la truite et ôter la peau des deux côtés. Dresser sur un plat de service. Pour la sauce, à ébullition, verser le jus de cuisson dans une casserole, ajouter la crème mélangée aux jaunes d'œufs. Assaisonner, faire épaissir, ajouter grains de raisins et baies de poivre rosé et napper la truite.

Exercise 1 **Un peu de diététique**

Avez-vous un bon équilibre alimentaire? Pour le savoir, testez-vous.

Cochez les cases qui correspondent à vos habitudes alimentaires.

VOS HABITUDES ALIMENTAIRES	Toujours	Parfois	Jamais
1 Vous buvez de l'eau tout au long de la journée?			
2 Vous optez pour les fruits et légumes?			
3 Vous restez raisonnable avec le gras et le sucre?			
4 Vous consommez des fibres?			
5 Vous préférez le poisson et les volailles?			
6 Vous consommez des céréales?			
7 Vous utilisez des huiles végétales?			
8 Vous déjeunez copieusement et dînez légèrement?			
9 Vous limitez votre consommation d'alcool?			
10 Vous mangez avec plaisir et en bonne compagnie?			

VOCAB

le gras *fat*
la volaille *poultry*
parfois *sometimes*

La solution:

Pour chaque question où vous avez coché la première colonne: accordez-vous 1 point; la deuxième colonne: 2 points; et la troisième: 3 points.

Et le verdict:

De 1 à 12 points: C'est bien! Vous avez un régime équilibré.

De 13 à 23 points: Encore un petit effort! Vous pouvez mieux faire et vous faire du bien.

De 24 à 30 points: C'est le désastre! Vous allez à la catastrophe à moins de faire quelque chose immédiatement.

Surfez sur le web

- Si vous aimez les bonnes recettes faciles à comprendre avec beaucoup d'illustrations allez demander conseils chez www.supertoinette.com. Vous y trouverez des centaines de recettes super.
- Si vous êtes au régime (*on a diet*) allez voir au bas de la page d'accueil: dans la rubrique 'recettes minceur', vous trouverez des dizaines de recettes avec le nombre de calories pour chaque plat.
- Choisissez 'Les pommes de terre farcies à la ricotta'. Vous m'en donnerez des nouvelles!

Web extension

Recette pommes de terre farcies à la ricotta

- 420 g de grosses pommes de terre (2)
- 130 g de ricotta
- 9 g d'ail
- Quelques brins de ciboulette (*chives*)
- Sel

Ingrédients | 2P | 1h15

- Poivre du moulin
- 5 g de vinaigre de Xérès
- 8 feuilles de basilic
- 2 pincées de cannelle (*cinnamon*)

Web extension exercise

Vrai ou Faux? Dans la recette des pommes de terre farcies à la ricotta:

1 *The potatoes are stuffed with camembert*
2 *Use 9 grams of shallots*
3 *Use a teaspoon of cinnamon*
4 *This is a recipe for one person*
5 *The potatoes should be cooked in the oven – not in the microwave (justify your answer)*

---

3 Des nouvelles de la famille
Family news

◄» **CD2, TR 41**

Tout le monde est encore à table, la truite au champagne est délicieuse, le vin est bon et on échange des nouvelles de la famille.

Listen to the recording and answer the questions.

a *Where is Daniel now?*
b *When is he coming back to France?*
c *Does he like it?*
d *Is he married?*

Listen again.

e *Who is Tante Eliane going to Canada with?*
f *Why is she going with her?*

Listen once more.

g *When are they leaving? From where?*
h *When are they returning?*

un ordinateur *a computer*
célibataire *single (applies to men or women)*
ma belle-sœur *my sister-in-law*
à cause de *because of*

Sarah	Au fait, comment va Daniel?
Tante Eliane	Il va bien, il voyage beaucoup … Euh … en ce moment il est au Japon mais il rentrera en France à Noël.
Sarah	Ah bon! Ça fait combien de temps qu'il est là-bas?
Tante	Oh, à peu près trois mois. Il travaille pour une firme qui fabrique des ordinateurs et en ce moment il passe trois mois en France et trois mois au Japon.
Sarah	Ça lui plaît?
Tante	Ah oui, énormément. Et puis tant qu'il est célibataire il n'y a pas de problèmes. Oh mais je ne vous ai pas dit? Cette fois-ci c'est moi qui pars en voyage!
Marie-Claire	Ah bon! Et où vas-tu?
Tante	Au Canada! J'y vais avec ma belle-sœur qui habite à Nantes. C'est un voyage organisé. Ils avaient acheté les billets et maintenant son mari ne peut pas y aller à cause de son travail alors j'y vais à sa place.
Guillaume	Et quand est-ce que tu pars?
Tante	Eh bien le départ de Nantes est le 12 octobre et nous rentrons le 21.
Marie-Claire	Bon, alors on te souhaite un bon voyage et n'oublie pas de nous envoyer une carte postale, hein!

Link the following English phrases to the equivalent French expressions.

1 How long has he been there?	**a** C'est un voyage organisé.
2 He works for a firm which manufactures computers.	**b** tant qu'il est célibataire…
3 as long as he is single…	**c** N'oublie pas de nous envoyer une carte postale.
4 I am going with my sister-in-law.	**d** Ça fait combien de temps qu'il est là-bas?
5 Don't forget to send a postcard.	**e** J'y vais avec ma belle-sœur.
6 It's a package tour.	**f** Il travaille pour une firme qui fabrique des ordinateurs.

Insight

Names of countries or continents are masculine or feminine and singular or plural: **le Canada, la France, les Etats-Unis, les Pays-Bas, la Hollande,** and to say 'in' we use either en or à: **au Canada, aux Etats-Unis, au Royaume-Uni / en Grande Bretagne, aux Pays-Bas / en Hollande, au Japon, en Australie, en Espagne**

Un peu de grammaire
A bit of grammar

QUI *OR* QUE?

These are relative pronouns. Although similar, they have two different functions:

▶ **Qui** who, which, *that represents people or objects. It acts as the subject of the verb:*
une firme qui fabrique des ordinateurs
c'est **moi qui** pars

In the two examples above **qui** represents the noun which precedes it and which is the subject of the sentence. **Qui** links two sentences, making one longer and more elegant sentence:

C'est ma belle sœur. Elle habite à Nantes. → **C'est ma belle sœur qui habite à Nantes.**

▶ Que/qu' *which, that, whom also links two sentences, but it represents the direct object of the sentence. It represents people or objects.*
Le voyage que je vais faire est un voyage organisé.

In this type of sentence **que** is placed immediately before the subject. This should be more obvious in the next two examples:

Regarde, c'est **le type que** j'ai   *Look, it's the guy I saw yesterday.*
    vu hier.

Here **que** represents **le type** (the object). **Que** precedes **j'** (the subject) who did the action of seeing the man (the object).

Regarde, c'est **le type qui** a vu   *Look, it's the guy who saw the*
    l'accident.   *accident.*

In this sentence **qui** represents **le type** (here the subject) who saw the accident (the object).

Qui is always followed by a verb, sometimes preceded by an indirect pronoun:

C'est toi **qui** lui as donné les clefs!   *It's you who gave her the keys!*

In the above example, **qui** represents the subject **toi**. In the following sentence **que** represents the object **les clefs** and precedes the subject **tu**. Note that as the object **les clefs** precedes the verb, the past participle agrees with the number and gender of the object (**données**):

Voici les clefs **que** tu lui as données.   *Here are the keys you gave him.*

Exercise 2 Remplissez les blancs

In each of the sentences fill the gap(s) with **qui, que** or **qu'**.

a   *Ce _____ j'aime ce sont les enfants _____ sont polis!*
b   *La recette _____ je préfère c'est celle de la truite aux amandes.*
c   *Le film _____ je voulais voir passe à la télé ce soir.*
d   *Ce sont les années _____ j'ai passées en Angleterre à apprendre l'anglais _____ me seront les plus utiles.*
e   *C'est toi _____ as les clefs?*
f   *Pourquoi est-ce que ce sont toujours les mêmes _____ décident?*

Insight

If you're still in doubt whether to use **qui** or **que** examine the sentence below:

Le seul magazine que j'achète régulièrement c'est le 'Nouvel Observateur', qui est un hebdomadaire. *The only magazine that I buy regularly is the 'Nouvel Observateur', which is a weekly magazine.*

1400 €
Départ de Nantes

PROGRAMME

JOUR 5
MONTRÉAL-QUÉBEC
Petit déjeuner à l'hôtel. Départ pour la visite guidée, métropole cosmopolite, Montréal présente mille et un visages, mille et un éclats. Vous découvrirez le centre-ville et ses gratte-ciel, le Vieux Montréal et ses rues recouvertes de gros pavés, le Vieux Port qui offre une fenêtre sur St-Laurent, l'Eglise Notre-Dame, le Mont-Royal, l'Ile Ste-Hélène, le Jardin Botanique et le Stade Olympique. Départ pour Québec. Déjeuner à la Cabane à Sucre Chez Pierre. Dîner de homard au restaurant le Monte Carlo. 5e nuit Hôtel LE COTTAGE ou similaire.

JOUR 6
QUÉBEC
Petit déjeuner à l'hôtel. Départ de l'hôtel pour la visite guidée de la ville Québec, berceau de la civilisation française en Amérique du Nord. La seule ville fortifiée au Nord du Mexique. Vous verrez le Vieux-Québec, le Château Frontenac, la Place Royale, la Colline Parlementaire et la Citadelle. Déjeuner et temps 'libre' dans le Vieux Québec pour découvrir ses boutiques et musées à pied. Dîner au restaurant La Cage aux Sports. 6e nuit Hôtel LE COTTAGE ou similaire.

JOUR 7
QUÉBEC-CHARLEVOIX
Petit déjeuner à l'hôtel. Départ pour la région de Charlevoix, nous ferons quelques arrêts, premier arrêt aux Chutes Montmorency (1 fois et demi la hauteur des Chutes du Niagara). Déjeuner à Tadoussac, suivi de temps libre pour visiter ce très beau petit village ou faire l'excursion des baleines (en option); pour les autres nous ferons la visite du Manoir Richelieu. Dîner à votre hôtel. 8e nuit au MANOIR CHARLEVOIX.

Exercise 3 **Un peu de lecture**
Tante Eliane shows her family what she is going to see in Canada.

Look at the schedule for Days 5, 6 and 7.

les gratte-ciel *skyscrapers*   **un homard** *a lobster*
des pavés *cobblestones*   **des baleines** *whales*

....

Insight

    Les gratte-ciel de Montréal *Montreal's sky-scrapers* (lit. *scratch sky*): regardless of the number of skyscrapers, both parts of the noun remain in the singular: **gratte** is a verb and as such cannot be pluralized as if it were a noun; **ciel** remains in the singular too because there is only one sky. The plural of **le ciel, les cieux,** has poetic connotations. It is also used in the Lord's prayer: **Notre père qui êtes aux cieux...**

....

Vrai ou faux?

Say whether the following statements based on the schedule are true or false.

  a *They will see skyscrapers in Tadoussac.*
  b *Québec is one of two fortified towns north of Mexico.*
  c *There is a lobster dinner at the end of day 7.*
  d *The excursion to see the whales is optional.*
  e *There will be some free time to see old Quebec.*
  f *Mont-Royal offers a window on the St Laurent.*
  g *Montmorency Falls are one and a half times higher than Niagara Falls.*
  h *There is a guided tour of Tadoussac.*
   i *Québec is the cradle of French civilization in North America.*
   j *L'Ile Ste Hélène is a church.*

Cherchez l'erreur
Attention: dans le texte pour le Jour 7 il y a **une petite erreur d'imprimerie** (*a small printing error*). L'avez-vous découverte?

Au Québec

Tante Eliane visitera le village historique de Tadoussac, le mieux connu des Français et pour cause! C'est le berceau (lit. *cradle*) de la Nouvelle-France. En 1535, Jacques Cartier jette l'ancre à Tadoussac, suivi quelques années plus tard par Pierre de Chauvin, qui y débarque en 1599. En 1600, on y érige le premier poste officiel de traite des fourrures (*fur trade*) en Nouvelle-France, ce qui en fait le plus vieux village en Amérique du Nord, plus vieux même que Québec. Pour en savoir plus visitez le sites des plus beaux villages du Québec: www.beauxvillages.qc.ca.

Vive le Québec libre! Comme vous pouvez le constater la France et le Québec sont très liés et des personnages politiques français l'ont souvent exprimé en ces termes, comme par exemple le général de Gaulle en juillet 1967 et Ségolène Royal, alors candidate à la présidence de la République, en janvier 2007.

Mais ce n'est pas tout! En 2008 Québec a fêté son 400e anniversaire.

De juin à septembre 2008, les Québécois ont vécu l'expérience mémorable du 400e anniversaire de Québec en découvrant la ville et son histoire sous un jour nouveau. Un livre pour se souvenir a été publié: 'Québec, ma ville, mon 400e'. Pour en savoir d'avantage sur Espace 400e, consultez les sites suivants www.monquebec 2008.com/fr/ espace 400e.phy ainsi que www.bonjourquebec.com.

Si vous avez envie de visiter d'autres pays francophones visitez www.francegazette.com et cliquez sur Planetantilles ou bien lisez les articles Francophonie. Si vous ne pouvez pas voyager, visitez-les virtuellement!

Web extension exercise
1 *What is the name of the best-known village of the province of Québec?*
2 *What happened in 2008 in Québec?*

TEST YOURSELF

Une carte postale de Québec

Use the groups of words below to complete the text of the postcard.

hier soir; j'ai préféré; je te raconterai; beaucoup aimé; ma semaine; avons été très touchés; de choses; ça ressemblait; partout dans le monde; cette carte postale; a débarqué; c'était drôle

Ma Chère Marie-Claire,

__ au Québec touche à sa fin. Nous avons fait tellement __ intéressantes que je n'ai pas le temps de tout dire sur __ mais __ tout en détails à mon retour. J'ai __ le vieux Montréal mais ce que __ ce sont tous les petits villages que nous avons visités. J'ai surtout adoré Tadoussac qui est le village où Jacques Cartier__ en 1535. Les villageois nous ont fait fête et nous __ de les rencontrer. J'adore la façon dont ils parlent le français, avec leur accent chantant. J'avais envie de parler comme eux.

__ nous sommes allés à un concert folklorique dans un vieux bar où il y avait un groupe de chanteurs qui s'appellent 'La Bottine Souriante'. __ parce que __ un peu à de la musique bretonne. Apparemment ils sont très connus __.

J'espère que tu vas bien et que ta petite blessure ne te cause plus d'ennuis.

Embrasse bien les enfants de ma part.

A bientôt

Tante Eliane

374

25

Si on achetait une maison?
What if we bought a house?

In this unit you will learn
- *how to express sadness and feeling depressed*
- *the order of pronouns*
- *about planning to buy a house in France*
- *some legal requirements when buying a property*

1 Avant le départ
Before the departure

◄» **CD2, TR 42**

Toute la famille accompagne Sarah à la gare du Nord d'où elle doit repartir pour Londres.

Listen to the recording once, and answer these questions.

   a *Why is Sarah feeling a bit low?*
   b *How does Ariane feel about Sarah's departure?*
   c *Is Sarah looking forward to going back to work?*

Listen again.

   d *Who is Marie-Claire going to 'phone tonight?*
   e *Why tonight?*

Listen once more.

f *What is Mrs Burgess planning to do? (two things)*
g *What does Guillaume suggest?*
h *Does Marie-Claire think it is a good idea?*

Now read the dialogue.

Sarah	Ah là là, je n'ai pas envie de rentrer!
Guillaume	Eh bien reste!
Sarah	Non … je ne peux pas, seulement j'ai toujours un peu le cafard quand je quitte la France.
Ariane	Moi non plus je ne veux pas que tu partes. On est triste quand tu t'en vas!
Marie-Claire	Tu regrettes de ne pas avoir accepté l'offre d'emploi chez Gallimard?
Sarah	Non, pas du tout, je n'y pensais même plus. Non, ce n'est pas grave, je suis un peu déprimée mais ce n'est tout de même pas la grosse dépression! C'est tout simplement que je n'ai pas la pêche quand il s'agit de reprendre le travail!
Marie-Claire	En fait de déprime il ne faut pas que j'oublie de téléphoner à Maman ce soir. C'est la rentrée pour elle aussi demain et, en général, elle non plus elle n'a pas le moral avant de reprendre les cours.
Sarah	Alors fais bien attention. Elle va sûrement te faire part de ses projets: elle voudrait prendre sa retraite à cinquante-cinq ans et s'acheter une petite maison dans le Midi.
Marie-Claire	Oui je sais, elle m'en a déjà parlé. Elle dit que cette idée, c'est toi qui la lui as donnée!
Guillaume	Et si on achetait une maison entre nous tous! On pourrait peut-être trouver quelque chose de pas trop cher à rénover …
Marie-Claire	Ah oui! Dis, Guillaume, et qui est-ce qui les ferait, ces rénovations?

Feeling depressed:
Il a le cafard
Il est déprimé
Il n'a pas la pêche (colloquial)
Il n'a pas le moral

triste *sad*
faire part de *to inform about*
un faire-part de naissance/mariage/décès *announcement of birth/ wedding/death*
Gallimard *one of the most important French publishing companies*

Link the following English phrases to the equivalent French expressions.

1 Do you regret turning down Gallimard's job offer?

2 I was no longer thinking about it.

3 before going back to school.

4 She has already spoken to me about it.

5 She would like to retire at 55.

a Elle m'en a déjà parlé.

b Elle voudrait prendre sa retraite à 55 ans.

c Je n'y pensais même plus.

d avant de reprendre les cours.

e Tu regrettes de ne pas avoir accepté l'offre d'emploi chez Gallimard?

Un peu de grammaire
A bit of grammar

ORDER OF PRONOUNS: LE, LA, LES AND LUI

In the following sequence, the nouns in the sentence are replaced by pronouns:

Tu as donné cette idée à Maman.
Tu lui as donné cette idée. (**lui** represents **à Maman**)
Tu l'as donnée à Maman. (**la/l'** represents **cette idée**)
Tu la lui as donnée.

Word order, especially the order of pronouns, may appear difficult but there is a simple principle which can help: **le, la** and **les** are weaker pronouns, in terms of sound, than **lui** and **leur**. They are always placed before **lui** or **leur**:

J'ai donné mon billet au contrôleur: Je le lui ai donné.
J'ai donné mon permis de conduire aux gendarmes: Je le leur ai donné.

In a negative sentence there are even more words to line up. The same principle applies:

Je ne le lui ai pas donné.
Je ne le leur ai pas donné.

In more slovenly speech there is a tendency to rush all the pronouns together and to drop **ne** (which is weaker than **pas**) and also **le**:

J'lui ai pas donné.

and in the affirmative too there is a tendency to drop **le**:

J'lui ai donné.

The two examples above are not what you are advised to say but you will hear them frequently.

MOI AUSSI *ME TOO* / MOI NON PLUS *ME NEITHER*

These two expressions are frequently used. They are strictly direct responses, agreeing with something someone else has said:

Je n'aime pas les départs!	Response: **Non, moi non plus.**
Elle adore les voyages!	Response: **Oui, moi aussi.**

Insight

Vous n'êtes pas d'accord avec votre interlocuteur? *You don't agree with the person you're talking to?*

Je n'aime pas les vacances d'hiver. Response: **Moi, si!**

J'aime les films de gangsters. Response: **Moi, pas! / Moi, non!**

This, from a song by Serge Gainsbourg and Jane Birkin (1969), is rather more ambiguous:

Je t'aime… moi non plus

A doubt is cast on the statement, similar to 'I love you – not!' (It literally means 'I love you… Me neither!')

Exercise 1 **Vous êtes d'accord**

◀) **CD2, TR 43**

Listen to the recording and react to what is being said. You agree with everything said:

Exemples:

Statements	Responses
Je n'ai jamais aimé le football.	Moi non plus!
Nous avons souvent visité la Bretagne.	Moi aussi! / Nous aussi!

2 Chez le notaire
At the notary's

◀) **CD2, TR 44**

Depuis plusieurs mois déjà, Dominique et son copain Gildas ont décidé d'acheter une petite maison dans le Finistère. Ils en ont trouvé une qu'ils aiment beaucoup mais avant de faire les démarches nécessaires ils ont décidé de s'adresser à Maître Le Corre, leur notaire.

Listen to or read the dialogue below and answer these questions.

    a *Why are Gildas and Dominique consulting a lawyer?*
    b *What would they like to find out?*

Listen to or read the dialogue again.

    c *How did they find the house?*
    d *Have they contacted the owner?*
    e *Have they seen the house?*
    f *What would they like the lawyer to do?*

Listen or read once more.

    g *Who would check the present owner's civic status?*
    h *What are Gildas and Dominique going to do?*

QUICK VOCAB

un notaire *notary, a lawyer who deals specifically with property and family transactions such as wills, donations, etc.*
Maître (abbreviation **Me**) *a notaire's title*
l'état civil *civic status*
l'urbanisme *town planning department*
recueillir des renseignements *to gather information/to do a search*
le compromis de vente: l'avant-contrat *the pre-contract*

Gildas	Nous avons trouvé une petite maison que nous aimerions acheter. Nous avons pensé qu'il serait peut-être préférable de nous adresser à vous d'abord.
Me Le Corre	Vous avez eu tout à fait raison. Il vaut toujours mieux s'adresser à un notaire puisque c'est obligatoirement le notaire qui se chargera de rédiger l'acte de vente.
Dominique	Comment pouvons-nous être certains qu'il n'y a aucun problème avec la propriété et les propriétaires actuels?
Me Le Corre	C'est le rôle du notaire de le découvrir. Mais comment avez-vous trouvé la maison en question?
Dominique	Nous avons vu une petite annonce dans le journal, tout simplement.
Gildas	Oui, nous sommes allés voir la maison et nous pensons que c'est exactement ce que nous cherchions. Jusqu'ici c'est tout.
Me Le Corre	Et vous n'avez pas pris contact avec les propriétaires?
Gildas	Non, pas encore. Nous avons préféré venir en discuter avec vous d'abord.
Dominique	Vous pourriez organiser une visite de la maison parce que pour le moment nous ne l'avons vue que de l'extérieur?
Me Le Corre	Oui bien sûr mais la mission du notaire va beaucoup plus loin que ça: si vous me chargez de l'affaire, je vous informe, je vous conseille, je vérifie l'état civil du vendeur, je peux aussi recueillir des renseignements d'urbanisme ...
Gildas	Pour vérifier s'il n'y a pas d'autoroute ou autres constructions en projet?
Me Le Corre	Exactement. Je vous préparerais le compromis de vente, c'est-à-dire un avant-contrat, et ensuite le contrat si tout va bien.
Gildas	Eh bien nous allons réfléchir mais de toute façon nous reviendrons vous voir.

Link the following English phrases to the equivalent French expressions.

1 It would be preferable to consult you first.

2 You were absolutely right.

3 The lawyer will take care of drawing up the deeds of sale.

4 We've only seen it from the outside.

5 if you ask me to take care of the business

6 We are going to think about it.

a Vous avez eu tout à fait raison.

b si vous me chargez de l'affaire

c Nous ne l'avons vue que de l'extérieur.

d Nous allons réfléchir.

e Il serait peut-être préférable de nous adresser à vous d'abord.

f Le notaire se chargera de rédiger l'acte de vente.

Vrai ou faux?
Say which of the following statements are true or false.

a *Dominique and Gildas have visited the house and they like it.*
b *They saw the advert in a newspaper.*
c *They have been in contact with the vendor.*
d *They have found exactly what they were looking for.*
e *They have asked the lawyer to start the search as soon as possible.*
f *She can get information from the planning department.*
g *By law the deed of sale has to be prepared by a lawyer.*
h *The notary's mission is to inform and to advise.*

Insight

The role of the **notaire** is to

se renseigner sur la propriété et les propriétaires actuels; recueillir des renseignements d'urbanisme; organiser une visite de la propriété; préparer le compromis de vente; rédiger le contrat de vente *to find out about the property and current owners; to gather the town planning information; to organize a visit to the property; to prepare the draft sales contract; to write or draft the sales contract.*

Acheter une maison

If you decide to buy a house in France it is wise to go through a **notaire**. If you don't know a **notaire** you may know someone who does or you can find one by looking out for a prominent oval brass sign with the symbol of justice embossed on it. You may find that you need a **notaire** who speaks English so that he/she can explain the details of the transaction to you. You might like to find a helpful **notaire** before you have a property in mind.

If you have found a house you would like to buy, you have to be absolutely sure that you want it and that you won't change your mind, because, once you have signed a pre-contract, **compromis de vente** or **avant-contrat**, there is no going back unless the search has revealed elements which would render the pre-contract null and void, such as the fact that the property is threatened by some planning development or that the vendor is not solvent.

On signing **le compromis de vente** you engage yourself to buy the property by paying a deposit, **le dépôt de garantie**, a sum of money between 5% and 10% of the value of the property.

Following the signing of **le compromis de vente** there is a mandatory delay for the lawyer to carry out the necessary checks and to prepare the deed of sale. Your financial position and the availability of a mortgage will also be checked. If the search reveals something untoward, the sale will be stopped and you will receive your deposit back. If all the conditions are fulfilled then the sale must go ahead. If for some external reasons you then breach the pre-contract, you lose your deposit to the vendor. On the other hand, if the vendor is no longer willing to sign the contract, **signer le contrat,** then the sale is dealt with by a tribunal. This means that **le compromis de vente** is a solid guarantee both for vendor and buyer. There is no gazumping in France. Specifically when buying an apartment you may see a notice saying **conforme à la Loi Carrez.** By law the seller is under obligation to declare the surface which is for sale – not including shared areas. Failure to do so accurately could mean that the buyer can declare the sale null and void even after the deed of sale has been signed.

Exercise 2 **Acheter ou vendre dans les meilleures conditions**
In the leaflet below read carefully the desirable and necessary stages which apply if you sell or buy a property.

QUICK VOCAB

conseil/avis *advice*
conseils patrimoniaux *advice on the property*
mise au point *preparation*
les frais *expenses*
le bien *the property*
l'achat/l'acquisition *the purchase*
la vente *the sale*

On the leaflet the first nine points can be referred to as **A** (**acquisition**) and the next nine **V** (**vente**). Indicate which stage of the proceedings the following statements refer to.

Exemple: Advice on opportunity to buy: 1A

a *Advice on the price of the property*
b *Cost evaluation (including legal cost)*
c *Advertising the offer*
d *Property evaluation*
e *Organization of the visit to the property*
f *Preparation of the pre-contract*
g *Preparation of the deed of sale*
h *Search for suitable property in the area*

ACHETER OU VENDRE DANS LES MEILLEURES CONDITIONS

La transaction immobilière notariale s'adresse à tous les particuliers, acquéreur ou vendeur d'un bien immobilier. En neuf étapes, le notaire vous assure un service rigoureux et professionnel, dans les meilleures conditions financières et de délai.

L'acquisition en 9 étapes

1. Conseils sur l'opportunité de l'achat.
2. Recherche des biens à vendre dans la région.
3. Organisation de la visite du bien.
4. Avis sur le prix et conseil personnalisé.
5. Evaluation des frais.
6. Information sur les meilleures conditions de crédit.
7. Mise au point de l'avant-contrat.
8. Elaboration et signature de l'acte authentique de vente.
9. Conseils patrimoniaux.

La vente en 9 étapes

1. Conseils sur l'opportunité de la vente.
2. Evaluation proposée du bien.
3. Examen des conditions de la vente.
4. Signature d'un mandat avec ou sans exclusivité.
5. Publicité de l'offre.
6. Accueil des acquéreurs potentiels et organisation de la visite du bien.
7. Mise au point de l'avant-contrat.
8. Elaboration et signature de l'acte authentique de vente.
9. Conseils patrimoniaux.

Exercise 3 **La maison de votre choix**

You too have decided to buy a small house in Brittany, so you have been looking at the small ads. Today's newspaper offers 13 properties for sale. Look at the adverts, reproduced below.

à aménager/aménageable *to modernize/convert*
agrandissement *extension*
une grange *a barn*
démolir *to pull down*
un grenier *an attic/loft*
de la pierre *stone*
jardin clos *enclosed garden/secluded*

Say which property would suit you if you were looking for the following:

(More than one advert may apply)

a *a small house by the sea*
b *a four-bedroom house*
c *ruins to renovate*
d *a secluded garden*
e *preferably a stone house in the centre of a small town or a village*
f *a house with potential for extension*
g *vacant property*
h *reduced legal costs*

VENTES MAISONS

1) Vends **GRANGE à démolir**, petite et grande portes + escalier en pierre de taille. Tél. 02.98.66.39.41

2) **PONT-DE-BUIS**, maison pierres, **2 niveaux**, terrain permis agrandissement, meublée. 102.200 € Libre. Tél. 02.98.77.31.66.

3) Particulier vend **GUISCRIFF**, maison, cuisine, chambre, sanitaires, grenier aménageable, terrain, dépendances. 60.500 € à débattre. Bon état. Tél. 02.97.44.61.37

4) **PONT-CROIX** place de l'Eglise, maison pierre 4 chambres, grenier aménageable, jardinet, dépendances à rénover, possibilité commerce. 187.000 € à débattre. Tél. 02.98.71.39.81

5) Vends maison **SAINT-MARTIN-DES-CHAMPS**, quartier calme, jardin clos, cave, garage extérieur, **6 CHAMBRES**, chauffage gaz. 194.400 € Tél. 01.60.66.31.71.

VENTES MAISONS

6) Idéal pour loisirs et retraite, **MOËLAN-SUR-MER**, aur cœur d'un village proche plage, commerce et port, maison traditionnelle, jardin et parking privés, **3 chambres**, séjour, kitchenette équipée, belles prestations, frais notaires réduits. 130.000 € Tél. 02.98.37.69.75

7) A saisir entre mer et campagne, dans un cadre exceptionnel, 200 m plage, entre **CONCARNEAU ET LA POINTE DE TRÉVIGNON**, maison plus terrain, chambres, séjour, cuisine, belle prestation, frais de notaire réduits, 180.000 € Tél. 02.98.27.69.39.

8) **FOREST-LANDERNEAU**, maison T5, 5 chambres, salon, séjour, cuisine, cheminée, grand sous-sol, jardin 1.300 m², chauffage électrique. Tél. 02.98.77.66.33.

9) Vends maison **CHATEAULIN**, **4 chambres**, salon, séjour, cuisine, cheminée, grand sous-sol, 1er étage à aménager, terrain arboré. 199.500 € Tél. 02.98.96.66.71

10) **LESCONIL**, sur plage, grande maison, standing, confortable, toute l'année, jardin clos, dépendances, 378.500 € Particulier. Tél. 02.98.44.65.66.

11) Vends maison **CHATEAULIN**, **3 CHAMBRES**, salon-séjour, cuisine, grand sous-sol, 1er étage à aménager, terrain arboré, 210.000 € Tél. 02.98.74.75.45

12) Vends région **PRIZIAC**, **2 maisons ruines superbes**, encadrements fenêtres, portes, terrain à proximité. Tél. 02.98.75.63.20.

13) **PONT-L'ABBÉ centre-ville**, vends maison pierre, jardin clos, calme, 205.500 € accès direct jardin public. Tél. 02.98.78.91.49 (heures repas).

Insight

Où situer sa maison? Quels sont vos critères? *Where do you want your house situated? What are your criteria?*

en bord de mer - entre mer et campagne - en centre ville - dans un quartier calme - proche d'une plage - sans vis-à-vis - avec vue sur… la mer, la montagne…

by the sea - between the sea and the countryside - in the centre of town - in a quiet area - near a beach - with an open outlook - with a view of… the sea, the mountains…

Exercise 4 Le notaire vous pose des questions

◀) CD2, TR 45

You are four different customers. Using the adverts above for guidance, answer Me Le Corre's question (she asks everyone the same thing):

Me Le Corre: **Qu'est-ce que vous recherchez exactement?**

Client(e) 1 *You are looking for a small stone house close to the coast.*

Client(e) 2 *You are looking for a five-bedroom house with a cellar.*

Client(e) 3 *You are looking for a small house with a secluded garden.*

Client(e) 4 *You are looking for a small house with a convertible loft.*

Exercise 5 **Trouvez les intrus** Find the odd ones out

a *In the ads above there is one property for sale which is never going to be liveable in. Which one is it?*

b *Which is the only one mentioning a fireplace?*

c *Which property has direct access to the park?*

d *Which property could be developed for commercial purposes?*

e *Which is the only one which already has building permission for an extension?*

Insight

How do you go about getting a house built?

Il faut… aller sur le site internet du Ministère de l'Écologie, de l'Aménagement et du Développement durable; se conformer à la loi du 1er octobre 2007; remplir un formulaire en ligne sur internet ou bien déposer le formulaire à la mairie; vérifier que le terrain est constructible; signer un contrat de construction.

You have to… go to the ministry's website; comply with the law of 1 October 2007; fill in a form on line or hand it in at the Town Hall; check that the site can be built on; sign a building contract.

Vous pouvez consulter le web pour trouver des maisons à acheter dans toutes les régions de France.

- www.seloger.com
  Ce site est facile à utiliser si vous savez exactement ce que vous voulez
- Si vous voulez construire votre maison ou bien en rénover une vieille, allez voir www.vivremamaison.com

Web extension

Les Sans Domiciles Fixes (SDF) en France
Malheureusement tout le monde ne peut pas acheter ou louer une maison. Dans la plupart des villes de France il y a de nombreux sans-abris ou SDF (*people without a roof over their heads*). En novembre 2006 une nouvelle association, **Les Enfants de Don Quichotte**, a été fondée pour faire pression sur le gouvernement. A Paris par exemple 200 tentes ont été distribuées pour abriter des SDFs parisiens et ont été installées le long du canal St Martin.

Voir http://fr.wikipedia.org/wiki/Les_Enfants_de_Don_Quichotte pour plus de détails.

TEST YOURSELF

Version moderne des Trois Petits Cochons *The Three Little Pigs - retold*

Il était une fois trois petits cochons qui voulaient construire leur maison: le premier avait décidé de bâtir une maison de paille, le deuxième, une maison de bois et le troisième, une maison de brique. Malheureusement les terrains qu'avaient choisis le premier et le deuxième petits cochons n'étaient pas constructibles et ils n'avaient ni permis de construire ni de contrats de construction et le grand méchant loup, invoquant la loi du 1er octobre 2007, leur a fait démolir leurs deux maisons. Le troisième petit cochon, qui avait procédé selon le règlement, vit heureux dans sa maison et il a beaucoup d'enfants.

Vrai ou faux?

1 *Le premier petit cochon n'avait pas de permis de construire.*

2 *Toutes les maisons étaient en bois.*

3 *Il est possible de faire bâtir une maison sans contrat de construction.*

4 *Tous les petits cochons avaient bâti une maison.*

5 *Tous les terrains étaient constructibles.*

6 *Le troisième petit cochon habite toujours dans sa maison.*

7 *Le grand méchant loup leur a refusé des contrats de construction.*

8 *Le grand méchant loup a fait démolir toutes les maisons.*

9 *Seule la maison de brique était conforme à la loi.*

10 *La loi du 1er octobre 2007 exige un terrain constructible, un permis de construire et un contrat de construction.*

Congratulations on finishing *Complete French*!

I hope you have enjoyed working your way through the course. I am always keen to receive feedback from people who have used the course, so why not contact me and let me know your reactions? I'll be particularly pleased to receive your praise, but I should also like to know if things could be improved. I always welcome comments and suggestions, and do my best to incorporate constructive suggestions into later editions.

You can contact me through the publishers at:
Teach Yourself Books, Hachette UK,
338 Euston Road, London NW1 3BH, UK.

Bonne chance!

Gaëlle Graham

Unité de révision

1 Profils
Profiles

🔊 **CD2, TR 46**

Listen to the recording several times. You will hear information
which should allow you to complete these profiles of two friends.
Fill them in in French. You may need to revise what you have
learnt so far.

1	2
Nom:	Nom:
Prénom:	Prénom:
Âge:	Âge:
Adresse:	Adresse:
Numéro de téléphone:	Numéro de téléphone:
Nationalité:	Nationalité:
Nationalité du père:	Nationalité du père:
Nationalité de la mère:	Nationalité de la mère:
Profession:	Profession:
Lieu de travail:	Lieu de travail:
Aime:	Aime:
N'aime pas:	N'aime pas:

(Unités 1 à 5)

2 Une promenade à Saint Malo
A walk in St Malo

Follow the directions on the map and say what your starting point is and where you are going.

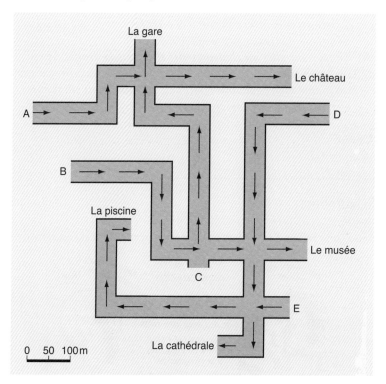

Exemple: Alors pour aller au musée vous allez vers la droite. Après cent cinquante mètres vous tournez à droite. Continuez sur cent mètres et vous tournez à gauche et le musée est à deux cents mètres.

Réponse: From **B** to the museum

1 *Pour aller à la gare vous allez tout droit. Après deux cents mètres vous tournez à gauche. Vous continuez encore sur cent mètres, puis vous tournez à droite et la gare est à cent mètres environ.*

2 *Pour aller à la piscine vous allez vers la gauche, vous allez tout droit sur deux cent cinquante mètres. Vous tournez à droite. Vous continuez sur cent mètres et vous tournez encore à droite. La piscine est à cinquante mètres.*

3 *Pour aller à la cathédrale? Vous allez vers la gauche. Vous tournez à gauche après cent mètres. Vous continuez sur trois cents mètres et vous tournez à droite. La cathédrale est à cinquante mètres.*

4 *Alors, pour aller au château vous allez vers la droite. Après cent mètres vous tournez à gauche. Vous tournez à droite après cinquante mètres et vous continuez sur deux cent cinquante mètres pour arriver au château.*

(Unité 5)

---

3 Numbers

Read the card and say what spelling rule applies for 20 and 100.

(Unités 4 et 5)

4 Grand jeu-concours

At 45 you are the managing director of a company from Rennes (Ille-et-Vilaine). You are representing your firm at an annual four-day conference in St Malo. Your firm has always favoured St Malo as a venue for this conference because of the excellent facilities and the range of activities available. You enjoy going to the swimming pool and going on your own around museums in your free time. You are staying in the conference centre hotel.

YOUR TASK:

Fill in the questionnaire on the next two pages as if you were the person described above and win the main prize in the competition.

1 *What is the main prize?*
2 *What is the deadline for entering the competition?*
3 *Who are the organizers of the competition?*

Grand JEU-CONCOURS

Jusqu'au 14 septembre

Bienvenue
à SAINT-MALO

Vous êtes de passage ou en vacances à SAINT-MALO, nous souhaitons mieux vous connaître, recueillir vos attentes et vos appréciations. C'est pourquoi **LA VILLE et L'OFFICE DU TOURISME** vous proposent de remplir ce questionnaire pour participer au **JEU-CONCOURS**.

Chaque semaine, GAGNEZ UN ALLER-RETOUR pour l'Angleterre pour 2 personnes et de nombreux autres lots.

Voir au dos

---

1 – COMMENT AVEZ-VOUS CONNU SAINT-MALO?

☐ Bouche à oreille
☐ Foires ou salons
☐ Reportages TV ou presse
☐ Guides touristiques ou Agences de voyage
☐ Office du Tourisme
☐ Excursions précédentes
☐ Déplacements professionnels

2 – FIDÉLISATION

☐ Premier séjour à Saint-Malo
☐ Visites occasionnelles à Saint-Malo
☐ Visites régulières à Saint-Malo

3 – ACTIVITÉS PRATIQUÉES
(Plusieurs réponses possibles)

☐ Culturelles   ☐ Autres: préciser
☐ Découvertes   ....
☐ Nautiques
☐ Sportives
☐ Animations gratuites
☐ Thermalisme
☐ Déplacements professionnels et congrès

4 – SATISFACTION:
Êtes-vous satisfait de votre séjour à Saint-Malo?

☐ Pas du tout   Justifier votre réponse_____
☐ Plutôt pas   _____
☐ Plutôt satisfait   _____
☐ Très satisfait

5 – DURÉE DU SÉJOUR:

☐ La journée   ☐ 2 à 3 jours   ☐ 4 à 8 jours
☐ 9 à 15 jours   ☐ 16 jours et plus

6 – MODE D'HÉBERGEMENT

☐ Hôtel   ☐ Camping-car   ☐ Camping
☐ Location meublée   ☐ Résidence secondaire ☐ Bateau
☐ Amis – Famille –   ☐ Gîtes – chambres   ☐ Famille d'accueil
   Parents   d'hôtes

7 – ÂGE

☐ - de 25 ans   ☐ 25/34 ans   ☐ 35/44 ans
☐ 45/54 ans   ☐ 55/65 ans   ☐ + de 65 ans

8 – ACCOMPAGNEMENT
(Êtes-vous venu à Saint-Malo...?)

☐ Seul ☐ En couple
☐ En famille ☐ Avec des amis

9 – CATÉGORIE SOCIO-PROFESSIONNELLE

☐ Agriculteur ☐ Chef d'entreprise,
☐ Cadre et profession libérale   commerçant, artisan
☐ Employé ☐ Cadre moyen
☐ Retraité ☐ Ouvrier
☐ Autres ☐ Scolaire et étudiant

10 – ORIGINE GÉOGRAPHIQUE

☐ Ille-et-Vilaine
☐ Autre département: ____/____ (n° du département)
☐ Étranger (Préciser la nationalité et la région)

Pour participer au JEU CONCOURS,
n'oubliez pas d'indiquer vos coordonnées ci-dessous:

NOM:... PRÉNOM:...

Adresse..

Lieu d'hébergement à Saint-Malo ....

Tél.:..

ATTENTION!

Toutes les rubriques du questionnaire doivent être remplies pour valider votre participation au JEU CONCOURS.

DÉPOSEZ VOS BULLETINS DANS L'URNE

NB:

Les renseignements font l'objet d'un traitement automatisé. Conformément aux prescriptions de la loi nous vous informons que:
• les informations recueillies sont destinées à l'Office du Tourisme et au service économique de la Ville de Saint-Malo.
• l'intéressé a la possibilité de consulter sa fiche informatisée auprès du service concerné.

(Unités 6 à 9)

5 Quelle attitude!

In Unit 9 the boy and the girl express their wishes differently:

Jeune garcon Moi je veux…
Jeune fille Je voudrais…

1 *What verbs and tenses do they use to express their respective wishes?*
2 *What do you think the difference indicates?*
3 *A boy asks for an ice cream. He might say a)* Je veux une glace *or b)* Je voudrais une glace. *To which request are you more likely to reply* Mais oui bien sûr!

6 Aujourd'hui c'est samedi

Cochez les cases – *Tick the boxes*

Go back to Unit 9 and read the dialogue entitled **C'est samedi matin** once more. Tick the correct boxes below, to make a meaningful sentence, in accordance with the dialogue.

Dimanche matin □ Lundi matin □ Aujourd'hui □
les parents et les trois enfants □ les parents □
toute la famille □ vont □ va □ au Mont Saint Michel □
à la plage □ au barrage de la Rance □

Now write down your complete sentence.

7 La voiture idéale

Neuf personnes (ou couples) avec des goûts bien individuels
Look at the cars below. In the second column of the grid indicate which car is most likely to belong to each of the nine people described. The third and fourth columns are jumbled. Choose where these people are mostly likely to live and what is likely to be their favourite eating place.

1. Une voiture safari pour aller partout et vivre l'aventure.	2. Une voiture sérieuse pour le confort et la sécurité.	3. Une voiture éclatante, agressive, qui ne passe pas inaperçue.

4. Une petite voiture nerveuse et maniable, pour se faufiler partout.	5. Une voiture-bus, pour transporter la famille, les amis.	6. Une voiture sport pour le plaisir de piloter et de conduire vite.

7. Une camionnette, pour l'utilité et l'économie.	8. Une voiture gag pour s'amuser et aller partout librement.	9. Une voiture futuriste conduite par ordinateur.

Neuf caractères très différents	La voiture de leurs rêves	Où habitent-ils?	Où mangent-ils?/ qu'est-ce qu'ils aiment?
1 André Morin a trente-cinq ans, célibataire. Il vient d'être nommé Directeur d'une grande banque parisienne. Il aime la vitesse, les avions, le ski, le ski nautique, etc. Quelle est la voiture de ses rêves?		**a** À Lyon dans une grande maison avec une piscine et un grand jardin.	**j** Ils adorent les pique-niques à la campagne.
2 Gérard Duigou a tout juste dix-huit ans. Il aime la mer, la plage et s'amuser avec ses copains. Quelle sera sa première voiture?		**b** Une petite maison dans la campagne pas loin de Toulouse	**k** Elle aime surtout les bons couscous de sa mère.
3 M. et Mme Dumas ont cinq enfants. Ils vont souvent chez leurs parents dans le Midi. Quelle voiture viennent-ils d'acheter?		**c** Dans une grande propriété à Deauville.	**l** À la cantine universitaire.

4 Jean-Yves et Florence Beaumont habitent à Toulouse où ils sont tous les deux enseignants dans un collège. Ils adorent passer leurs week-ends à explorer les Pyrénées. Leur rêve est d'aller en Afrique. Quelle est leur voiture?	**d** Dans un élégant appartement du seizième arrondissement de Paris.	**m** Chez Maxime ou à la Tour d'Argent, les deux restaurants les plus chers de Paris.
5 Etienne Vaillant a habité à Grenoble toute sa vie. Il est maintenant chercheur à l'université de Grenoble où il travaille sur un prototype de voiture futuristique.	**e** Dans un studio avec vue sur le vieux port.	**n** À McDonald's aussi souvent que possible!
6 Bernard Fargeon est fermier. Il a une ferme d'élevage de poulets dans le Finistère. Il y a cinq ans il a acheté un véhicule pratique pour transporter la nourriture pour la volaille et aussi pour transporter sa mère qui est Bigoudène.	**f** Il partage un appartement avec des copains.	**o** Chez Maxime ou à la Tour d'Argent, les deux restaurants les plus chers de Paris.
7 Olivier Dubois est le PDG (Président Directeur Général) d'une chaîne d'hypermarchés. Il aime le confort, le luxe et tout ce qui est solide. Quelle voiture a-t-il choisi?	**g** Il habite toujours chez ses parents. Sa chambre a un décor de science-fiction.	**p** Dans les restaurants chics du quartier de l'Opéra Garnier.
8 Laurent Dubois, le fils de M. Dubois, ne travaille pas mais avec l'argent de son père il s'est acheté une vieille Cadillac rouge, remise à neuf.	**h** Une ferme dans un village sur la Baie d'Audierne.	**q** Une soupe bien chaude après une longue promenade en montagne.
9 Adidja Ahmed est docteur à Marseille. Elle a choisi une petite voiture rapide et pratique pour aller visiter ses patients. Quelle est sa voiture?	**i** Il habite à Paris avec son amie qui est chanteuse à l'Opéra.	**r** Il aime un bon poulet rôti cuit à la ferme.

(Unités 10 à 16)

8 Les jeunes et l'emploi

Read carefully this short newspaper article about three young students.

1 ÉTUDIANTES STAGIAIRES

VIE QUOTIDIENNE
«Il ne suffit pas de cocher des cases»
Étudiants stagiaires

Que faisiez-vous du 28 août au 25 octobre? Et bien, pendant que certains profitaient encore de leurs dernières semaines de vacances, Jenny, Maria et Nathalie bossaient. Etudiantes en maîtrise A.G.E. (traduisez Administration et Gestion d'Entreprise), elles ont effectué durant huit semaines un stage non rémunéré à la Caisse d'Allocations Familiales (CAF) de Brest. Premier contact avec le monde du travail.

elles bossaient *they worked*
bosser *to work* (slang)
cocher des cases *to tick boxes* (as in multiple choice questions)

Now answer these questions.

 a *What did the three students do from 28 August to 25 October?*
 b *What is their area of study?*
 c *Were they paid for their work?*
 d *Was the work experience carried out in term time?*
 e *What did this type of work do for them in terms of experience?*

2 LA CHASSE AUX JOBS

Read the article below about the search for a part-time job. Then turn to the grid opposite and fill in the jobs in the order in which they appear in the article. The contents of the grid are jumbled so match each list of points with the correct job category and the correct heading. (Don't worry if you can't understand it all – just try to get the gist of the article.)

LA CHASSE AUX JOBS

Maigres bourses ou parents compréhensifs ne suffisent plus à subvenir à vos besoins? La chasse aux jobs est ouverte toute l'année. La concurrence est rude et mieux vaut se pointer devant votre employeur avec une bonne dose de motivation et une idée précise de ce que vous voulez. Conseils et idées en vrac.

Fast-foods et cafétérias
C'est payé tout juste le SMIC et les pourboires sont interdits. Cadences infernales, patrons omniprésents et cuisines aseptisées. Les grandes chaînes recrutent également assez régulièrement et le rythme y est légèrement plus supportable. Pour postuler, présentez-vous directement dans chaque restaurant (mais pas au moment du rush) ou envoyez lettre de candidature et CV avec photo. Un conseil: écumez les centres commerciaux. Il est rare qu'ils ne contiennent pas un ou deux points de restauration. Pour les emplois de serveur(se), les jobs sont mieux payés en général, pourboires aidant.

Télémarketing et sondages
Les horaires sont très modulables. Il vous suffit de faire preuve d'amabilité au téléphone et de ne pas être allergique à la répétition. Les sociétés de télémarketing préfèrent que le premier contact s'établisse par téléphone. Un excellent moyen pour elles de mesurer vos capacités et d'opérer une première sélection.

Distribution de prospectus
Lisez les journaux gratuits pour trouver une annonce. Avoir le pied

solide et posséder une voiture sont deux atouts. L'étudiant est payé au nombre de journaux ou tracts distribués.

Pensez aussi aux grandes surfaces, parkings, gardiennages, livraisons à domicile…

3 main job categories (List them in the order they appear in the article)	Requirements to secure a job	Advantages (if any)	Disadvantages (if any)
1)	a • Flexitime	b • Large fast food firms recruit regularly • Serving jobs are better paid • Tips allowed	c • Go and introduce yourself directly • Send a letter of application + CV • Check all the shopping centres
2)	d • Only paid minimum wage • Tips are not allowed • Fast rhythm of work • Bosses always present	e • Paid according to number of newspapers or leaflets distributed	f • Good if you have two assets: solid feet and a car
3)	g • Selection over the telephone • Need a good telephone manner	h • Read the free press for job adverts	i • Very repetitive job

(Unités 17 à 20)

9 Paris et le tourisme

◄》 **CD2, TR 47**

Vrai ou faux? Ecoutez le débat à la radio et dites si les phrases suivantes sont vraies ou fausses:

1 *On a besoin d'un seul billet pour tout déplacement.*
2 *Il n'y a pas de transport la nuit.*
3 *Les enfants de dix ans doivent payer plein tarif.*
4 *On peut voyager jusqu'à Disneyland.*
5 *On peut choisir un seul billet pour la zone 1 à 6.*
6 *Il ne faut pas de photo d'identité.*
7 *La carte Paris-Visite n'est pas valable pour le funiculaire de Montmartre.*
8 *On peut acheter un billet valable 4 jours.*

(Unité 20)

10 Les loisirs et vous: sondage d'opinion
Leisure activities and you: opinion poll

This is a real French opinion poll. For part A pretend you are Stéphane Jacquelin:

▶ *You like science-fiction films and psychological drama*
▶ *You enjoy TV programmes on classical music, religion and philosophy. You also like TV games shows*
▶ *You regularly read history magazines*

Put a circle around **1** (**oui**) for all the activities mentioned above and circle **2** (**non**) for all the others.

A. **Aimez-vous?**

Une réponse par ligne. Entourez le 1 ou le 2.

		oui	non
a	*Les films d'arts martiaux (karaté, kung fu ...).*	1	2
b	*Les films de science-fiction.*	1	2
c	*Les films musicaux, disco, rock...*	1	2
d	*La musique pop, le rock.*	1	2
e	*Les variétés, les chansons.*	1	2
f	*Les livres érotiques ou suggestifs.*	1	2
g	*Je suis intéressé(e) par les émissions TV et les magazines sur la musique classique.*	1	2
h	*Je suis intéressé(e) par les émissions TV sur la religion, la philosophie.*	1	2
i	*J'aime les journaux sur la santé, les informations médicales.*	1	2
j	*J'aime les émissions de jeux à la télévision.*	1	2
k	*Je lis régulièrement un ou des magazines (revues) d'histoire.*	1	2

B **Les sports**

For part B circle as many answers as you like to find out if you are sporty, or a TV sports fan.

Parmi les sports suivants, lesquels pratiquez-vous et lesquels aimez-vous regarder? Répondez à chaque colonne. Autant de réponses que vous voulez.

	Je pratique	**Je regarde**
Tennis, autres sports à raquettes.	1	2
Cyclisme.	1	2
Courses de voiture et de motos.	1	2
Jogging ou athlétisme.	1	2

Vous totalisez entre 7 et 8 points: vous êtes un fanatique de sport!

11 Encore une bonne recette, simple et rapide à réaliser
Another good recipe: simple and quick to make

QUICK VOCAB

en dés *diced*
des pignons de pin *pine kernels*
un brin de menthe *a leaf of mint*
un four à micro-ondes *microwave oven*

Read the recipe and answer the questions.

COUSCOUS PILAF

PRÉPARATION: 20 minutes
CUISSON: 5 minutes
POUR 2 PERSONNES

- ○ 1 petite pomme évidée, épluchée et coupée en dés
- ○ 50 g de céleri blanc en petits morceaux
- ○ 50 g de jeunes oignons en fines rondelles
- ○ 1 cuillère à soupe de raisins secs blancs
- ○ 2 moitiés d'abricot sec en petits morceaux
- ○ 30 g de pignons de pin grillés
- ○ 2 cuillères à café de margarine, 175 ml d'eau
- ○ 75 ml de nectar d'abricots ou de poires
- ○ ½ cuillère à café de curry en poudre
- ○ 40 g de couscous

Pour la garniture: un brin de menthe

RÉALISATION
Mettez la pomme, le céleri, les oignons, les raisins, les abricots, les pignons de pin et la margarine dans le plat et mélangez. Placez le plat à couvert au four à micro-ondes pendant 2 minutes. Ajoutez l'eau, le nectar et le curry au mélange et remettez le plat, à couvert, 3 minutes au four. Incorporez le couscous au mélange aux fruits, couvrez le plat et laissez gonfler le couscous pendant 5 minutes. Disposez le couscous pilaf sur un plat et garnissez avec la menthe.

a *How long does it take to prepare from beginning to end?*
b *How much liquid is required in all?*
c *How do you prepare the onions?*
d *How much curry powder is needed?*
e *What can you use if you don't have apricot juice?*
f *How many raisins do you need?*
g *What is the mint for?*
h *What do you add the water and juice to?*
i *At what stage do you add the couscous?*
j *How long does the dish need to rest before serving?*

(Unités 21 à 25)

Transcripts

Only the scripts of listening comprehensions or other listening exercises which are not already printed in the units are to be found in this section.

UNIT 2

Exercise 1: **D'où êtes-vous?**

Lucien	Bonjour, je m'appelle Lucien. Et vous comment vous appelez-vous?
Vous	Je m'appelle Françoise.
Lucien	Enchanté de faire votre connaissance. D'où êtes-vous?
Vous	Je suis de Boulogne. Et vous?
Lucien	Je suis de Bruxelles

Exercise 2: **Le Loto**

Et maintenant voici le tirage du Loto. Les numéros gagants sont le 21, le 45, le 53, le 65, le 9, le 50, le 11, le 24 et le 37.

Exercise 3: **Quel âge avez-vous?**

1 J'ai 21 ans. 2 Il a 38 ans. 3 Elle a 69 ans. 4 Il a 40 ans.

UNIT 4

Exercise 3: **C'est combien?**

Dominique	C'est combien les cigarettes?
Sarah	Euh… c'est 48 € les dix paquets.
Dominique	Et le whisky?
Sarah	C'est 22 €.
Dominique	Et le gin?
Sarah	C'est 16 €.
Dominique	Et le Cognac?
Sarah	C'est 27 €.

UNIT 5

Exercise 4: **Répondez aux touristes**
   a *Pour aller à la piscine s'il vous plaît? C'est à droite.*
   b *Le musée s'il vous plaît? C'est à 200 m.*
   c *La cathédrale, c'est loin? Non, c'est tout près.*
   d *Pour aller à l'office de tourisme s'il vous plaît? C'est tout droit.*
   e *Pour aller au château? C'est à gauche.*

UNIT 6

3 À l'heure française

Femme	En général je me lève à sept heures et demie. Je déjeune à midi et demi et je me couche à onze heures. Le dimanche je me lève entre dix heures et dix heures et demie.
Homme	Je me lève à sept heures. Je prends mon déjeuner entre une heure et une heure et demie. Je me couche vers minuit.
Fille	Alors je me lève à sept heures et quart. Je déjeune à midi et je me couche à vingt-deux heures.
Garçon	Je me lève à six heures quarante-cinq. Je prends mon déjeuner à midi et demi et je me couche à neuf heures. Quelquefois le week-end je me couche à minuit.

Exercise 2: **Quelle heure est-il?**
a Il est dix-sept heures cinq. b Il est midi et demi. c Il est huit heures cinquante-six. d Il est sept heures moins le quart. e Il est une heure vingt. f Il est trois heures. g Il est onze heures quinze. h Il est minuit moins le quart.

Exercise 3: **Matin ou après-midi?**

Jean-Pierre	Allô oui?
Martine	Salut Jean-Pierre, c'est Martine.
Jean-Pierre	Tu sais quelle heure il est? Il est quatre heures du matin ici!
Martine	Oh pardon! Il est deux heures de l'après-midi ici en Australie!

UNIT 8

Exercise 5: Écoutez et écrivez
1 *Sylvie Lécaille: Je m'appelle Mademoiselle Sylvie Lécaille.*
   Lécaille ça s'épelle L-é-c-a-i-l-l-e.
2 *Gaétan Leberre: Alors mon nom c'est Gaétan Leberre. Gaétan*
   ça s'épelle G-a-é-t-a-n et Leberre L-e-b-e-r-r-e.
3 *Yannick Tanguy: Je m'appelle Yannick Tanguy. Yannick ça*
   s'épelle Y-a-n-n-i-c-k et Tanguy T-a-n-g-u-y.

UNIT 9

Exercise 3: J'ai besoin de … / Je voudrais …
1 *Je voudrais du jambon et du pâté.*
   Vous: Allez à la charcuterie!
2 *J'ai besoin de médicaments*
   Vous: Allez à la pharmacie!
3 *Je voudrais acheter des journaux*
   Vous: Allez à la Maison de la Presse!
4 *J'ai besoin de timbres poste*
   Vous: Allez à la poste!
5 *Je voudrais du pain et des gâteaux*
   Vous: Allez à la boulangerie-pâtisserie!
6 *J'ai besoin d'un plan de la ville*
   Vous: Allez à l'Office de Tourisme!

UNIT 10

Exercice 1: **La cuisine française**

Pierre	Je crois que la cuisine française est la meilleure du monde.
Lionel	Oui, moi je suis tout à fait d'accord avec vous. Nous avons les meilleurs chefs et les meilleurs restaurants.
Pierre	Vous avez raison et la preuve c'est que nos chefs sont demandés partout dans le monde.
Pascale	Eh bien moi je ne suis pas d'accord avec vous. Je crois qu'il y a de la bonne cuisine partout dans le monde. Qu'est-ce que vous pensez de la cuisine chinoise ou de la cuisine italienne par exemple? Moi je pense que c'est une question de goût, c'est tout!

Exercice 3: **Le souper marin**

Michel	C'est quel jour le souper marin?
Vous	Le 15 août.
Michel	C'est à quelle heure?
Vous	C'est à partir de 19h30.
Michel	Qu'est-ce qu'il y a au menu?
Vous	Soupe de poissons, moules, frites et dessert.
Michel	C'est combien?
Vous	10 €.

UNIT 11

Exercice 2: **Où sont-ils en vacances?**

1 *Bonjour, je m'appelle Fabienne. Dans la ville où je suis le temps est couvert et les températures sont entre 15 et 21 degrés.*

2 *Bonjour, je m'appelle Jérôme. Dans la ville où je suis il fait de l'orage et les températures sont entre 21 et 29 degrés.*

3 *Bonjour, je m'appelle Stéphanie. Dans la ville où je suis il fait de l'orage et les températures sont entre 7 et 12 degrés.*

4 *Bonjour, je m'appelle Alexandre. Dans la ville où je suis il fait de l'orage et les températures sont entre 12 et 23 degrés.*

UNIT 12

Exercise 3: Bon appétit!

Serveuse	Monsieur-dame, qu'est-ce que vous avez choisi?
Florence	Moi j'adore les fruits de mer. Je prends le menu à 45 €.
Serveuse	Excellent! Et pour Monsieur?
Luc	Alors moi je vais prendre le menu à 20 €.
Serveuse	Oui … et qu'est-ce que vous prendrez comme entrées?
Luc	Alors, comme entrée je prends la Coquille St Jacques à la Bretonne et puis comme plat principal je prends la Brochette de joues de Lotte à la Diable avec salade de saison.
Serveuse	Très bien. Vous prendrez le plateau de fromage ou un dessert?
Luc	Je vais prendre un dessert … une glace si vous en avez.
Serveuse	Certainement Monsieur.
Une autre table … vous, un autre client	
Serveuse	Vous avez choisi? Qu'est-ce que vous allez prendre?
Vous	Je vais prendre le menu à 25 €.
Serveuse	Et qu'allez-vous prendre comme entrée?
Vous	Je vais prendre les six huîtres chaudes avec cocktail d'algues.
Serveuse	Oui, et comme plat principal?
Vous	Je vais prendre la Brochette de St Jacques au beurre blanc.
Serveuse	Et après le plateau de fromage vous prendrez un dessert?
Vous	Oui, une glace à la fraise, s'il vous plaît.

UNIT 13

Exercise 3: À la station service

Marc	Le plein de gazole pour la camionnette SVP.
Sandrine	Mettez vingt litres de super dans ma vieille voiture de sport SVP.
Martine	Trente litres d'essence sans plomb SVP.

3 Les informations: un weekend meurtrier sur les routes françaises

'Le weekend du quinze août a été marqué par de nombreux accidents de la route. L'accident le plus grave s'est produit sur la route nationale dix lorsqu'un car portugais a percuté un camion débouchant d'une route privée. Sur les 42 passagers huit ont été tués et 24 autres ont été blessés.

À St Nazaire un cycliste a été tué dans une collision avec une voiture et sur la D 940 entre Calais et Boulogne huit personnes ont été blessées dans un accident impliquant quatre voitures.'

UNIT 14

Exercise 2: **Un coup de téléphone**

Propriétaire	Allô, j'écoute!	
1 Vous	J'ai vu une annonce pour un studio dans *Libé*. C'est bien ici?	
Propriétaire	Oui, c'est bien cela.	
2 Vous	C'est à quel étage?	
Propriétaire	C'est au sixième.	
3 Vous	Il y a un ascenseur?	
Propriétaire	Euh, non mais monter et descendre les escaliers est excellent pour la santé!	
4 Vous	Il y a le chauffage central?	
Propriétaire	Non, le chauffage est électrique.	
5 Vous	Il y a une cuisine?	
Propriétaire	Oui il y a une cuisine moderne toute équipée.	
6 Vous	C'est bien 400 € toutes charges comprises?	
Propriétaire	C'est bien cela. Vous pouvez visiter aujourd'hui?	
7 Vous	Je viendrais cet après-midi si vous êtes disponible.	

UNIT 16

Exercise 2: À votre tour de poser des questions

a Vous	Vous êtes allée au Maroc avec le groupe?
Adidja	Oui, j'y suis allée.
b Vous	Combien de jeunes sont allés au Maroc?
Adidja	Dix-huit. Huit filles et dix garçons.
c Vous	Vous êtes restés combien de temps?
Adidja	Nous sommes restés trois semaines.
d Vous	Ils ont rencontré des jeunes marocains?
Adidja	Oui, beaucoup. C'était formidable.

UNIT 17

Exercise 2: À l'A.N.P.E.

a Employé	Quel genre de métiers vous intéresse?
Vous	Je m'intéresse aux métiers de l'hôtellerie.
b Employé	Qu'est-ce qui vous intéresse?
Vous	Je m'intéresse aux métiers de la photographie.
c Employé	Qu'est-ce qui vous intéresse?
Vous	Je m'intéresse aux métiers de la restauration.
d Employé	Quel genre de métiers vous intéresse?
Vous	Je m'intéresse aux métiers de la santé.
e Employé	A quoi vous intéressez-vous?
Vous	Je m'intéresse aux métiers de l'habillement.

UNIT 18

Exercise 2: **Ça prend combien de temps…?**
Exemple:

Question Ça prend combien de temps pour aller de Paris à Marseille par le TGV?
Vous Ça prend deux heures cinquante-cinq.

a *Ça prend combien de temps pour aller à Nantes?*
Ça prend deux heures.
b *Ça prend combien de temps pour aller à Toulouse?*
Ça prend cinq heures.
c *Ça prend combien de temps pour aller à Lyon?*
Ça prend une heure cinquante-cinq.
d *Ça prend combien de temps pour aller à Lille?*
Ça prend exactement une heure.

Exercise 3: **À vous de réserver un billet**
a Vous Je voudrais réserver un billet pour Paris SVP.
Employée Vous voyagez aujourd'hui?
b Vous Non, je voyage demain.
Employée Vous prenez le train de quelle heure?
c Vous Je prends le train de 7h 05.
Employée Vous prenez un billet aller-retour?
d Vous Non, je prends un billet simple. C'est combien?

Exercise 1: **Vous passez beaucoup trop de temps au téléphone!**

a *À quelle heure avez-vous téléphoné à Nadine?*
Je lui ai téléphoné à onze heures trente.

b *À quelle heure avez-vous téléphoné à Mathieu?*
Je lui ai téléphoné à midi.

c *À quelle heure avez-vous téléphoné à Chantal et à Marc?*
Je leur ai téléphoné à 17h15.

d *À quelle heure avez-vous téléphoné à votre sœur?*
Je lui ai téléphoné à 18h45.

e *À quelle heure avez-vous téléphoné à vos parents?*
Je leur ai téléphoné à 20h10.

f *À quelle heure avez-vous téléphoné à votre fiancé(e)?*
Je lui ai téléphoné à 22h45.

Exercise 2: **Les maux et blessures**

Marie-José	J'ai mal au dos.
Alain	Je suis blessé aux genoux.
Adrienne	J'ai mal à la tête.
Benoît	J'ai mal aux dents.
Elise	Je crois que je me suis cassé le bras.
Julien	Je me suis brûlé la main avec le fer à repasser.
Cécile	Je me suis coupé le pied en marchant sur une bouteille cassée.
Didier	J'ai des piqûres de moustiques infectées.

Exercise 4: **Jacques a dit...**
  1 *Jacques a dit 'levez le bras droit'*
  2 *Baissez le bras*
  3 *Grattez la tête*
  4 *Jacques a dit 'touchez la bouche avec la main gauche'*
  5 *Jacques a dit 'baissez le bras droit'*
  6 *Levez le pied droit*
  7 *Frappez le nez*
  8 *Dansez*
  9 *Jacques a dit 'chantez'*
  10 *Jacques a dit 'touchez le pied gauche'*
  11 *Jacques a dit 'levez la main droite'*
  12 *Asseyez-vous*

   UNIT 21

Exercise 2: **Qu'est-ce que vous feriez?**
  a *Qu'est-ce que vous feriez si vous gagniez le gros lot au Loto?*
     J'aurais une grande maison en Bretagne, j'aurais un bateau,
     j'irais à la pêche et le soir je regarderais la télé.
  b *Est-ce que vous feriez des voyages?*
     Je ferais un voyage autour du monde.

Exercise 5: **Vous avez coché?**
Et voici les numéros gagnants pour le deuxiéme tirage du Loto: le
35, le 8, le 15, le 28, le 13, le 45, le 11, le 25, et le 12 est le numéro
complémentaire.

UNIT 22

Exercise 2: Oui, c'est le mien

1 *Ce sac, c'est à vous?*
Oui, c'est le mien.

2 *Ce sont vos clefs?*
Oui, ce sont les miennes.

3 *C'est votre montre?*
Oui, c'est la mienne.

4 *Ce sont vos patins à roulettes?*
Oui, ce sont les miens.

UNIT 25

Exercise 1: Vous êtes d'accord

1 *J'adore la cuisine française.*
Moi aussi.

2 *Je n'aime pas les voyages organisés.*
Moi non plus.

3 *Nous aimons beaucoup la Bretagne.*
Moi aussi.

4 *Je n'aime pas la rentrée.*
Moi non plus.

5 *Je déteste prendre l'avion.*
Moi aussi.

6 *Je préfère rester chez moi.*
Moi aussi.

Exercise 4: Le notaire vous pose des questions

Me Le Corre Qu'est-ce que vous recherchez exactement?

1 Je cherche une petite maison de pierre près de la côte.

2 Je cherche une maison de cinq chambres avec cave.

3 Je cherche une petite maison avec un jardin clos.

4 Je cherche une petite maison avec un grenier aménageable.

UNITÉ DE RÉVISION

1 Profils
1 Je m'appelle Sarah Burgess. J'ai 28 ans. J'habite 12 Stella Avenue, Londres SW2. Mon numéro de téléphone est le 020 8476 5656. Je suis de nationalité britannique, mon père est de nationalité britannique, ma mère est de nationalité française. Je suis éditrice chez Hodder & Stoughton. J'aime les voyages, le cinéma, la lecture. Je n'aime pas le sport à la télévision. **2** Je m'appelle Dominique Périer. J'ai 36 ans. J'habite 5 Avenue de la Vieille Ville à St Nazaire en France. Mon numéro de téléphone est le 02 40 45 18 11. Je suis de nationalité française, mon père et ma mère sont de nationalité française. Je suis professeur de philosophie au lycée de St Nazaire. J'aime beaucoup les chats, l'opéra et les musées d'art. Je n'aime pas la télévision. Je n'aime pas les voitures.

9 Paris et le tourisme

Présentateur du programme	Et vous pensez que Paris est accessible à tous nos visiteurs?
Représentante de la RATP	Mais certainement avec Paris-Visite les touristes peuvent allez partout dans Paris et la région parisienne.
Présentateur	C'est quoi Paris-Visite?
Représentante	Eh bien c'est un seul et unique billet qui permet de voyager à volonté sur tous les modes de transport: métro, bus, tram, funiculaire de Montmartre, Noctambus pour voyager la nuit…
Présentateur	Ça c'est bien mais pour ce qui est de la banlieue qu'est-ce que vous leur proposez aux touristes?
Représentante	Eh bien toujours avec ce même billet ils peuvent prendre les trains de banlieue, suivant les zones qu'ils ont choisis soit zone 1 à 3 ou bien la zone 1 à 8. Ils peuvent se rendre avec le même billet jusqu'à Disneyland, Versailles et jusqu'aux aéroports parisiens.
Présentateur	Il faut acheter un nouveau billet tous les jours?
Représentante	Non, pour une visite de cinq jours ont peut acheter un billet qui sera valable cinq jours, en fait il y a

quatre possibilités: un billet pour un jour, deux, trois ou cinq jours.

Présentateur Il y a des réductions pour les enfants?

Représentante Bien sûr, il y a un tarif réduit pour les enfants de 4 à 11 ans.

Présentateur Et cela est compliqué comme démarche? Ça prend beaucoup de temps?

Représentante Pas du tout! Vous voyagez sans perdre de temps, un seul achat et pas besoin de photo!

Présentateur Alors j'espère que les touristes seront nombreux dans la capitale!

Représentante Merci!

Key to the exercises

Unit 1

Exercise 1 a Bonjour Madame Corre! **b** Au revoir Marie-Claire. **c** Bonne nuit Paul! **d** Bon après-midi Mademoiselle! **e** À tout à l'heure / à bientôt Monsieur Jarre. Comment ça va? Monsieur Blanchard is feeling fine; Madame Lebrun is feeling so so. **Exercise 2** 1c 2a 3e 4f 5d 6b
Exercise 3 Dialogue 1: c New Year **Dialogue 2:** b Françoise's birthday **Dialogue 3:** a Estelle and Paul's wedding **Exercise 4 D1c D2b D3c**
Exercise 5 a un kilo de pommes **b** cinq euros **c** un sandwich au fromage **d** une bière **e** la gare **5** Dans la rue **a** the post office **b** the tourist office **c** the supermarket **d** the Citroën garage **Web exercise: 1** Mariage **2** Bonne Fête **3** Fêtes → Fêtes Nationales

Test yourself 1 A) 2/5, 3, 1, 4 B) 1 bon appétit 2 C'est combien? 3 Bon anniversaire 4 L'addition SVP 5 Vive la mariée

Unit 2

1 Enchanté de faire votre connaissance **a** Alain **b** Claire **c** Paris **d** Marseille **e** Je suis de Paris. **f** Enchanté de faire votre connaissance.
Exercise 1 a Je m'appelle Françoise. **b** Je suis de Boulogne. Et vous?
Exercise 2 a Between 2 and 10 **b** Twenty numbers for each draw **c** 3 € for two draws and 1,5 € for one **d** The winning numbers are: 21, 45, 53, 65, 9, 50, 11, 24, 37. 2 Je suis la mère d'Isabelle **a** Isabelle's mother **b** David's **c** no – she's French **d** Mark Thompson **e** in England **f** J'habite en Angleterre. **g** La tante de David. **h** Je vous présente Madame ... **i** Mon fils. **j** Ma fille. 3 Tu as quel âge? **a** J'ai douze ans. **b** Mon frère, il a quatorze ans. **c** Je n'ai pas de frère. **d** Moi aussi! **e** Tu as quel âge?
Exercise 3 a J'ai vingt et un ans. **b** Il a trente-huit ans. **c** Elle a soixante-neuf ans. **d** Il a quarante ans. 4 Vous parlez français? **a** French and English **b** Both **c** French **d** Il est professeur de français. **e** Cela dépend. **f** Je parle français ou anglais. **g** Je parle français à la maison. **h** Les enfants parlent couramment les deux langues. **i** Il parle bien le français.
Exercise 4 1c 2e **3d** 4a **5b Exercise 5 a** Grand-mother **b** Father **c** Aunt **d** Cousin **e** Brother **Exercise 6** 5 is the odd one out – *mon oncle* is the only male.

Test yourself 2 1 Sophie 2 Anne Thompson 3 M. Norbert 4 Lucien 5 Camille 6 Hélène Lejeune 7 Mark Thompson 8 Danielle 9 Isabelle 10 La Loterie Nationale

Unit 3

2 Natalie **a** 36 **b** yes **c** two **d** Yes **e** Cinema, travelling, reading, photography **f** Je suis professeur d'histoire. **g** J'aime voyager. **h** J'habite à Vannes en Bretagne. **i** J'aime aller au cinéma. **j** Je n'aime pas faire le ménage. 3 Antoine **a** 29 **b** Paris **c** German **d** Watching films and sports on TV, photography and travelling **e** Je demeure **à** Paris. **f** J'aime bien regarder des films à la télé. **g** J'ai horreur des voitures. **h** Je vais au travail à vélo. Grammar Alors moi: so; Alors je vais au travail à vélo: therefore 4 Monique **a** 45 **b** Her husband **c** At the post office **d** A little **e** She hates it **f** Je travaille à la poste. **g** Je parle un peu l'anglais. **h** Je n'ai pas d'enfants. **i** J'apprends le vietnamien. **j** il est au chômage. 5 Pierre **a** 52 **b** Monique **c** At Renault **d** In Dijon **e** Ma mère est veuve. **f** Je travaille chez Renault. **g** Elle habite chez nous. **h** J'adore les voyages et la lecture. **i** Je n'aime pas la télé sauf les documentaires. **j** Je comprends un peu l'anglais. **Exercise 1** Je m'appelle Anne-Marie Pélerin. J'ai quarante-cinq ans. J'habite à Boulogne. Je suis dentiste. Je parle français, anglais et allemand. J'adore le football et la photographie. **Exercise 2**:

NAMES	QUESTIONS	ANSWERS
Natalie		Je m'appelle Natalie
Antoine		J'ai vingt-neuf ans
Natalie	Quelle est votre profession?	
Monique		Je travaille à la poste
Pierre	Où habitez-vous?	
Antoine	Quelles langues parlez-vous?	
Monique	Vous aimez le sport?	
Pierre		Oui, je suis marié avec Monique

Exercise 3 a Faux **b** Faux **c** Vrai **d** Vrai **e** Vrai **f** Faux **Exercise 4 f**

Test yourself 3 A) 1 Antoine 2 Natalie 3 Antoine 4 Monique 5 Pierre B) 1 Antoine 2 Natalie 3 Monique 4 Natalie 5 Monique

Unit 4

1 Au pont cinq **a** five **b** eight **c** Information desk. Deck 7 **d** It's in the evening (they say bonsoir) **e** 017 Linked phrases: **1d** 2e **3a** 4b **5c** **Exercise 1 1d** 2f **4g** 6b **7c** 11a **12h** 13j **15e** 17i **Exercise 2 a** C'est au pont sept. **b** C'est au pont neuf. **c** C'est au pont neuf. **d** C'est au pont neuf. **e** C'est au pont sept. 2 Est-ce qu'il y a un cinéma? **a** Yes, there are two **b** No **c** Le Come-back **d** 22.30 **e** 10 € Linked phrases: 1c, 2d, 3a, **4b** **Exercise 3 a** 27 € **b** 22 € **c** 15 € for 10 packets **d** 16 €

Test yourself 4 1 deux / cabine / trouve / huit / voiture / est / pont cinq 2 Hugh Grant 3 Octante 4 fermière / boulanger

Unit 5

1 Pour aller à... a2 b2 c3 Linked phrases: **1e** 2c **3a** 4f **5d** 6b 2 Vous tournez à gauche **a** Dominique **b** A passer-by **c** 500 metres **d** Not at all Linked phrases: **1f** 2g **3a** 4b **5c** 6d **7e Exercise 1 a** Et toi tu connais? **b** Vous allez/vous tournez **Exercise 2 1c** 2a **3c Exercise 3** Q1: Le petit aquarium SVP? Q2: La cathédrale SVP? Q3: Le Musée SVP? **Exercise 4 a** C'est à droite. **b** C'est à 200 m. **c** Non, c'est tout près. **d** C'est tout droit. **e** C'est à gauche.

Test yourself 5 1 le 2 la 3 la 4 les / la 5 le 6 la 7 la 8 l' 9 le 10 le 11 le 12 les 13 l' 14 les 15 le 16 la 17 la 18 le 19 le 20 l'

Unit 6

1 Où stationner? 1 2 hours 2 There's a special tariff for residents. 3 Your receipt 2 Tu as de la monnaie? 1a 2 3 to 4 hours 3 4 € 4 With the following coins: **a** 50c x 1, **b** 1 € x 1 **c** 2 € x 1 **d** 20c x 2 **e** 10c x 1 Linked phrases: **1e** 2d **3f** 4a **5c** 6b **Exercise 1 a** monnaie **b** me repose **c** reste **d** argent **e** argent 3 À l'heure française a votre déjeuner, ton déjeuner

b	Q1	Q2	Q3
Femme		12.30	11.00
Homme	7.00		about midnight
Fille	7.15		10.00
Garçon		12.30	9.00

c The woman **d** Midnight **Exercise 2 1e** 2h **3a** 4b **5c** 6g **7f** 8d
Exercise 3 a 4 a.m. **b** 2 p.m. **Exercise 4 a** 5th channel **b** Saturday 9 August
at 2.30 p.m. and Wednesday 13 August at 12.30 p.m. **c** At what altitude do
giant pandas live? **Exercise 5 a** 1 July to 31 August **b** No, there are no guided
tours at the weekend between 1 September and 30 June **c** 10 a.m. to 11.30
and 2.30 to 6 p.m. **d** From 10 a.m. to 3 p.m. **e** School parties and groups of
10+ if they pre-book **f** It's free **g** Musée ouvert toute l'année, Tous les jours
du 1er juillet au 31 août **h** In French, unless names for the days of the week
and the months of the year are at the beginning of a sentence, they are spelt
without capital letters. **Web extension exercise: 1** 7 **2** 4 **3** 3 **4** 2

Test yourself 6 A) tick 2, 3, 4, 5 B) 1 un billet de 5€, une pièce de vingt
centimes et une de dix. 2 25,40€ 3 3 pièces d'1€ et une de 10 centimes
(more than one answer possible) 4 50,25€

Unit 7
1 Choisir un hôtel **1c** 2e **3f** 4b **5a** 6d Symbols **1h** 2j **3k** 4m **5b** 6c **7n**
8a **9i** 10d **11e** 12g **13f** 14l 2 Quelques renseignements 1 One room
for two people for one night, in a 3 star hotel with sea view 2 A hotel
where he/she can take a small dog 3 One room for one person in **a** not
too expensive hotel with restaurant and swimming pool 4 A large room
for three people in a hotel with a lift (disabled daughter in wheelchair)
Exercise 1 a Je voudrais une chambre pour une personne avec vue
sur la mer. **b** Je voudrais une chambre double dans un hôtel. **c** Nous
cherchons un hôtel avec piscine. **d** On voudrait une chambre d'hôtel
pour le week-end Chambre d'hôtes **a** Chez des agriculteurs **b** Pour une
ou plusieurs nuits **c** Un petit déjeuner campagnard **d** Vos hôtes vous
serviront Services 'plus' **a** dentifrice **b** chauffe biberon **c** sèche-cheveux
d brosse **à** dents **e** crème à raser **f** télécopie 4 Un petit hôtel **a** Yes **b**
No, there are plenty of restaurants in St Malo. **c** Yes **d** No but they can
phone to check availability. **e** Cela devrait être possible. **f** Pouvez-vous
nous renseigner? **g** Vous vous chargez des réservations? **h** Non, je suis
désolé madame! **i** Nous passons quelques jours dans la région.
Exercise 2 a (inside the old town) **b** 18 **c** Yes, they have English TV
channels **d** A lift **e** Between 45 € and 79 €

Test yourself 7 1 voudrions 2 dois 3 sert 4 dois 5 voudrions 6 voudrais /
charge 7 chargez 8 servent 9 doit 10 voudrais

Unit 8

1 Quel hôtel choisir? **a** Station Hotel **b** It's convenient, easy with luggage and it's the cheapest. **c** Near the station **d** Madame Olivier **e** More comfortable Linked phrases: **1c** 2a **3f** 4e **5b** 6h **7d Exercise 1 a** Faux **b** Vrai **c** Faux **Exercise 2 a** Café des Amis **b** Café du Port **c** Café de la Vieille Ville **d** Café de l'Europe

Exercise 3

```
C Q A D H B G T I C R V
H A P D E O U Y T N H I
S Q F X G L T W T T Y E
H O T E L D U P O R T I
R E G T O F M E D A W L
T G H W A E F P F M F L
A N G L A I S V I L L E
A M G L B I S Q C R U P
B C V N F T H W A Q S F
```

2 À l'hôtel de la Plage **a** yes **b** two nights **c** third floor **d** 25 **e** from 8 to 10 a.m. **f** at 11 p.m. Linked phrases: **1e** 2d **3a** 4f **5g** 6c **7b Exercise 4** 1 Lécaille 2 Gaétan Leberre 3 Yannick Tanguy **Exercise 5 a** Je prends/peux, Tu peux/prends, Il/elle/on prend/peut, Nous prenons, Vous prenez, Ils/elles peuvent/prennent **b** Vous prendrez … Oui nous le prendrons **c** Where there is a will there is is a way. Un entretien avec … 1 dogs, cats and rabbits 2 She has a diploma 3 When a dog owner collects his/her dog and leaves the salon proud of the dog.

Test yourself 8 A) 1 moins cher / moins 2 plus cher que / plus **B)** croissants / pain / confiture / eau minérale / café au lait / yaourts aux fruits

Unit 9

1 C'est à côté du… **a** Try to find a post office **b** Yes (PTT) **c** A tour of the ramparts **d** 2 An hour's time Linked phrases: **1e** 2a **3f** 4h **5g** 6c **7d** 8b Vrai ou faux? **a** Faux **b** Vrai **c** Faux **d** Faux **e** Faux

Exercise 1

A	B	C	D
1 M & Mme Olivier	vont	choisir	des cartes postales
2 Tu	vas	téléphoner	à ton frère
3 Sarah Burgess	va	prendre	le petit déjeuner au lit
4 Vous	allez	visiter	la vieille ville
5 Je	vais	rester	à St Malo
6 On	va	chercher	du travail
7 Les enfants	vont	faire	une promenade
8 Nous	allons	voir	le dernier film de Spielberg

2 Une si jolie petite ville! **4f** 7a **8d** 10c **15b** 16e **17g** Directions from Pl. de la République Passant: camping municipal Vous: camping … charcuterie Passant: mairie Vous: bibliothèque 3 Qu'est-ce qu'on va faire? **a** Mum **b** The girl **c** Take the little train in St Malo **d** Dad **e** What they will do tomorrow Linked phrases **1d** 2e **3a** 4b **5f** 6c **Exercise 2** **a** The intra-muros (the old town) and places around St Malo **b** It is the starting place and the end of the train ride **c** No, only in July and August **Exercise 3** 1 Allez à la charcuterie! 2 Allez à la pharmacie! 3 Allez à la Maison de la Presse! 4 Allez **à** la Poste! 5 Allez à la boulangerie-pâtisserie! 6 Allez à l'Office de Tourisme! **Web extension** Porte St Vincent is in St Malo, at the foot of the ramparts, 50m away from the tourist office, 10km from Dinard, 32km from Dinan, 15km from Cancale, 56km from Mont St Michel and roughly an hour away from Jersey and Guernsey.

Test yourself 9 1 centre / entre / en face 2 pain / croissants / derrière 3 renseignements / à côté / derrière 4 lait / sucre / devant / à côté 5 timbres / en face 6 entre

Unit 10
1 Où est-ce qu'on mange? **a** A picnic **b** The other side of the street **c** 10,50 € all included Linked phrases: **1g** 2e **3a** 4f **5b** 6h **7d** 8c **Exercise 1 a** Chauvinism **b** When it is a question of cuisine/cookery **c** two **d** The chefs and French restaurants **e** China and Italy **f** one 2 Les repas… **a** Fine food and good meals **b** Christening, communion or confirmation, a wedding, an exam result, a birthday, Christmas and the New Year. **c**

7 to 8 p.m. **d** Children **e** *Souper* is later than *dîner* and it is also a lighter meal. **f** At the canteen, cafeteria, restaurant or at home if they live close to their work place. **Exercise 2 a** 4 and 6, **b** 1 and 5, **c** 4, **d** 2 and 3, **e** 7, **f** 4, **g** 7, **h** 3, **i** 5, **j** 6 4 Le goûter à la ferme **a** Orchards and cider making **b** Apple juice or cider **c** jams or preserves **d** Every afternoon from 1 May to 15 September **e** You need to book **Exercise 3 a** Le 15 août **b** A partir de 19h30 **c** Soupe de poissons, moules, frites et dessert **d** dix euros **Exercise 4** Les Belges sont amateurs de moules-frites qu'ils mangent dans des restaurants ou des brasseries. Le chanteur et poète Jacques Brel a célébré cette coutume nationale dans ses chansons.

Test yourself 10 1 Elise 2 Christophe 3 Jean-Michel 4 Jacques

Unit 11
1 Il va faire de l'orage **a** This afternoon **b** To listen to the weather forecast **c** The Pyrenees, the Alps and Corsica d3 e4 f2 g2 **h** 2 and 3 Un peu de géographie 1 Bretagne, Caen 2 Lille 3 Strasbourg, Nord-est 4 Poitou-Charentes, Limousin 5 Bordeaux 6 Auvergne, Lyon 7 Marseille, Nice, Corse **Exercise 1 a** Poitou-Charentes, Centre, Limousin, Aquitaine, Midi-Pyrénées, Auvergne, Rhône-Alpes **b** Bretagne, Pays de la Loire, Normandie, Nord-Picardie, Ile-de-France, Nord-Est, Bourgogne, Franche-Comté **c** The same as the areas with thunderstorms **d** & **e** Nord-Picardie, Ile de France **f** Pourtour méditerranéen, Corse **g** Nord-Est, Bourgogne, Franche-Comté **h** Bretagne, Pays de la Loire, Normandie **Exercise 2 a** 1 à Dublin 2 à Athènes 3 à Moscou 4 à Oslo **b** 1 A Varsovie le temps est ensoleillé 2 Il fait de l'orage **Web extension exercise** 1 heat waves 2 coup de soleil 3 rhume des foins

Test yourself 11 Aujourd'hui, ce matin, en ce moment: **c** / **e** / **f** / **i** / **k** / **l** Demain, après-demain, en fin de semaine: **a** / **b** / **d** / **g** / **h** / **j**

Unit 12
1 Un peu de lecture **1b** 2c **3a** 4c **5b Exercise 1** 1 Je viens d'arriver à Paris. 2 Tu viens de finir tes examens. 3 Jean-Paul vient de gagner le gros lot au Loto. 4 Nous venons de visiter St Malo. 5 Vous venez de choisir un menu. 6 Elles viennent de voir un bon film. **Exercise 2** 1 J'ai écouté les infos à la radio. 2 Tu as fini ton travail. 3 On a mangé des moules-frites. 4 Nous avons choisi un hôtel pas trop cher. 5 Vous avez posté vos

cartes postales. 6 S & D ont réservé une cabine. 2 Au café de la Baie **a** No Sarah orders a draft beer and Dominique a shandy **b** Ice cream **c** No, she is on a diet **d** Sarah **e** Dominique. Sarah paid last time **f** 9,50 € Yes 50c **g** Je vous apporte la carte **h** Prends un sorbet; il y a moins de calories **i** Une glace à la fraise et un sorbet au citron **j** Tu as payé la dernière fois **k** Quelques minutes plus tard **l** Un peu plus tard Perfect tense: Vous avez choisi, tu as payé; Present tense: je vous sers, je conduis, je vous apporte, tu prends, je suis, il y a, paie, c'est, fait; Immediate future: je vais prendre, nous allons prendre. 3 Au restaurant **a** A table by the window **b** No, they ask for the menu **c** A children's menu **d** Yes **e** It's only available at lunch time **f** Two menus at 20 €, two children's menus and a bottle of Muscadet **Web extension exercise:** Vrai – especially if you chose *une brasserie*

Exercise 3

	Menus (prix)	First course	Second course	Cheese	Dessert
Luc	20 €	Scallops	Monkfish	No	Ice cream
Florence	45 €	Sea food platter	Lobster	Cheese	Choice of dessert
Vous	25 €	6 huîtres chaudes avec cocktail d'algues	brochette de St Jaques au beurre blanc	fromage	glace à la fraise

Test yourself 12 Perfect tense: Je n'ai pas trouvé / Josiane a pris / nous avons fait / Elle m'a présentée / j'ai goûté / j'ai appris / j'ai nagé / nous avons fait / je n'ai pas lu / tu m'as prêté; Future: Je le lirai / Je te verrai; Present: (il y a) / je finis / mon avion part

Unit 13
1 Il y a une déviation **a** There is a diversion in 500 m **b** 50 km/hour **c** Service station **d** On the right Linked phrases: **1e** 2h **3g** 4b **5f** 6a **7c** 8d **Exercise 1** 1 **a** or **c** 2e **3d** 4b **5f** 6 **a** or **c Exercise 2** 3 Vérifier la pression des pneus **Exercise 3** 1 C, 2 A, 3 B, 4 a full tank of diesel, 20 litres of leaded 4 star petrol, 30 litres of unleaded petrol **Exercise 4 a** A16 **b** N43 **c** D940 2 Les panneaux **a** The end of the area where the

signs apply **b** Blue **c** Red **d** A blue square Checklist 1 3 4 6 7 9 10

3 Les informations...

Accidents	Type of vehicle involved in the accident	Place where accident occurred	No. of people killed	No. of people injured
1	Portuguese coach and lorry	RN10	8	24
2	Bicycle and a car	St Nazaire	1	–
3	Four cars	D940 Calais–Boulogne	0	8

Exercise 5 1f 2g **3a** 4d **5e** 6c **7b**

Test yourself 13 1 Non, il n'y en a pas 2 Non, je n'en ai pas acheté 3 Non, il n'en a pas lu 4 Non, ils n'en ont pas mangé 5 Non, il n'y en a pas 6 Non, je n'en écris pas 7 Oui, il en faut 8 Oui, il y en a 9 Si, j'en prends 10 Si, il y en a

Unit 14

1 L'appart de Dominique **a** Fourth floor **b** No **c** Yes, the view is great, it's cheap and the neighbours are quiet **d** There is no lift **e** Going up and down stairs **f** Dominique and her boyfriend **g** The sea Linked phrases: **1h** 2e **3g** 4k **5b** 6c **7d** 8f **9j** 10a **11i** Grammar 1 je le loue; si, les voilà; l'à décoré; tu la vois? 2 appartement; clefs; appartement; mer. **Exercise 1** 2, 3, 5, 6, 7, 9, 10, 14, 16, 17, 20 2 Où loger? **a** Her mother **b** A room in the university campus **c** Rent a studio flat or share a flat with one or two girl friends. **d** She is going to find a holiday job. Linked phrases: **1d** 2f **3a** 4e **5c** 6b 3 Corinne cherche... 1 4: a, b, **d** and **j** 2b 3 **k** and **g** (although **g** is too expensive for her) 4 400–550 € **5a Exercise 2 1e** 2g **3a** 4f **5d** 6c **7b**

Test yourself 14 1 Nous la regardons... 2 Ils le volent 3 Je l'achète... 4 Il l'emmène... 5 Je finis de le lire / je le finis 6 Oui, nous le prendrons au lit / non, nous ne le prendrons pas au lit. 7 Je l'ai fini 8 Il ne l'a pas fini 9 Oui, nous la connaissons / non, nous ne la connaissons pas

Unit 15

1 Rien dans le frigo **a** Milk, cheese, yogurts, butter, bread, fish, fruit and vegetables, washing-up liquid and tins of cat food **b** Her cat **c** Her neighbour **d** Film for her camera, batteries for her torch, white wine and a cake **e** For Sarah and Dominique's evening meal **f** A pair of shoes and a pullover **g** No **h** Green **i** Fish counter Linked phrases: **1e** 2f **3h** 4b **5c** 6a **7d** 8g Dom. plaisante Sarah has just told Dominique that red does not suit her. In reply Dominique suggests that they move on to the fish counter, saying that she hopes they don't sell goldfish. The French word for goldfish is *poisson rouge* (lit. red fish). On va à quel rayon? 3, 12, 13, 21, 22, 23, 24, 25, 26, 28, 33, 36 and 40 **Exercise 1 1e** 2f **3a** 4b **5d** 6c **Exercise 2 a** White nectarines **b** 1 to 3 August **c** A Sunday **d** In the town centre on Tuesday 12 and Wednesday 13 August **e** Bedding **f** 4800 € **g** Wednesday 6 August **h** Furniture 2 Au rayon charcuterie Bayonne ham: six slices; garlic sausage: 12 slices; farmhouse pâté: 250 g; Greek mushrooms: 200 g; scallops: 4

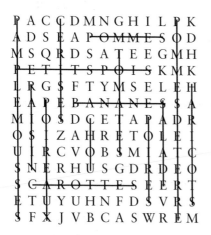

Test yourself 15 1i 2j **3a** 4h **5c** 6d **7f** 8b **9g** 10e

Unit 16

1 Je suis animateur **1b** 2c 3 Sports, photography, music and travel 4 Morocco 5 three weeks 6 18 young people and 3 adults 7 With their families 8 Young Moroccans Linked phrases **1h** 2f **3e** 4g **5a** 6b **7d** 8c **Exercise 1 1c** Djamel is the youth worker who organized the journey.

2e Sarah and Dominique arrived at Gildas's. **3f** I went up the Eiffel Tower. **4a** The young people went to Morocco. **5b** You went away with a group of young people? **6d** The group stayed three weeks in Morocco. **Exercise 2 a** Vous aussi, vous êtes allée au Maroc avec le groupe? **b** Combien de jeunes y sont allés/sont allés au Maroc? **c** Vous êtes restés combien de temps? **d** Vous avez rencontré des jeunes marocains? 2 Je suis né en France **a** If it was the first time he had been to Morocco **b** In France **c** His parents and sisters **d** About ten times **e** Arabic **f** Three: Arabic, French and English **Exercise 3 1c** 2e **3a** 4b **5d** Exercise 4 **a** 50 %: cinquante pour cent **b** 48 %: quarante-huit pour cent **c** 65 %: soixante-cinq pour cent **d** 32 %: trente-deux pour cent **Web extension exercise:** 1 French footballer 2 Paris suburbs 3 Because they are negative towards young people of the « banlieues ». 4 Interior Minister 5 Thuram has not lived there for many years.

Test yourself 16 Perfect tense with être: Nous sommes arrivés à M / (ils) sont partis / (ils) sont restés / (Yousef) est parti / (Nadima) s'est installée / La tante est venue / (Saïd) s'est cassé la figure; Present tense: Les jeunes qui ont des contacts / tout va bien; Future: (elle) la ramènera / Je t'enverrai; Gerund: en faisant l'idiot

Unit 17

1 Mon père était professeur **a** It's very good **b** Sarah is bilingual **c** Her mother and her father **d** He died **e** Five years ago **f** Fine **g** Because he is tiring Sarah out with his questions **h** Her room **i** Two years ago

Noms	profession/métier	profession/job
Dominique ✓	Prof de Philo	Philosophy teacher
Sarah ✓	Editrice	Editor
Mme Périer	Pharmacienne	Pharmacist
M. Périer	Viticulteur	Wine grower
Mr. Burgess	Professeur d'allemand	German teacher
Mrs. Burgess ✓	Professeur de français	French teacher

Exercise 1 a Je dansais **b** Je skiais/je faisais du ski **c** Je faisais du basket **d** J'allais à la pêche **e** Je faisais de la planche à roulettes **f** Je jouais du piano 2 À l'ANPE **a** He does not know **b** He was a baker's apprentice **c** He works full-time as a baker **d** Go out to clubs in the

evening **e** 5 a.m. **f** In a pharmacy Linked phrases: **1d** 2f **3a** 4c **5b** 6e
3 Le contrat 1 Between 16 and 26 2 two years 3 It can be extended to
three and reduced to one 4 Two months 5 The contract can be broken
6 Five weeks 7 Six weeks before the date of birth and ten afterwards
8 **a** four days **b** three days 9 General and technical 10 Between one
and two weeks per month **Exercise 2 a** Je m'intéresse aux métiers de
l'hôtellerie. **b** Je m'intéresse à la photographie. **c** Je m'intéresse aux
métiers de la restauration. **d** Je m'intéresse aux métiers de la santé. **e**
Je m'intéresse aux métiers de l'habillement. **Exercise 3 a** Job offers **b**
You can look up all adverts for the last fortnight **c** You can send your CV
immediately via the Internet **d** Sales assistants, doorman, confectioner,
waitresses, apprentice (in a delicatessen), home helps **e** Secretarial jobs
or accountancy, sales, electrician **f** At least 26 **g** You must be dynamic,
motivated and interested in information technology **h** Maths, physics,
chemistry, economics or management

Test yourself 17 quand / étais / ma / racontait / incroyables / était /
chez / grand / mangeait / les / pouvait / toujours / faim / jour / pâtissier /
mais / punir /fait / énorme / anniversaire

Unit 18
1 Vous prenez le TGV? **a** She has to go back to work **b** Bordeaux, les
Landes and the local wine **c** She likes it a lot **d** To Paris **e** By train (TGV)
f 3 hours **g** 12 hours **h** To make her train reservation **i** Between 3 and
4 p.m. **j** Her sister Linked phrases: **1d** 2f **3a** 4g **5b** 6c **7h** 8e **Exercise 1**
1b 2c **3d** 4a **5f** 6e **Exercise 2 a** Ça prend deux heures **b** Ça prend cinq
heures **c** Ça prend une heure cinquante-cinq **d** Ça prend exactement
une heure 2 Au guichet de la gare **a** 1h45 **b** return tickets **c** on Thursday
d 10.09 **e** 10.37 **f** It arrives at Poitiers just in time for lunch **g** No **h** Book
her ticket at the ticket machine Linked phrases: **1d** 2e **3b** 4h **5a** 6c **7f**
8g **Exercise 3 a** Je voudrais réserver un billet pour Paris SVP. **b** Non, je
voyage demain. **c** Je prends le train de sept heures cinq. **d** Non, je prends
un billet simple. C'est combien? **Exercise 4 a** une soirée **b** ans **c** jours **d**
ans 3 Les points de vente… **a** Vrai **b** Faux **c** Vrai **d** Vrai **e** Faux **f** Faux **g**
Vrai

Web extension exercise: 1 No 1 2 weekly 3 all rail news (equipment, technology and people who matter) 4 On the internet – click on *Vous Abonner* or by telephone

```
A R R I V E E S A R T Y U C V B M B T A
Z E F G H N M K L O S E R A T A Z C V L
D S I M P L E F S D F G H O R A I R E L
R E W A S V B G N M J D E P A R T S V E
G R A N D E S L I G N E S D I A S W B R
T V S A F T F E D D T Y U I N G S A N I
F A A W E G A H F E S V O Y A G E G D R
V T S S D G U J I U Y T R D G F A O F E
B I L L E T T E R I E S F F R D X N G T
C O F F G I O K L Y F D F G A S C R T O
V N D U W R M D G T R R M I N I T E L U
N E E J E G A R E S F F F U D B F S Y R
G U I C H E T F Z A G F G K E J G T U A
M F D H A B I L L E T D U Y V K H A E E
O G F N S S Q H G L N S I T I U J U A I
P B H F S A U K E R K G K F T T H R D O
V A L A B L E L K L H U U D E R T A F U
N P O I N T S D E V E N T E S D S N C F
F H W E T G G U I T H U T D S E F T G Y
G S D M O N T P A R N A S S E S R S E A
```

Test yourself 18 1e 2a/f/h 3a/f/h **4c** 5b **6d** 7a/f/h **8g**

Unit 19

1 Sarah téléphone à sa sœur **a** 19.15 **b** 19.05 She will not get compensation (her train was less than 30 minutes, late) **c** No **d** To telephone her sister **e** a mobile phone 2 Allô! **a** her mobile phone **b** 01–48 05 39 16 **c** At the hospital **d** Opening a tin of cat food **e** Not really **f** Marie-Claire's children **g** Get a taxi **h** No, she knows her way very well
Linked phrases: **1d** 2g **3e** 4h **5b** 6c **7a** 8f

Exercise 1

Names	Questions on the recording	Your answer
Nadine	A quelle heure avez-vous téléphoné à Nadine?	Je lui ai téléphoné à onze heures trente
Mathieu	… à Mathieu?	Je lui ai téléphoné à midi
Chantal et Marc	… à Chantal et Marc?	Je leur ai téléphoné à dix-sept heures quinze
Votre sœur	… à votre sœur?	Je lui ai téléphoné à dix-huit heures quarante-cinq
Vos parents	… à vos parents?	Je leur ai téléphoné à vingt heures dix
Votre fiancé/e	… à votre fiancée?	Je lui ai téléphoné à vingt-deux heures quarante-cinq

Exercise 2 1g mal au dos **2e** blessé aux genoux **3d** mal à la tête **4b** mal aux dents **5f** bras cassé **6c** main brûlée avec un fer **7h** coupé le pied en marchant sur une bouteille cassée **8a** piqûres de moustiques infectées 4 J'ai mal au ventre **a** No **b** Stomach **c** 38.2 degrees (it's slightly high) **d** appendicitis **e** Nothing at all **f** Breakfast **g** 10 a.m. **h** She should be kept at the hospital for observation Linked phrases: **1c** 2a **3d** 4e **5f** 6b **Exercise 3 a** Wednesday 21 March 2007 at 8.30 p.m. **b** Dr Friat **c** Backache **d** Salle polyvalente (village hall) **e** C.H.U. of Brest **Exercise 4** 1 lift right arm 2 nothing 3 nothing 4 touch mouth with left hand 5 lower right arm 6 nothing 7 nothing 8 nothing 9 sang 10 touch left foot 11 lift right hand 12 nothing **Web extension exercise:** 1 from age 5. 2 Jacques a dit 3 he/she is no longer in the game 4 the winner becomes Jacques

Test yourself 19 1c 2a **3a** 4c **5b** 6c **7a** 8a **9b** 10a

Unit 20
1 Je te prie… Calendar of events **a** Chatting to her sister **b** Will take the children out to the Bois de Boulogne zoo and go for a walk **c** All go to the cinema **d** Lunch at Tante Eliane **e** Gare du Nord: register train ticket **f** Takes Eurostar back to London **g** Starts work in London Linked phrases: **1c** 2e **3g** 4h **5b** 6a **7d** 8f **Exercise 1 a** Il n'y a pas de mal **b** Ce n'est

pas grave **c** Ne vous inquiétez pas **d** Cela ne fait rien **Web extension exercise** 1 Since 2002 2 four to five weeks in July and August 3 On the right bank of the Seine 4 The traffic 2 Acheter des tickets **a** No they have got some **b** Half-fare **c** Children **d** She needs to think which kind of ticket she needs to buy **e** A carnet of tickets **f** Direction Porte de Vincennes **g** Because they may be able to have a ride on the little train at the Bois de Boulogne Linked phrases: **1c** 2e **3f** 4b **5a** 6d **Exercise 2 a** Card A **b** B is for museums and monuments, C is for Disneyland **c** In all RER and RATP stations **d** Marne-la-Vallée/Chessy (Disneyland station) **e** Card A **f** For 1, 3 or 5 days **g** All metro and RER stations, bus terminals, shops and tobacconists with the RATP sign, ticket machines **h** 6,50 €

Test yourself 20 1j 2c **3f** 4a **5i** 6b **7g** 8h **9e** 10d

Unit 21
On pourrait sortir **b** c **d** f **g** Marie-Claire is feeling much better and she will be careful **h** More time and money Linked phrases: **1b** 2d **3e** 4a **5f** 6c **Exercise 1 1g** 2d **3a** 4h **5c** 6e **7b** 8f 2 Qu'est-ce que tu ferais? **a** Marie-Claire is imagining what she would do if she won the jackpot. **b** A large apartment in Paris and a house on the Mediterranean. **c** Because she loves Paris. **d** No, she would have all the time to herself. **e** Every morning. **f** She would go to the cinema, theatre, opera, fine restaurants. **g** All her family including Sarah **Exercise 2** 1 J'aurais une grande maison en Bretagne, j'aurais un bateau, j'irais à la pêche et le soir je regarderais la télé. 2 Je ferais un voyage autour du monde. **Exercise 3 a** Three identical sums of money on the card and you win that amount **b** 2 € **c** you win 20 000–1 000 000 € on the wheel **Exercise 4 a** Wednesdays and Saturdays **b** 16,8 € **c** 33,6 € **d** 10 **e** 5 **Exercise 5** Winning numbers: 35, 8, 15, 28, 13, 45, 11, 25; bonus number is 12 3 Un peu de littérature **a** She would go and meet her parents **b** In a hotel room at 41 Boulevard Ornano **c** Her journey **d** Nation. Simplon **e** One **f** A cinema **g** 1945 **h** A quest for the identity of people and their painful and enigmatic past **Web extension exercise:** la vue, l'ouïe, le toucher, l'odorat et le goût.

Test yourself 21 1 continuerais 2 j'achèterais / ferais 3 aurait / pourraient 4 . j'achèterais / passerais 5 j'emploierais / j'exigerais / seraient / vieillirions

Unit 22

1 C'est le mien **a** Over a game **b** He left it at his grandmother's **c** Ariane's **d** Pierre **e** That it is his game **f** To go and sit down in the living-room and watch TV **g** Because she says she does not like animals **h** She kicks Pierre **i** Go to bed Linked phrases: **1d** 2f **3g** 4h **5a** 6b **7c** 8e **Exercise 1 a** Non ce n'est pas le mien. **b** Oui ce sont les miens. **c** Oui ce sont les miennes. **d** Non ce n'est pas le mien. **e** Oui ce sont les miennes. **f** Oui c'est le mien. **g** Non ce n'est pas la mienne. **Exercise 2** Q1: Ce sac est à vous? R1: Oui c'est le mien. Q2: Ce sont vos clefs? R2: Oui ce sont les miennes. Q3: C'est votre montre? R3: Oui c'est la mienne. Q4: Ce sont vos patins à roulettes? R4: Oui ce sont les miens. **2** On regarde la télé **a** From Sunday **b** It might affect her return journey **c** Good, she can stay in Paris! **d** A film called Ridicule **e** Mots-Croisés **f** Because she is interested in politics Linked phrases: **1f** 2e **3d** 4a **5b** 6c À vous de choisir **a** Channel 5 (ARTE) at 20.45 **b** F2 at 20.55 **c** F2: 23.55/F3: 22.50/C+: 22.15 **d** F2: 22.35 **e** TF1: 22.55 **f** M6: 20.45 **g** Cable TV: 20.30 **h** If you had cable TV **i** Mensuel **j** 'Which school for our children?' **3** Le retour de Loft Story **a** 13 **b** Bedrooms, dining rooms, sitting room, a gym and the « confessional » **c** the confessional **d** it is on the second floor and is used for individuals to address TV audience **e** 22 cameras and 55 microphones **f** use the gym **g** the filming of the competitors **h** 7000 **4** Que disent les journaux? **1** Will this strike snowball to the other towns in France? **2** 15 **3** in La Seine-Saint-Denis **4** Personal itineraries/programmes to motivate pupils and give a taste for life-long learning **5** The new initiatives, because changes have had to be made to the timetable. They object to French, Maths, History and Geography having to be cut by two hours a week. **6** They want an extra 6000 teachers for La Seine–Saint-Denis.

Test yourself 22 **1** Ce portable c'est le vôtre? Non, ce n'est pas le mien, c'est celui de mon fils. **2** Ces patins en ligne ce sont les vôtres? Non, ce ne sont pas les miens, ce sont ceux de ma fille. **3** Cette voiture c'est la vôtre? Non, ce n'est pas la mienne, c'est celle de mon mari. **4** Ces valises ce sont les vôtres? Non, ce ne sont pas les miennes, ce sont celles de mes enfants. **5** Cet ordinateur c'est le vôtre? Non, ce n'est pas le mien, c'est celui de ma professeure. **6** Ces livres ce sont les vôtres? Non, ce ne sont pas les miens ce sont ceux de collège. **7** Ces cigarettes ce sont les vôtres? Non, ce ne sont pas les miennes, ce sont celles de mon copain.

Unit 23
1 Moi, j'en ai ras-le-bol!

Saturday	**Marie-Claire**	**Guillaume**	**Sarah**	**Ariane**	**Pierre**
Morning	Housework Shopping	**Bercy Sports centre, playing tennis with his office friends**	Housework and shopping	Housework and shopping	Housework and shopping
Afternoon	**Having a rest at home**	Football match	**Cinema**	**Cinema**	**Cinema**
Evening	Cinema	**At home looking after the children**	**Cinema**	At home	**At home**

Linked phrases: **1d** 2f **3e** 4c **5a** 6b **Exercise 1 1d** 2f **3g** 4a **5h** 6e **7b** 8c **Exercise 2 a** Around 10 **b** Car rally, horse racing, rugby, running (marathon and 20 km), martial arts, tennis, football, waiters' races, cycling: Tour de France, vintage cars race **c** In June **d** From the Champs-Elysées to Bastille **e** On a Sunday during first two weeks of April **f** A 20 km run

Exercise 3 Est-ce que vous connaissez bien les deux meilleurs footballeurs français?

1. Prénom: Zinédine
2. Nom: Zidane
3. Nationalité: française
4. Date de naissance: 23 juin 1972
5. Lieu de naissance: Marseille
6. Taille: 1,85 m
7. Poste: milieu de terrain
8. Club avant la coupe du Monde: Real Madrid

1. Prénom: Thierry
2. Nom: Henry
3. Nationalité: française
4. Date de naissance: 17 août 1977
5. Lieu de naissance: Paris
6. Taille:1,88m
7. Poste: attaquant
8. Club avant la coupe du Monde: Arsenal FC

2 Aller au cinéma **a** when she is in London she gets more opportunities to go to the cinema than M-C. **b** *Paris je t'aime* has just come out on

DVD and M-C will give a copy to Sarah for her birthday **c** Hors de Prix
Exercise 4 a a Je voudrais voir Paris je t'aime parce que j'adore Paris. **b**
j'aime beaucoup les films de Luc Besson. **c** c'est intéressant de voir un fil
américains sur l'histoire de France **d** l'histoire, l'animation et la musique
sont très belles. **Exercise 5 a** 40% discount **b** 5 issues for 17€ **c** cheque,
postal order or credit card

Test yourself 23 **1g** 2f **3e** 4b **5h** 6i **7a** 8d **9j** 10c

Unit 24

1 Mettre le couvert **a** To help her lay the table **b** Her crockery and her
glasses **c** The corkscrew **d** White wine **e** Menu de Tante Eliane: Melon,
Melon, Truite au champagne et raisins, Trout in Champagne with grapes,
Pommes de terre sautés, Sauté potatoes, Salade, Salad, Fromage,
Cheese, Tarte aux pommes, Apple Tart Le couvert **a** un verre **b** une
assiette **c** un couteau **d** une fourchette **e** une cuillère **f** la vaisselle **g** un
tire-bouchon Linked phrases: **1d** 2e **3f** 4a **5c** 6b 2 Une bonne recette
Ingredients: **1c** 2e **3a** 4f **5d** 6b Utensils: **7h** 8g **9i** 10j Preparation of
ingredients: **11k** 12o **13m** 14n **15l** What to do: **16p** 17u **18r** 19s **20v**
21y **22q** 23w **24x** 25t **26z** Lisez la recette! **a** 6 to 8 **b** 45 minutes **c** Half
a bottle **d** Heated **e** Once or twice during the cooking time **f** They need
to be wrapped in aluminium paper 3 Des nouvelles de la famille **a** In
Japan **b** For Xmas **c** Yes **d** No, he is single **e** Her sister-in-law **f** Because
her brother-in-law cannot go **g** 12 October, from Nantes **h** 21 October
Linked phrases: **1d** 2f **3b** 4e **5c** 6a **Exercise 2 a** que, qui **b** que **c** que **d**
que, qui **e** qui **f** qui **Exercise 3 a** Faux **b** Faux **c** Faux **d** Vrai **e** Vrai **f** Faux
g Vrai **h** Faux **i** Vrai **j** Faux Printing error: In the last sentence for Day 7 of
the visit it refers to la **8e** nuit instead of 7e. **Web extension exercises**
– Recette pommes de terre farcies **à** la ricotta 1 Faux (ricotta) 2 F (9g of
garlic) 3 F (2 pinches) 4 F (2 people) 5 Vrai (1h15 minutes of cooking)
Au Québec 1 Tadoussac 2 4th centenary of Québec

Test yourself 24 Ma semaine / de choses / cette carte postale / je te
raconterai / beaucoup aimé / j'ai préféré / a débarqué / nous avons été
très touchés / Hier soir / C'était drôle / ça ressemblait / partout dans le
monde

Unit 25

1 Avant le départ **a** Because she is leaving **b** sad **c** No **d** Their mother **e** Because she too is going back to work tomorrow **f** Retire at 55 and buy a small house in the South of France **g** All buy a house together and renovate it **h** Not really Linked phrases: **1e** 2c **3d** 4a **5b** **Exercise 1** 1 S: J'adore la cuisine française R: Moi aussi 2 S: Je n'aime pas les voyages organisés R: Moi non plus 3 S: Nous aimons beaucoup la Bretagne R: Nous/moi aussi 4 S: Je n'aime pas la rentrée R: Moi non plus 5 S: Je déteste prendre l'avion R: Moi aussi 6 S: Je préfère rester chez moi R: Moi aussi 2 Chez le notaire **a** Because they intend to buy a house **b** Whether there are any problems **c** An advert in a newspaper **d** No, not yet **e** Yes **f** Arrange a visit **g** The lawyer **h** Think about it Linked phrases: **1e** 2a **3f** 4c **5b** 6d Vrai ou faux? **a** Vrai **b** Vrai **c** Faux **d** Vrai **e** Faux **f** Vrai **g** Vrai **h** Vrai **Exercise 2 a** 4A **b** 5A **c** 5V **d** 2V **e** 3A **f** 7A **g** 8A and 8V **h** 2A **Exercise 3 a** 6 and 7 **b** 4, 9 **c** 12 **d** 5 10 13 **e** 2, 4, 13 **f** 2 (also 3, 9), **g** 2, **h** 6 **Exercise 4** C1: Je cherche une petite maison de pierres près de la côte. C2: Je cherche une maison de cinq chambres avec cave. C3: Je cherche une petite maison avec un jardin clos. C4: Je cherche une petite maison avec grenier aménageable **Exercise 5 a** 1 **b** 8 **c** 13 **d** 4 **e** 2

Test yourself 25 1V 2F 3F 4V 5F 6V 7F 8F 9V 10V

Unité de révision

1 Profiles 1 Nom: Burgess; Prénom: Sarah; Âge: 28 ans; Adresse: 12 Stella Avenue, Londres SW2; Numéro de téléphone: 020 8476 5656; Nationalité: britannique; Nationalité du père: britannique; Nationalité de la mère: française; Profession: éditrice, Lieu de travail: Hodder & Stoughton, Londres, Aime: les voyages, le cinéma, la lecture; N'aime pas: le sport à la télévision 2 Nom: Périer; Prénom: Dominique; Âge: 36 ans; Adresse: 5 Avenue de la Vieille Ville; St Nazaire; France; Numéro de téléphone: 02 40 45 1811; Nationalité: française, Nationalité du père: française; Nationalité de la mère: française; Profession: professeur de philosophie; Lieu de travail: lycée de St Nazaire; Aime: les chats, l'opéra, les musées d'art; N'aime pas: la télévision, les voitures

2 Une promenade à St Malo (1) from **c** to the station, (2) from **e** to the swimming pool, (3) from **d** to the cathedral, (4) from **a** to the castle

3 Orthographe des nombres *vingt* and *cent* only have s in the plural if they come at the end of the number e.g. *deux cents*, *quatre vingts*, but *deux cent trois*, *quatre-vingt-cinq*

4 Grand jeu-concours 1 A trip to England for two 2 14 September 3 The town and the tourist office.

5 Quelle attitude! 1 They both use the verb *vouloir: je veux* is the present tense and *je voudrais* is the conditional. 2 The difference shows 2 different attitudes: *je veux* is likely to be perceived as impolite 3 To b)

6 Aujourd'hui c'est samedi Aujourd'hui les parents et les trois enfants vont au barrage de la Rance/Aujourd'hui toute la famille va au barrage de la Rance

7 La voiture idéale 1 6-d-m/o 2 8-f-n 3 5-a-j 4 1-b-q 5 9-g-l 6 7-h-r 7 2-c-m/o 8 3-i-p 9 4-e-k

8 Les jeunes et l'emploi 1 **a** Work experience **b** Administration and management **c** No **d** It was eight weeks of their holidays **e** It gave them their first contact with the world of work 2 1 Fast food and cafeteria: **c b d** 2 Telephone marketing and opinion polls: **g a i** 3 Leaflet distribution: **h** f **e**

9 Paris et le tourisme 1 V 2 F there is a night bus, 3 F children of 4 to 11 pay a reduced rate, 4 V 5 F the zones are 1 to 3 and 1 to 8 6 V 7 F 8 F tickets are for 1, 2, 3 or 5 days

10 Les loisirs et vous 1A Oui: b g h j l Non: a c d e f i

11 Encore une bonne recette a 25 minutes **b** 175 cl of water + 75 cl of juice **c** Thin slices **d** Half a teaspoon **e** Pear juice **f** One soup spoon **g** Garnish **h** The mixture **i** After the fruit mixture is cooked **j** Five minutes

A quick guide to French pronunciation

A language is primarily something that you hear and something that you speak. When learning a new language the most important thing to do is to listen to it. Reading about the way it sounds is not really satisfactory but I shall attempt to describe the sounds comparing them with English sounds where possible and giving a very simple description of the position of the tongue in relation to the palate and the position of the lips and jaws. In order to describe it, it is necessary to divide the tongue into three broad areas: the tip of the tongue, the front of the tongue (more or less the centre of the blade) and the back of the tongue.

There is an important difference between the hard palate and the soft palate. You need only feel the roof of your mouth with your tongue in order to discover the difference between the two.

Reading through the list of words and practising how to say them, taking into account the position of the lips, tongue, palate and jaws should give you awareness of how sounds are formed. And try to listen to French as often as you can.

VOWELS

French examples	Similar English sounds	Characteristic position of tongue (T), Lips (L), jaw (J)
idée (idea) ami (friend) ici (here)	be, meet (the French sound is shorter)	T: The whole tongue is raised towards the hard palate, as high as possible, L: spread, J: together
été (summer) assez (enough) aller (to go) et (and)	ready, play (with a Scottish accent)	T: The front of the tongue is raised towards the middle of the hard palate, L: neutral, J: nearly together

mais (but) sept (seven) même (even) béret rester (stay) scène les (the)	men set maim ray Seine lay	T: The front of the tongue is slightly lifted towards the hard palate, L: neutral, J: slightly open
là (there) la (the) malade (sick)	cap, pat,	T: Front is only very slightly lifted (passage between tongue and palate is wide), L: neutral, J: wide.
pâté là-bas (over there) pas (not)	dark, father	T: The tip is kept against the lower teeth. The back part is slightly raised towards soft palate, L: not rounded, J: wide open.
rue (street) plus (more) futur	there is no very similar sound in English: 'dew' with very rounded lips	T: Very similar to i, L: rounded and pouting. Try practising i and u, first li, then lu, keeping the same tongue position, but rounding your lips for lu (like in 'Lully'), J: not far apart
deux (two) peu (little) heureux (happy) œufs (eggs)	no satisfactory comparison: 'adieu' with very rounded lips	T: Stretched but not raised, L: rounded and pouting, but open wider than for u, J: not far apart
heure (hour) seul (alone) œuf (egg)	something between the 'ur' in 'turn' and 'er' in 'butter'	T: Stretched but not raised, L: rounded but not pouting.
ouvert (open) sous (under) où (where)	hoot, two, do	T: Back is raised towards the soft palate, L: rounded and closed, as for u, J: not far apart

gros (big) beau (beautiful) rôle chaud (hot)	as in 'go', but very much shorter	T: Back is retracted towards the pharynx, L: very rounded, J: not far apart
homme (man) mort (dead)	hot, dog	T: Back slightly raised towards the larynx, L: rounded as for o, but with a wider opening, J: not far apart

NASALISED VOWELS

These are very common in French. The **m** or **n** is swallowed, and the preceding vowel is pronounced in a nasal fashion (i.e. through the nose).

French examples	Similar English sounds	Characteristic position of tongue (**T**), Lips (**L**), jaw (**J**)
camp grand (tall) emblème	calm, part (pronounced in a nasal fashion)	T: Back slightly raised towards the larynx, L: not rounded, J: wide apart. The soft palate is lowered
fin (end) pain (bread) plein (full) simple	pet (nasalised)	T: Back slightly raised towards the larynx, L: spread, J: wide apart. The soft palate is lowered
brun (brown) lundi (Monday) humble	turn (nasalised)	T: Back slightly raised towards the larynx, L: rounded, J: apart. The soft palate is lowered.
bon (good) nom (name) long	song (nasalised)	T: Back slightly raised towards the larynx, L: closely rounded, J: not far apart. The soft palate is lowered

SEMI-VOWELS

French examples	Similar English sounds	Characteristic position of tongue (T), Lips (L), jaw (J)
briller (shine) travail (work) pied (foot) mayonnaise	yellow, young	T: Back moves towards the hard palate, sides touch the upper teeth each side of the mouth, L: neutral, J: not far apart
lui (him) puis (then) bruit (noise)		T: It is stretched and raised toward the hard palate, L: rounded, J: not far apart.
oui (yes) ouest (west)	'w' as in 'walk', 'west'	T: The back forms a narrow passage against the soft palate, L: very rounded, J: not far apart.
loi (law) moi (me) quoi (what) poële (frying pan)	the 'wo' sound in 'wonder'	T: similar to 'wonder', L: rounded, J: Not far apart

CONSONANTS

Although there are some differences between French and English, it is not difficult to produce the correct sounds, even if you have never heard them before. (The position of the tongue, lips and jaw are only mentioned if relevant.)

French examples	Similar English sounds	Characteristic position of tongue (T), Lips (L), jaw (J)
port papier (paper)	port, bump	not aspirated (no puff of air after the 'p')
bon (good) beau (beautiful)	boy, bat	

tout (all) porte (door)		not aspirated (no puff of air after the 't')
dans (in) monde (world)	day, pad	
quai (platform) carotte	cup, cook	not aspirated (no puff of air after the 'c/qu')
gauche (left) vague	go, gag	
moment mère (mother)	man, jam	
noir (black) fini (finished)	new,	
digne (dignified) agneau	onion, Tanya	
lourd (heavy) ville (town) pluriel (plural)	let, little	a tight sound, like the first, not the last 'l' in 'little'
café photo	telephone, friend	
vert(green) avant (before)	virus, have	
savoir (to know) ça (this) passé (past)	save, place	
maison (house) rose zone	zany, roses	's' between two vowels has the sound 'z'
chat (cat) chercher (to look for)	shine, fresh	
jeune (young) mangeons (we eat) garage	's' in 'pleasure', or 'Jane' in English without the 'd' sound at the beginning	there is no hard 'dj' sound in French

rouge (red) nourriture (food) amour (love)	difficult to compare with an English 'r'	There are many varieties of **r**. The sound varies according to individuals and regions. In a Parisian **r**, the back of the tongue is raised to form a narrow passage against the soft palate.

Although many words have the same spelling in both French and English, the pronunciation is usually entirely different. When trying to pronounce a word, it is important to bear the following points in mind:

1 *Final consonants are usually silent (except for* **c, f, l, r**). **h** *is not normally pronounced.* **e** *is silent at the end of a word, except for words of one syllable.*
2 *Stress mainly falls on the last syllable of a word.*
3 *The written accents in French are:*
é *acute,* ê *circumflex,* è *grave*
ë *tréma is used to separate the sounds of 2 consecutive vowels, e.g. in 'Noël'.*
cedilla ç, *which changes the sound /k/ into /s/ before* **u, a** *and* **o**.

Accents may be omitted when capital letters are used.

LINKING WORDS

Two consecutive words can be pronounced as one by linking the last letter of the first word to the first letter of the second when the first word ends in a consonant and the second words begins with a vowel or **h**.

Examples:

mes amis	mezami	*my friends*
tout est fini	tutay fini	*it's all over*

vous habitez à Paris	vuzabitezapari	*you live in Paris*
	vuzabite apari	
un œuf	unœf	*an egg*
des œufs	dezeu	*eggs*

These expressions are pronounced as if they were one word:

jmappelle (je m'appelle – *my name is*)
jai (j'ai – *I have*)
jabite (j'habite – *I live*)
jaime (j'aime – *I love / like*) / **jnai**me pas (je n'aime pas – *I don't like*)
ilya (il y a – *there is*)

Try these three examples of **liaison**: two words linked together because of the last letter of the first one:

Je suis amoureux / amoureuse (*I am in love*). This should be pronounced: je **suiza**moorer / je **suiza**moorerze

Bonjour mes amis (*hello my friends*), pronounced bonjour **meza**mi (the **s** at the end of **amis** is silent)

Bon appétit, pronounced **bon**appeti (the **t** at the end of **appétit** is silent)

INTONATION

Intonation (variation in the tone of voice), for example when raising your voice in order to ask a question, reveals the intentions and feelings of the speaker. The same sentence can be uttered differently according to circumstances.

Grammar summary

ADJECTIVES

Adjectives are used to provide more information about nouns. In English they can appear in front of a noun or they can stand on their own after a verb such as to *be/to look/to seem*:

The new school opens today.   *It looks good.*

In French, adjectives have the same function but their spelling is affected by the noun they are linked with. Also they stand either before or after the nouns and in some cases the meaning of the adjective changes slightly according to where it is placed. The two factors which affect the spelling of adjectives are the gender and number of the noun:

un joli petit village   *a pretty little village*
une jolie petite ville   *a pretty little town*

In French, village is masculine and town feminine. -e indicates the feminine form except if the adjective finishes with an -e in its generic form:

un quartier tranquille   *a quiet district*
une région tranquille   *a quiet area*

Adjectives linked to plural nouns tend to take an -s but in some cases (as for the feminine) there are more drastic changes. If there is already an -s at the end of the adjective, it does not change in the plural form:

J'aime un bon verre de cidre   *I like a good glass of fresh cider*
     frais avec des moules bien   *with very fresh mussels.*
     fraîches.

| **J'aime une bonne bière bien fraîche avec des fruits de mer bien frais.** | *I like a good cool beer with very fresh seafood.* |

Examples of a few adjectives which change more drastically:

Quel beau château!	*What a beautiful castle!*
Quelle belle journée!	*What a beautiful day!*
Quels beaux enfants!	*What beautiful children!*
C'est le tarif normal.	*It's the normal price.*
Ce sont des gens normaux.	*They are normal people.*
Ils mènent une vie normale.	*They lead a normal life.*
Ce sont des attitudes tout à fait normales.	*These are perfectly normal attitudes.*

Possessive adjectives: For the full list of words such as **mon, ma, mes** *my*, **son, sa, ses**, *her/his*, **votre** *your*, see Unit 22.

ADVERBS

Just as adjectives provide more information about nouns, so adverbs tend to provide more information about verbs or adjectives:

Il marche vite.	*He walks fast.*
Le voyage s'est bien passé.	*The journey went well.*
Ils ne sont nullement fatigués.	*They are not at all tired.*

For easy recognition of a large number of French adverbs you need to note the following pattern: adjective in feminine form + **-ment** (equivalent of **-ly** in English):

| **Heureusement qu'il fait beau.** | *Luckily the weather is good.* |
| **Les gendarmes sont arrivés rapidement.** | *The policemen arrived rapidly.* |

An adverb can also provide information about another adverb:

| **Ils conduisent trop vite.** | *They drive too fast.* |

ARTICLES

The definite article

This term is given to *the* in English and to **la, le, l'** and **les** in French. **Le** is used in front of masculine nouns, **la** with feminine nouns, **l'** if a noun starts with a vowel or a mute **h**; **les** is used in front of nouns in the plural form:

À la naissance d'un enfant il faut déclarer la date, le lieu de naissance, le nom et les prénoms de l'enfant et les noms des parents.

When a child is born you have to declare the date, the place of birth, the surname and first names of the child and the names of the parents.

The indefinite article

This is the term given to the words a and an in English and to un, une, des in French:

Il y a des jours où un rien me donne un mal de tête ou une migraine.

There are some days when nothing much can give me a headache or a migraine.

AUXILIARY VERBS

Auxiliary verbs are used as a support to the main verb, for example, I *am* working, you *are* working. Here *am* and *are* are used to support the verb *work*. By its very nature an auxiliary verb does not normally stand on its own, because it is the main verb which carries the meaning. *Working* gives us the information as to what activity is going on. **Avoir** *to have* and **être** *to be* are the main auxiliary verbs in the two languages and are mainly used to form past tenses. Others are **pouvoir** *can*, **venir de** ... *to have just* ..., also *to do* in English.

Est-ce que vous travaillez le samedi?
Do you work on Saturdays?

Je viens de voir un très bon film.
I have just seen a very good film.

J'ai perdu ma montre.
I have lost my watch.

Pourriez-vous m'indiquer la bonne route?	*Could you show me the right way?*
Ils sont partis de bonne heure.	*They left early / They have left early.*

COMPARATIVES

When we make comparisons, we need the comparative form of the adjective. In English this usually means adding **-er** to the adjective or putting more, less or as in front of it. In French you add plus, **moins** or **aussi** in front of adjectives:

Tu es plus fort que moi.	*You are stronger than me.*
Il est plus intelligent que son frère et beaucoup moins beau. Mais ils ont aussi mauvais caractère.	*He is more intelligent than his brother and less good-looking but they are just as bad tempered.*

CONJUNCTIONS

Conjunctions are words such as and and although. They link words, or clauses or sentences:

Nous sommes allés à Paris mais nous n'avons pas vu la tour Eiffel.	*We went to Paris but we did not see the Eiffel Tower.*
Nous avons fait une promenade bien qu'il pleuve.	*We went for a walk although it was raining.*
Je vous téléphonerai plus tard si vous voulez.	*I'll call you later if you want.*

GENDER

In English, grammatical gender is only used for male and female persons or animals, so for example we refer to a man as *he* and a woman as *she*. Objects of indeterminate sex are referred to as having *neuter* gender. So a table is referred to as *it*. In French all nouns have a gender which is either masculine or feminine and although the gender of the word is linked to the sex of the person or the animal in most cases, there are very few guide lines to help you guess whether other nouns are feminine or masculine.

Le vélo de Paul et **la bicyclette** de Pierre: both words mean *bike* although one is masculine and the other feminine. In this case it is likely that **bicyclette** is feminine because it ends with -**ette** and words ending with -**ette** are usually feminine words e.g **une fillette** *a little girl*. It is not normally so easy to rationalize the reason for the gender of words. It is important to remember that it is the word which is feminine or masculine, not the object it refers to.

IMPERATIVE

The imperative is the form of the verb used to give orders, commands or advice:

Viens ici!	*Come here! (order)*
Roulez à droite.	*Drive on the right. (command)*
Faites attention en traversant la rue.	*Be careful when you cross the road. (advice)*
Écoutons les informations.	*Let's listen to the news.*
Regarde la télé.	*Watch TV.*
N'attrape pas froid!	*Don't catch a cold!*

The imperative is used for notices everywhere to direct or guide our actions:

Poussez!	*Push!*
Tirez!	*Pull!*
Cochez les cases.	*Tick the boxes.*
Ralentissez!	*Slow down!*

INFINITIVE

The infinitive is the basic form of the verb. This is the form that you will find in the dictionary. In English the infinitive is usually accompanied by the word *to*, e.g. *to go, to play*.

In French the infinitive form of a verb is noticeable by its ending. There are three major groups of verbs: -er verbs (ending in -er: **chercher, regarder, manger**), -ir verbs (ending in -ir: **choisir, finir**) and -re and -oir verbs (ending in -re: **prendre, attendre** or -oir: **vouloir, pouvoir**).

Verbs are used in the infinitive in two particular types of circumstances:

Je vais acheter du fromage.   *I am going to buy some cheese.*

A second verb is always in the infinitive, except when the first verb is **avoir** or **être**. A verb following a preposition such as **à, de, sans,** etc is always in the infinitive form.

J'ai passé toute la journée à   *I spent the whole day tidying up*
   ranger mes placards   *my cupboards.*

NOUNS

Nouns are words like **maison** *house*, **pain** *bread*, **beauté** *beauty*. A useful test of a noun is whether you can put **le, la** or **les** *the* in front of it.

OBJECT

The term 'object' expresses the 'receiving end' relationship of a noun and a verb. So, for instance, **le facteur** *the postman* is said to be the object at the receiving end of the biting in the sentence:

Le chien a mordu le facteur.   *The dog bit the postman.*
J'ai donné des fleurs à ma mère. *I gave flowers to my mother.*

In this particular example **des fleurs** is referred to as the direct object because there is nothing between it and the verb, and **ma mère** is referred to as the indirect object because it is linked to the verb with a preposition (**à, de,** etc).

It is important to know whether a noun is a direct or indirect object when it comes to using a pronoun to replace the noun.

Some verbs don't need an object:

Le chien a aboyé.   *The dog barked.*

PAST PARTICIPLE

This is the name for the part of the verb which follows the auxiliary verbs **avoir** and **être** in the perfect and pluperfect tenses. Verbs ending with -er in the infinitive tend to have a past participle ending with -é. Other endings for past participles are **-i** for most **-ir** verbs, **-u** for most **-oir** verbs and **-is** for most **-re** verbs:

J'ai regardé la télé.	(**regarder**, *to watch*)
Yannick a fini son travail.	(**finir**, *to finish*)
Les garçons ont voulu partir en Angleterre.	(**vouloir**, *to want*)
Ariane a mis le couvert.	(**mettre**, *to put / to set the table*)

PREPOSITIONS

Words like **à** *at*, **avec** *with*, **de** *of*, **dans** *in*, **chez** *at someone's house*, **pour** *for*, **sans** *without*, **sous** *under*, **sur** *on* are called prepositions. Prepositions often tell us about positions or relationships. They are normally followed by a noun or pronoun:

Ton livre est sur la table.	*Your book is on the table.*
Il a laissé son parapluie dans le train.	*He left his umbrella in the train.*
Voici un cadeau pour toi.	*This present is for you.*
Elle est sortie avec son copain.	*She went out with her boyfriend.*

PRESENT PARTICIPLE

The part of a French verb which is often equivalent to *-ing* in English:

Ils sifflent en travaillant.	*They whistle while working.*
En réfléchissant bien…	*Thinking about it…*
La chance aidant il a réussi son examen.	*With the help of luck he has passed his exam.*

PRONOUNS

Pronouns fulfil a similar function to nouns and often stand in the place of nouns which have already been mentioned:

La maison a plus de 200 ans.	*The house is over 200 years old.*
Elle est très belle.	*It is very beautiful.*

(House is the noun and it is the pronoun.)

TABLE OF PRONOUNS

Subject pronouns	Reflexive pronouns	Direct object pronouns	Indirect object pronouns	Emphatic pronouns
je	me/m'	me/m'	me/m'	moi
tu	te/t'	te/t'	te/t'	toi
il	se/s'	le/l'	lui	lui
elle	se/s'	la/l'	lui	elle
on	se/s'			soi
nous	nous	nous	nous	nous
vous	vous	vous	vous	vous
ils	se/s'	les	leur	eux
elles	se/s'	les	leur	elles

For more explanations of pronouns, please refer to the following sections of the book: Unit 12 (emphatic pronouns), Unit 19 (indirect object pronouns), Unit 22 (possessive pronouns) and Unit 25 (order of pronouns). For relative pronouns see relative clauses.

REFLEXIVE VERBS

When the subject and the object of a verb are one and the same, the verb is said to be reflexive:

Jean se lève à 6 heures.	*John gets (himself) up at 6 a.m.*
Je me lave bien.	*I wash myself thoroughly.*
Florence s'est blessée.	*Florence hurt herself.*

In French nearly all verbs can be reflexive if they are preceded by a reflexive pronoun:

Il a lavé sa chemise.	*He has washed his shirt.*
Il s'est lavé les mains.	*He has washed his (own) hands.*
Je regarde la télé.	*I watch TV.*
Je me regarde dans le miroir.	*I look at myself in the mirror.*

When reflexive verbs are used in the perfect tense, they are always used with **être**. But when the same verb is not in its reflexive form, it takes **avoir** in the perfect tense.

Hélène a coupé du bois.	*Helen cut some wood.*
Hélène s'est coupé la main avec la scie.	*Helen cut her hand with the saw.*
J'ai vu la télé.	*I saw the TV.*
Je me suis vue à la télé.	*I saw myself on TV.*

RELATIVE CLAUSES AND RELATIVE PRONOUNS

A relative pronoun such as **que** *which/that* or **qui** *who* can be used to provide more information about a noun which has just been mentioned. The resulting clause is called a relative clause:

Je connais la personne qui habite à côté de chez toi.	*I know the person who lives next door to you.*
La voiture que je conduis a presque dix ans.	*The car (which) I drive is nearly ten years old.*

(In French it is not possible to omit the relative pronoun **que**.) See Unit 24 for more about relative pronouns.

SUBJECT

The term 'subject' expresses a relationship between a noun and a verb. The subject is the person or thing doing the action, as here for instance:

Le chien a mordu le facteur. *The dog bit the postman.*

Because it is the dog that does the biting, the dog is said to be the subject of the verb **mordre** *to bite*.

SUPERLATIVES

The superlative is used for the most extreme version of a comparison:

Ce magasin est le moins cher de tous. *This shop is the cheapest of all.*

C'est la plus belle femme du monde. *She is the most beautiful woman in the world.*

Le champion du monde de Formule Un, c'est le meilleur pilote du monde. *The Formula One champion is the best driver in the world.*

TENSE

Most languages use changes in the verb form to indicate an aspect of time. These changes in the verb are referred to as 'tense', and the tense may be present, past or future. Tenses are often reinforced with expressions of time:

Past: **Hier je suis allé à Londres.** *Yesterday I went to London.*
Present: **Aujourd'hui je reste à la maison.** *Today I am staying at home.*
Future: **Demain je prendrai l'avion pour Berlin.** *Tomorrow I'll be flying to Berlin.*

The course introduces verbs in the present tense. This includes the subjunctive – a verbal form referred to as a 'mood', mostly used in the present to express regrets, doubts and uncertainties. Several past tenses are used throughout the course: the perfect tense, the imperfect and the pluperfect. The future tense also features in the course.

The conditional is used to indicate that if certain conditions were fulfilled something else would happen.

VERBS

Verbs often communicate actions, states and sensations. So, for instance, the verb **jouer** *to play* expresses an action, the verb exister *to exist* expresses a state and the verb **voir** *to see* expresses a sensation. A verb may also be defined by its role in the sentence or clause. It usually has a subject:

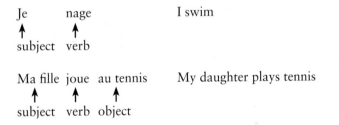

Je	nage	I swim
↑	↑	
subject	verb	

Ma fille	joue	au tennis	My daughter plays tennis
↑	↑	↑	
subject	verb	object	

IRREGULAR VERBS

Life would be easier if all verbs behaved in a regular fashion. Unfortunately, all European languages have verbs which do not follow a set pattern and which are therefore commonly referred to as irregular verbs.

There are 30 useful verbs in the verb table which follows. Most are irregular but, all the same, most can be used as a pattern for a few other verbs.

Verb tables

Trente verbes utiles (*Thirty useful verbs*)

1 Four regular verbs (with subject pronouns: *je, tu, il, elle, on, nous, vous, ils, elles*)

Parler *to speak, to talk* Past participle: **parlé** Present participle: **parlant**

Present indicative / Présent de l'indicatif	Perfect / Passé composé	Imperfect / Imparfait	Conditional / Conditionnel	Future / Futur	Present subjunctive / Présent du subjonctif	Imperative / Impératif
je parle	j'ai parlé	je parlais	je parlerais	je parlerai	(que) je parle	
tu parles	tu as parlé	tu parlais	tu parlerais	tu parleras	tu parles	parle
il/elle parle	il a parlé	il parlait	il parlerait	il parlera	il parle	
nous parlons	nous avons parlé	nous parlions	nous parlerions	nous parlerons	nous parlions	parlons
vous parlez	vous avez parlé	vous parliez	vous parleriez	vous parlerez	vous parliez	parlez
ils/elles parlent	ils ont parlé	ils parlaient	ils parleraient	ils parleront	ils parlent	

Remplir *to fill* Past participle: *rempli* Present participle: **remplissant**

Present indicative / Présent de l'indicatif	Perfect / Passé composé	Imperfect / Imparfait	Conditional / Conditionnel	Future / Futur	Present subjunctive / Présent du subjonctif	Imperative / Impératif
je remplis	j'ai rempli	je remplissais	je remplirais	je remplirai	(que) je remplisse	
tu remplis	tu as rempli	tu remplissais	tu remplirais	tu rempliras	tu remplisses	remplis
il/elle remplit	il a rempli	il remplissait	il remplirait	il remplira	il remplisse	
nous remplissons	nous avons rempli	nous remplissions	nous remplirions	nous remplirons	nous remplissions	remplissions
vous remplissez	vous avez rempli	vous remplissiez	vous rempliriez	vous remplirez	vous remplissiez	remplissez
ils/elles remplissent	ils ont rempli	ils remplissaient	ils rempliraient	ils rempliront	ils remplissent	

Present indicative	Perfect	Imperfect	Conditional	Future	Present subjunctive	Imperative

Vendre *to sell* Past participle: **vendu** Present participle: **vendant**

Present indicative	Perfect	Imperfect	Conditional	Future	Present subjunctive	Imperative
je vends	j'ai vendu	je vendais	je vendrais	je vendrai	(que) je vende	
tu vends	tu as vendu	tu vendais	tu vendrais	tu vendras	tu vendes	vends
il/elle vend	il a vendu	il vendait	il vendrait	il vendra	il vende	
nous vendons	nous avons vendu	nous vendions	nous vendrions	nous vendrons	nous vendions	vendons
vous vendez	vous avez vendu	vous vendiez	vous vendriez	vous vendrez	vous vendiez	vendez
ils/elles vendent	ils ont vendu	ils vendaient	ils vendraient	ils vendront	ils vendent	

Se lever *to get up* Past participle: **levé** Present participle: **levant**.

Note that there is an accent on the first e of **lever** when the following syllable has a neutral sound, e.g. **je me lève, je me lèverai**

Present indicative	Perfect	Imperfect	Conditional	Future	Present subjunctive	Imperative
je me lève	je me suis levé(e)	je me levais	je me lèverais	je me lèverai	(que) je me lève	
tu te lèves	tu t'es levé(e)	tu te levais	tu te lèverais	tu te lèveras	tu te lèves	lève-toi
il/elle se lève	il(elle) s'est levé(e)	il se levait	il se lèverait	il se lèvera	il se lève	
nous nous levons	nous nous sommes levés(es)	nous nous levions	nous nous	nous nous lèverons	nous nous levions	levons-nous
vous vous levez	vous vous êtes levé(s)(es)(e)	vous vous leviez	vous vous lèveriez	vous vous lèverez	vous vous leviez	levez-vous
ils/elles se lèvent	ils se sont levés elles se sont levées	ils se levaient	ils se lèveraient	ils se lèveront	ils se lèvent	

2 Twenty-six irregular verbs

Aller *to go* Past participle: **allé** Present participle: **allant**

Present indicative	Perfect	Imperfect	Conditional	Future	Present subjunctive	Imperative
je vais	suis allé(e)	allais	irais	irai	aille	
tu vas	es allé(e)	allais	irais	iras	ailles	va
il/elle va	est allé(e)	allait	irait	ira	aille	
nous allons	sommes allés(e)	allions	irions	irons	allions	allons
vous allez	êtes allé(e)(s) (es)	alliez	iriez	irez	alliez	allez
ils/elles vont	sont allés(es)	allaient	iraient	iront	aillent	

S'asseoir *to sit* **assis – asseyant**

Present indicative	Perfect	Imperfect	Conditional	Future	Present subjunctive	Imperative
je m'assieds	me suis assis(e)	m'asseyais	m'assiérais	m'assiérai	m'asseye	
tu t'assieds	t'es assis(e)	t'asseyais	t'assiérais	t'assiéras	t'asseyes	assieds-toi
il/elle s'assied	s'est assis(e)	s'asseyait	s'assiérait	s'assiéra	s'asseye	
nous nous asseyons	nous sommes assis(es)	nous asseyions	nous assiérions	nous assiérons	nous asseyions	asseyons-nous
vous vous asseyez	vous êtes assis (e)(es)	vous asseyiez	vous assiériez	vous assiérez	vous asseyiez	asseyez-vous
ils/elles s'asseyent	se sont assis(es)	s'asseyaient	s'assiéraient	s'assiéront	s'asseyent	

Avoir *to have*: eu – ayant

Present indicative	Perfect	Imperfect	Conditional	Future	Present subjunctive	Imperative
j'ai	ai eu	avais	aurais	aurai	aie	
tu as	as eu	avais	aurais	auras	aies	aie
il/elle a	a eu	avait	aurait	aura	ait	
nous avons	avons eu	avions	aurions	aurons	ayons	ayons
vous avez	avez eu	aviez	auriez	aurez	ayez	ayez
ils/elles ont	ont eu	avaient	auraient	auront	aient	

Boire *to drink*: bu – buvant

Present indicative	Perfect	Imperfect	Conditional	Future	Present subjunctive	Imperative
je bois	ai bu	buvais	boirais	boirai	boive	
tu bois	as bu	buvais	boirais	boiras	boives	bois
il/elle boit	a bu	buvait	boirait	boira	boive	
nous buvons	avons bu	buvions	boirions	boirons	buvions	buvons
vous buvez	avez bu	buviez	boiriez	boirez	buviez	buvez
ils/elles boivent	ont bu	buvaient	boiraient	boiront	boivent	

Commencer *to begin*: commencé – commençant
(ç is necessary to keep the sound /s/ before a, o or u)

Present indicative	Perfect	Imperfect	Conditional	Future	Present subjunctive	Imperative
je commence	ai commencé	commençais	commencerais	commencerai	commence	
tu commences	as commencé	commençais	commencerais	commenceras	commences	commence
il/elle commence	a commencé	commençait	commencerait	commencera	commence	
nous commençons	avons commencé	commencions	commencerions	commencerons	commencions	commençons
vous commencez	avez commencé	commenciez	commenceriez	commencerez	commenciez	commencez
ils/elles commencent	ont commencé	commençaient	commenceraient	commenceront	commencent	

Conduire *to drive*: conduit – conduisant

Present indicative	Perfect	Imperfect	Conditional	Future	Present subjunctive	Imperative
je conduis	ai conduit	conduisais	conduirais	conduirai	conduise	
tu conduis	as conduit	conduisais	conduirais	conduiras	conduises	conduis
il/elle conduit	a conduit	conduisait	conduirait	conduira	conduise	
nous conduisons	avons conduit	conduisions	conduirions	conduirons	conduisions	conduisons
vous conduisez	avez conduit	conduisiez	conduiriez	conduirez	conduisiez	conduisez
ils/elles conduisent	ont conduit	conduisaient	conduiraient	conduiront	conduisent	

Present indicative	Perfect	Imperfect	Conditional	Future	Present subjunctive	Imperative

Connaître *to know:* **connu – connaissant**

Present indicative	Perfect	Imperfect	Conditional	Future	Present subjunctive	Imperative
je connais	ai connu	connaissais	connaîtrais	connaîtrai	connaisse	
tu connais	as connu	connaissais	connaîtrais	connaîtras	connaisses	connais
il/elle connaît	a connu	connaissait	connaîtrait	connaîtra	connaisse	
nous connaissons	avons connu	connaissions	connaîtrions	connaîtrons	connaissions	connaissons
vous connaissez	avez connu	connaissiez	connaîtriez	connaîtrez	connaissiez	connaissez
ils/elles connaissent	ont connu	connaissaient	connaîtraient	connaîtront	connaissent	

Croire *to believe:* **cru – croyant**

Present indicative	Perfect	Imperfect	Conditional	Future	Present subjunctive	Imperative
je crois	ai cru	croyais	croirais	croirai	croie	
tu crois	as cru	croyais	croirais	croiras	croies	crois
il/elle croit	a cru	croyait	croirait	croira	croie	
nous croyons	avons cru	croyions	croirions	croirons	croyions	croyons
vous croyez	avez cru	croyiez	croiriez	croirez	croyiez	croyez
ils/elles croient	ont cru	croyaient	croiraient	croiront	croient	

Devoir *to have to (I must):* **dû – devant**

Present indicative	Perfect	Imperfect	Conditional	Future	Present subjunctive	Imperative
je dois	ai dû	devais	devrais	devrai	doive	
tu dois	as dû	devais	devrais	devras	doives	dois
il/elle doit	a dû	devait	devrait	devra	doive	
nous devons	avons dû	devions	devrions	devrons	devions	devons
vous devez	avez dû	deviez	devriez	devrez	deviez	devez
ils/elles doivent	ont dû	devaient	devraient	devront	doivent	

Dire *to say:* **dit – disant**

Present indicative	Perfect	Imperfect	Conditional	Future	Present subjunctive	Imperative
je dis	ai dit	disais	dirais	dirai	dise	
tu dis	as dit	disais	dirais	diras	dises	dis
il/elle dit	a dit	disait	dirait	dira	dise	
nous disons	avons dit	disions	dirions	dirons	disions	disons
vous dites	avez dit	disiez	diriez	direz	disiez	dites
ils/elles disent	ont dit	disaient	diraient	diront	disent	

Entendre *to hear*: entendu – entendant

Present indicative	Perfect	Imperfect	Conditional	Future	Present subjunctive	Imperative
j'entends	ai entendu	entendais	entendrais	entendrai	entende	
tu entends	as entendu	entendais	entendrais	entendras	entendes	entends
il/elle entend	a entendu	entendait	entendrait	entendra	entende	
nous entendons	avons entendu	entendions	entendrions	entendrons	entendions	entendons
vous entendez	avez entendu	entendiez	entendriez	entendrez	entendiez	entendez
ils/elles entendent	ont entendu	entendaient	entendraient	entendront	entendent	

Envoyer *to send*: envoyé – envoyant

Present indicative	Perfect	Imperfect	Conditional	Future	Present subjunctive	Imperative
j'envoie	ai envoyé	envoyais	enverrais	enverrai	envoie	
tu envoies	as envoyé	envoyais	enverrais	enverras	envoies	envoie
il/elle envoie	a envoyé	envoyait	enverrait	enverra	envoie	
nous envoyons	avons envoyé	envoyions	enverrions	enverrons	envoyions	envoyons
vous envoyez	avez envoyé	envoyiez	enverriez	enverrez	envoyiez	envoyez
ils/elles envoient	ont envoyé	envoyaient	enverraient	enverront	envoient	

Être *to be*: été – étant

Present indicative	Perfect	Imperfect	Conditional	Future	Present subjunctive	Imperative
je suis	ai été	étais	serais	serai	sois	
tu es	as été	étais	serais	seras	sois	sois
il/elle est	a été	était	serait	sera	soit	
nous sommes	avons été	étions	serions	serons	soyons	soyons
vous êtes	avez été	étiez	seriez	serez	soyez	soyez
ils/elles sont	ont été	étaient	seraient	seront	soient	

Faire *to do, to make*: fait – faisant

Present indicative	Perfect	Imperfect	Conditional	Future	Present subjunctive	Imperative
je fais	ai fait	faisais	ferais	ferai	fasse	
tu fais	as fait	faisais	ferais	feras	fasses	fais
il/elle fait	a fait	faisait	ferait	fera	fasse	
nous faisons	avons fait	faisions	ferions	ferons	fassions	faisons
vous faites	avez fait	faisiez	feriez	ferez	fassiez	faites
ils/elles font	ont fait	faisaient	feraient	feront	fassent	

Present indicative	Perfect	Imperfect	Conditional	Future	Present subjunctive	Imperative

Falloir to be necessary (impersonal only): Past participle: **fallu** No present participle

Present indicative	Perfect	Imperfect	Conditional	Future	Present subjunctive	Imperative
il faut	il a fallu	il fallait	il faudrait	il faudra	(qu')il faille	

Manger to eat: mangé – mangeant
(e is added after the g in order to keep the soft sound before a, o and u)

Present indicative	Perfect	Imperfect	Conditional	Future	Present subjunctive	Imperative
je mange	ai mangé	mangeais	mangerais	mangerai	mange	
tu manges	as mangé	mangeais	mangerais	mangeras	manges	mange
il/elle mange	a mangé	mangeait	mangerait	mangera	mange	
nous mangeons	avons mangé	mangions	mangerions	mangerons	mangions	mangeons
vous mangez	avez mangé	mangiez	mangeriez	mangerez	mangiez	mangez
ils/elles mangent	ont mangé	mangeaient	mangeraient	mangeront	mangent	

Mettre to put: mis – mettant

Present indicative	Perfect	Imperfect	Conditional	Future	Present subjunctive	Imperative
je mets	ai mis	mettais	mettrais	mettrai	mette	
tu mets	as mis	mettais	mettrais	mettras	mettes	mets
il/elle met	a mis	mettait	mettrait	mettra	mette	
nous mettons	avons mis	mettions	mettrions	mettrons	mettions	mettons
vous mettez	avez mis	mettiez	mettriez	mettrez	mettiez	mettez
ils/elles mettent	ont mis	mettaient	mettraient	mettront	mettent	

Ouvrir to open: ouvert – ouvrant

Present indicative	Perfect	Imperfect	Conditional	Future	Present subjunctive	Imperative
j'ouvre	ai ouvert	ouvrais	ouvrirais	ouvrirai	ouvre	
tu ouvres	as ouvert	ouvrais	ouvrirais	ouvriras	ouvres	ouvre
il/elle ouvre	a ouvert	ouvrait	ouvrirait	ouvrira	ouvre	
nous ouvrons	avons ouvert	ouvrions	ouvririons	ouvrirons	ouvrions	ouvrons
vous ouvrez	avez ouvert	ouvriez	ouvririez	ouvrirez	ouvriez	ouvrez
ils/elles ouvrent	ont ouvert	ouvraient	ouvriraient	ouvriront	ouvrent	

Present indicative	Perfect	Imperfect	Conditional	Future	Present subjunctive	Imperative

Pleuvoir *to rain* (impersonal only): **plu – pleuvant**

Present indicative	Perfect	Imperfect	Conditional	Future	Present subjunctive	Imperative
il pleut	il a plu	il pleuvait	il pleuvrait	il pleuvra	(qu')il pleuve	

Pouvoir *to be able to (I can)*: **pu – pouvant**

Present indicative	Perfect	Imperfect	Conditional	Future	Present subjunctive	Imperative
je peux	ai pu	pouvais	pourrais	pourrai	puisse	
tu peux	as pu	pouvais	pourrais	pourras	puisses	
il/elle peut	a pu	pouvait	pourrait	pourra	puisse	
nous pouvons	avons pu	pouvions	pourrions	pourrons	puissions	
vous pouvez	avez pu	pouviez	pourriez	pourrez	puissiez	
ils/elles peuvent	ont pu	pouvaient	pourraient	pourront	puissent	

Prendre *to take*: **pris – prenant**

Present indicative	Perfect	Imperfect	Conditional	Future	Present subjunctive	Imperative
je prends	ai pris	prenais	prendrais	prendrai	prenne	
tu prends	as pris	prenais	prendrais	prendras	prennes	prends
il/elle prend	a pris	prenait	prendrait	prendra	prenne	
nous prenons	avons pris	prenions	prendrions	prendrons	prenions	prenons
vous prenez	avez pris	preniez	prendriez	prendrez	preniez	prenez
ils/elles prennent	ont pris	prenaient	prendraient	prendront	prennent	

Savoir *to know*: **su – sachant**

Present indicative	Perfect	Imperfect	Conditional	Future	Present subjunctive	Imperative
je sais	ai su	savais	saurais	saurai	sache	
tu sais	as su	savais	saurais	sauras	saches	sache
il/elle sait	a su	savait	saurait	saura	sache	
nous savons	avons su	savions	saurions	saurons	sachions	sachons
vous savez	avez su	saviez	sauriez	saurez	sachiez	sachez
ils/elles savent	ont su	savaient	sauraient	sauront	sachent	

Present indicative	Perfect	Imperfect	Conditional	Future	Present subjunctive	Imperative

Sortir *to go out:* **sorti – sortant**

Present indicative	Perfect	Imperfect	Conditional	Future	Present subjunctive	Imperative
je sors	suis sorti(e)	sortais	sortirais	sortirai	sorte	
tu sors	es sorti(e)	sortais	sortirais	sortiras	sortes	sors
il/elle sort	est sorti(e)	sortait	sortirait	sortira	sorte	
nous sortons	sommes sortis(es)	sortions	sortirions	sortirons	sortions	sortons
vous sortez	êtes sorti(e)(s) (es)	sortiez	sortiriez	sortirez	sortiez	sortez
ils/elles sortent	sont sortis(es)	sortaient	sortiraient	sortiront	sortent	

Venir *to come:* **venu – venant**

Present indicative	Perfect	Imperfect	Conditional	Future	Present subjunctive	Imperative
je viens	suis venu(e)	venais	viendrais	viendrai	vienne	
tu viens	es venu(e)	venais	viendrais	viendras	viennes	viens
il/elle vient	est venu(e)	venait	viendrait	viendra	vienne	
nous venons	sommes venus(es)	venions	viendrions	viendrons	venions	venons
vous venez	êtes venu(e)(s) (es)	veniez	viendriez	viendrez	veniez	venez
ils/elles viennent	sont venus(es)	venaient	viendraient	viendront	viennent	

Voir *to see:* **vu – voyant**

Present indicative	Perfect	Imperfect	Conditional	Future	Present subjunctive	Imperative
je vois	ai vu	voyais	verrais	verrai	voie	
tu vois	as vu	voyais	verrais	verras	voies	vois
il/elle voit	a vu	voyait	verrait	verra	voie	
nous voyons	avons vu	voyions	verrions	verrons	voyions	voyons
voys voyez	avez vu	voyiez	verriez	verrez	voyiez	voyez
ils/elles voient	ont vu	voyaient	verraient	verront	voient	

Vouloir *to want:* **voulu – voulant**

Present indicative	Perfect	Imperfect	Conditional	Future	Present subjunctive	Imperative
je veux	ai voulu	voulais	voudrais	voudrai	veuille	
tu veux	as voulu	voulais	voudrais	voudras	veuilles	veuille
il/elle veut	a voulu	voulait	voudrait	voudra	veuille	
nous voulons	avons voulu	voulions	voudrions	voudrons	voulions	veuillons
vous voulez	avez voulu	vouliez	voudriez	voudrez	vouliez	veuillez
ils/elles veulent	ont voulu	voulaient	voudraient	voudront	veuillent	

French–English vocabulary

à *prep to; at; with*

abonné *nmf subscriber; season ticket holder*

abonnement *nm subscription; season ticket*

d'abord *phr first*

absolument *adv absolutely*

accident *nm accident; hitch; mishap*

accompagner *vtr to accompany, to go with*

accord *nm agreement;* **je suis d'~** *I agree*

accueil *nm welcome, reception; reception desk*

accueil *adj* **page d'** *– home page (computer)*

accueillant, -e *adj hospitable, welcoming*

accueillir *vtr to welcome; to receive; to greet*

acheter *vtr to buy*

acheteur, -euse *nmf buyer, purchaser*

acquéreur *nm buyer, purchaser*

acquérir *vtr to acquire; to purchase*

acquisition *nf purchase*

acteur, -trice *nmf actor/actress*

actif, -ive *adj active;* **la vie active** *working life*

activité *nf activity*

actuel, -elle *adj present, current*

addition *nf bill*

adieu *goodbye, farewell*

adorer *vtr to adore*

adresse *nf address*

s'adresser à qn *v refl (+ v être) to speak to sb*

aéroport *nm airport*

affiche *nf poster*

agaçant, -e *adj annoying, irritating*

âge *nm age*

agence *nf agency;* ~ **immobilière** *estate agents*

agglomération *nf town; (smaller) village*

agir *to act;* **s'agir de** *v impers* **de quoi s'agit-il**? *what is it about?; what's the matter?*

agréable *adj nice, pleasant*

aider *vtr to help*

ail, *pl* ~**s** *or* **aulx** *nm garlic*

ailleurs *adv elsewhere* **d'ailleurs** *phr besides*

aimable *adj pleasant; kind; polite*

aimer *vtr to love; to like, to be fond of*

ainsi *adv thus*

ajouter *vtr to add (à to)*

alcool *nm alcohol*

alentour *adv* **la ville et la région** ~ *the town and surrounding area*

alimentation *nf food;* **magasin d'** ~ *food shop, grocery store*

Allemagne *nf Germany*

allemand, ~**e** *adj German; nm (lang) German*

aller *vi to go; v aux* **je vais**

apprendre l'italien *I'm going to learn Italian* **comment ça va**? *how are you? to go;* **s'en aller** *v refl (+ v être) to go, to leave*

allumer *vtr to light*

alors *adv then*

améliorer *vtr* **s'améliorer** *refl (+ v être) to improve*

aménagement *nm development*

aménager *vtr to convert; to do up [house, attic]*

amener *vtr to accompany, to bring sb*

américain *adj American*

ami, -e *nmf friend*

amitié *nf friendship*

amusant, ~**e** *adj entertaining; funny*

amuser *vtr to entertain;* **s'amuser** *v refl (+ v être) to have fun, to play;* **pour s'**~ *for fun*

an *nm year*

ancien, -ienne *adj old*

anglais, ~**e** *adj English*

Anglais, ~**e** *nmf Englishman/Englishwoman*

Angleterre *nf England*

animal, ~**e**, *mpl* **-aux** *animal*

animateur, -trice *nmf coordinator*

animer *vtr to lead*

année *nf year*

anniversaire *nm birthday*

ANPE *nf (abbr =* **Agence nationale pour l'emploi**) *French national employment agency*

août nm August

apercevoir vtr to make out; to catch sight of

apéritif nm drink

à-peu-près nm inv approximation

appareil nm appliance; telephone; ~ photo camera

appartement nm flat

appeler vtr to call

s'appeler v refl (+ v **être**) **comment t'appelles-tu**? what's your name?

appétit nm appetite

apprendre vtr to learn

apprenti ~e nmf apprentice

apprentissage nm apprenticeship

après adv afterward(s), after; later

après-midi nm/nf inv afternoon

argent nm money; silver

arrêter vtr to stop

arrière adj inv back

arriver (+ v **être**) vi to arrive

arrondissement nm administrative division

s'asseoir v refl (+ v **être**) to sit down

assez adv enough

attendre vtr to wait for

au prep (= **à le**) see **à**

auberge nf inn; ~ **de jeunesse** youth hostel

aujourd'hui adv today

aussi adv too, as well, also

aussitôt adv immediately

auteur nm author

autocar nm coach

automne nm autumn

autoroute nf motorway

autour de phr around

autre other

avant adv before

avant-hier adv the day before yesterday

avec prep with

avenir nm future

averse nf shower (rain)

avion nm plane

avis nm inv opinion

avocat nm lawyer

avoir vtr to have

avril nm April

bagage nm piece of luggage

baguette nf French stick

bain nm bath

balcon nm balcony

banlieue nf suburbs

bar-tabac nm café (selling stamps and cigarettes)

bas, **basse** adj low

bateau nm boat, ship

bâtonnier nm president of the Bar

bavarder vi to talk to, to chatter

beau, **belle** adj beautiful; handsome; good; fine

beaucoup adv a lot

beau-frère nm brother-in-law

Belgique nf Belgium

belle-mère nf mother-in-law

belle-sœur nf sister-in-law

besoin nm need **avoir** ~ **de** to need

bête adj stupid, silly

beur *nmf second-generation North African (living in France) (slang)*
beurre *nm butter*
bibliothèque *nf library*
bicyclette *nf bicycle*
bien *adj inv good; adv well*
bien que *phr although*
bière *nf beer*
bijou *nm piece of jewellery*
bilan *nm outcome, result*
bilingue *adj bilingual*
blanc, blanche *adj white*
blessé, ~e *nmf injured or wounded man/woman*
blessure *nf injury*
bleu ~e *adj blue*
bois *nm inv wood*
boisson *nf drink*
boîte *nf box; tin*
bon, bonne *adj good*
bonne-maman *nf grandma*
bord *nm* **le ~ de la mer** *the seaside*
bouche *nf mouth*
bouche-à-oreille *nm inv* **le ~** *word of mouth*
boucher, -ère *nmf butcher*
boucherie *nf butcher's shop*
bouchon *nm cork*
bouillir *vi to boil*
boulanger, -ère *nmf baker*
boulangerie *nf bakery*
bout *nm end; tip*
briser *vtr to break*
brouillard *nm fog*
bruit *nm noise*
brûler *vtr to burn*

bureau *nm office*
ça *that; this*
caisse *nf cash desk*
carrefour *nm crossroads*
carte *nf card;* **~ à puce** *smart card*
en tout cas *phr in any case*
case *nf box (on form)*
casserole *nf saucepan, pan*
cave *nf cellar*
céder *vtr* **~ le passage** *to give way*
celui / celle / ceux / celles *pron the one(s)*
celui-ci / celle-ci / ceux-ci / celles-ci *this one; these*
celui-là *pron that one*
cent *adj a hundred*
chacun, -e *each*
chambre *nf bedroom; room*
champignon *nm mushroom*
change *nm exchange rate*
chaque *each, every*
charcuterie *nf pork butcher's*
se charger *v refl (+ v* **être***)* **se ~ de** *to take responsibility for*
chat *nm cat*
château *nm castle*
chaud *adj hot*
chaussure *nf shoe*
chauvin ~e *adj chauvinistic*
cher, chère *adj dear*
chercher *vtr to look for*
cheveu *nm hair*
chèvre *nm goat('s cheese)*
chez *prep* **~ qn** *at sb's place*
chien *nm dog*
chiffre *nm figure*

chinois, ~e *adj* Chinese

chômage *nm* unemployment

chose *nf* thing

chou *nm* cabbage

ciel *nm* sky

clos *adj* closed

cocher *tr* to tick

coffre *nm* (of car) boot

coin *nm* corner

collège *nm* secondary school

combien de how many, how much

comme *conj* as

comment *adv* how

comprendre *vtr* to understand

compter *vtr* to count

concours *nm inv* competition

conduire *vtr* to drive

conduite *nf* (of vehicle) driving

confiture *nf* jam

connaître *vtr* to know

conseil *nm* advice

contre *prep* against

convenu, -e *adj* agreed

copain, copine *nmf* friend; boyfriend/girlfriend

corps *nm inv* body

à côte *phr* nearby

se coucher *v refl* (+ *v* **être**) to go to bed

coup blow; **donner un ~ de pied** to kick

couper *vtr* to cut; **se couper** to cut oneself

couramment *adv* fluently

courir *vi* to run

courriel *nf* e-mail

court ~e *adj* short

couteau *nm* knife

coûter *vtr* to cost

couvert *adj* [sky] overcast; **mettre le ~** to lay the table

crêpe *nf* pancake

crever *vtr* puncture

croire *vtr* to believe

cuillère *nf* spoon

cuillerée *nf* spoonful

cuire *vtr* to cook

cuisine *nf* kitchen; cooking

dans *prep* in

déboucher *vtr* to uncork

début *nm* beginning; start

découvrir *vtr* to discover

défense *nf* '~ **de fumer**' 'no smoking'

défi *nm* challenge

dehors *adv* outside

déjà *adv* already

déjeuner *vi* to have lunch; *nm* lunch

demain *adv* tomorrow

demander *vtr* to ask for

déménagement *nm* moving house

déménager *vtr* to move (furniture)

demeurer to reside, to live

demi, ~e *nmf* half

demi-heure *nf* half an hour

demi-tarif *adv* half-price

dent *nf* tooth

dentifrice *nm* toothpaste

dépanner *vtr* to fix [car, machine]

départ *nm* departure

déprimer *vtr* to depress; *vi* to be depressed

depuis *adv since*

dernier, -ière *adj last*

derrière *prep behind*

dès que *phr as soon as*

descendre *vtr (+ v **avoir**) to go down, to come down sth; vi to go down (+ v **être**)*

désolé *pp adj sorry*

dessous *adv underneath;* **en dessous** *phr underneath*

dessus *adv on top*

devant *prep in front of*

devenir *vi (+ v **être**) to become*

deviner *vtr to guess*

devoir *v aux to have to*

diététique *adj dietary; nf dietetics*

dingue *adj (person) crazy (slang)*

dire *vtr to say*

doigt *nm finger*

donc *conj so, therefore*

donner *vtr to give*

dormir *vi to sleep*

dos *nm inv back;* **mal de ~** *backache*

douche *nf shower*

droit, -e *adj straight*

droite *nf right;* **tourner à ~** *to turn right*

dur, -e *adj hard*

durée *nf length*

eau *nf water*

ébullition *nf boiling*

école *nf school*

écrire *vtr to write*

éditeur, -trice *nmf editor, publisher*

en effet *phr indeed*

église *nf church*

embouteillage *nm traffic jam*

embrasser *vtr to kiss*

embrumé, ~e *adj misty*

emmener *vtr to take*

emploi *nm job; employment*

employé, ~e *nmf employee*

emporter *vtr to take [object];* **pizzas à** *takeaway pizzas*

en *prep in; into*

encore *adv still; again*

endroit *nm place*

enfant *nmf child*

enfin *adv finally*

ennuyeux, -euse *adj boring*

enregistrer *vtr to check in (baggage)*

enseignant, ~e *nmf teacher*

enseigner *vtr to teach*

ensoleillé *adj sunny*

ensuite *adv then*

entendre *vtr to hear*

entier, -ière *adj whole*

entre *prep between*

entrée *nf entrance; starter*

entrer *vi to come in*

envie *nf* **avoir ~ de qch** *to feel like sth*

envoyer *vtr to send*

épais, épaisse *adj thick*

épicerie *nf grocer's (shop)*

éplucher *vtr to peel*

époux *nm inv husband*

équilibre *nm balance*

équipage *nm crew*

équipe *nf team*

escalier *nm staircase; stairs*

Espagne *nf Spain*

espagnol, -e *adj Spanish nm* l'
Spanish
espérer *vtr to hope*
essayer *vtr to try*
essence *nf petrol*
essuie-glace *nm windscreen*
wiper
étage *nm floor*
été *nm summer*
être *vi (+ v avoir) to be*
étudiant, -e *nmf student*
extrait *nm (from book, film)*
extract
fabriquer *vtr to make*
en face de *phr* **en ~ de** l'église
opposite the church, across
from the church
facile *adj easy*
façon *nf way;* **de toute ~** *anyway*
faim *nf hunger* **avoir ~** *to be*
hungry
faire *vtr to make*
faire-part *nm inv announcement*
faisable *adj* **c'est ~** *it can be*
done
au fait *phr by the way*
falloir *v impers* **il faut qch/qn** *we*
need sth/sb
familial, -e *adj (meal, life, firm)*
family
famille *nf family*
fatigant, ~e *adj tiring*
fatiguer *vtr to make [sb/sth] tired*
fauteuil *nm armchair;* **roulant**
wheelchair
faux, fausse *adj wrong*
féliciter *vtr to congratulate*
femme *nf woman*

fenêtre *nf window*
fer *nm iron;* **~ à repasser** *iron*
ferme *nf farm, farmhouse*
fermer *vtr to close*
fête *nf public holiday; name-day*
feu *nm fire*
février *nm February*
fille *nf daughter; girl*
fillette *nf little girl*
fils *nm inv son*
fin, fine *adj fine; [slice, layer] thin*
finir *vtr to finish*
fois *nf inv (with numerals)* **une ~**
once; **deux ~** *twice*
fort, ~e *adj strong*
fou, folle *adj mad*
four *nm oven*
fourchette *nf fork*
frais, fraîche *adj cool; cold; fresh*
fraise *nf strawberry*
framboise *nf raspberry*
frère *nm brother*
frigo *nm fridge*
froid, -e *adj cold*
fromage *nm cheese*
gagner *vtr to win*
galette *nf pancake*
Galles *nf pl* **le pays de ~** *Wales*
gamin, -e *nmf kid*
garçon *nm boy*
gâteau, *pl* **-x** *nm cake*
gauche *nf left*
genou, *pl* **-x** *nm knee*
genre *nm sort, kind, type*
gens *nm pl people*
gestion *nf management*
gîte *nm shelter;* **~ rural** *self-*
catering cottage

gonflé, -e *adj* inflated
gonfler *vtr* to inflate [tyre]
goût *nm* taste; palate
goûter *nm* snack
grand, -e *adj* [person, tree, tower] tall
grand-mère *nf* grandmother
grand-père *nm* grandfather
gras, grasse *adj* [substance] fatty
gratter *vtr* to scratch
gratuit, -e *adj* free
grave *adj* [problem, injury] serious
gris, -e *adj* grey
gros, grosse *adj* big, large; thick
habiller *vtr* to dress; **s'habiller** *v refl (+ v* **être***)* to get dressed
habitation *nf* house
halle *nf* covered market
haricot *nm* bean; **~ vert** French bean
haut, -e *adj* high; tall
hébergement *nm* accommodation
héberger *vtr* to put [sb] up
heure *nf* hour; **l'~ d'arrivée** the arrival time; **~s d'ouverture** opening times
hier *adv* yesterday
histoire *nf* history
hiver *nm* winter
homme *nm* man
hors-d'œuvre *nm inv* starter
humide *adj* damp
ici *adv* here
immatriculation *nf* registration
immeuble *nm* building
immobilier *nm* **l' ~** property

imprimerie *nf* printing
incendie *nm* fire
infirmier *nm* male nurse
infirmière *nf* nurse
information *nf* **écouter les ~s** to listen to the news
inquiet, -iète *adj* anxious; worried.
s'inquiéter *v refl (+ v* **être***)* to worry
interdit, -e *pp adj* prohibited, forbidden
intéresser *vtr* to interest **ça ne m'intéresse pas** *I'm not interested*
irlandais, -e *adj* Irish *nm* Irish
italien, -ienne *adj* Italian *nm* Italian
jamais *adv* never
jambe *nf* leg
jambon *nm* ham
jardin *nm* garden
jaune *adj* yellow
je (**j'** before vowel or mute **h**) I
jeu, *pl* **-x** *nm* game
jeu-concours *nm* competition
jeudi *nm* Thursday
jeune *adj* young
jeunesse *nf* youth
joli -e *adj (gen)* nice; [face] pretty
jouer *vtr* to play
jour *nm* day
journal, *pl* **-aux** *nm* newspaper
journée *nf* day
juillet *nm* July
jus *nm inv* juice
jusque-là *adv* until then, up to here

juste adv right, just
justement adv precisely
là adv there; here
là-bas adv over there
laisser vtr to leave
lait nm milk
lancer vtr to throw
large adj broad; wide
lavabo nm washbasin, washbowl
laver vtr to wash **se laver** v refl
  (+ v **être***)* to wash; **se ~ les**
  mains to wash one's hands
le, la (**l'** before vowel or mute **h**),
  pl **les** the
lecture nf reading
léger, -ère adj light
lent, -e adj slow
lequel / laquelle / lesquels /
  lesquelles adj who; which
se lever v refl *(+ v* **être***)* to get up
liaison nf link
librairie nf bookshop
libre-service adj inv self-service
lieu nm place; **au lieu de** phr
  instead of
lire vtr to read
livre nm book
locataire nmf tenant
location nf renting
logement nm accommodation
loin adv a long way, **c'est trop ~**
  it's too far
loisir nm spare time; leisure
Londres n London
longtemps adv a long time
louer vtr [owner, landlord] to let;
  to rent out
lourd, -e adj heavy

lumière nf light
lundi nm Monday
lune nf moon
lunettes nf pl glasses; **~ de soleil**
  sunglasses
lycée nm secondary school
  *(school preparing students
  aged 15-18 for the Baccalau-
  réat)*
madame, pl **mesdames** Mrs; a
  *woman whose name you do
  not know*
mademoiselle, pl **mesdemoi-**
  selles Miss; a woman whose
  name you do not know
magnétophone nm tape re-
  corder
magnétoscope nm video re-
  corder, VCR
maigre adj [person] thin;
  [cheese] low-fat
main nf hand
mairie nf town council
mais conj but
maison nf house; home
mal, pl **maux** adj bad, wrong; nm
  pain; **avoir ~ partout** to ache
  all over; **avoir ~ à la tête** to
  have a headache
malade adj [person] ill, sick
malgré prep in spite of, despite
malheureusement adv unfortunately
Manche nf the Channel; **le**
  tunnel sous la ~ the Channel
  tunnel
manger vtr to eat; **il n'y a rien à**
  ~ dans la maison there's no

food in the house

manière *nf* way; **d'une ~ ou d'une autre** *in one way or another*

manoir *nm* manor (house)

manquer *vtr* to miss

manquer de *v + prep* to lack; **on ne manque de rien** *we don't want for anything*

manteau, *pl* -x *nm* coat

marcher *vi* to walk; to work; **ma radio marche mal** *my radio doesn't work properly*

mardi *nm* Tuesday

marée *nf* tide; **à ~ haute/basse** *at high/low tide*

marémoteur, -trice *adj* tidal; **usine marémotrice** *tidal power station*

mari *nm* husband

marié, -e *pp adj* married

se marier *v refl* (+ *v* **être**) to get married (**avec qn** *to sb*)

mars *nm inv* March

matin *nm* morning

mauvais, -e *adj* bad

mécanicien, -ienne *nmf* mechanic

Méditerranée *nf* la (mer) ~ the Mediterranean

meilleur, -e *adj* better; best; **le ~ des deux** *the better of the two*

mélanger *vtr* to mix

même *adj* same; *adv* even; *phr* **agir** or **faire de** ~ to do the same

ménage *nm* household; house-

work; **faire le** ~ to do the cleaning

mensuel, -elle *adj* monthly; *nm* monthly magazine

menteur, -euse *nmf* liar

mentir *vi* to lie, to tell lies

mer *nf* sea

merci *nm* thank you

mercredi *nm* Wednesday

mère *nf* mother

météo *nf* weather forecast

métier *nm* job; profession

métro *nm* underground

mettre *vtr* to put

meuble *nm* **des ~s** furniture

meublé *nm* furnished flat

meubler *vtr* to furnish

miam-miam *excl* yum-yum!

micro-ondes *nm inv* microwave

midi *nm* twelve o'clock, midday, noon; lunchtime; **le Midi** the South of France

miel *nm* honey

le mien, la mienne, les miens, les miennes mine

mieux *adj inv* better; **le ~, la ~, les** ~ the best

milieu *nm* middle; **au ~ de la nuit** in the middle of the night

mille *adj inv* a thousand, one thousand

milliard *nm* billion

mince [person, leg] slim, slender

minuit *nm* midnight

mi-temps *nm inv* part-time job; **elle travaille à** ~ she works part-time

mobilier, -ière *adj* **biens ~s** *movable property*

mobylette® *nf moped*

moi *I, me;* **c'est ~** *it's me*

moi-même *myself*

moins *minus;* **il est huit heures ~ dix** *it's ten (minutes) to eight; adv (comparative) less*

à moins de *phr unless*

au moins *phr at least*

mois *nm inv month*

moitié *nf half;* **à ~ vide** *half empty*

môme *nmf kid; brat (slang)*

mon, ma *pl* **mes** *my*

monde *nm world; people;* **tout le ~** *everybody*

moniteur, -trice *nmf group leader*

monnaie *nf currency; change*

monsieur, *pl* **messieurs** *nm Mr*

montagne *nf mountain*

monter *vtr (+ v* **avoir***) to go up sth; vi (+* **être***);* **tu es monté à pied?** *did you walk up?*

montrer *vtr to show*

mordre *vtr to bite*

morsure *nf bite*

mort *nf death*

mort, -e *adj dead;* **je suis ~ de froid** *I'm freezing to death*

mot *nm word*

moule *nf mussel*

mourir *vi (+ v* **être***) to die*

moyen, -enne *adj [height, size] medium; medium sized; [price] moderate*

municipal, ~e *adj [council] local, town*

mur *nm wall*

musée *nm museum; art gallery*

nager *vtr to swim*

nageur, -euse *nmf swimmer*

naissance *nf birth*

naître *vi (+ v* **être***) to be born;* **elle est née le 5 juin** *she was born on 5 June*

naturellement *adv naturally*

né, -e *pp see* **naître**

nécessaire *adj necessary*

neige *nf snow*

neiger *v impers to snow;* **il neige** *it's snowing*

n'est-ce pas *adv* **c'est joli, ~?** *it's pretty, isn't it?*

net, nette *adj [price, weight] net*

nettoyage *nm cleanup*

neuf *nine*

neuf, neuve *adj new*

neveu, *pl* **-x** *nm nephew*

nez *nm nose*

ni *conj nor, or*

Noël *nm Christmas;* **'Joyeux ~'** *Merry Christmas*

noir *adj black*

nom *nm name;* **~ et prénom** *full name*

nombre *nm number*

nombreux, -euse *adj numerous, many*

non *adv no*

nord *adj inv north; northern*

nord-africain, -e *adj North African*

nord-ouest *adj inv northwest*

notaire *nm notary public*

notre, *pl* **nos** *our*

nourriture *nf food*

nous *(subject) we; (object) us*

nous-même, *pl* **nous-mêmes**
ourselves

nouveau (**nouvel** *before vowel or
mute* **h**), **nouvelle** *adj new*

nouveau-né *adj newborn*

nuage *nm cloud*

nuageux, **-euse** *adj [sky] cloudy*

nuit *nf night*

nulle part *phr nowhere*

nullement *adv not at all*

numéro *nm number* **~ de téléphone** *telephone number*
~ d'abonné *customer's
number;* **~ d'appel gratuit**
freefone number

obligatoire *compulsory; inevi-
table*

occupant, **-e** *occupant*

occupé, **~e** *[person, life] busy;
[seat] taken; [phone] en-
gaged*

s'occuper *v refl (+ v* **être***)* **s'~ de**
*to see to, to take care of [din-
ner, tickets]*

œil, *pl* **yeux** *nm eye*

offre *nf offer;* **répondre à une
~ d'emploi** *to reply to a job
advertisement*

oignon *nm onion*

oiseau, *pl* **-x** *nm bird*

oncle *nm uncle*

onze *eleven*

orage *nm storm*

orageux, **-euse** *stormy; thundery*

ordinaire *adj ordinary*

ordinateur *nm computer*

oreille *nf ear*

oreiller *nm pillow*

organisateur, **-trice** *nmf organ-
izer*

orthographe *nf spelling*

os *nm inv bone*

ou *conj or*

où *adv where*

oublier *vtr to forget [name, date,
fact]*

ouf *phew!*

oui *yes*

outil *nm tool*

ouvert, **-e** *adj open*

ouvrable *adj [day] working;
[hours] business*

ouvre-boîtes *nm inv tin-opener*

ouvrier, **-ière** *nmf worker; work-
man*

ouvrir *vtr to open*

paiement *nm payment*

pain *nm bread*

pancarte *nf notice*

panier *nm basket*

panneau *nm sign;* **~ indicateur**
signpost

pantalon *nm trousers*

papeterie *nf stationer's (shop),
stationery shop*

papier *nm paper*

Pâques *nm, nf pl Easter*

par *prep* **elle est arrivée ~ la
droite** *she came from the
right;* **régler** *or* **payer ~ carte
de crédit** *to pay by credit
card*

paradis *nm inv heaven; paradise*

paraître vi to appear, to seem, to look

parapluie nm umbrella

parc nm park

parce que phr because

pardon nm forgiveness; pardon; **je te demande** ~ I'm sorry ~! sorry!

pare-chocs nm inv bumper

pareil, **-eille** adj similar

paresse nf laziness

paresseux, **-euse** adj lazy

parfait, **-e** adj perfect

parfaitement adv perfectly

parfois adv sometimes

parier vtr to bet

parisien, **-ienne** adj Parisian

parler vtr to speak

parmi prep among, amongst

part nf (of food) slice, helping

partager vtr to share

partir vi (+ v **être**) to leave

partout adv everywhere

pas adv **je ne prends** ~ **de sucre** I don't take sugar

passager, **-ère** nmf passenger

passant, **-e** nmf passer-by

passer vtr to cross; to go through

patin nm skate; ~ **à roulettes** roller skate

pâtissier, **-ière** nmf confectioner, pastry cook

patron, **-onne** nmf boss

pauvre adj poor

payer vtr to pay for

pays nm country

péage nm toll

peau nf skin

pêche nm peach; **avoir la** ~ to be feeling great

pêcher vtr to go fishing for

peine nf sorrow, grief; **avoir de la** ~ to feel sad or upset

pellicule nf film

se pencher v refl (+ v **être**) to lean

pendant prep for; **je t'ai attendu** ~ **des heures** I waited for you for hours

penser vtr to think

Pentecôte nf Whitsun

perdre vtr to lose

père nm father

permettre vtr ~ **à qn de faire** to allow sb to do

permis nm ~ **de conduire** driver's licence

petit, **-e** adj small, little; short

petite-fille nf granddaughter

petit-fils nm grandson

petits-enfants nm pl grandchildren

peu adv not much

peut-être adv perhaps, maybe

phare nm headlight

pharmacie nm chemist's (shop)

pharmacien, **-ienne** nmf (dispensing) chemist

pièce nf room

pied nm foot

pierre nf stone

piéton, **-onne** adj pedestrianized; nmf pedestrian

piqûre nf injection, shot; sting; bite

placard nm cupboard

plage *nf* beach
plaisanter *vi* to joke
plan, *nm* map; (in building) plan, map
planche *nf* ~ **à voile** windsurfing board
plateau, *pl* **-x** tray (**de** of)
plein, -e *adj* full
pleurer *vi* to cry
pleuvoir *v impers* to rain; **il pleut** it's raining
pluie *nf* rain
la plupart *nf inv* most
plus *adv* more; **le ~** the most; **de plus** *phr* furthermore; **une fois de ~** once more, once again
plusieurs *adj* several
plutôt *adv* rather; fairly
pluvieux, -ieuse *adj* wet, rainy
pneu *nm* tyre
poids *nm inv* weight
poignée *nf* ~ **de main** handshake
point *nm* ~ **de suture** (Med) stitch; ~ **de vue** point of view
pointure *nf* shoe size
poire *nf* pear
pois *nm* **petit ~** (garden) pea
poisson *nm* fish
poivre *nm* pepper
poivrer *vtr* to add pepper to [sauce]
poli, -e *adj* polite
pomme *nf* apple; ~ **de terre** potato; ~**s frites** chips
pompe *nf* ~ **à essence** petrol pump

pompier, -ière *nm* fireman
pont *nm* bridge; deck
populaire *adj* working-class
portail *nm* gateway, portal (computer)
portefeuille *nm* wallet
porter *vtr* to carry
portugais *adj* Portuguese *nm* Portuguese
poulet *nm* chicken
pour *prep* to; ~ **faire** to do; in order to do; for; **le train ~** *Paris* the train for Paris
pourquoi why
pourtant *adv* though
pousser *vtr* to push
pouvoir *v aux* to be able to; **peux-tu soulever cette boîte?** can you lift this box?
pratique *adj* practical; convenient
pratiquer *vtr* to play [tennis]; to practise
préavis *nm inv* notice; **déposer un ~ de grève** to give notice of strike action
premier, -ière *adj*; first
prendre *vtr* to take; **je vais ~ du poisson** I'll have fish; **aller ~ une bière** to go for a beer
prénom *nm* first name, forename
près *adv* close; **à peu ~ vide** *phr* practically empty
presque *adv* almost, nearly
prêt, -e *adj* ready
preuve *nf* proof
prévenir *vtr* to tell; to warn
prévision *nf* forecasting; ~**s**

météorologiques *weather forecast*

printemps *nm inv spring*

prix *nm inv price*

prochain, ~e *adj next*

proche *adj nearby*

produit *nm product*

professeur *nm (in school) teacher*

profil *nm profile*

se promener *v refl (+ v* **être***) to go for a walk/drive/ride*

promettre *vtr* ~ **qch à qn** *to promise sb sth*

prononcer *vtr to pronounce*

propos *nm inv* **à ~, je...** *by the way, I...*

propre *adj clean*

prouver *vtr to prove*

PTT *nf pl (abbr =* **Administration des postes et télécommunications et de la télédiffusion***) French postal and telecommunications service*

puis *adv then*

quai *nm quay; river bank*

quand *conj when*

quart *nm quarter*

quartier *nm area; district*

Québécois, -e *nmf Quebecois, Quebecker*

quel, quelle *who; what; which*

quelque *some; a few; any;*

quelquefois *adv sometimes*

quelqu'un *someone, somebody; anyone, anybody*

qui *who; whom*

quitter *vtr to leave [place, person, road]*

quoi *what;* **à ~ penses-tu?** *what are you thinking about?*

quotidien, -ienne *adj daily; nm daily (paper)*

raccrocher *vtr to hang [sth] back up* ~ **le combiné** *to put the telephone down.*

raisin *nm grape*

raison *nf reason;* ~ **d'agir** *reason for action*

ralentir *vtr, vi to slow down*

rallye *nm (car) rally*

ranger *vtr to put away; to tidy*

rapide *adj quick, rapid*

rapidement *adv quickly; fast*

se raser *v refl (+ v* **être***) to shave*

rasoir *nm* ~ **électrique** *electric shaver*

rater *vtr to miss*

rayon *nm department*

recette *nf* ~ **(de cuisine)** *recipe*

recevoir *vtr to receive, to get*

reconnaître *vtr to recognize; to identify*

réfléchir à *vtr + prep to think about*

réfrigérateur *nm refrigerator*

regarder *vtr to look at [person, scene, landscape]*

régime *nm diet;* **être au ~** *to be on a diet*

région *nf region; area;* **le vin de la ~** *the local wine*

regretter *vtr to be sorry about, to regret*

rejoindre *vtr to meet up with*

remarquer *vtr to point out*

remercier *to thank (***de qch** *for sth)*

remplir *vtr to fill (up) [container]; to fill in or out [form]*

rencontre *nf meeting; encounter*

rencontrer *vtr to meet [person]*

rendez-vous *nm inv appointment*

renseignement *nm information*

renseigner *vtr ~ ***qn** *to give information to sb*

rentrée *nf (general) return to work (after the slack period of the summer break, in France)*

réparer *vtr to repair, to mend, to fix*

repasser *vtr to iron*

répétitif, -ive *adj repetitive*

répondre *vtr to answer, to reply*

réponse *vtr answer, reply*

repos *vtr rest*

reposer *vtr to rest; ***se reposer** *v refl (+ v ***être***) to have a rest, to rest*

réserver *vtr to reserve, to book [seat, ticket]*

respirer *vtr to breathe in [air]; vi to breathe*

rester *vi (+ v ***être***) to stay, to remain*

résultat *nm result*

retard *nm lateness; ***un ~ de dix minutes** *a ten-minute delay; ***avoir de** *~ to be late*

retour *nm return; (***billet de***) ~ return ticket*

retraite *nf retirement*

se retrouver *v refl (+ v ***être***) to meet (again); ***on s'est re-*** trouvé en famille *the family got together*

réunion *nf meeting*

réussir *vtr to achieve ~ ***à un exa-men** *to pass an exam*

rêve *nm dreaming; dream*

se réveiller *v refl (+ v ***être***) to wake up*

revoir *vtr to see again*

au revoir *phr goodbye, bye*

rien *nothing; ***se disputer pour un** *~ to quarrel over nothing*

rire *vi to laugh*

rond, -e *adj [object, table, hole] round*

rond-point *nm roundabout*

roue *nf wheel*

rouge *adj red*

route *nf road, highway*

routier *nm lorry driver*

sage *adj wise, sensible; good, well-behaved*

saison *nf season*

salade *nf lettuce; salad; ~ ***verte** *green salad*

salaire *nm salary; wages*

salle *room; hall; ~ ***d'attente** *waiting room; ~ ***de bains** *bathroom; ***~ de jeu(x)** *(for children) playroom ~ ***à man-ger** *dining room; ~ ***de séjour** *living room*

sans *adv without*

santé *nf health; ***à votre** *~! cheers!*

saucisse *nf sausage*

saucisson *nm ~ ***à l'ail** *garlic sausage*

sauf *prep* except, but

savoir *vtr* to know [truth, answer]

sécurité *nf* security; **en toute ~** in complete safety

selon *prep* according to

semaine *nf* week

sens *nm inv* direction, way

sentinelle *nf* sentry

sentir *vtr* to smell

serveur, -euse *nmf* waiter/waitress

servir *vtr* to serve; **qu'est-ce que je vous sers (à boire)?** *what would you like to drink?*

se servir *v refl (+ v* **être)** *(at table)* to help oneself

seul, -e *adj* alone, on one's own

seulement *adv* only

si *nm inv* if; *adv* yes; so **c'est un homme ~ agréable** *he's such a pleasant man*

siffler *vtr* to whistle [tune]

sinon otherwise, or else

skier *vi* to ski

sœur *nf* sister

soif *nf* thirst; **avoir ~** to be thirsty

soir *nm* evening; night

soirée *nf* evening; **dans** or **pendant la ~** in the evening

en solde *phr* **acheter une veste en ~** to buy a jacket in a sale

soldes *nm pl* sales; sale

sommaire *nm* contents

sommeil *nm* sleep; **avoir ~** to be or feel sleepy

son, sa, *pl* **ses** his/her/its

sondage d'opinion *nm* opinion poll

sortir *vi (+ v* **être)** to go out; to come out; **être sorti** to be out

sous *prep* under, underneath

souvent *adv* often

stage *nm* professional training; work experience

studio *nm* studio flat

sud *adj inv* south

suffire *vi* to be enough; **ça suffit (comme ça)!** *that's enough!*

suivant, ~e *adj* following; next; **le ~** the following one; the next one

sur *prep* on; **~ la table** on the table

sympathique *adj* nice; pleasant

syndicat *nm* trade union

tabac *nm* tobacco

taille *nf* size

tant *adv (so)* much

tante *nf* aunt

tard *adv* late; **plus ~** later

tarif *nm* rate

tarte *nf (food)* tart; **~ aux fraises** strawberry tart

tasse *nf* cup; **~ à thé** teacup; **~ de thé** cup of tea

tel, telle *adj* such; **je n'ai jamais rien vu de ~** *I've never seen anything like it*

télécopieur *nm* fax machine, fax

tellement *adv* so

temps *nm inv* weather; time

tenir *vtr* to hold

terrain *nm* ground

terrasse *nf* terrace; **s'installer à la ~ d'un café** to sit at a table outside a café

tête *nf head*

tien, tienne, le tien, la tienne, les tiens, les tiennes *yours*

timbre *nm stamp*

tirer *vtr to pull*

toi *pron you*

toile *nm fabric, web (computer)* – **d'araignée** *spider's web*

tomber *vi (+ v **être**) to fall*

tonnerre *nm thunder*

tort *nm **avoir** ~ to be wrong*

tôt *adv [start] early*

toujours *adv always*

tourner *vtr to turn*

tout ~e *mpl* **tous** *fpl* **toutes** *everything; all; anything*

trafic *nm traffic*

tranquille *adj [person, life, street, day] quiet*

tranquillement *adv quietly*

travail *nm work;* **chercher du/ un** ~ *to look for work/a job*

travailler *vtr to work*

traverser *vtr to cross*

très *adv very*

triste *adj sad*

trop *adv too; too much*

trouver *vtr to find*

tutoyer *vtr to address [sb] using the 'tu' form*

université *nf university*

urgence *nf urgency;* **le service des** ~s, **les** ~s *the casualty department*

utile *adj useful*

utiliser *vtr to use*

vacances *nf pl holiday*

vache *adj mean, nasty (slang)*

nf cow

vachement *adv really;* **il a** ~ **maigri** *he's lost a hell of a lot of weight*

valise *nf suitcase*

véhicule *nm vehicle*

vélo *nm bike;* ~ **tout terrain, VTT** *mountain bike*

vendeur, -euse *nmf shop assistant*

vendre *vtr to sell*

vendredi *nm Friday*

venir *v aux* **venir de faire** *to have just done;* **elle vient de partir** *she's just left; vi (+ v **être**) to come*

vent *nm wind*

vente *nf sale*

ventre *nm stomach;* **avoir mal au** ~ *to have stomach ache*

vérifier *vtr to check*

verre *nm glass*

vers *prep toward(s)*

vert, ~e *adj green*

vêtement *nm piece of clothing*

veuf, veuve *adj widowed*

viande *nf meat*

vide *adj empty*

vie *nf life*

vieux, vieille *adj old*

ville *nf town; city*

vin *nm wine*

virage *nm bend*

vite *adv quickly;* ~! *quick!*

vitesse *nf speed*

vivre *vi to live*

voici *prep here is, this is; here are*

voilà *prep here is, this is; here are*

voir *vtr to see*

voisin, ~e *nmf neighbour*

volant *nm steering wheel*

vomir *vtr to vomit*

votre, *pl* **vos** *your*

vôtre: mes biens sont ~s *all I have is yours*

vouloir *vtr to want*

vous *you*

vous-même *yourself*

vouvoyer *vtr to address [sb] using the 'vous' form*

voyage *nm trip; journey*

voyager *vi to travel*

voyageur, -euse *nmf passenger*

vrai, ~e *true; real, genuine*

y *it;* **il ~ a** *there is/are;* **il ~ a du vin? il n'~ en a plus** *wine? there's none left;* **il n'~ a qu'à téléphoner** *just phone*

yaourt *nm yoghurt*

yeux *nm pl see* **œil**

zéro *nm zero, nought*

zone *nf zone, area;* **~ d'activités** *business park*

zut *damn!*

English–French vocabulary

a *adjective*
adv *adverb*
aux *auxiliary*
conj *conjunction*
excl *exclamation*
f *feminine*
i *intransitive*
m *masculine*
n *noun*

phr *phrase*
pl *plural*
prep *preposition*
pron *pronoun*
qch *quelque chose (something)*
rel *relative*
tr *transitive*
v *verb*

---

a, an **un, une**; *a man,* **un homme**; *an apple,* **une pomme**

able a. **capable, compétent, habile**

aboard **adv. à bord**; *to go a.,* **monter à bord**

about **adv. & prep. autour (de); au sujet de;** *while you are a. it,* **pendant que vous y êtes**

above **adv. & prep. au dessus (de)**

abroad **adv. à l'étranger**

accelerate **v.tr. accélérer**

accompany **v.tr. accompagner**

account **n. compte m**; *my bank a.,* **mon compte en banque**

accurate **a. exact, juste, précis**

ache **n. mal m, douleur f**

acquire **v.tr. acquérir**

across **adv. & prep. en travers (de)** *to walk a. (a street),* **traverser (une rue)**

acute **a. 1. aigu. 2. (douleur) aiguë**

add **v.tr. ajouter**

address **n. adresse f**

adequate **a. suffisant**

admit **v.tr. admettre**

adventure **n. aventure f**

advice **n. conseil(s) m**

advise **v.tr. conseiller**

aerial **n. antenne f**

afford **v.tr. (usu. with can) avoir les moyens**

afraid **a. effrayé;** *to be a.,* **avoir peur**

Africa **l'Afrique f**

African **a. & n. africain, -aine**

after **adv. après;** *the day a. tomorrow,* **après-demain**

again **de nouveau, encore;** *once a.,* **encore une fois**

against **prep. contre**

agenda **programme m (d'une réunion)**

ago **adv.** *ten years a.,* **il y a dix ans**

agree **v.i. & tr. consentir**

alas **excl. hélas!**

alcohol **n. alcool m**

alike **a. semblable, pareil**

alive **adj. vivant**

all **a., pron., & adv. tout;** *a. day,* **(pendant) toute la journée;** *a. men,* **tous les hommes**

allow **v.tr. (permit) permettre**

alone **a. seul**

along **prep. le long de;** *to go a. a street,* **suivre une rue**

aloud **adv. à haute voix**

already **adv. déjà**

also **adv. aussi**

altogether **adv. (wholly) entière-ment, tout à fait;** *how much a.?* **combien en tout?**

always **adv. toujours**

America **l'Amérique f;** *North, South, A.,* **l'Amérique du Nord, du Sud**

American **a. & n. américain, -aine**

amiable **a. aimable**

amid(st) **prep. au milieu de; parmi**

among(st) **prep. parmi, entre**

and **conj. et**

anger **n. colère f**

angry **a. fâché, en colère**

animator **n. animateur, -trice (d'un groupe, d'un club)**

anniversary **n. anniversaire m**

another **a. & pron. encore;** *a. cup of tea,* **encore une tasse de thé;** *(a similar)* **une(e) autre, un(e) second(e)**

answer **n. 1. réponse; 2. solution**

f (d'un problème)

anxious **adj. inquiet**

anything **pron. & n. quelque chose**

anyway **adv. & conj. en tout cas, de toute façon**

anywhere **adv. n'importe où**

apartment **appartement m**

apple **n. pomme f**

apprentice **n. apprenti, -ie**

apricot **n. abricot m**

April **n. avril m**

area **n. région f**

arm **n. bras m;** *armchair,* **n. fauteuil**

around **adv. autour, à l'entour**

artichoke **n. artichaut m**

as **adv. aussi, si;** *you're as tall as I am, as me,* **vous êtes aussi grand que moi**

ash **n. cendre(s);** *ashtray* **n. cendrier m**

ask **v.tr. & i. demander**

asleep **adv. & a. endormi**

assault **v.tr. attaquer;** *to be as-saulted,* **être victime d'une agression**

assist **v.tr. aider**

astonish **v.tr. étonner**

at *at table, at school,* **à table, à l'école**

attend *to a. a meeting* **assister à une réunion**

August **n. août m**

aunt **n. tante f**

autumn **n. automne m**

average **n. moyenne f**

avoid **v.tr. éviter**

awake v.i. s'éveiller, se réveiller

away adv. loin; au loin

back n. dos m

bad a. mauvais

bag n. sac m

baggage n. bagages mpl

bake v.tr. cuire, faire cuire (qch.)

ball n. balle f

bank n. banque f

bargain n. affaire f

barrister n. avocat m

basket n. panier m

be v.i. être

beach n. plage f

bean n. haricot m

beautiful a. beau, belle; magnifique

because conj. parce que

become v.i. devenir

bed n. lit m; *twin beds*, lits jumeaux; *double b.*, grand lit

bee n. abeille f

beef n. bœuf m

beer n. bière f

beetroot n. betterave f

before adv. avant; devant

begin v.tr. & i. commencer

behind adv. derrière

Belgian a. & n. belge (mf)

Belgium la Belgique

believe v.tr. croire

bell n. cloche f

belly n. ventre m

belong v.i. appartenir

below adv. en bas, (au-)dessous

belt n. ceinture f

bench n. banc m

bend n. (of road) virage m;

bends for 3 miles, virages sur 5 kilomètres

beneath adv. dessous, au-dessous, en bas

best a. & n. (le) meilleur, (la) meilleure; le mieux

better adj. meilleur

between prep. entre

beverage n. boisson f

big a. (large) grand; (bulky) gros

bill n. (in restaurant) addition f

black a. noir

blood n. sang m

blue a. bleu

boat n. bateau m

body n. corps m

boil v.i. bouillir

bone n. os m

book n. livre m

boss n. patron, chef m

bottle n. bouteille f

box n. boîte f

boy n. garçon m

brake n. frein m; *hand b.*, frein à main

bread n. pain m

break v.i. casser

breakfast n. (petit) déjeuner m

Britain Great B., la Grande-Bretagne

British a. britannique

Brittany la Bretagne

broken a. cassé

brother n. frère m

brown a. brun; marron

build v.tr. bâtir (une maison)

burn v.tr. & i. brûler

business n. affaire f
busy a. affairé, occupé; actif
but conj. mais
butcher n. boucher m
butter n. beurre m
by prep. (near) (au)près de, à
    côté de
bye(-bye) au revoir!
cake n. gâteau m
call v.tr. appeler
can1 n. boîte f (de conserves,
    de bière)
can2 v. aux. pouvoir
car n. auto(mobile) f, voiture f;
    rail: voiture, wagon m
card n. carte f
carpet n. tapis m
carry v.tr. porter
cat n. chat
chair n. chaise f
Channel la Manche
cheap a. bon marché
child n. enfant mf
China la Chine
Christmas n. Noël m
church n. église f
clean a. propre, net
clear a. clair
clock n. (large) horloge f;
    (smaller) pendule f
close v.tr. fermer
clothes n.pl. vêtements mpl
cloud n. nuage m
code the Highway C., le code de
    la route
coffee n. café m
coin n. pièce f de monnaie
cold a. froid

colour n. couleur f
come v.i. venir, arriver
computer n. ordinateur nm
construct v.tr. construire; bâtir
cook v.tr. (faire) cuire
cool a. frais, f. fraiche
cost v.i. coûter
count v.tr. compter
country n. pays m, région f
crash (car) accident m
cross v.tr. traverser (la rue)
crowd n. foule f
cry v.tr. pleurer
cup n. tasse f; c. of tea, tasse de
    thé
customs (bureaux de la) douane
cut v.tr. couper
dairy d. produce, produits lai-
    tiers mpl
dark a. sombre, obscur
day n. jour m
dead a. mort; he's d., il est mort
dear a. cher
death n. mort f
deep a. profond
Denmark le Danemark
depart v.i. s'en aller, partir
depth n. profondeur f
die v.i. mourir
dinner n. dîner m
discover v.tr. découvrir, trouver
do v. aux., v.i., v.tr. faire
dog n. chien m
door n. porte f
down adv. en bas; to go d.,
    descendre
dozen n. douzaine f
dream n. rêve m

dress n. **robe f**
drive n. *left-hand d.*, **conduite f à gauche;** v.tr. **conduire (une auto)**
drunk a. **ivre**
dry a. **sec, f. sèche**
duck n. **canard m**
duty n. **devoir m**
each a. **chaque;** *e. day,* **chaque jour; tous les jours**
ear n. **oreille f**
early a. **de bonne heure**
earth n. **terre f; monde m**
Easter n. **Pâques m;** *E. Day,* **le jour de Pâques**
easy a. **facile**
eat v.tr. **manger**
egg n. **œuf m;** *boiled e.,* **œuf à la coque**
eight **huit (m);** *to be e. (years old),* **avoir huit ans**
elbow n. **coude m**
eleven **onze (m)**
e-mail n. **courriel nm**
emergency n. **cas urgent m**
end n. **fin f**
engine n. **moteur m**
England **l'Angleterre f;** *in E.,* **en Angleterre**
English a. & n. **anglais, -aise**
enjoy v.tr. **aimer,** *to e. oneself,* **s'amuser**
enough a. **assez**
enter v.i. **entrer**
entrance n. **entrée f**
envelope n. **enveloppe f**
eve n. **veille f;** *Christmas E.,* **la veille de Noël**

even adv. **même**
evening n. **soir m; soirée f**
event n. **événement m**
ever adv. **jamais**
every a. **chaque**
except prep. **excepté; sauf**
exhaust pipe, **tuyau m d'échappement**
exit n. **sortie f**
expense n. **dépense f;** *expensive,* a. **coûteux, cher;** *to be e.,* **coûter cher**
explain v.tr. **expliquer**
eye n. **œil m, pl. yeux;** *to have blue eyes,* **avoir les yeux bleus**
fall v.i. **tomber**
false a. **faux**
family n. **famille f**
famous a. **célèbre, renommé**
far adv. *(of place)* **loin**
fare n. **prix m du voyage, de la place**
fast a. **rapide; vite,** *not so f.!* **pas si vite! doucement**
fasten v.tr. **attacher**
fat a. **gros; gras**
father n. **père m**
fault n. **défaut m; imperfection f**
fear n. **peur f**
February n. **février m**
feel v.tr. **toucher**
fetch v.tr. **aller chercher**
few a. **peu de;** *he has f. friends,* **il a peu d'amis**
field n. **champ m**
fill v.tr. **remplir**

find v.tr. trouver, rencontrer, découvrir

finger n. doigt m

finish v.tr. finir, terminer

fire n. feu m

first a. premier; *the f. of April*, le premier avril

fish n. poisson m

five cinq (m)

flag n. drapeau m

flat a. plat; horizontal; *f. roof*, toit plat

flight n. vol m

flower n. fleur f

flu n. grippe f

fly v.i. voler

fog n. brouillard m

follow v.tr. suivre

food n. nourriture f; aliments mpl

foot n. pied m

for prep. pour

forbid v.tr. défendre, interdire; *smoking forbidden*, défense de fumer

forget v.tr. oublier

fork n. fourchette f

fortnight n. quinzaine f; quinze jours m

forty quarante (m)

forward adv. en avant

four quatre (m)

free a. & adv. libre; *is this table f.?* est-ce que cette table est libre?; gratuit

French a. français

Friday n. vendredi m

fridge n. réfrigérateur m

friend n. ami, f amie

from prep. de

full a. plein, rempli

fun n. amusement m

furniture n. meubles mpl

further davantage, plus; *furthermore* adv. de plus

gale n. coup m de vent; *it's blowing a g.*, le vent souffle en tempête

game n. jeu m

garden n. jardin m

garlic n. ail m

gas n. gaz m; *g. cooker*, cuisinière f à gaz

gate n. porte f (de ville); portail m

genuine a. authentique, véritable

Germany l'Allemagne f.

get v.tr. obtenir; *if I g. the time*, si j'ai le temps; *to g. dressed*, s'habiller

gift n. cadeau m

girl n.f. jeune fille; *little g.*, petite fille

give v.tr. donner

glad a. heureux, content

glass n. verre m

go v.i. aller; *come and go*, aller et venir

gold n. or m

good a. bon

grape n. raisin m; *bunch of grapes*, grappe f de raisin

grass n. herbe f

great a. grand

green a. vert

grey adj. gris (m)

grow v.i. (of plant) pousser; (of pers.) grandir

guess v.tr. deviner

guest n. invité

habit n. habitude f, to be in the h. of doing…, avoir l'habitude de faire…

hair n. (of head) cheveu m; to do one's h., se coiffer

half n. moitié f

ham n. jambon m; h. and eggs, œufs au jambon

hand n. main f

happen v.i. arriver; se passer

happy a. heureux

hat n. chapeau m

have v.tr. avoir, posséder; he has no friends, il n'a pas d'amis

he pron. il

head n. tête f; headache, n. mal m de tête; headlamp n. phare f

hear v.tr. entendre

heat n. chaleur f

heavy a. lourd

height n. hauteur f

hello excl. bonjour!

help n. aide f, assistance f, secours m; with the h. of a friend, avec l'aide d'un ami

her pron. la, lui, elle; adj. son, sa, ses

here adv. ici

hers pron. le sien, la sienne, les sien(ne)s

herself pron. elle-même

hide v.tr. cacher

high a. haut

him pron. le, lui

himself pron. lui-même

hire v.tr. louer (une voiture)

his a. son, sa, ses; pron. le sien, la sienne, les sien(ne)s

hit v.tr. frapper

holiday n. fête f; jour m férié; the holidays, les vacances; a month's h., un mois de vacances f; where did you spend your h.? où avez-vous passé vos vacances?

home n. chez-soi m; at h., à la maison, chez soi

home page n. accueil nm

honey n. miel m

hope v.i. espérer

horse n. cheval, -aux m

hot a. chaud

hour n. heure f; an h. and a half, une heure et demie; half an h., une demi-heure

house n. maison f

how adv. comment

however adv. toutefois, cependant, pourtant

huge a. énorme

hundred cent (m)

hunger n. faim f; to be hungry, avoir faim

hurry v.tr. hâter, presser

hurt v.tr. blesser

husband n. mari m

I pron. je

ice n. glace f

idea n. idée f

if conj. si

ill a. mauvais; malade

impede v.tr. empêcher

in prep. en, à, dans; *in Europe,* en Europe; *in Japan,* au Japon; *in Paris,* à Paris; *in the country,* à la campagne

include v.tr. comprendre, renfermer; *we were six including our host,* nous étions six y compris notre hôte

income n. revenu m

indeed adv. en effet; vraiment

India l'Inde f

indoor n. intérieur m

inside n. dedans m; intérieur m

instance n. exemple m, cas m; *for i.,* par exemple

instead prep. phr. au lieu de

interview n. entrevue f

into prep. dans, en; *to go i. a house,* entrer dans une maison

iron n. fer m

island n. île f

it pron. il, f. elle

Italian a. italien

Italy l'Italie f

its adj. son, sa, ses

itself pron. lui-même, elle-même

jam n. confiture f; *strawberry j.,* confiture(s) de fraises

jaw n. mâchoire f

jewel n. bijou m

job n. tâche f; travail m

joke n. plaisanterie f, farce f

juice n. jus m

July n. juillet m

June n. juin m

keep v.tr. garder

key n. clef f, clé f

kind a. bon, aimable, bienveillant; *kindness* n. bonté f

king n. roi m

kitchen n. cuisine f

knee n. genou m

knife n. couteau m

know v.tr. & i. connaître

lady n. dame f; *ladies and gentlemen!* mesdames, mesdemoiselles, messieurs!

lager n. bière blonde f

lake n. lac m

land n. terre f; *by l. and sea,* sur terre et sur mer

lane n. route f; voie f; *four l. highway,* route à quatre voies

large a. grand; gros; fort; *to grow l.,* larger, grossir, grandir

last a. dernier; *the l. but one,* l'avant-dernier

late a. *I am l.,* je suis en retard

laugh n. rire m; v.i. rire

launderette n. laverie f automatique

law n. loi f

lawn n. pelouse f; gazon m

lazy a. paresseux

lean a. maigre

learn v.tr. apprendre

leather n. cuir m; *l. shoes,* chaussures f en cuir

leave v.tr. laisser; *to l. the door open,* laisser la porte ouverte; quitter

left **a. gauche;** *on the l. bank,* **sur la rive gauche; adv.** *turn l.,* **tournez à gauche**

leg **n. jambe f**

lemon **n. citron m**

length **n. longueur f**

less **n. moins m; adv.** *l. known,* **moins connu;** *l. and l.,* **de moins en moins**

life **n. vie f;** *it's a matter of l. and death,* **c'est une question de vie ou de mort**

light1 **n. lumière f;** *traffic lights,* **feux de circulation**

light2 **a.** *it is l.,* **il fait jour**

like1 **a. semblable, pareil, tel;** *l. father, l. son,* **tel père, tel fils**

like2 **v.tr. aimer;** *I l. him,* **je l'aime bien**

lip **n. lèvre f**

listen **v.i. écouter**

little **a. petit**

live **a. vivant; en vie**

lock **n. serrure f**

loft **n. grenier m**

look **n. regard m; v.i. & tr. regarder;** *to l. out of the window,* **regarder par la fenêtre**

lose **v.tr. perdre**

lot **beaucoup**

love **n. amour m**

low **a. bas, basse;** *l. tide,* **marée basse**

luck **n. hasard m, chance f, fortune f;** *good l.,* **bonne chance**

luggage **n. bagage(s) m(pl)**

mad **a. fou**

mail **n. courrier m; la poste**

main **a. principal; premier, essentiel**

make **v.tr. faire;** *to m. a noise,* **faire du bruit**

man **n. homme m**

manner **n. manière f, façon f**

manor **n. m.** *(house),* **manoir m**

map **n. carte f**

March **n. mars m;** *in M.,* **au mois de mars**

market **n. marché m**

marmalade **n. confiture f d'oranges**

may1 **aux.** *might, I m. do it with luck,* **avec de la chance je peux le faire;** *he m. miss the train,* **il se peut qu'il manque le train;** *m. I?* **vous permettez?**

May2 **n. mai m;** *in M.,* **en mai; au mois de mai**

me **pron. me, moi**

meal **n. repas m**

mean **v.tr. vouloir dire; signifier**

meat **n. viande f**

medium **n. milieu m; a. moyen**

meet **v.tr. rencontrer**

memory **n. mémoire f**

middle **a. du milieu;** *m. size,* **grandeur moyenne;** *the m. class(es),* **la classe moyenne**

milk **n. lait m**

mine **pron. le mien, la mienne, les mien(ne)s**

mislay **v.tr. égarer (ses clefs, etc.)**

mispronounce **v.tr. mal prononcer**

mist **n. brume f**

mistake **n. erreur f; faute f**

Monday **n. lundi m**

money **n. monnaie f; argent m**

month **n. mois m**

moon **n. lune f**

more **a. plus;** m. than ten men, **plus de dix hommes;** some m. bread, **encore du pain**

Morocco **le Maroc**

most **a. le plus**

mother **n. mère f**

mountain **n. montagne f**

mouth **n. bouche f**

move **v.tr. déplacer; bouger**

much **a. beaucoup;** with m. care, **avec beaucoup de soin**

mum **n. maman f**

must **modal aux.** you m. hurry up, **il faut vous dépêcher**

my **adj. mon, f. ma, pl. mes**

myself **pron. moi(-même)**

name **n. nom m;** full n., **nom et prénoms**

near **adv. près, proche**

neck **n. cou m**

need **n. besoin m**

never **adv. jamais**

new **a. nouveau, nouvelle**

news **n. nouvelle(s) f(pl);** n. (bulletin), **informations fpl**

next **a. prochain**

no **non**

nobody **pron. personne**

noise **n. bruit m**

none **pron. aucun**

nor **conj. (ne, ni…) ni;** he has neither father n. mother, **il n'a ni père ni mère**

Normandy **la Normandie**

north **n. nord m**

nose **n. nez m**

not **adv. pas**

nothing **n. or pron. rien**

noun **n. substantif m, nom m**

November **n. novembre m**

now **adv. maintenant**

nowhere **adv. nulle part**

number **n. nombre m; numéro m**

nurse **n. infirmière f**

obvious **a. évident, clair, manifeste**

occur **v.i. (of event) avoir lieu; arriver; se produire**

October **n. octobre m**

of **prep. de**

office **n. bureau m**

oil **n. huile f;** olive o., **huile d'olive**

old **a. vieux; âgé**

on **prep. sur**

once **adv. une fois**

one **adj. & n. un**

only **a. seul, unique;** o. son, **fils unique; adv. seulement;** if o. I knew! **si seulement je le savais!**

open **a. ouvert**

opposite **a. en face**

other **a. autre;** the o. one, **l'autre;** the o. day, **l'autre jour**

our **poss.a. notre, pl. nos**

ours **pron. le/la nôtre, les nôtres**
ourselves **pron. nous-mêmes**
out **adv. dehors;** *to go o.,* **sortir**
outside **n. extérieur m**
outskirts **n. banlieue f**
outward the o. voyage, **l'aller m**
oven **n. four m**
owe **v.tr. devoir**
own **v.tr. posséder**
oyster **n. huître f**
paint **n. peinture f**
pan **n. casserole f**
paper **n. papier m; journal m;**
    weekly p., **hebdomadaire m**
partner **n. associé, -ée; partenai-**
    re mf
pay **v.tr. payer**
pea **n. pois m;** *green peas,* **petits**
    pois
peace **n. paix f**
pen **n. stylo m**
pencil **n. crayon m**
people **n. peuple m; habitants**
    mpl (d'une ville)
permit **v.tr. permettre**
petrol **n. essence f**
pig **n. porc m, cochon m**
pillow **n. oreiller m;** *p.-case,* **taie**
    f d'oreiller
pink **adj. & n. rose (m)**
plate **n. assiette f**
platform **quai m;** *departure p.,*
    (quai de) départ m; *arrival*
    p., **(quai d')arrivée f**
play **n. jeu; v.i. jouer**
please (if you) p., **s'il vous plaît**
plum **n. prune f**
pool **n.** *swimming p.,* **piscine f**

poor **a. pauvre**
pork **(viande f de) porc m**
portal **n. portail nm**
poultry **n. volaille f**
prepay **v.tr. payer d'avance**
present **n. cadeau m**
pretty **a. joli; beau**
prevent **v.tr. empêcher**
previous **a. préalable**
price **n. prix m**
pronounce **v.tr. prononcer**
property **n. propriété f**
proprietor **n. propriétaire mf**
proud **a. fier, orgueilleux**
pub **n. bistro(t) m**
pull **v.i. & tr. tirer**
punish **v.tr. punir**
pupil **n. élève mf**
push **v.tr. pousser**
put **v.tr. mettre**
quarrel **n. querelle f, dispute f**
quarter **n. quart m**
query **n. question f**
quick **a. rapide**
quiet **n. tranquillité f, repos**
    m, calme m; a. tranquille,
    calme, silencieux; *be q.!*
    taisez-vous!
quite **adv. tout à fait; entière-**
    ment
rabbit **n. lapin m**
rain **n. pluie f**
rather **adv. plutôt; un peu; as-**
    sez; *r. pretty,* **assez joli**
read **v.tr. lire;** *to teach s.o. to r.,*
    apprendre à lire à qn
ready **a. prêt**
real **adj. vrai**

rebate n. **rabais m**

receipt n. **reçu m, quittance f**

receive v.tr. **recevoir**

recipe n. **recette f**

recover to r. one's health, v.i. **guérir**

red a. & s. **rouge (m)**

reduce v.tr. **réduire**

refrigerator n. **réfrigérateur m**

remain v.i. **rester**

remember v.tr. **se souvenir; se rappeler**

rent n. **loyer m;** v.tr. **(a)** *(let)* **louer (une maison); (b)** *(hire)* **louer, prendre en location (une maison)**

repair n. **réparation f**

reply n. **réponse f**

report n. **rapport m**

request **demande f, requête f**

rescue n. **sauvetage m**

resort n., *seaside r.* **station balnéaire, plage f**

respond v.i. **répondre**

rest n. **repos m**

return n. **retour m;** *the r. to school,* **la rentrée (des classes)**

reward n. **récompense f**

rice n. **riz m**

ride n. **promenade f (à cheval, à vélo)**

right **à droite**

river n. **fleuve m; rivière f**

road n. **route f**

roast v.tr. **rôtir, faire rôtir**

rob v.tr. **voler**

rock n. **rocher m**

roof n. **toit m, toiture f**

rope n. **corde f**

round a. **rond, circulaire**

run v.i. **courir**

Russia **la Russie**

safe a. *s. and sound,* **sain et sauf; sans danger**

sale n. **vente f**

salt n. **sel m**

same a. & pron. **(le, la) même, (les) mêmes;** *he's the s. age as myself,* **il a le même âge que moi**

sand n. **sable m**

Saturday n. **samedi m;** *he comes on Saturdays,* **il vient le samedi**

sausage n. **saucisse f**

save v.tr. **sauver**

say v.tr. **dire**

school n. **école f**

Scot n. **Écossais, -aise;** *she's a S.,* **c'est une Écossaise**

screen n. **écran m**

sea n. **mer f**

season n. **saison f**

seat n. **siège m**

see v.tr. **voir**

seem v.i. **sembler, paraître**

sell v.tr. **vendre**

send v.tr. **envoyer**

seven a. & n. **sept (m)**

shave to have a s., **se raser;** v.tr. **raser**

she pron. **elle**

sheet n. **drap m (de lit); feuille f (de papier)**

shoe n. **chaussure f;** *I shouldn't*

like to be in his shoes, **je ne voudrais pas être à sa place**

shop **n. magasin m**

short **a. court**

show **n. spectacle m (de théâtre)**

shower **n. averse f;** *to take a s.,* **prendre une douche**

shriek **n. cri m**

shy **a. timide**

sick **a. malade;** *she's still s.,* **elle est toujours malade**

side **n. côté m**

sight **n. vue f**

silver **n. argent m;** *s. spoon,* **cuiller f d'argent**

similar **a. semblable, pareil**

since **adv. depuis**

single **a. seul, unique**

sink **n. évier m (de cuisine)**

sit **v.i. s'asseoir; être assis**

site **n. emplacement m**

size **n. dimension f; taille (de vêtements); pointure f (de chaussures)**

skin **n. peau f**

skirt **n. jupe f**

sleep **n. sommeil m**

slice **n. tranche f**

slow **a. lent**

small **a. petit**

smart **a. élégant, distingué, chic**

smell **n. odeur f; parfum m**

smile **n. sourire m**

smoke **n. fumée f**

snow **n. neige f**

so **adv. si, tellement; tant, aussi**

soap **n. savon m**

soft **a. doux;** *s. voice,* **voix douce**

solicitor **n. notaire m**

some **a. quelque**

somebody, someone **n. or pron. quelqu'un**

something **n. or pron. quelque chose m**

sometimes **adv. quelquefois, parfois**

somewhere **adv. quelque part**

son **n. fils m**

song **n. chant m; chanson f**

soon **adv. bientôt, tôt**

sore **a. douloureux;** *to be s. all over,* **avoir mal partout**

sound **n. son m, bruit m;** *s. engineer,* **ingénieur m du son**

south **a. & n. sud (m)**

space **n. espace m, intervalle m**

Spain **l'Espagne f**

Spanish **a. espagnol**

spare **s. parts, pièces f de rechange, pièces détachées**

speak **v.i. parler**

spectacles **n. pl. lunettes f**

speed **n. vitesse f**

spend **v.tr. dépenser**

spice **n. épice f**

spinach **n. épinards mpl**

spine **n. colonne vertébrale; dos m**

spoon **n. cuiller f, cuillère f**

spring **n. printemps m;** *in (the) s.,* **au printemps**

staff **n. personnel m;** *teaching s.,* **personnel enseignant**

stamp **n. timbre m**

stand **v.i. être debout**

star n. **étoile f**

starve *I'm starving,* **je meurs de faim**

state *the United States of America,* **les États-Unis d'Amérique**

station n. *service s.,* **station-service f;** *(railway)* s., **gare f**

stay n. **séjour m; visite f**

steeple n. **clocher m**

step n. **pas m**

stomach n. **estomac m;** *s. ache,* **douleurs fpl d'estomac**

stop n. **arrêt m;** *bus s.,* **arrêt d'autobus**

storey n. **étage m (d'une maison)**

storm n. **orage m**

story n. **histoire f, récit m**

straight a. **droit;** *s. line,* **ligne droite**

strawberry n. **fraise f**

street n. **rue f**

strike n. **grève f**

strong a. **fort**

subscribe *to s. to a newspaper,* **s'abonner, prendre un abonnement, à un journal**

such a. **tel, pareil, semblable**

sudden a. **soudain, subit**

sugar n. **sucre m**

sum n. **somme f**

summer n. **été m**

sun n. **soleil m**

sure a. **sûr, certain**

surgeon n. **chirurgien, -ienne**

Sweden **la Suède;** *Swede,* n. **Suédois, -oise**

swim v.i. & tr. **nager**

switch n. **interrupteur m**

take v.tr. **prendre**

talk v.i. **parler;** *to learn to t.,* **apprendre à parler**

tall a. **grand**

tap n. **robinet;** *t. water,* **eau f du robinet**

taste n. **goût m**

tax n. **impôt m;** *income t.,* **impôt sur le revenu**

tea n. **thé m;** *t. bag,* **sachet m de thé**

teach v.tr. **enseigner**

team n. **équipe f**

tell v.tr. **dire;** *to t. the truth,* **dire la vérité**

ten a. & n. **dix (m)**

term n. **trimestre m**

than conj. **que**

thank n.pl. *thanks,* **remerciement(s) m**

that1 pron., pl. *those;* **cela, ça;** *what's t.?* **qu'est-ce que c'est que ça?**

that2 rel. pron. (for subject) **qui;** (for object) **que**

that3 conj. **que**

the **le, la**

their a. **leur, pl. leurs**

theirs pron. **le/la leur, les leurs**

them pron. **les; eux**

themselves pron. **eux-mêmes**

then adv. **alors**

there adv. **là**

they pron. **ils, elles**

thick a. **épais**

thief n. **voleur, -euse**

thin **a. mince**

thing **n. chose f**

think **v.tr. & i. penser, réfléchir**

third **adj. troisième**

thirst **n. soif f**

thirteen **a. & n. treize (m)**

thirty **a. & n. trente (m)**

this **pron. ceci; ce**

though **conj. quoique, bien que**

thought **n. pensée; idée f**

thousand **a. & s. mille (m)**

three **a. & n. trois (m)**

throat **n. gorge f;** *to have a sore t.,* **avoir mal à la gorge**

through **prep. à travers**

thunder **n. tonnerre m**

Thursday **n. jeudi m**

tide **n. marée f;** *high, low, t.,* **marée haute, basse**

till **prep. jusqu'à**

time **n. temps m**

tip **n. pourboire m**

to **prep. à**

together **adv. ensemble**

toll **n. péage m**

tomorrow **adv. & n. demain (m);** *t. night,* **demain soir**

tonight **adv. & n. cette nuit; ce soir**

too **adv. trop;** *t. much money,* **trop d'argent**

tooth **n. dent f;** *toothache,* **n. mal m de dents**

towel **n. serviette f (de toilette)**

town **n. ville f**

toy **n. jouet m**

traffic **n. trafic m**

travel **n. voyages mpl**

tree **n. arbre m**

trip **n. excursion f; voyage m**

trousers **n.pl. pantalon m**

true **a. vrai**

truth **n. vérité f**

try **v.tr. essayer;** *to t. a dish,* **goûter**

twelve **a. & n. douze (m);** *t. o'clock,* **midi m, minuit m**

twenty **a. & n. vingt (m)**

twice **adv. deux fois**

twin **a. & n. jumeau, jumelle**

two **a. & n. deux (m)**

tyre **n. pneu m**

umbrella **n. parapluie m**

uncork **v.tr. déboucher (une bouteille)**

under **prep. sous; au-dessous de;** *to swim u. water,* **nager sous l'eau**

undo **v.tr. défaire**

unfair **a. (of pers.) injuste**

unhappy **a. malheureux, triste**

union **n. (trade) u., syndicat m**

unknown **a. inconnu**

unless **conj. à moins que**

unpleasant **a. désagréable**

untidy **a. (of room) en désordre**

until **prep. jusqu'à**

up **adv. vers le haut;** *to go up,* **monter**

us **pron. nous**

use **n. emploi m, usage m**

vacuum **n. v. cleaner, aspirateur m**

van **n. camionnette f**

vanilla **n. vanille f**

vegetable **n. légume m**

vehicle n. véhicule m, voiture f
very adv. très
view n. vue f
voice n. voix f
wage n. salaire m, paie f
wait v.i. attendre
wake to w. (up), se réveiller
Wales le Pays de Galles
walk v.i. marcher
wall n. mur m
wallet n. portefeuille m
want v.i. désirer, vouloir; he knows what he wants, il sait ce qu'il veut
war n. guerre f
warm a. chaud
wash v.tr. laver; to w. oneself, se laver
watch v.tr. observer; regarder; to w. television, regarder une émission de télévision
water n. eau f
way n. chemin m, route f
we pron. nous
weak a. faible
wear v.tr. porter (un vêtement)
weather n. temps m; in all weathers, par tous les temps
web n. (computer) toile nf
Wednesday n. mercredi m
week n. semaine f
weep v.i. pleurer
welcome v.tr. souhaiter la bienvenue
well adv. bien; to work w., bien travailler
Welsh a. & n. gallois, du Pays de Galles

west n. ouest m
wet a. mouillé; humide
what a. (rel.) (ce) que, (ce) qui
wheel n. roue f
when adv. quand? w. will you go? quand partirez-vous?
where adv. où? w. am I? où suis-je?
which a. quel, f. quelle, pl. quels, quelles
while conj. pendant que, tandis que
white a. blanc, f. blanche
who pron. qui
whole a. entier; complet
whom pron. qui? (rel.) que
why adv. pourquoi?
wide a. large
wife n. femme f, épouse f
win v.tr. & i. gagner; a. winning number, numéro gagnant
wind n. vent m
window n. fenêtre f
wine n. vin m
winner n. gagnant, -ante
winter n. hiver m
wish v.i. désirer, souhaiter
with prep. avec
within prep. à l'intérieur de
without prep. sans
woman n. femme f
wood n. bois m
wool n. laine f
word n. mot m
work n. travail, -aux m
worry v.i. s'inquiéter
worse a. & n. pire
worst a. (le) pire

wound **n. blessure f**
wrong **a. mauvais; faux, f.**
    fausse
Xmas **n. Noël m**
year **n. année f**
yellow **a. jaune**
yes **adv. oui**
yet **adv. déjà; jusqu'ici;** *not y.,*
    pas encore
you **pron. tu, te, toi, vous**
young **a. jeune**
your **adj. ton, ta, votre; pl tes,**
    vos
yours **pron. le/la tien(ne), le/la**
    vôtre; pl les tien(ne)s, les
    vôtres
yourself, yourselves **pron. toi-**
    même, vous-même(s)
youth **n. jeunesse f;** *y. hostel,*
    auberge f de la jeunesse
zip z. *fastener,* **fermeture f éclair**

Credits